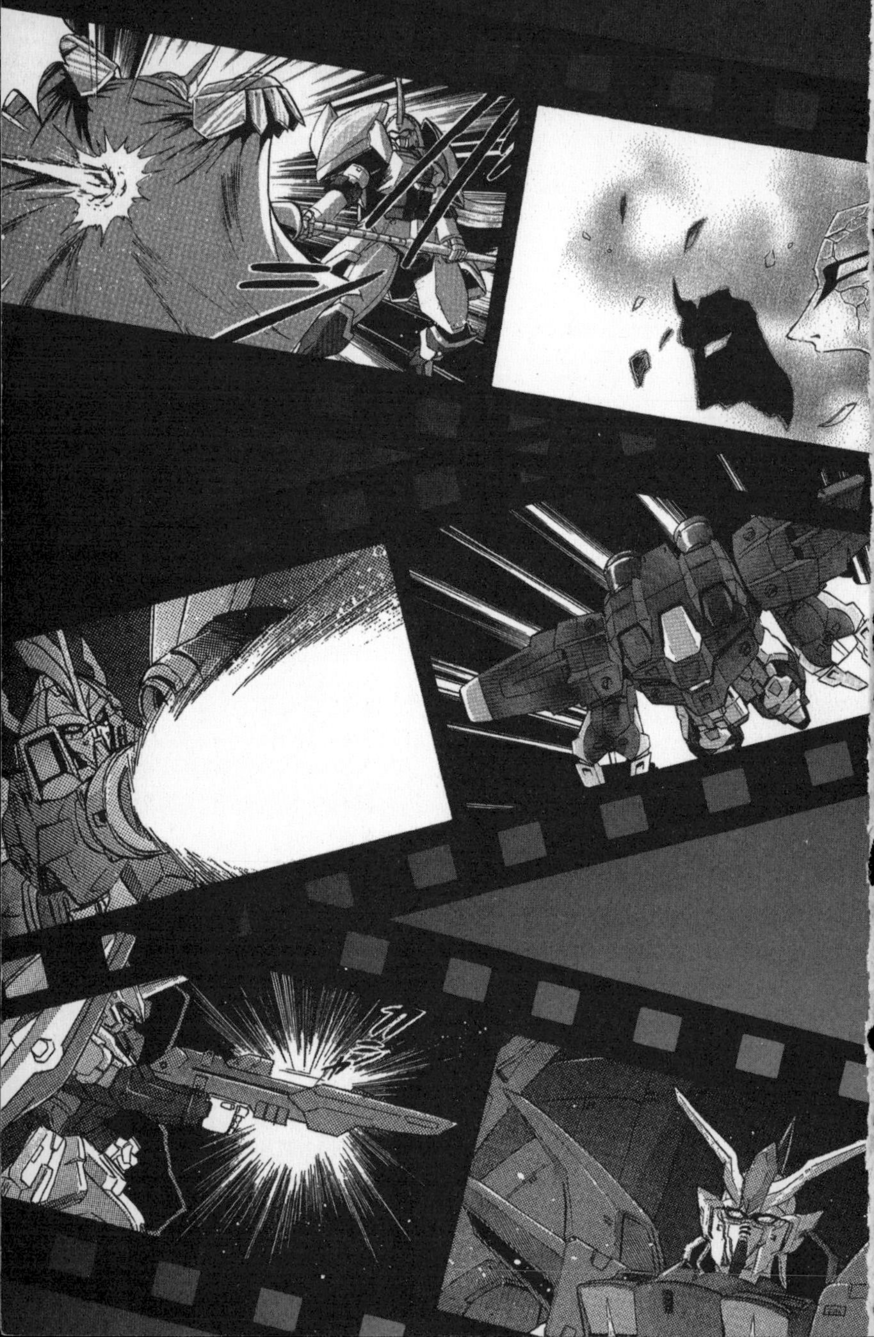

ALSO AVAILABLE FROM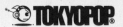

MANGA

ACTION

ANGELIC LAYER*
CLAMP SCHOOL DETECTIVES* (April 2003)
DIGIMON (March 2003)
DUKLYON: CLAMP SCHOOL DEFENDERS* (September 2003)
GATEKEEPERS* (March 2003)
GTO*
HARLEM BEAT
INITIAL D*
ISLAND
JING: KING OF BANDITS* (June 2003)
JULINE
LUPIN III*
MONSTERS, INC.
PRIEST
RAVE*
REAL BOUT HIGH SCHOOL*
REBOUND* (April 2003)
SAMURAI DEEPER KYO* (June 2003)
SCRYED* (March 2003)
SHAOLIN SISTERS* (February 2003)
THE SKULL MAN*

FANTASY

CHRONICLES OF THE CURSED SWORD (July 2003)
DEMON DIARY (May 2003)
DRAGON HUNTER (June 2003)
DRAGON KNIGHTS*
KING OF HELL (June 2003)
PLANET LADDER*
RAGNAROK
REBIRTH (March 2003)
SHIRAHIME:TALES OF THE SNOW PRINCESS* (December 2003)
SORCERER HUNTERS
WISH*

CINE-MANGA™

AKIRA*
CARDCAPTORS
KIM POSSIBLE (March 2003)
LIZZIE McGUIRE (March 2003)
POWER RANGERS (May 2003)
SPY KIDS 2 (March 2003)

ANIME GUIDES

GUNDAM TECHNICAL MANUALS
COWBOY BEBOP
SAILOR MOON SCOUT GUIDES

ROMANCE

HAPPY MANIA* (April 2003)
I.N.V.U. (February 2003)
LOVE HINA*
KARE KANO*
KODOCHA*
MAN OF MANY FACES* (May 2003)
MARMALADE BOY*
MARS*
PARADISE KISS*
PEACH GIRL
UNDER A GLASS MOON (June 2003)

SCIENCE FICTION

CHOBITS*
CLOVER
COWBOY BEBOP*
COWBOY BEBOP: SHOOTING STAR* (June 2003)
G-GUNDAM*
GUNDAM WING
GUNDAM WING: ENDLESS WALTZ*
GUNDAM: THE LAST OUTPOST*
PARASYTE
REALITY CHECK (March 2003)

MAGICAL GIRLS

CARDCAPTOR SAKURA
CARDCAPTOR SAKURA: MASTER OF THE CLOW*
CORRECTOR YUI
MAGIC KNIGHT RAYEARTH* (August 2003)
MIRACLE GIRLS
SAILOR MOON
SAINT TAIL
TOKYO MEW MEW* (April 2003)

NOVELS

SAILOR MOON
SUSHI SQUAD (April 2003)

ART BOOKS

CARDCAPTOR SAKURA*
MAGIC KNIGHT RAYEARTH*

TOKYOPOP KIDS

DISNEY CLASSICS (June 2003)
STRAY SHEEP (September 2003)

MOBILE SUIT
GUNDAM
THE LAST OUTPOST

Volume 2 of 3

**Art by
Koichi Tokita
Created by
Hajime Yadate &
Yoshiyuki Tomino**

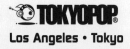
Los Angeles • Tokyo

Translator - Yuki Ichimura
English Adaption - Jake Forbes
Retouch and Lettering - Tom Misuraca
Cover Artist - Raymond Swanland
Cover Layout - Anna Kernbaum

Senior Editor - Jake Forbes
Managing Editor - Jill Freshney
Production Manager - Jennifer Miller
Art Director - Matt Alford
VP of Production & Manufacturing - Ron Klamert
President & C.O.O. - John Parker
Publisher - Stuart Levy

Email: editor@TOKYOPOP.com
Come visit us online at www.TOKYOPOP.com

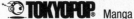 Manga
TOKYOPOP® is an imprint of Mixx Entertainment Inc.
5900 Wilshire Blvd. Suite 2000, Los Angeles, CA 90036

ISBN: 1-931514-82-8

First TOKYOPOP® printing:February 2003

10 9 8 7 6 5 4 3 2 1

Printed in Canada

CONTENTS

MOBILE SUIT GUNDAM
THE LAST OUTPOST

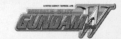

The Story So Far...

The remote asteroid colony MO-V is under attack from the OZ force known as "Prize." Cut off from the rest of the solar system, the people of MO-V must defend themselves. Their only hope rests in two pilots, the Bernett brothers Odin and Odel. Using the MO-V developed Gundam G-Units, modular Mobile Suits with incredible powers, they might have stood a chance.

But in the last attack, things went wrong...very wrong. Odel, the older and better pilot, was shot down by Prize and is presumed dead. To make matters worse, MO-V's top scientist, the brilliant Dr. Berg, has been spying for Prize and defected to their ship. With all hope lost, the people of MO-V prepare their last defense...

CHARACTER DOSSIERS

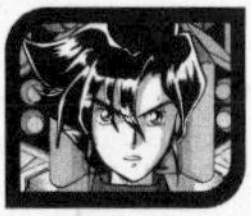

Odin Bernett

The younger Bernett brother, Odin is frustrated at living in the shadow of his brother. Impulsive and brash, Odin hasn't been able to master the self-control needed to take full advantage of the new G-Unit and its PX system, but he's still an ace pilot.

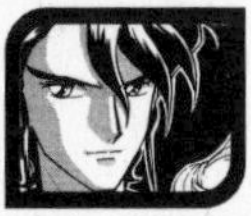

Odel Bernett

The older of the Bernett brothers, Odel is the top MS pilot at MO-V. He is distrustful of the OZ delegates who come to his home.

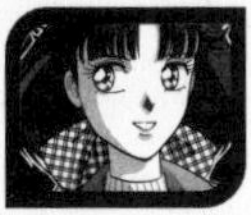

Lucille Aisley

Lucille is the lead programmer at MO-V, whose computer skills are invaluable in the development of the new G-Units. She's also Odin's girlfriend, although it's hard to tell that, as they are always bickering.

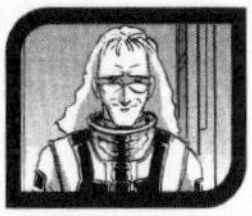

Dr. Berg

The inventor of the G-Units, Dr. Berg is a brilliant scientist. He seems more interested in protecting his work than the people of MO-V.

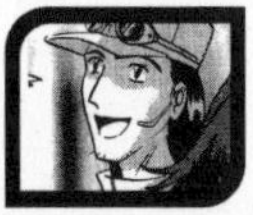

Dick Hidasaki

Chief Mechanic on MO-V, Dick can usually be found in the hanger with Lucille working on the G-Units.

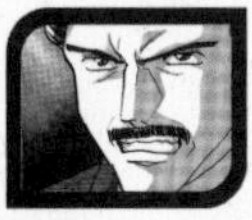

Roga Herman

The elected official of MO-V, Roga is a humble leader who rellies, perhaps too much, on the advice of his communications officer Tricia Farrell. The current assault has left him understandably stressed.

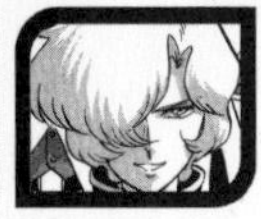

Roche Nattono

Leader of the elite OZ group Prize, Roche is arrogant, cruel, and an ace MS pilot. His assistant, Aretha, is enamored with him, but he is blind to her affections.

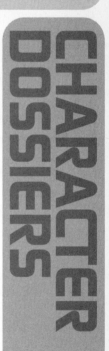

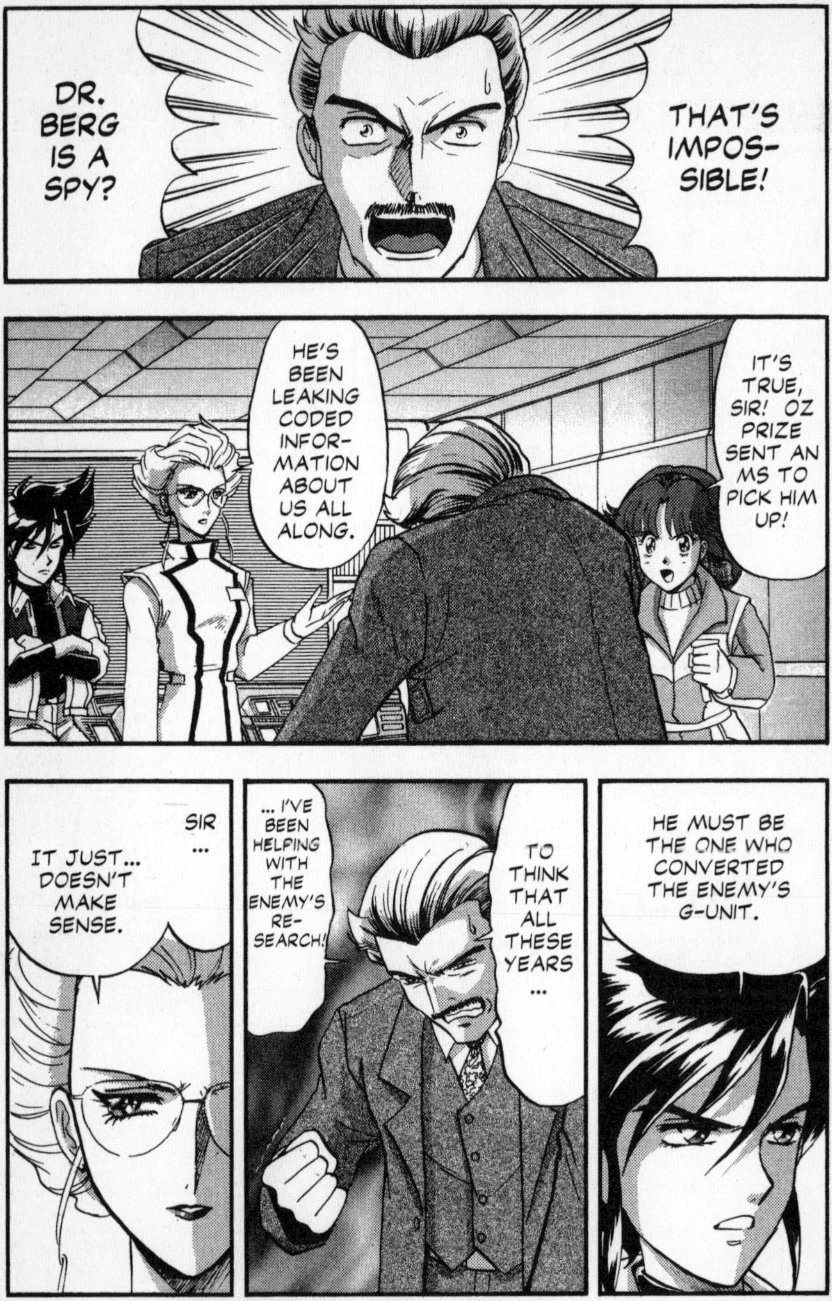
THAT'S IMPOS-SIBLE!
DR. BERG IS A SPY?
IT'S TRUE, SIR! OZ PRIZE SENT AN MS TO PICK HIM UP!
HE'S BEEN LEAKING CODED INFOR-MATION ABOUT US ALL ALONG.
HE MUST BE THE ONE WHO CONVERTED THE ENEMY'S G-UNIT.
TO THINK THAT ALL THESE YEARS ...
... I'VE BEEN HELPING WITH THE ENEMY'S RE-SEARCH!
SIR ...
IT JUST... DOESN'T MAKE SENSE.

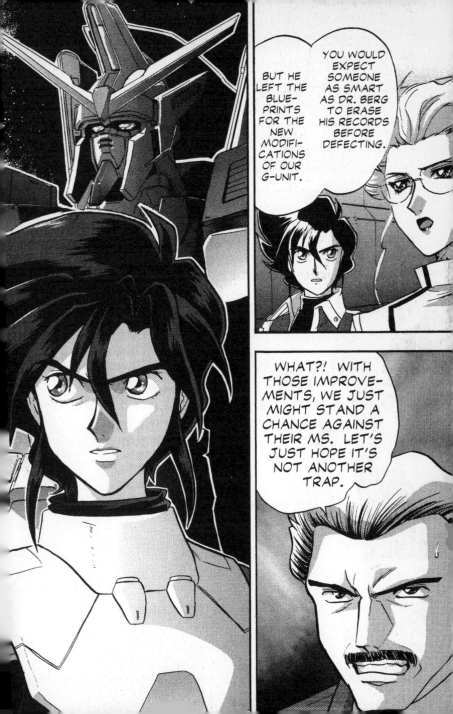

YOU WOULD EXPECT SOMEONE AS SMART AS DR. BERG TO ERASE HIS RECORDS BEFORE DEFECTING.

BUT HE LEFT THE BLUE-PRINTS FOR THE NEW MODIFICATIONS OF OUR G-UNIT.

WHAT?! WITH THOSE IMPROVEMENTS, WE JUST MIGHT STAND A CHANCE AGAINST THEIR MS. LET'S JUST HOPE IT'S NOT ANOTHER TRAP.

#5 The Man with the Silver Mask

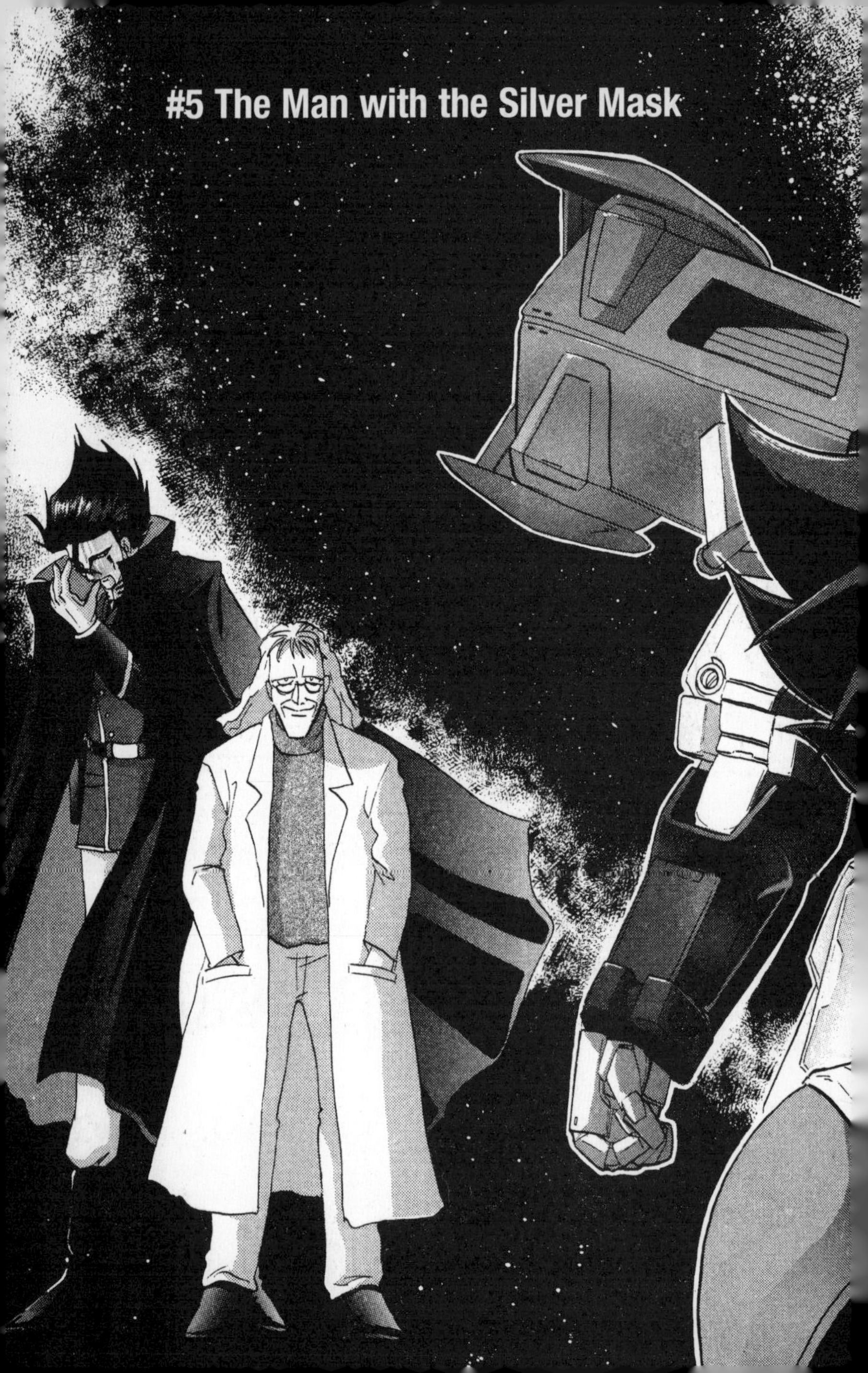

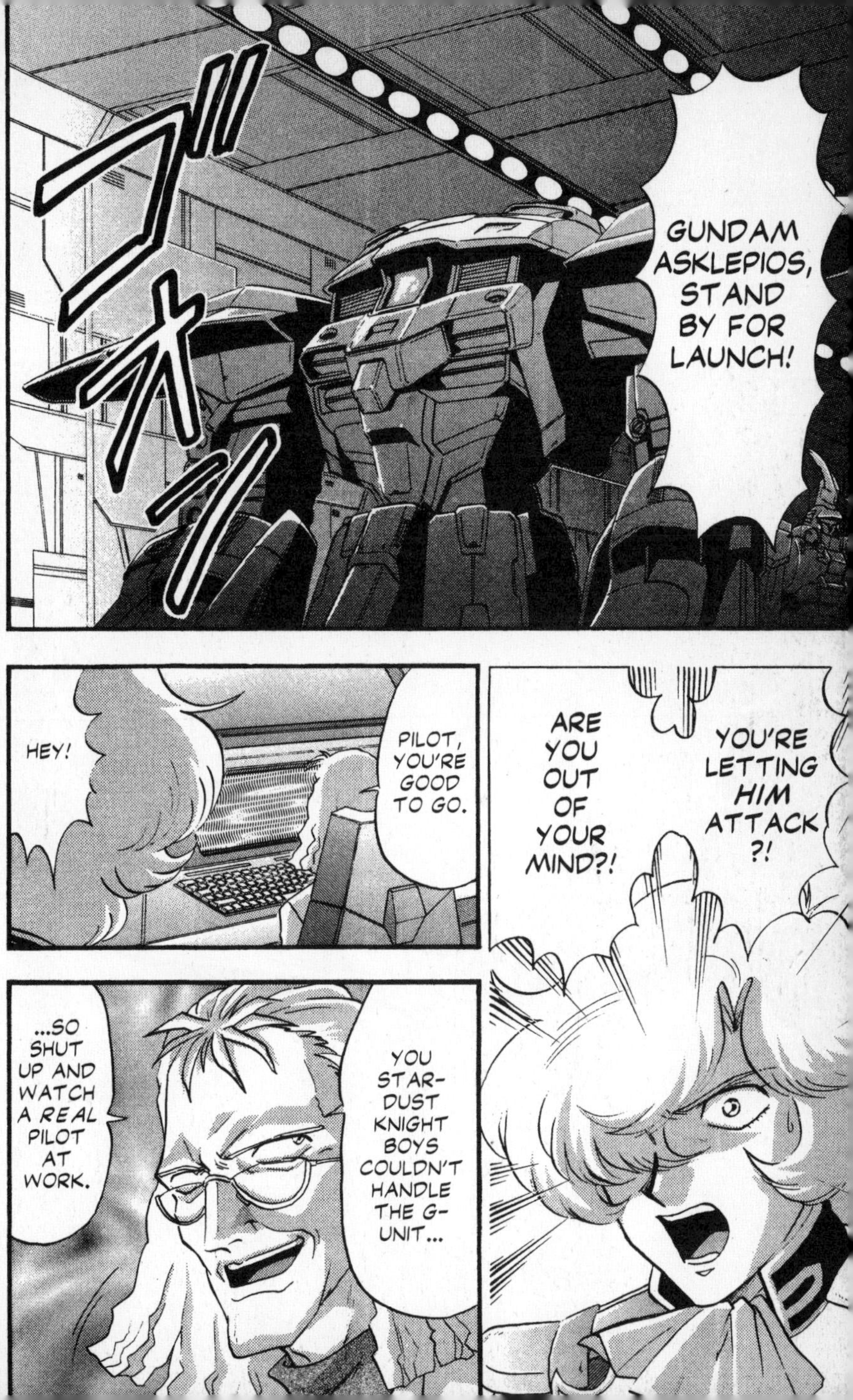
ゴオン
GUNDAM ASKLEPIOS, STAND BY FOR LAUNCH!
YOU'RE LETTING HIM ATTACK?!
ARE YOU OUT OF YOUR MIND?!
PILOT, YOU'RE GOOD TO GO.
HEY!
YOU STAR-DUST KNIGHT BOYS COULDN'T HANDLE THE G-UNIT...
...SO SHUT UP AND WATCH A *REAL* PILOT AT WORK.

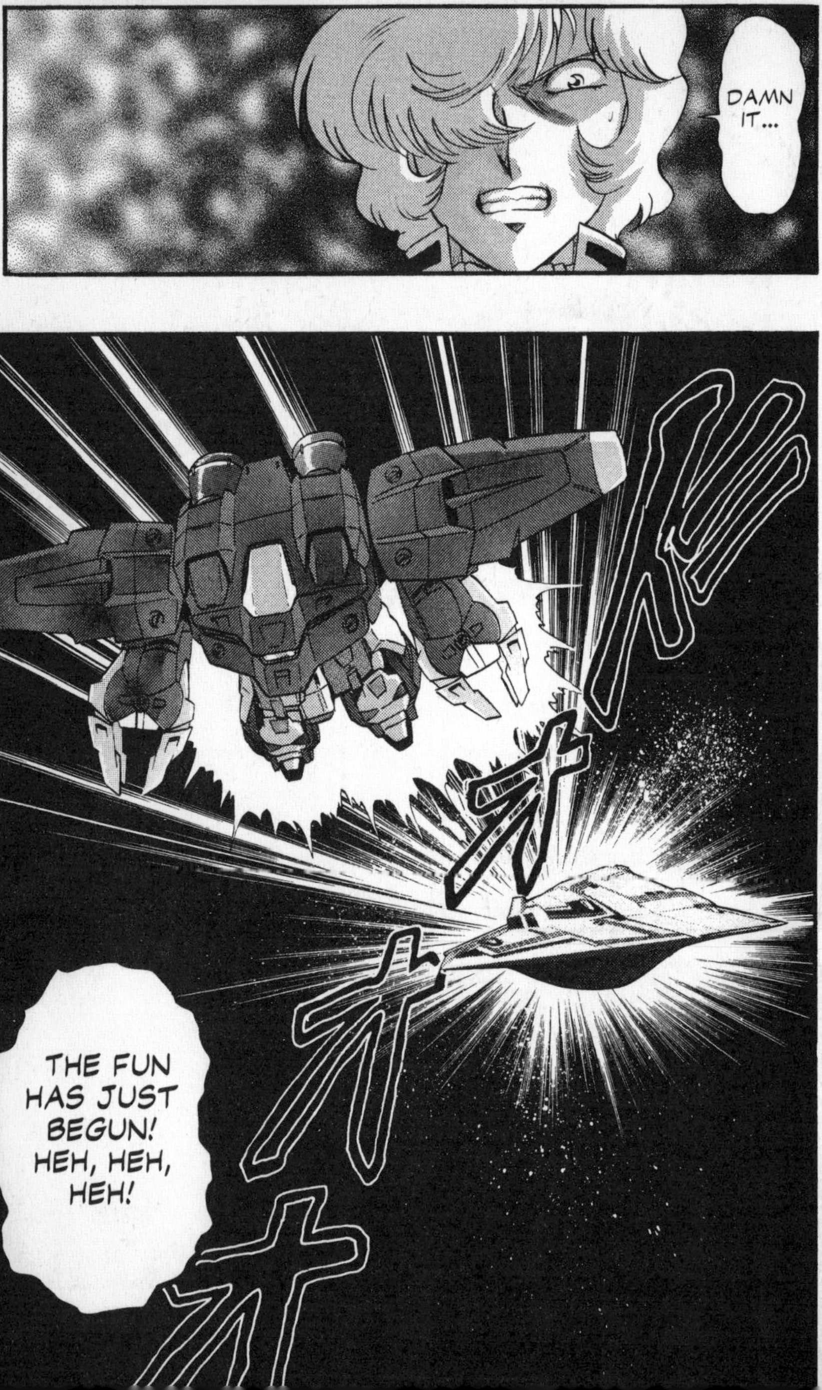
DAMN IT...
THE FUN HAS JUST BEGUN! HEH, HEH, HEH!

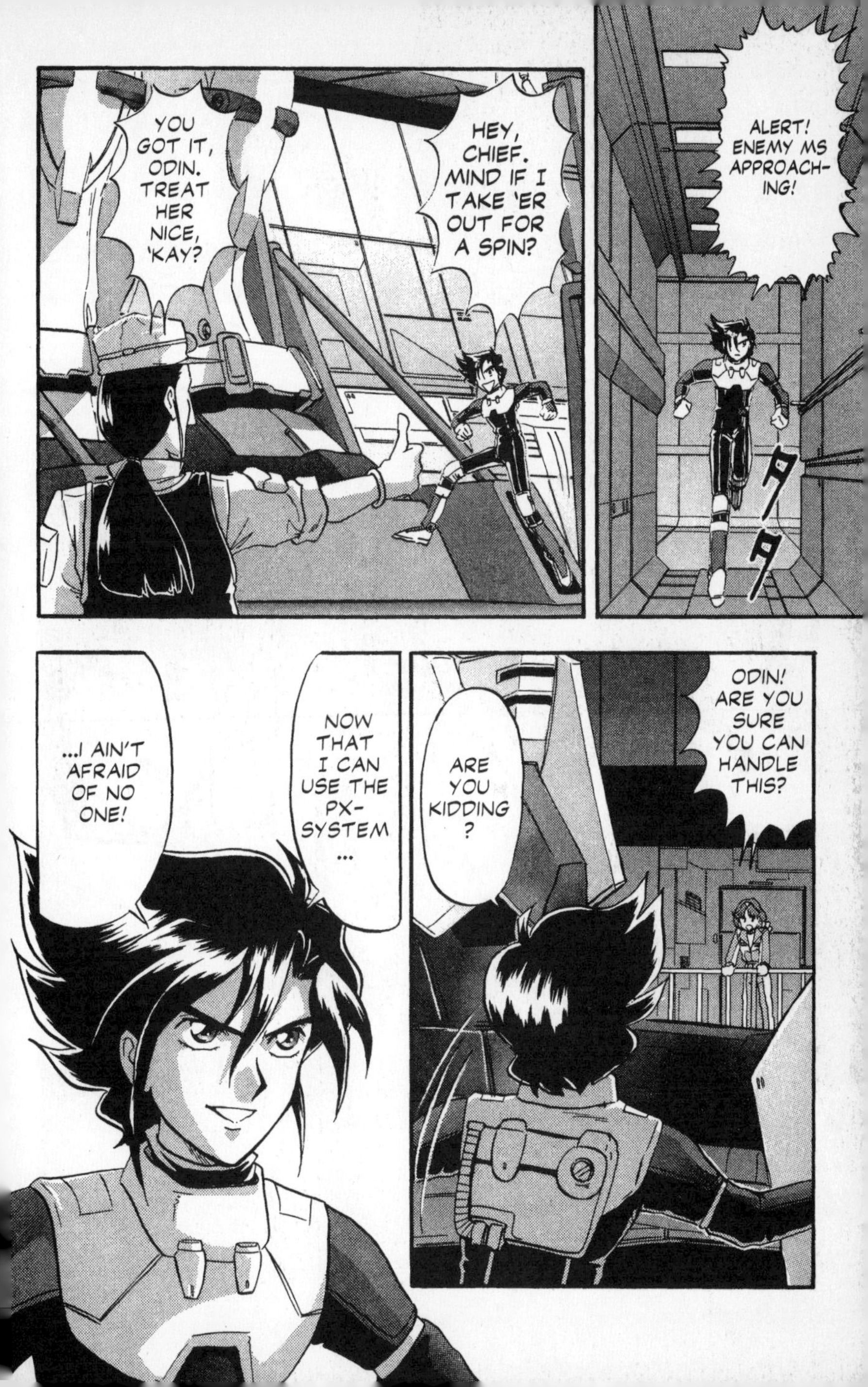
ALERT! ENEMY MS APPROACH-ING!
HEY, CHIEF. MIND IF I TAKE 'ER OUT FOR A SPIN?
YOU GOT IT, ODIN. TREAT HER NICE, 'KAY?
ODIN! ARE YOU SURE YOU CAN HANDLE THIS?
ARE YOU KIDDING?
NOW THAT I CAN USE THE PX-SYSTEM ...
...I AIN'T AFRAID OF NO ONE!

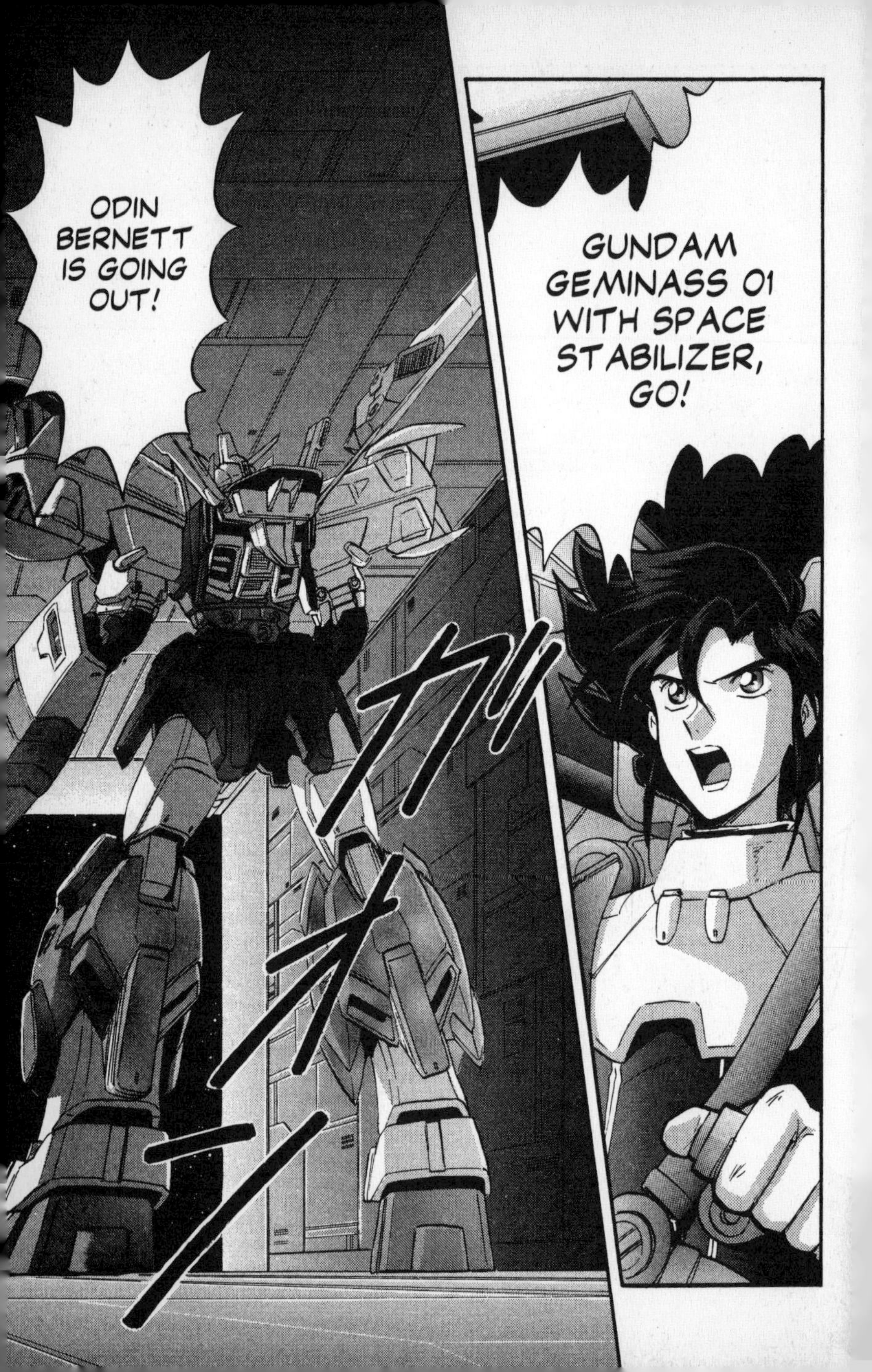
GUNDAM GEMINASS 01 WITH SPACE STABILIZER, GO!
ODIN BERNETT IS GOING OUT!

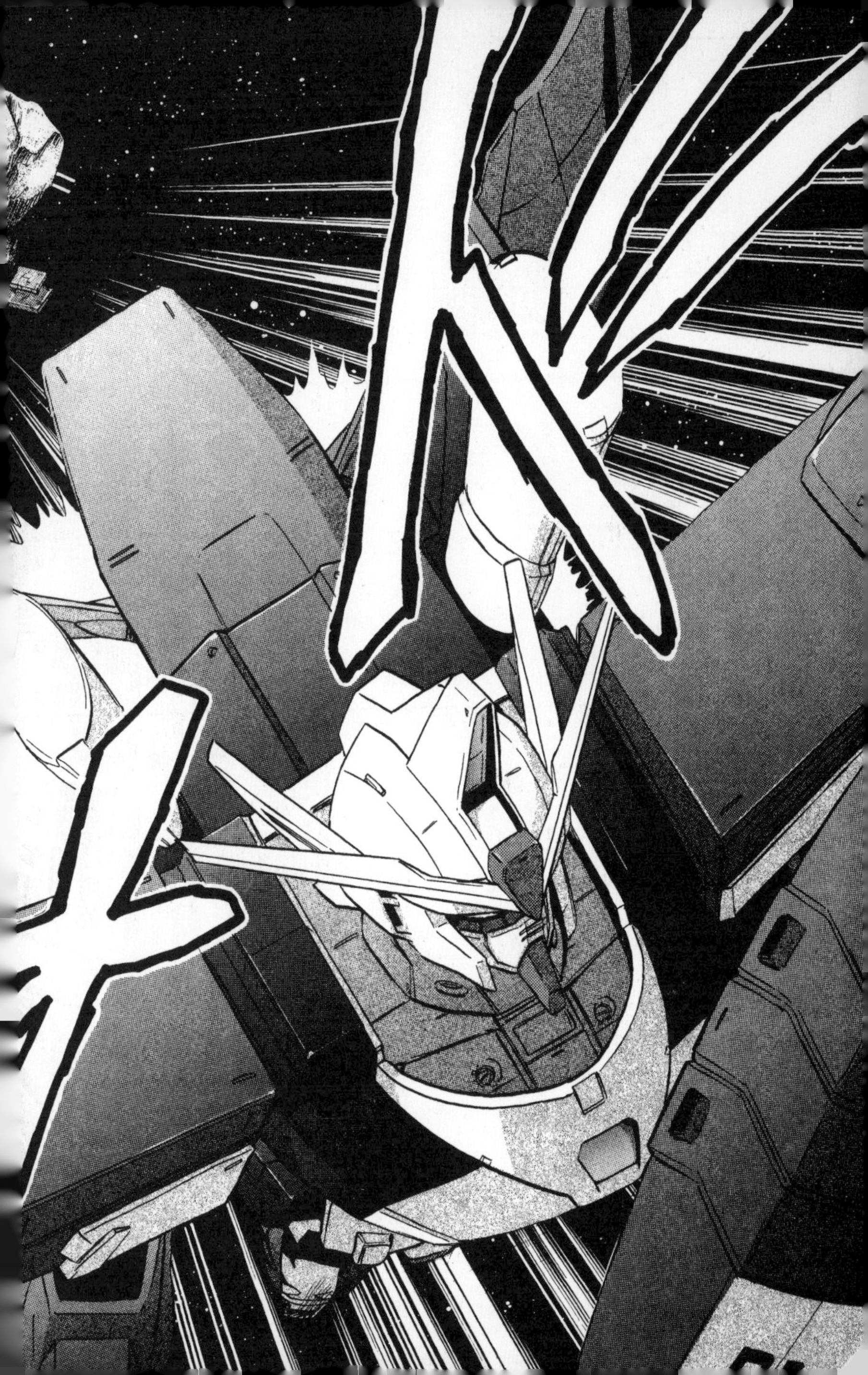

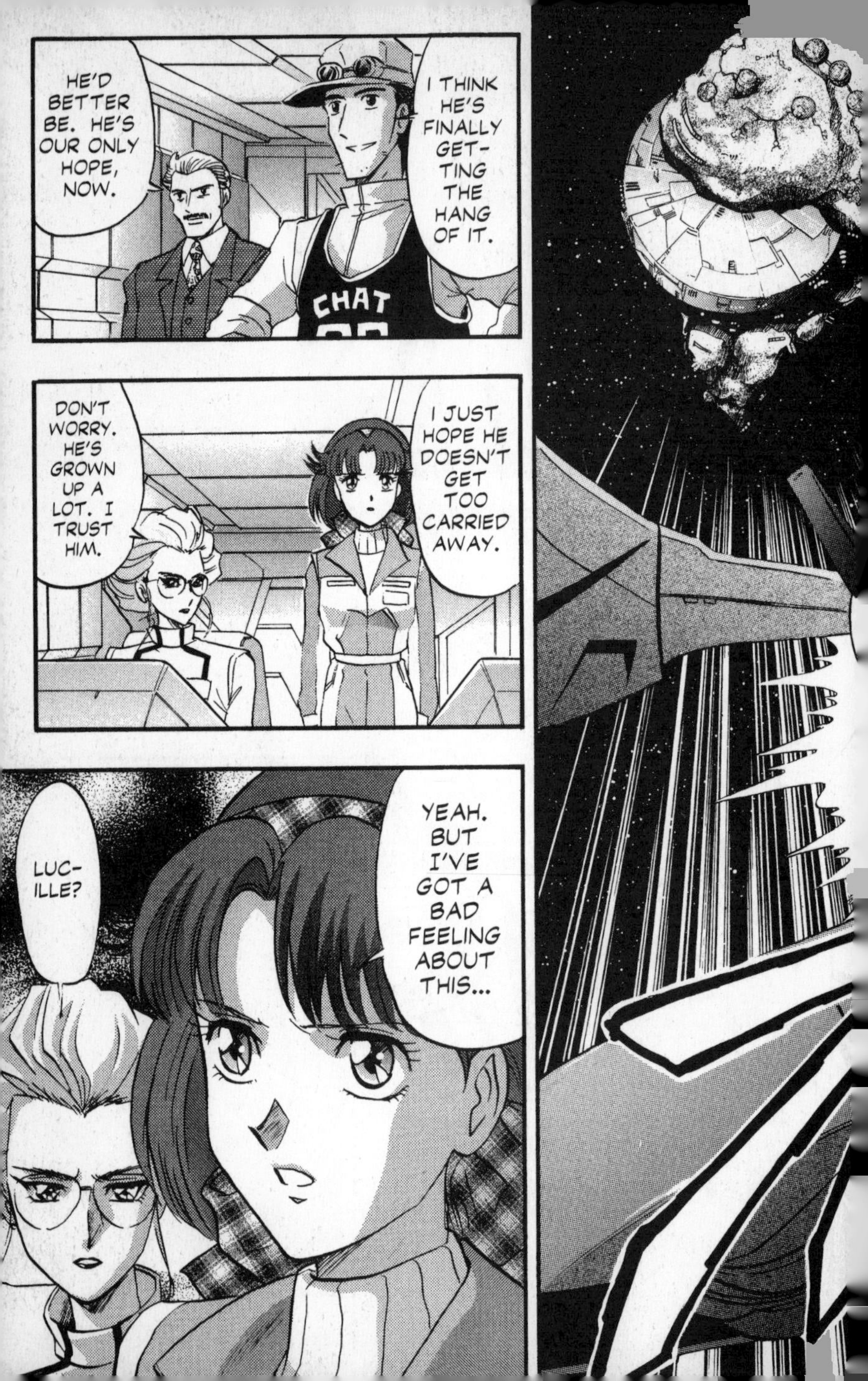
I THINK HE'S FINALLY GET-TING THE HANG OF IT.
HE'D BETTER BE. HE'S OUR ONLY HOPE, NOW.
I JUST HOPE HE DOESN'T GET TOO CARRIED AWAY.
DON'T WORRY. HE'S GROWN UP A LOT. I TRUST HIM.
YEAH. BUT I'VE GOT A BAD FEELING ABOUT THIS...
LUC-ILLE?

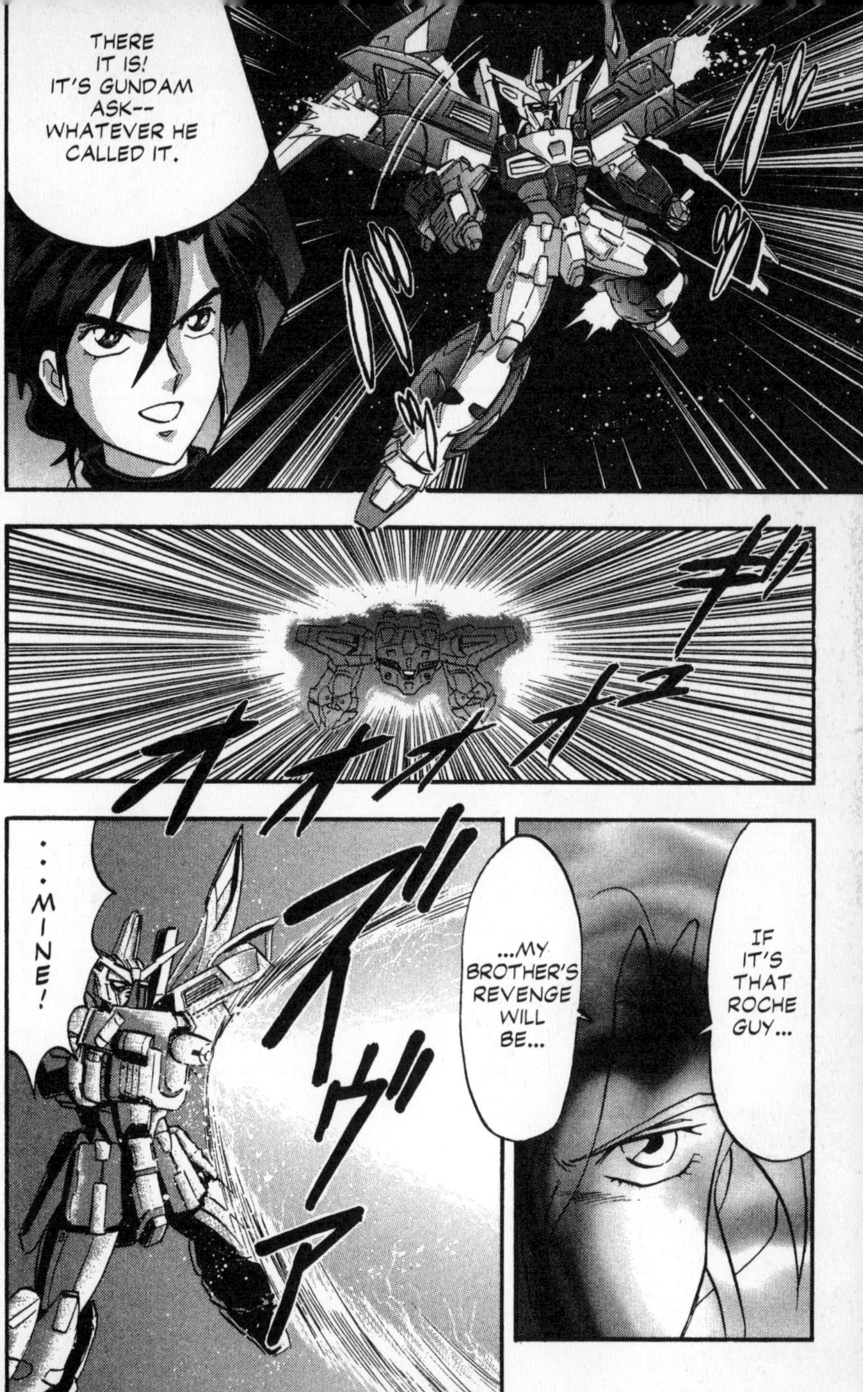
THERE IT IS! IT'S GUNDAM ASK-- WHATEVER HE CALLED IT.
IF IT'S THAT ROCHE GUY...
...MY BROTHER'S REVENGE WILL BE...
...MINE!

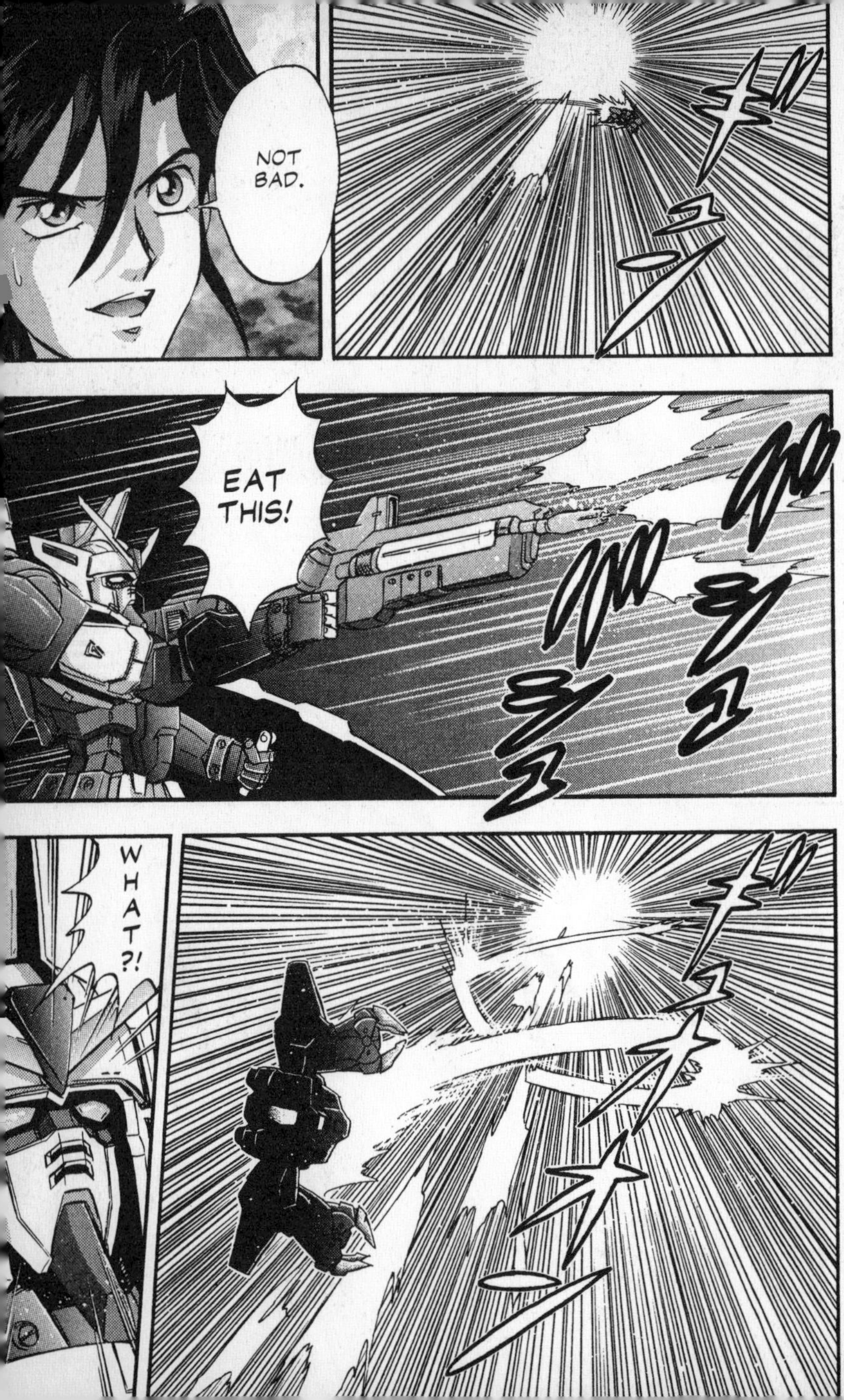
NOT BAD.
EAT THIS!
WHAT?!

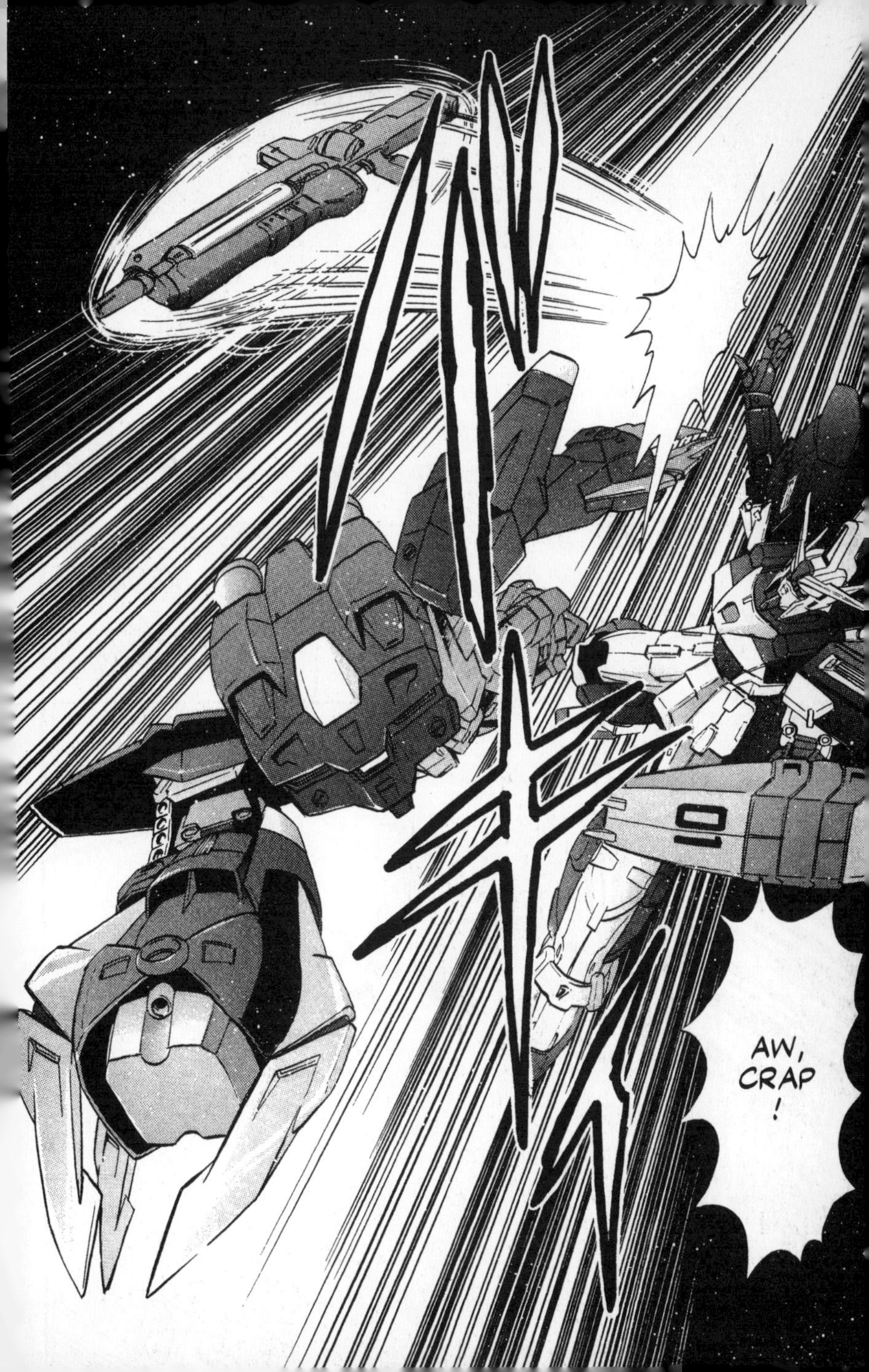
AW, CRAP!

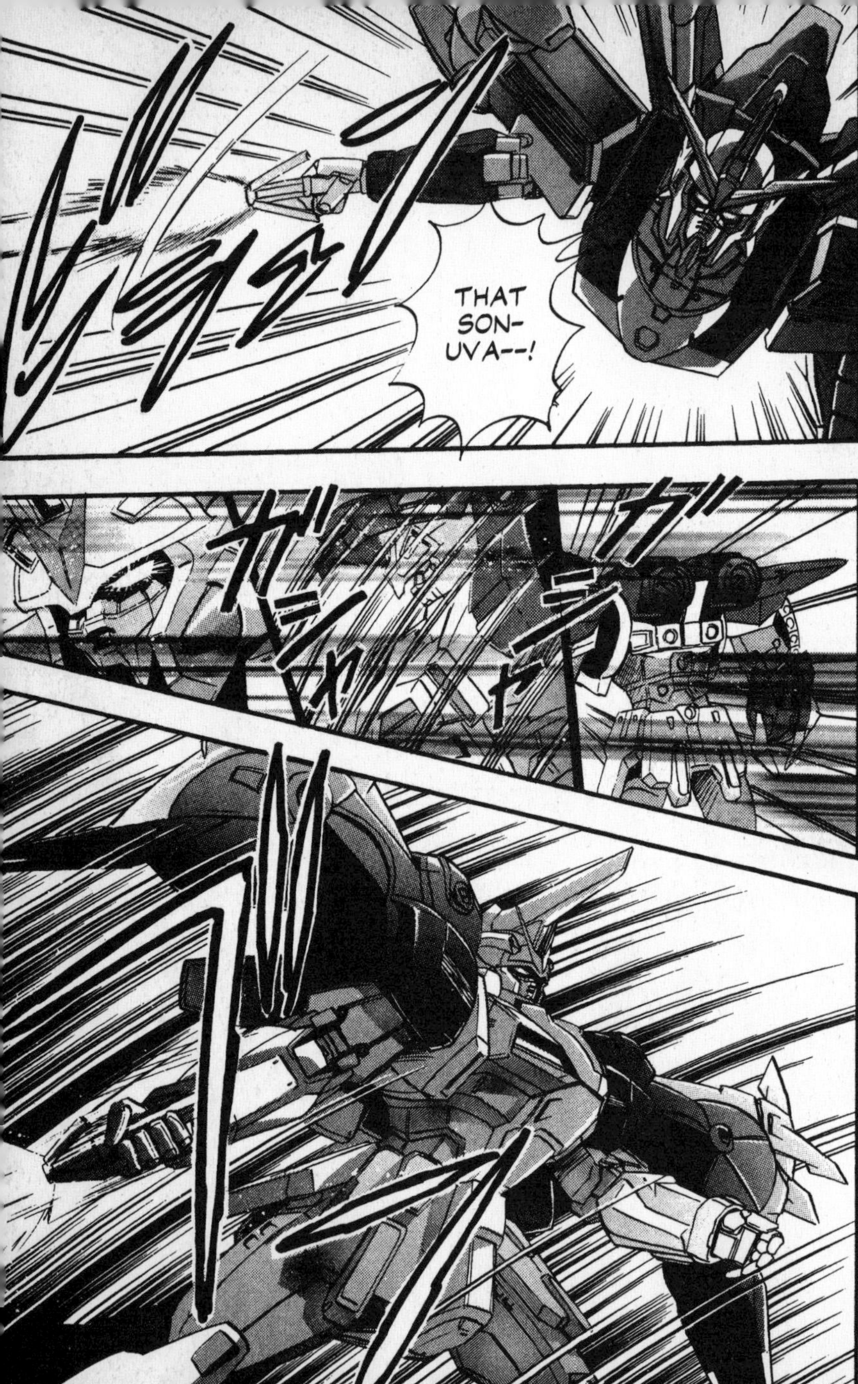
THAT SON-UVA--!

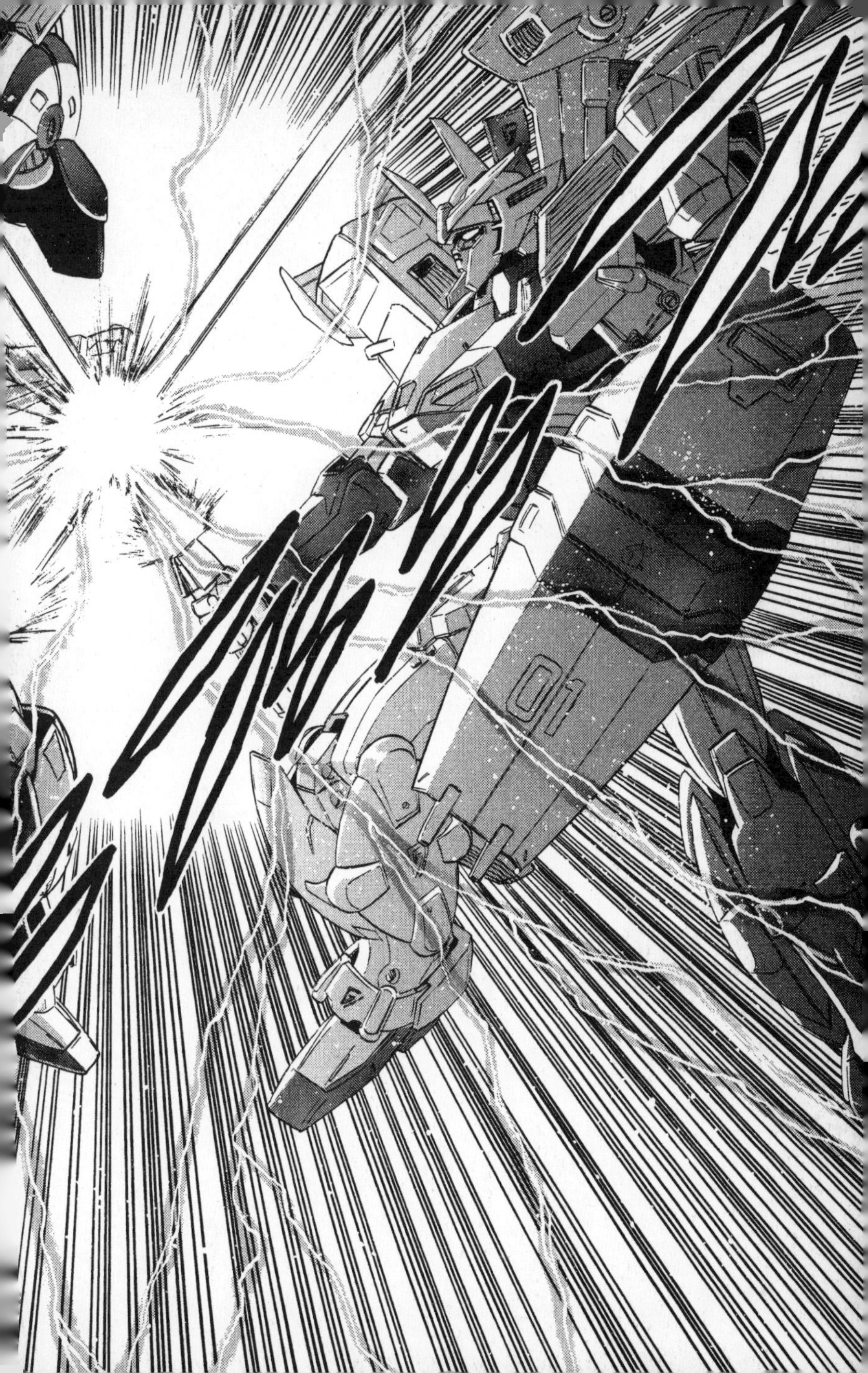

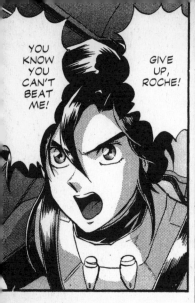

YOU KNOW YOU CAN'T BEAT ME!

GIVE UP, ROCHE!

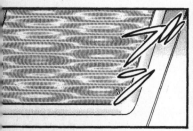

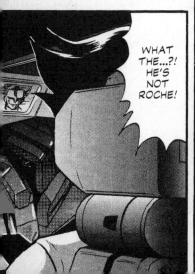

WHAT THE...?! HE'S NOT ROCHE!

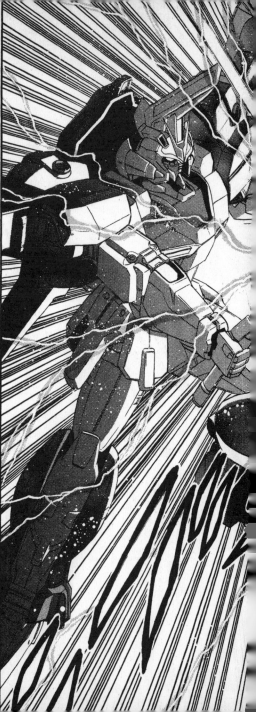

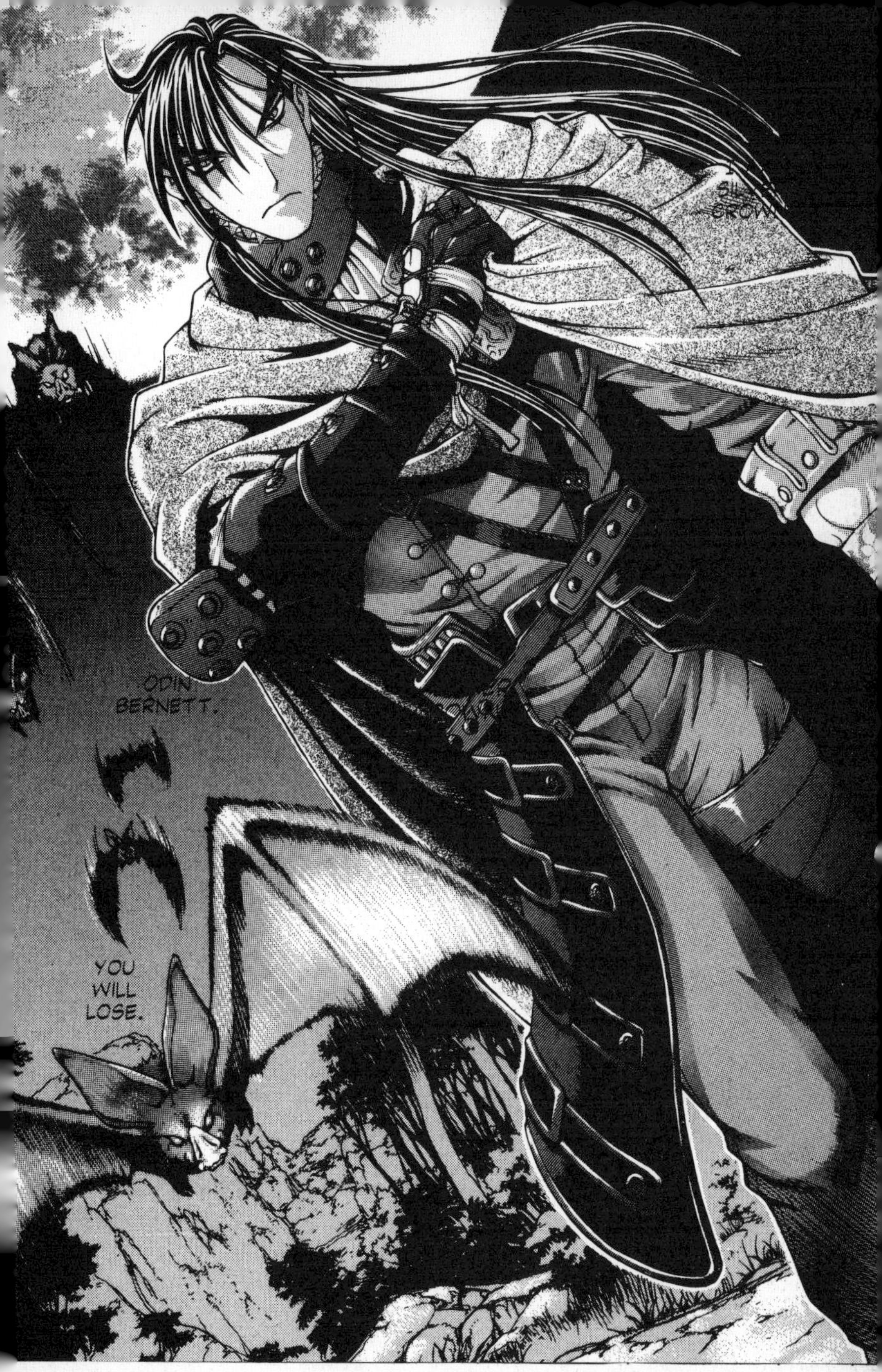
SIL
CROW
ODIN BERNETT.
YOU WILL LOSE.

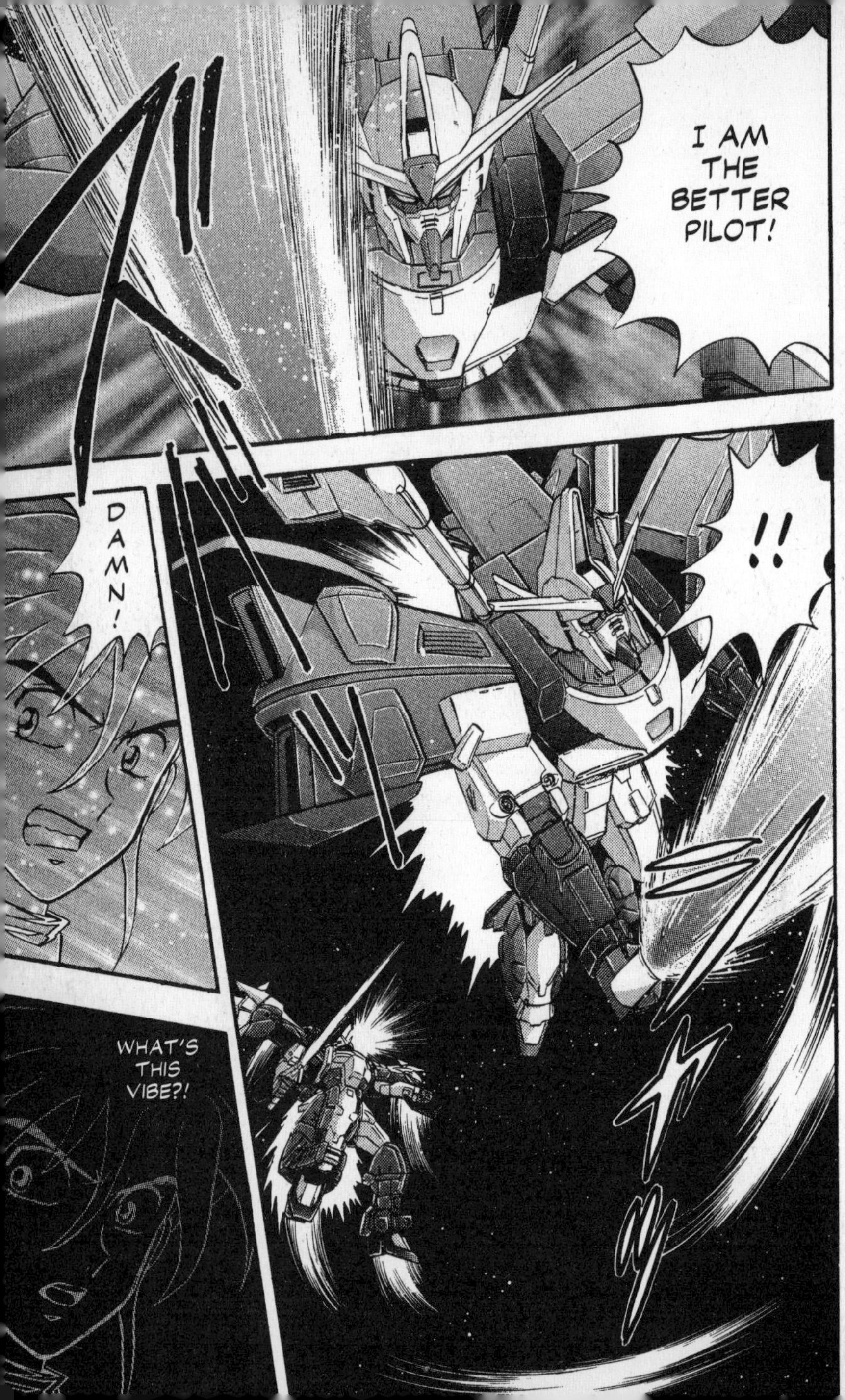
I AM THE BETTER PILOT!
!!
DAMN!
WHAT'S THIS VIBE?!

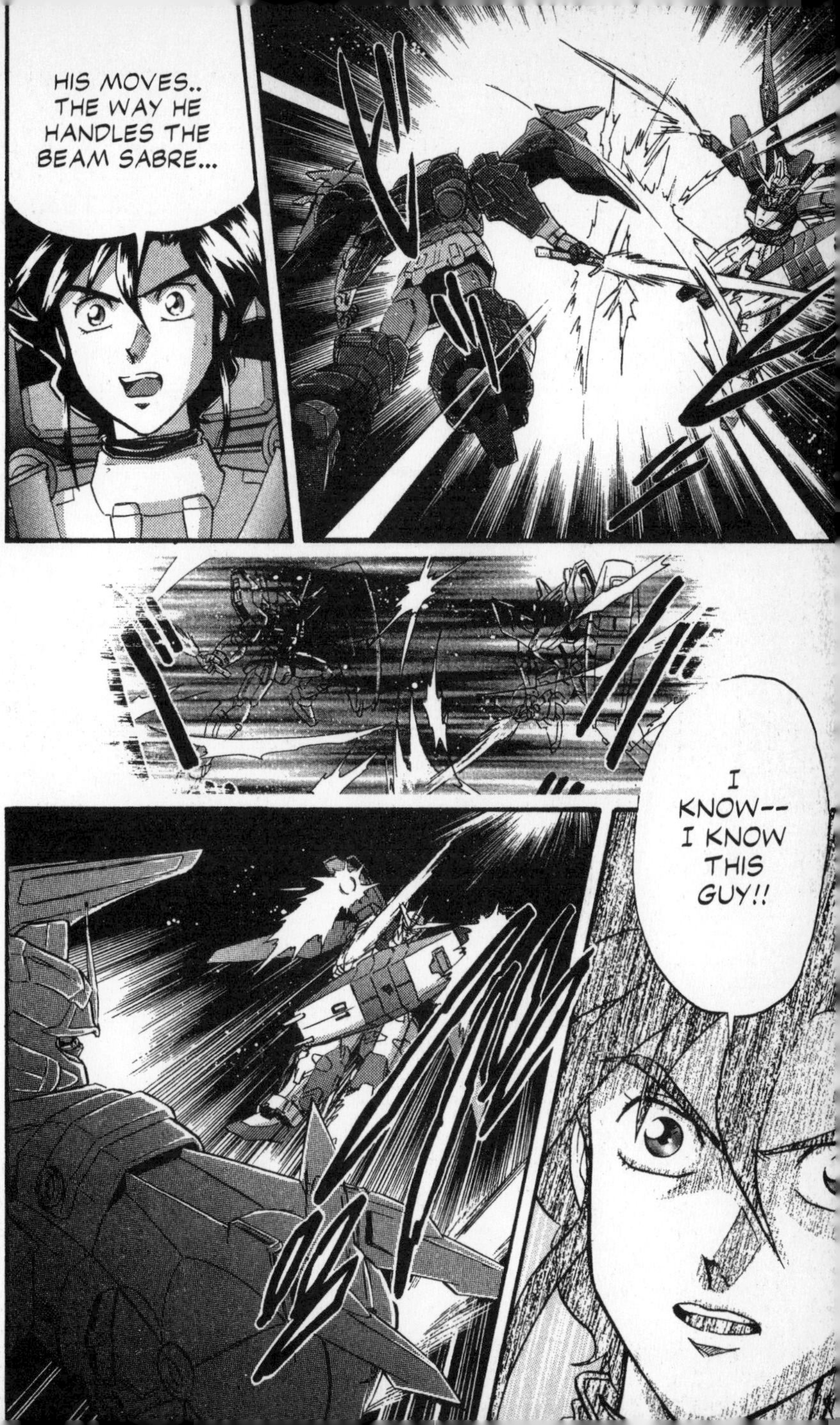
HIS MOVES.. THE WAY HE HANDLES THE BEAM SABRE...
I KNOW-- I KNOW THIS GUY!!

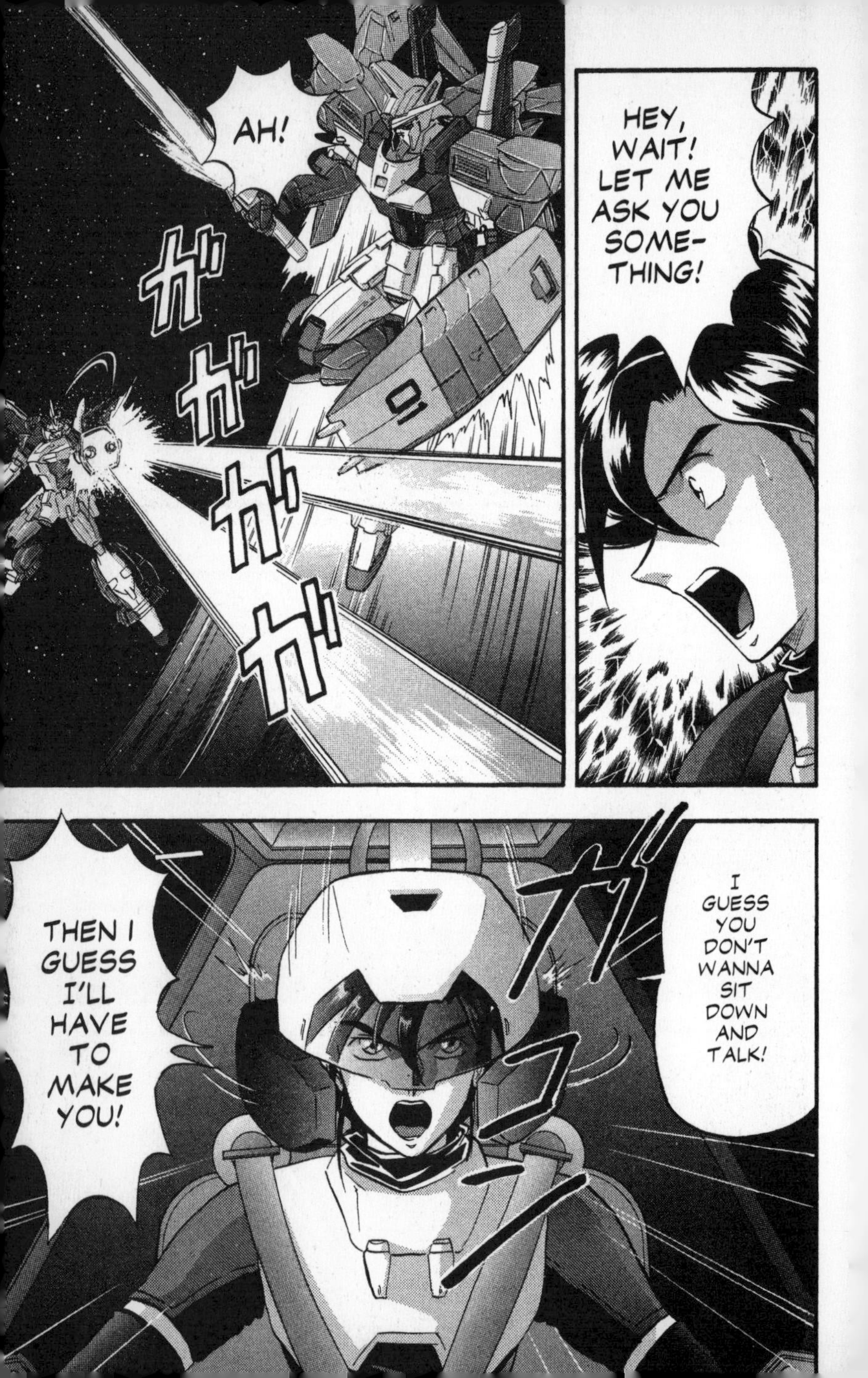
HEY, WAIT! LET ME ASK YOU SOME-THING!
AH!
ガガガガ
I GUESS YOU DON'T WANNA SIT DOWN AND TALK!
THEN I GUESS I'LL HAVE TO MAKE YOU!

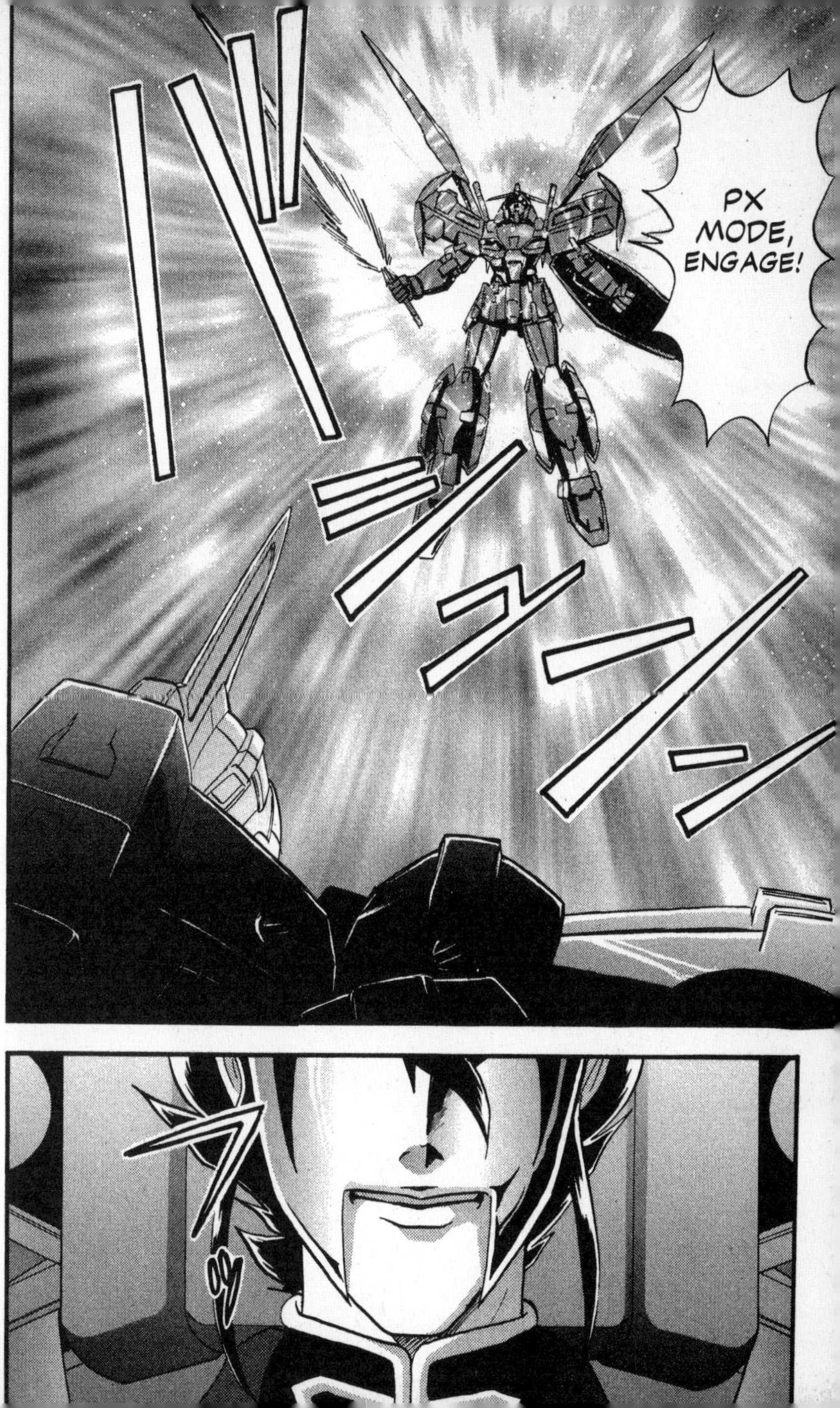
PX MODE, ENGAGE!

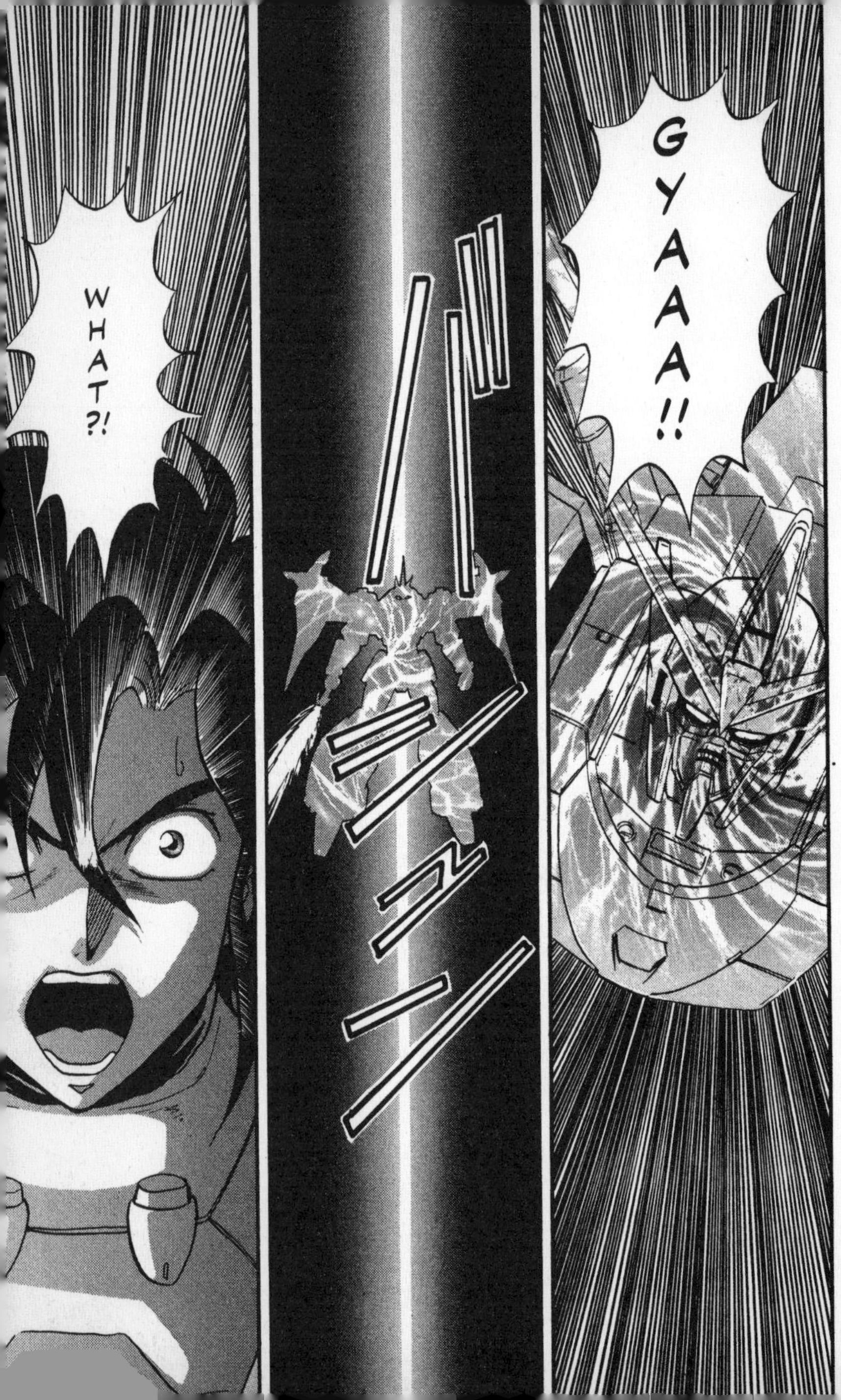
GYAAA!!
WHAT?!

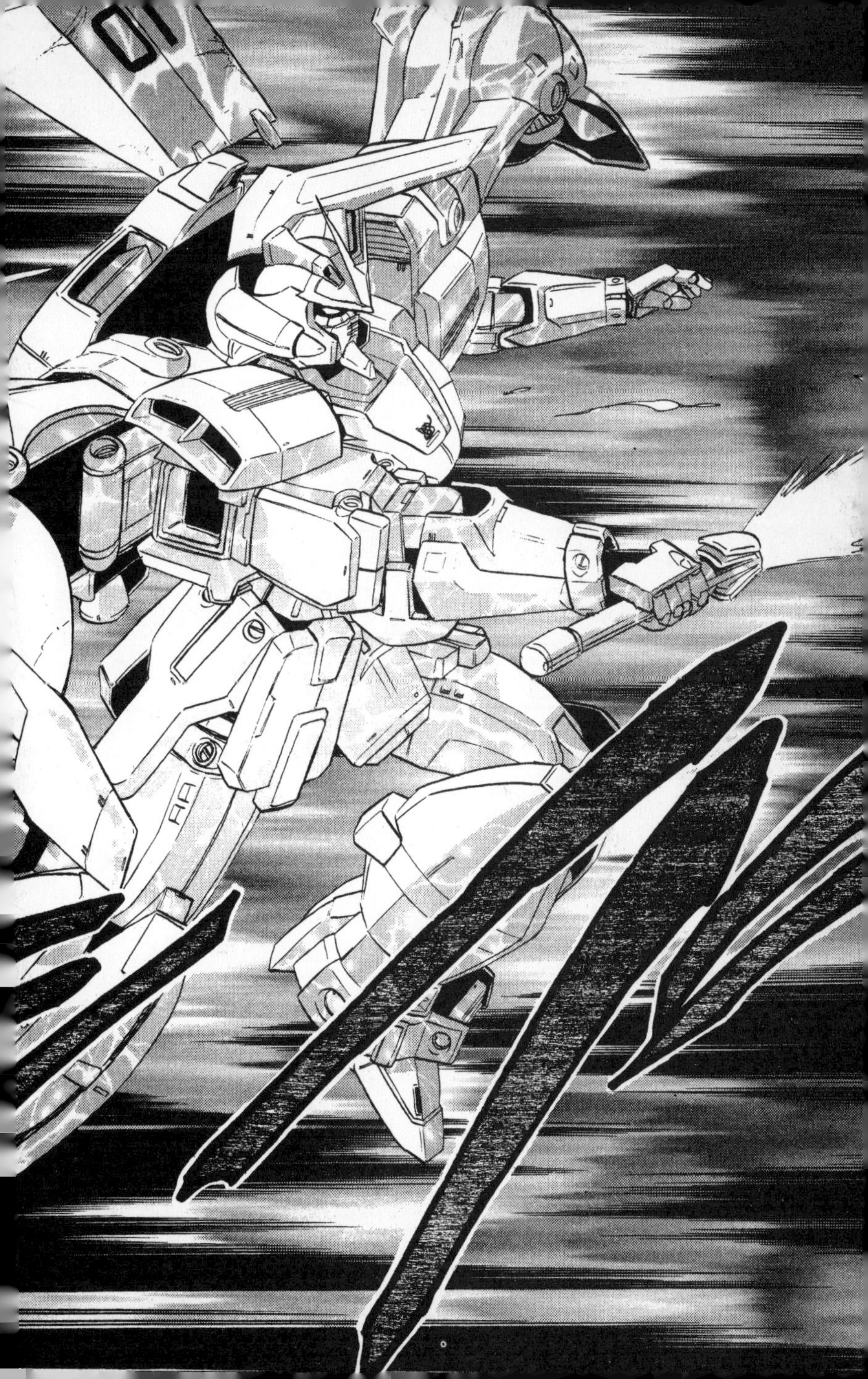

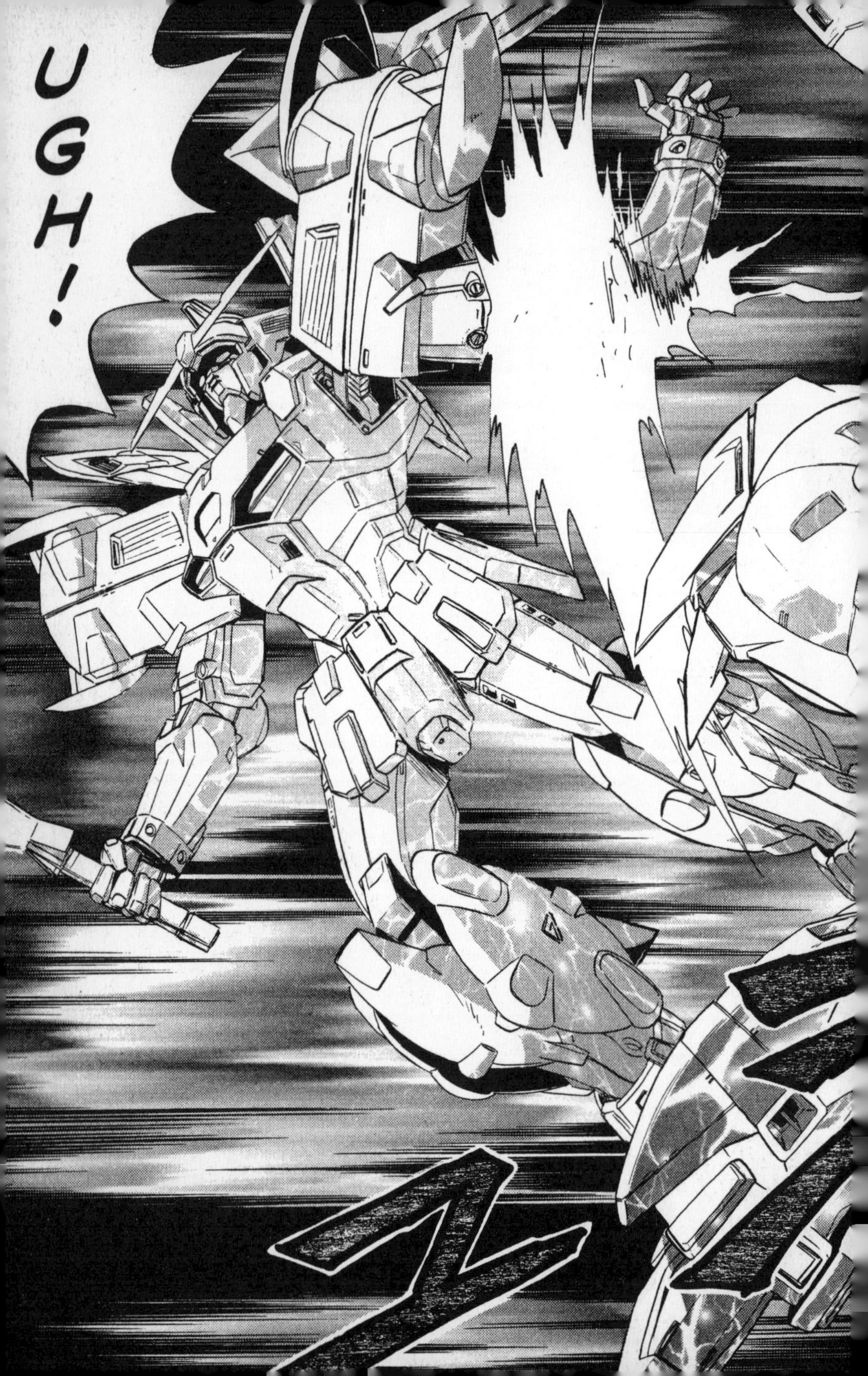
UGH!

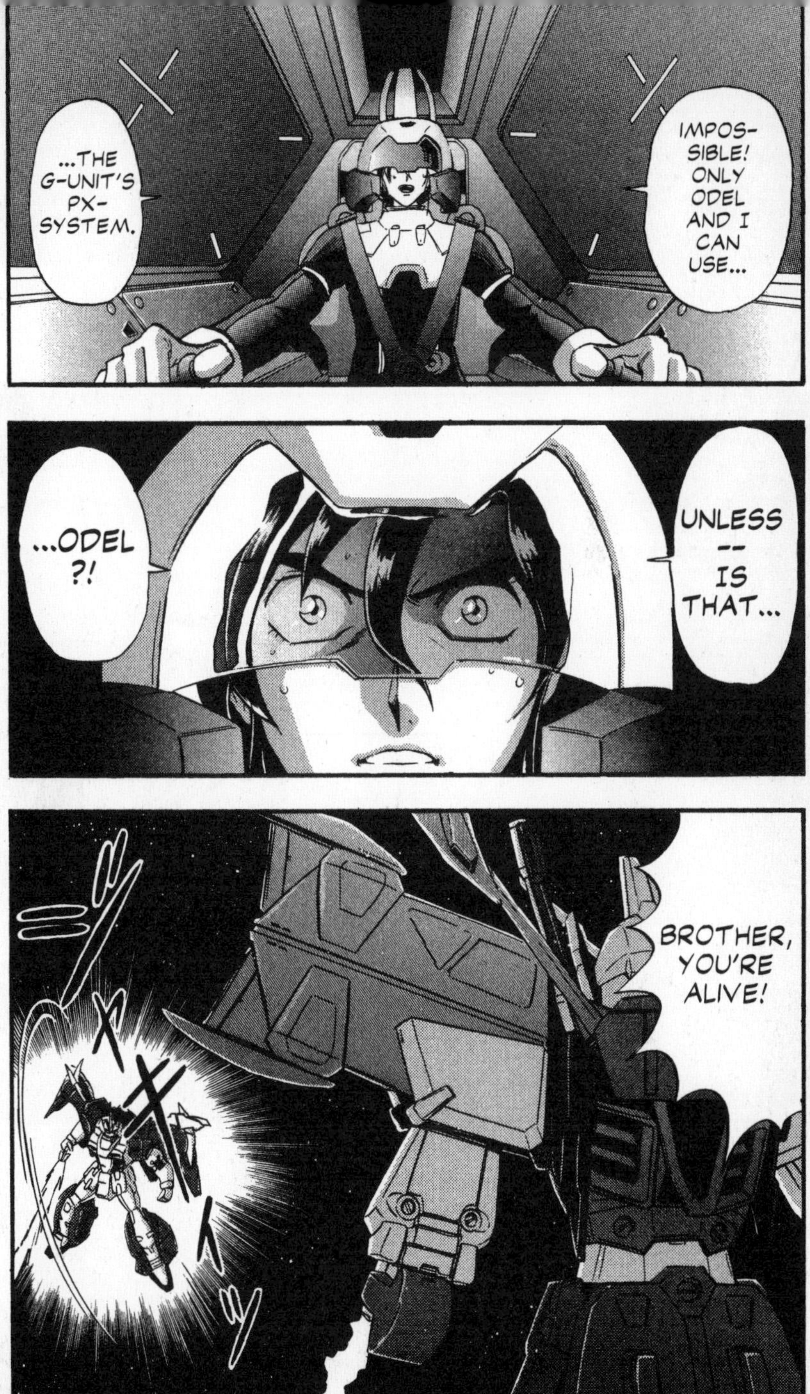
IMPOS-SIBLE! ONLY ODEL AND I CAN USE...
...THE G-UNIT'S PX-SYSTEM.
UNLESS -- IS THAT...
...ODEL ?!
BROTHER, YOU'RE ALIVE!

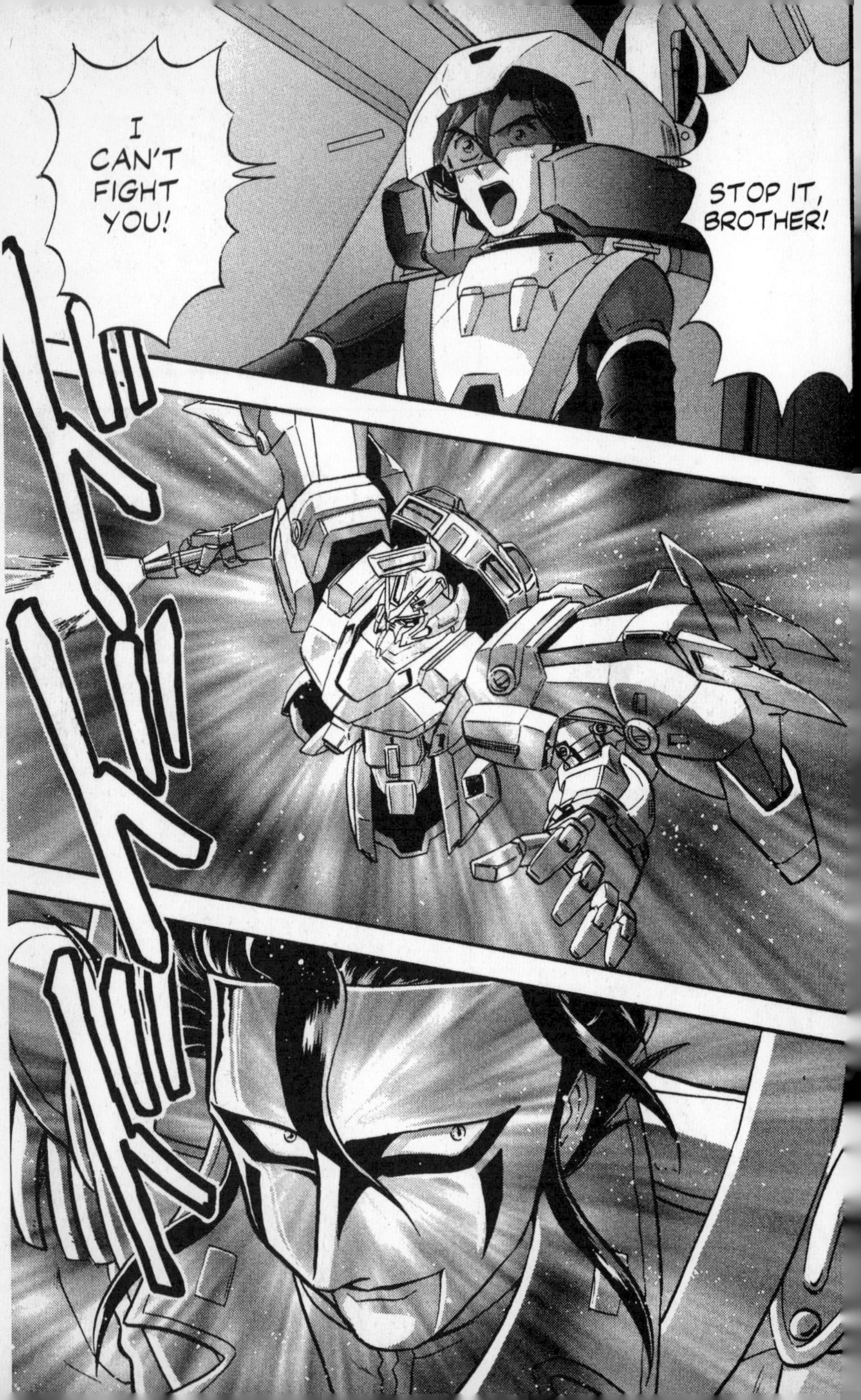
STOP IT, BROTHER!
I CAN'T FIGHT YOU!

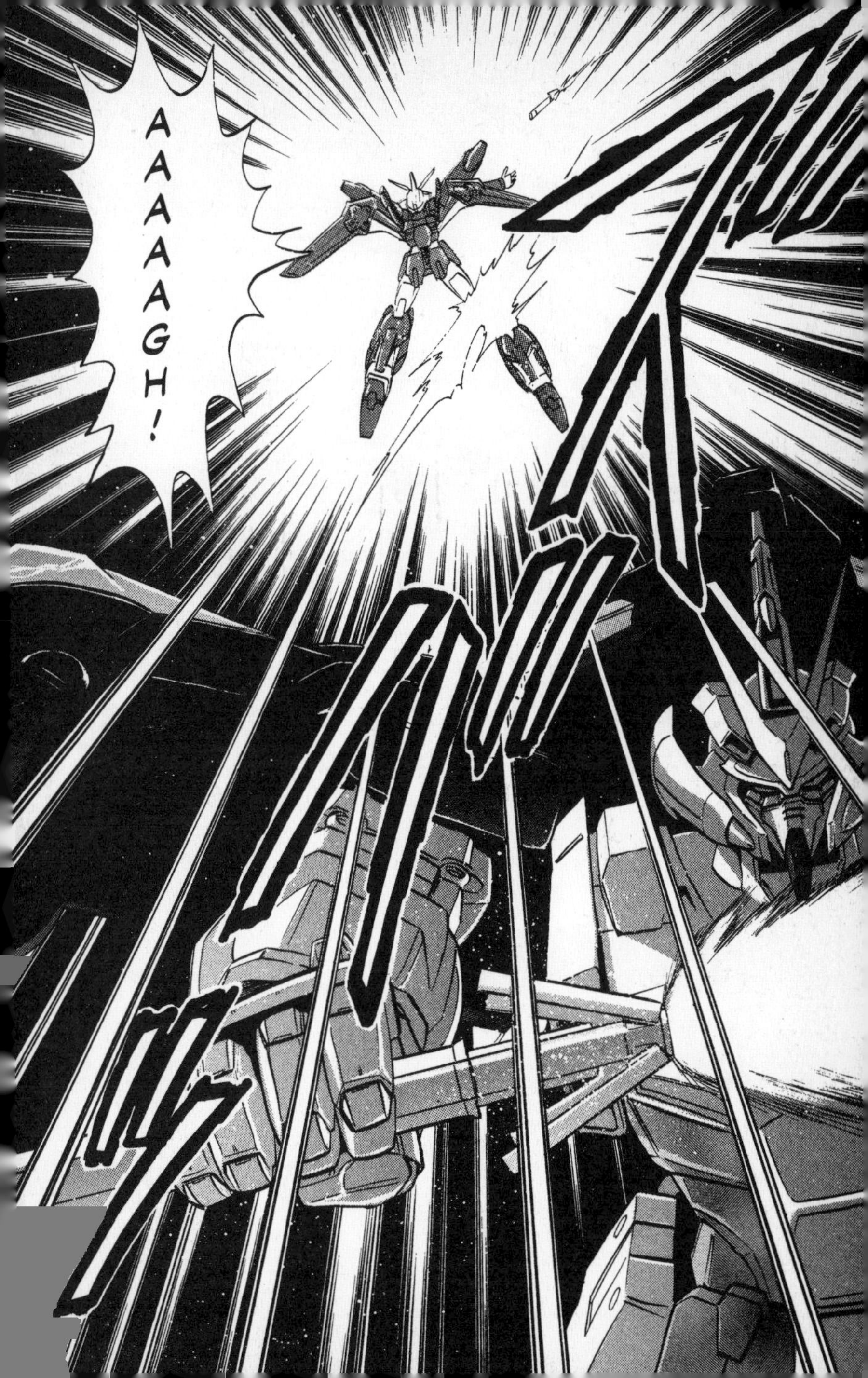
AAAAAGH!

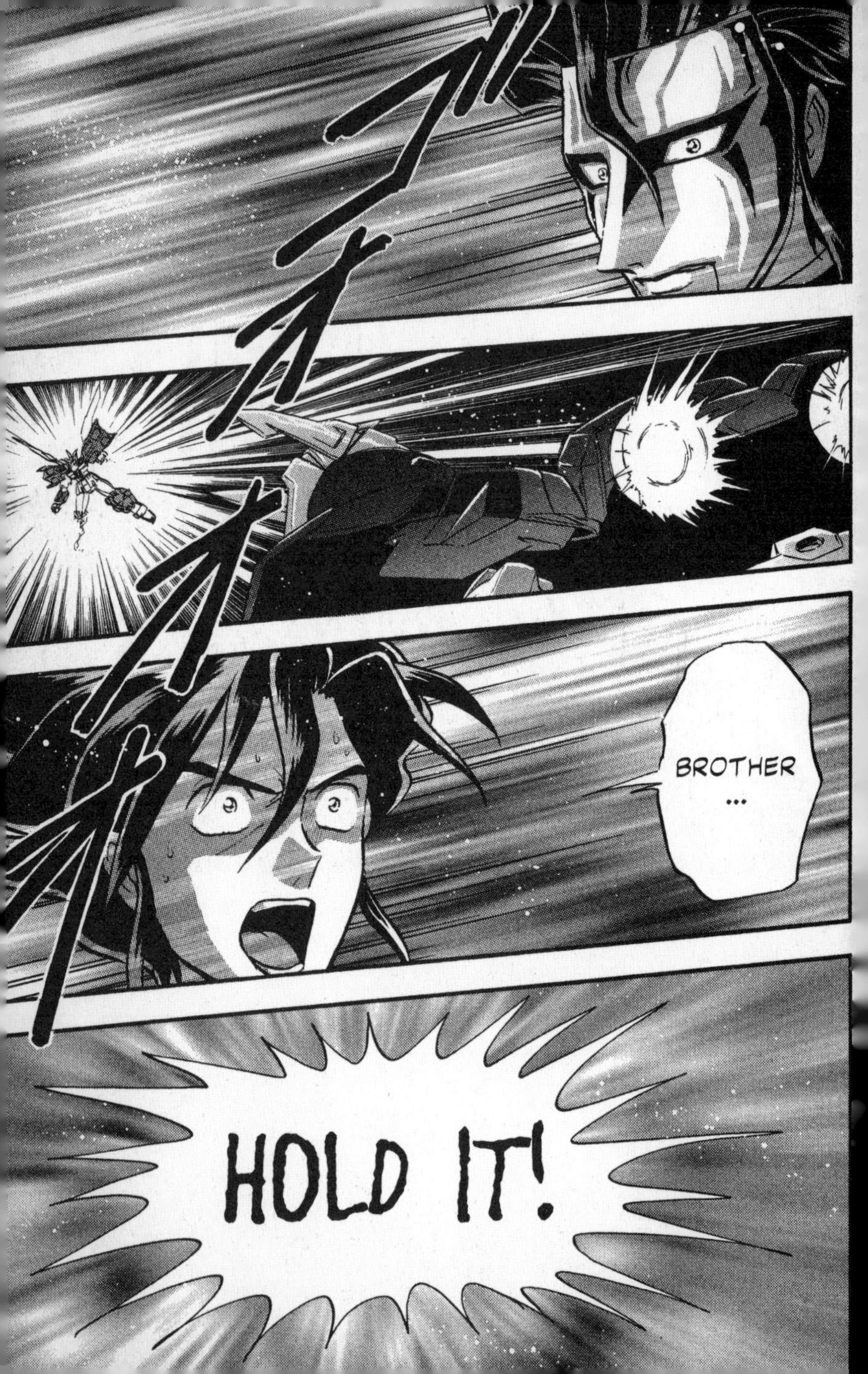
BROTHER ...
HOLD IT!

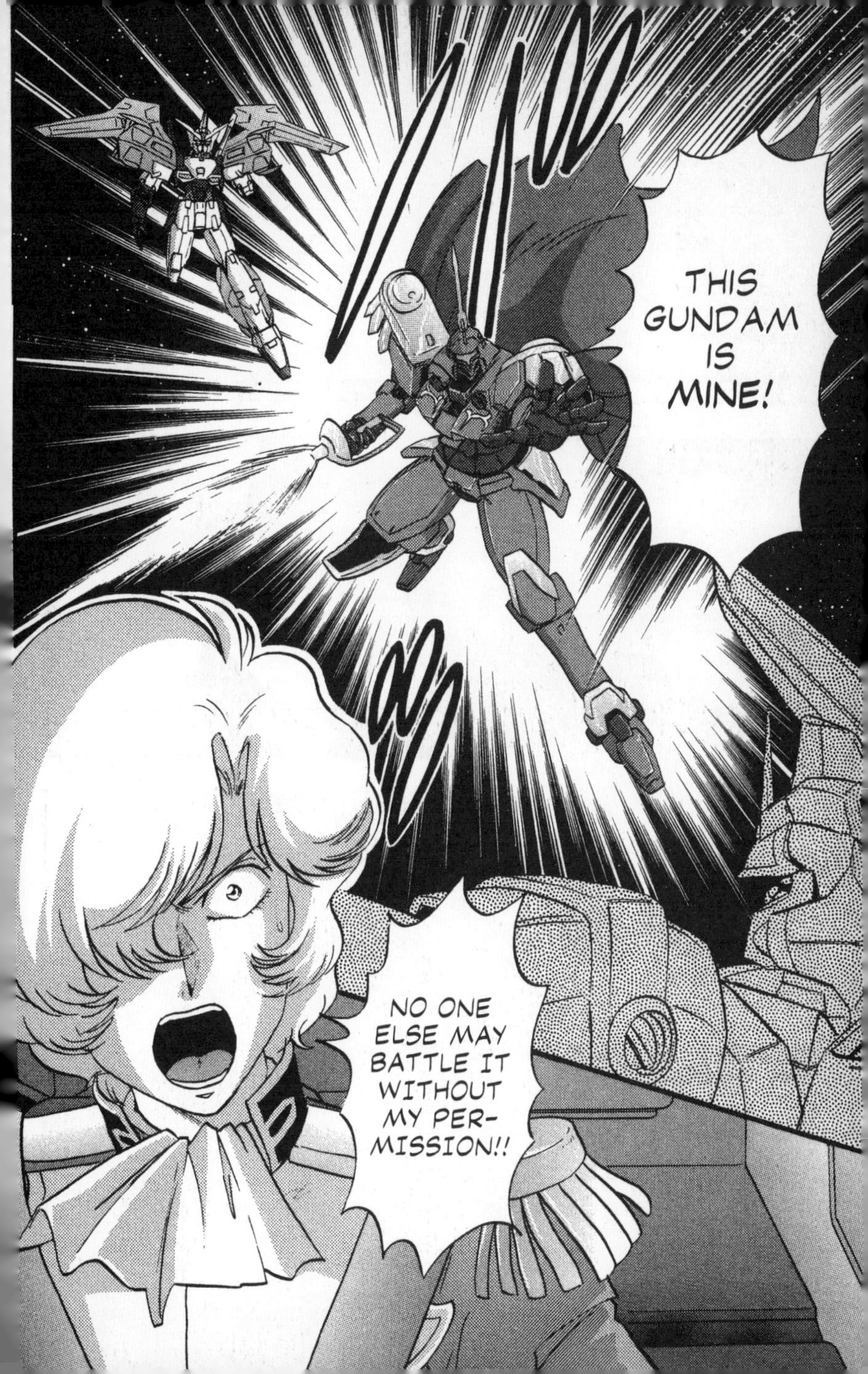
THIS GUNDAM IS MINE!
NO ONE ELSE MAY BATTLE IT WITHOUT MY PER-MISSION!!

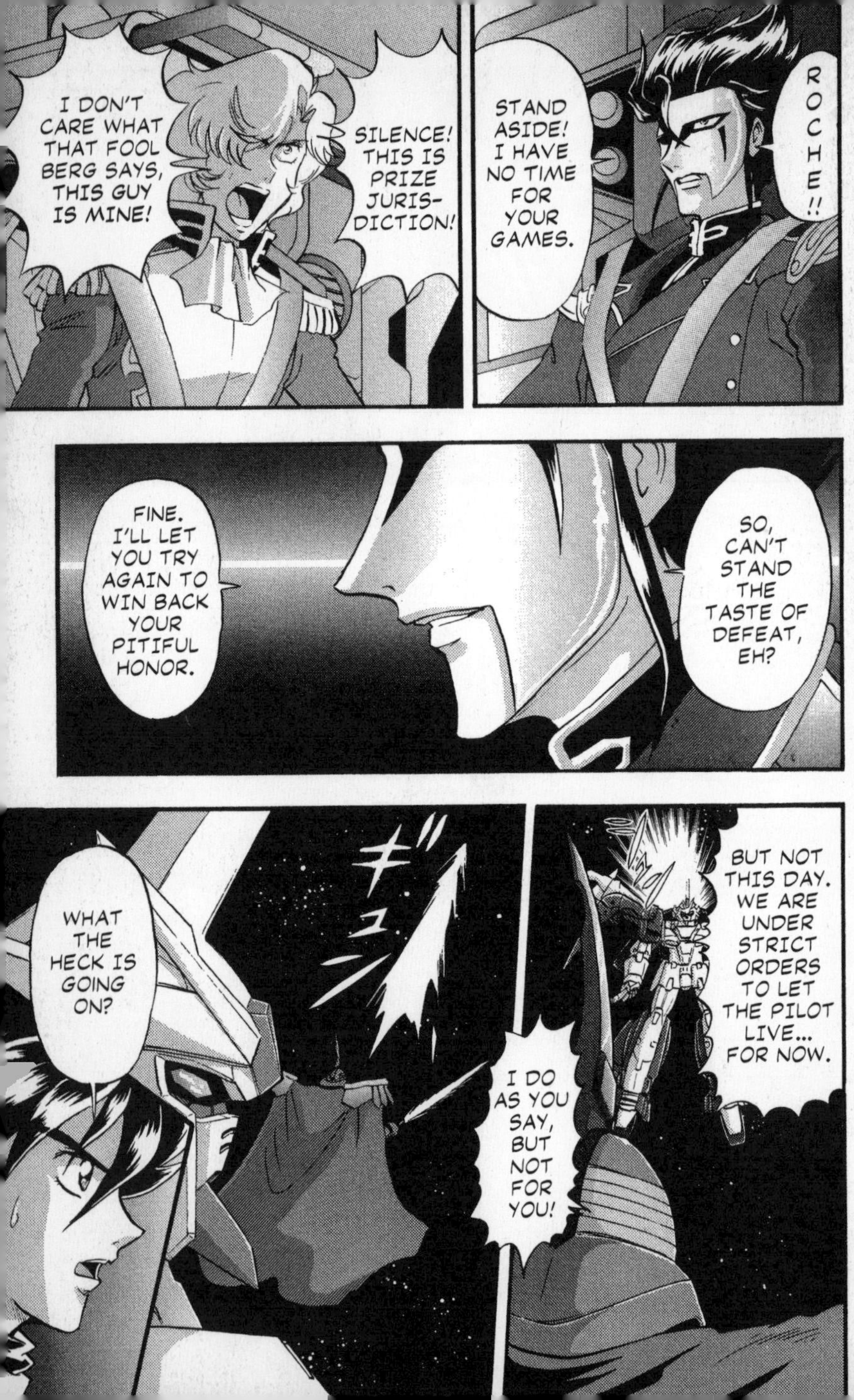
ROCHE!!
STAND ASIDE! I HAVE NO TIME FOR YOUR GAMES.
SILENCE! THIS IS PRIZE JURISDICTION!
I DON'T CARE WHAT THAT FOOL BERG SAYS, THIS GUY IS MINE!
SO, CAN'T STAND THE TASTE OF DEFEAT, EH?
FINE. I'LL LET YOU TRY AGAIN TO WIN BACK YOUR PITIFUL HONOR.
BUT NOT THIS DAY. WE ARE UNDER STRICT ORDERS TO LET THE PILOT LIVE... FOR NOW.
I DO AS YOU SAY, BUT NOT FOR YOU!
ギュ
WHAT THE HECK IS GOING ON?

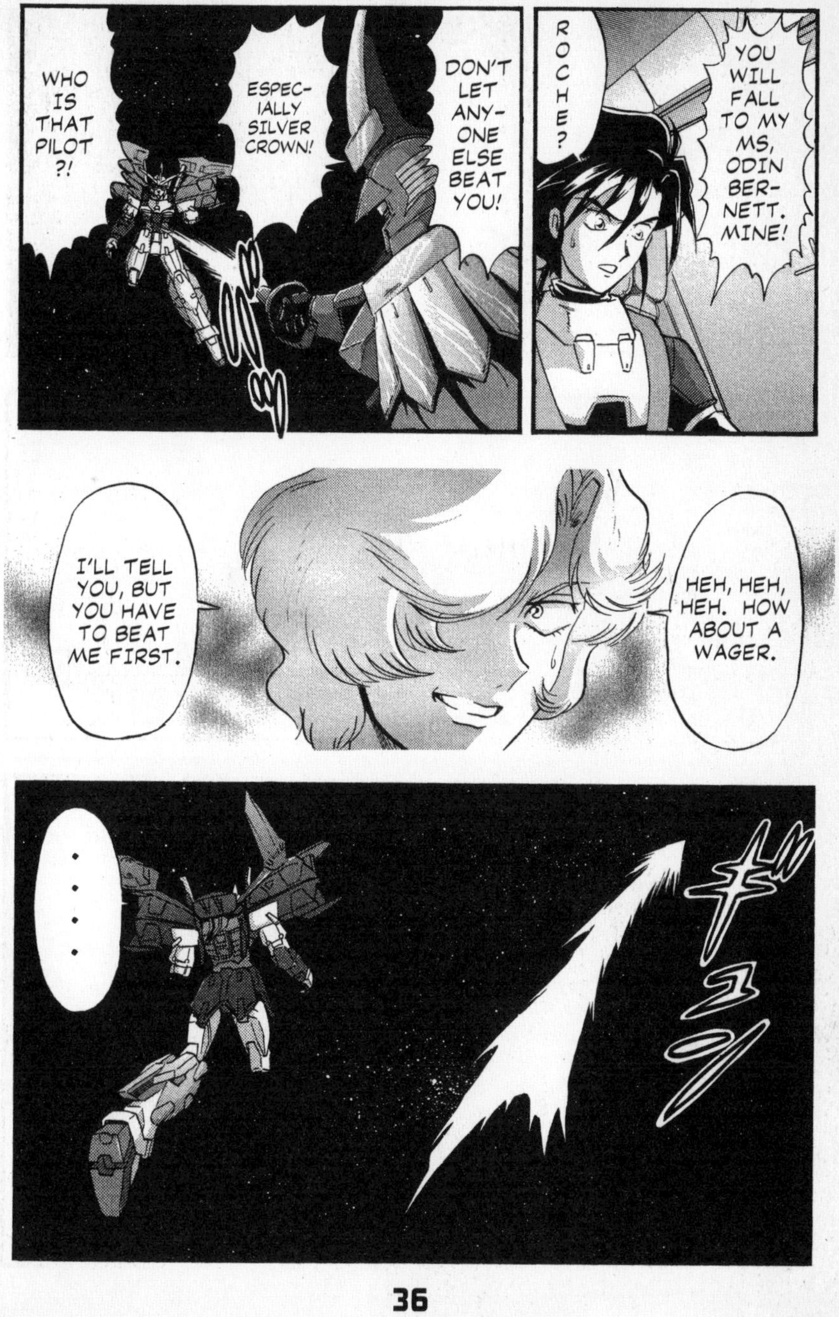
YOU WILL FALL TO MY MS, ODIN BERNETT. MINE!
ROCHE?
DON'T LET ANYONE ELSE BEAT YOU!
ESPECIALLY SILVER CROWN!
WHO IS THAT PILOT?!
HEH, HEH, HEH. HOW ABOUT A WAGER.
I'LL TELL YOU, BUT YOU HAVE TO BEAT ME FIRST.
....

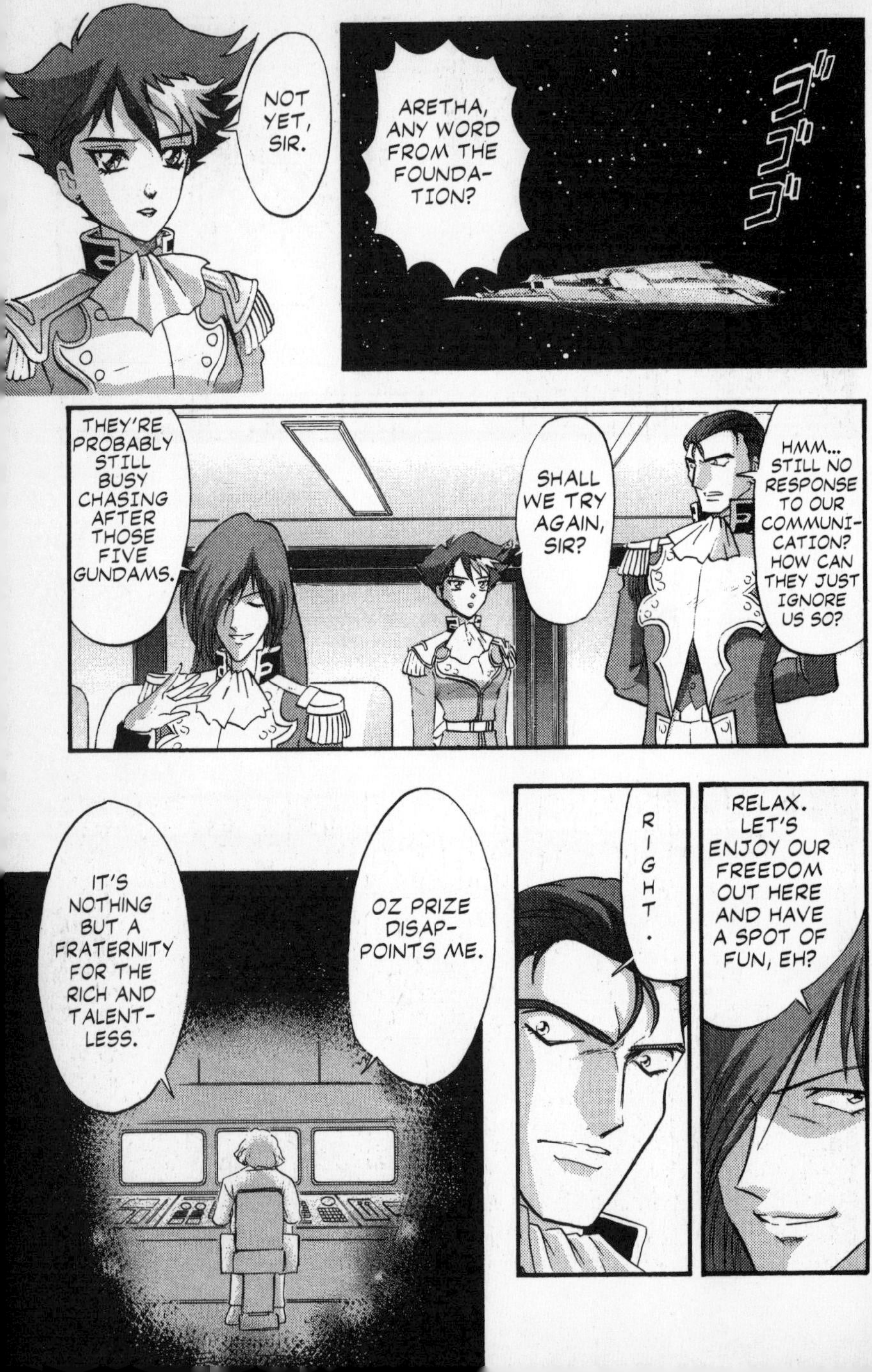
ゴゴゴゴ
ARETHA, ANY WORD FROM THE FOUNDATION?
NOT YET, SIR.
HMM... STILL NO RESPONSE TO OUR COMMUNICATION? HOW CAN THEY JUST IGNORE US SO?
SHALL WE TRY AGAIN, SIR?
THEY'RE PROBABLY STILL BUSY CHASING AFTER THOSE FIVE GUNDAMS.
RELAX. LET'S ENJOY OUR FREEDOM OUT HERE AND HAVE A SPOT OF FUN, EH?
RIGHT.
OZ PRIZE DISAPPOINTS ME.
IT'S NOTHING BUT A FRATERNITY FOR THE RICH AND TALENTLESS.

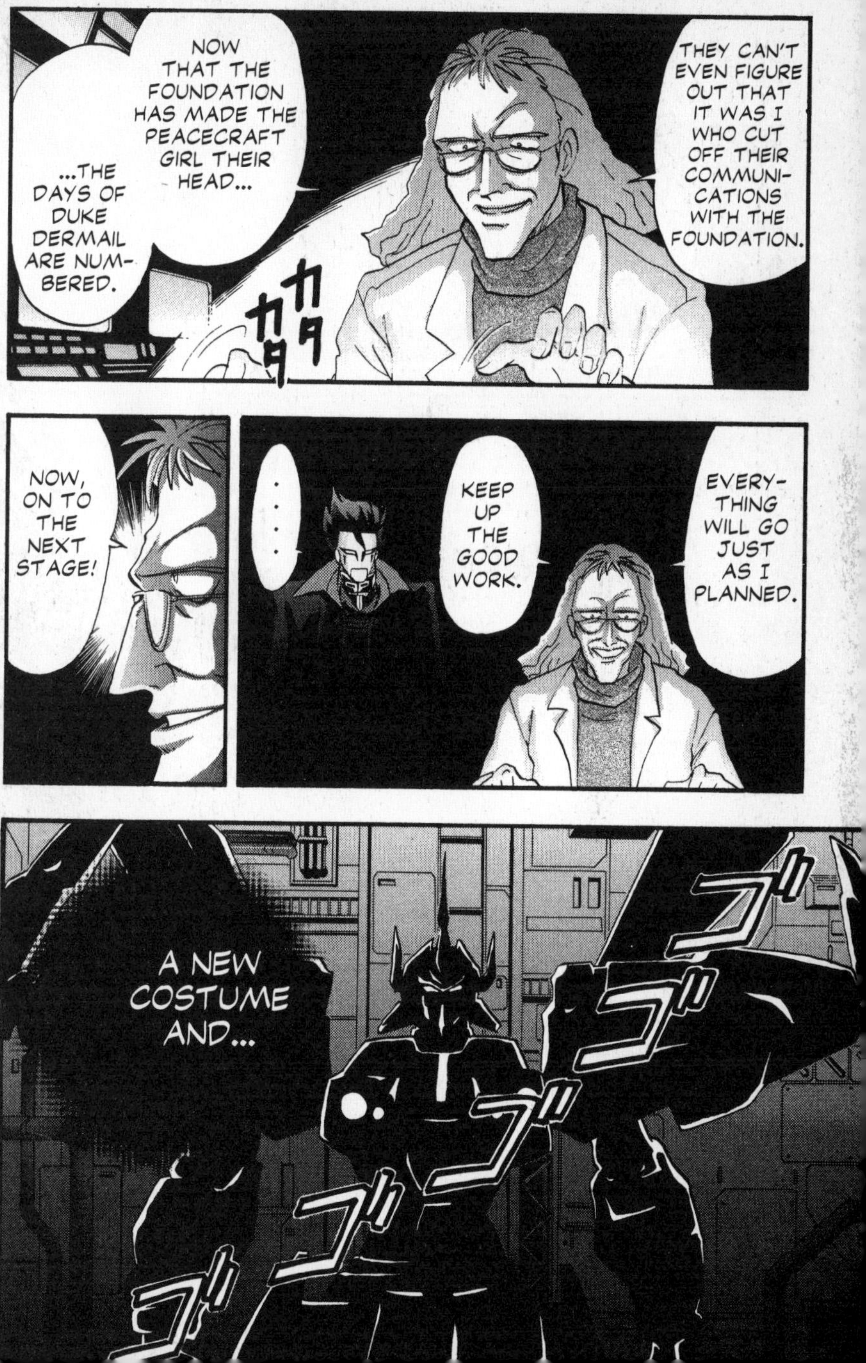
THEY CAN'T EVEN FIGURE OUT THAT IT WAS I WHO CUT OFF THEIR COMMUNI-CATIONS WITH THE FOUNDATION.
NOW THAT THE FOUNDATION HAS MADE THE PEACECRAFT GIRL THEIR HEAD...
...THE DAYS OF DUKE DERMAIL ARE NUM-BERED.
カタカタ
EVERY-THING WILL GO JUST AS I PLANNED.
KEEP UP THE GOOD WORK.
....
NOW, ON TO THE NEXT STAGE!
A NEW COSTUME AND...
ゴゴゴゴゴゴ

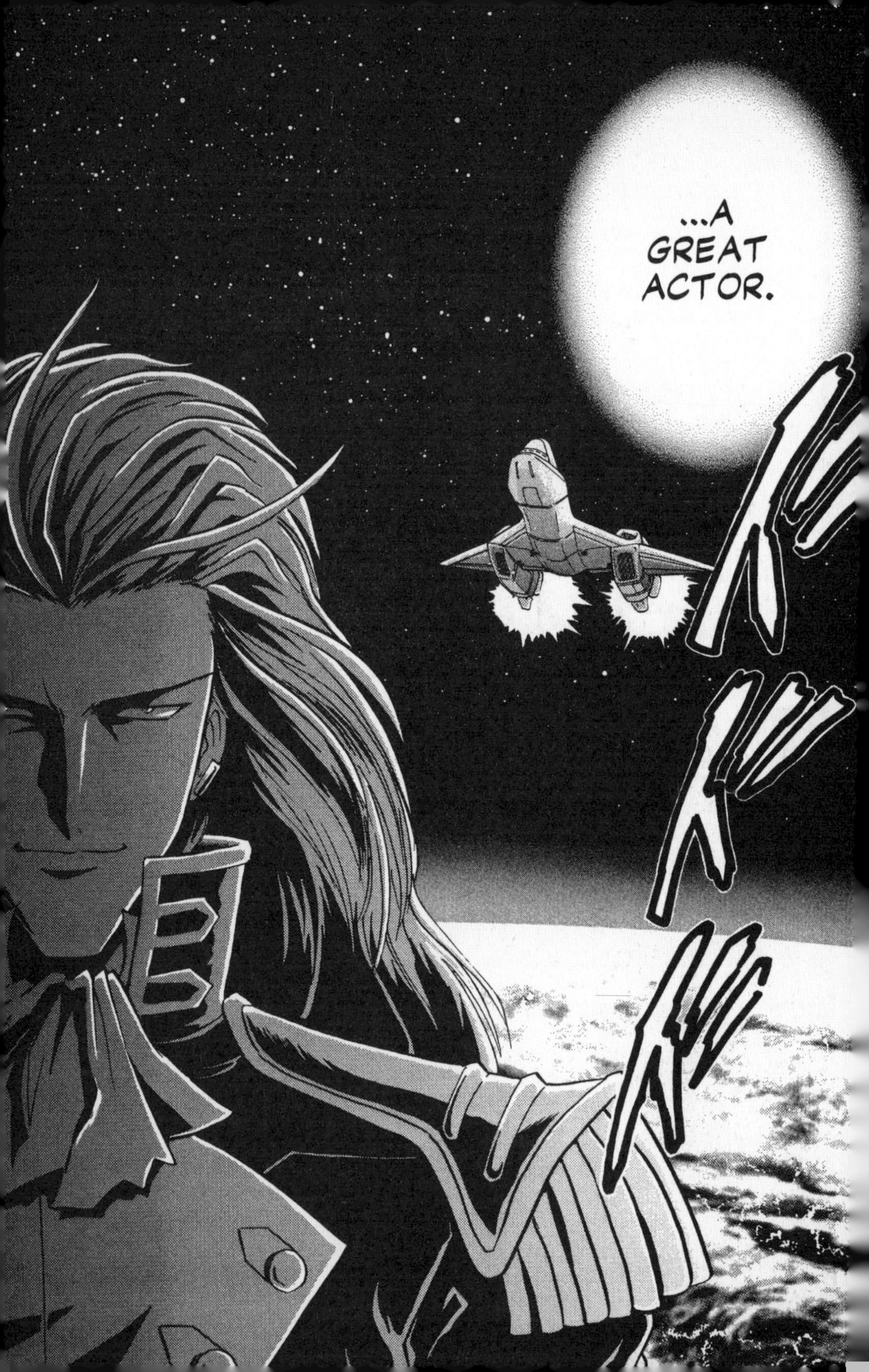
...A GREAT ACTOR.

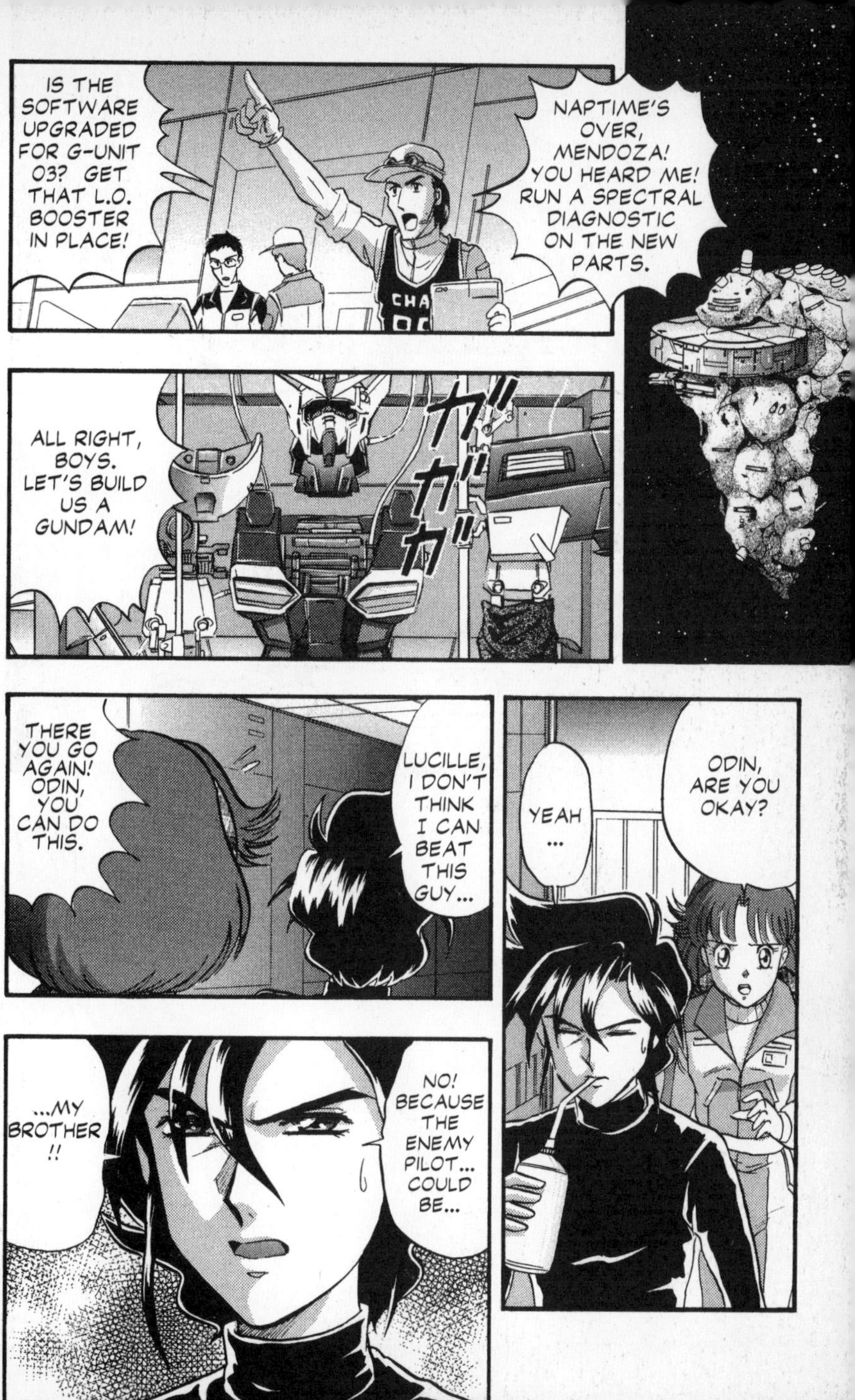
NAPTIME'S OVER, MENDOZA! YOU HEARD ME! RUN A SPECTRAL DIAGNOSTIC ON THE NEW PARTS.
IS THE SOFTWARE UPGRADED FOR G-UNIT 03? GET THAT L.O. BOOSTER IN PLACE!
ガガガ
ALL RIGHT, BOYS. LET'S BUILD US A GUNDAM!
ODIN, ARE YOU OKAY?
YEAH ...
LUCILLE, I DON'T THINK I CAN BEAT THIS GUY...
THERE YOU GO AGAIN! ODIN, YOU CAN DO THIS.
NO! BECAUSE THE ENEMY PILOT... COULD BE...
...MY BROTHER !!

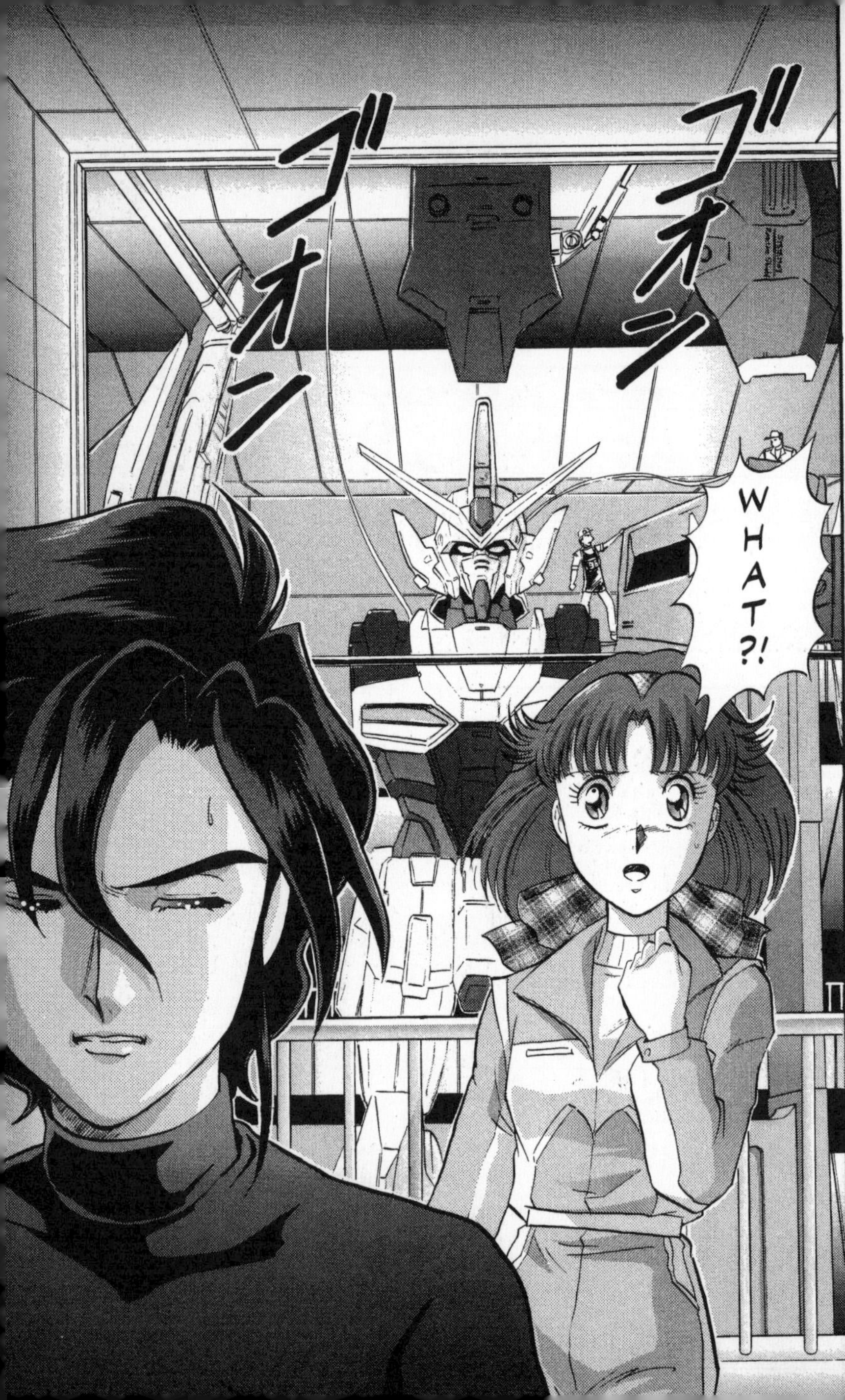
ゴォン
ゴォン
WHAT?!

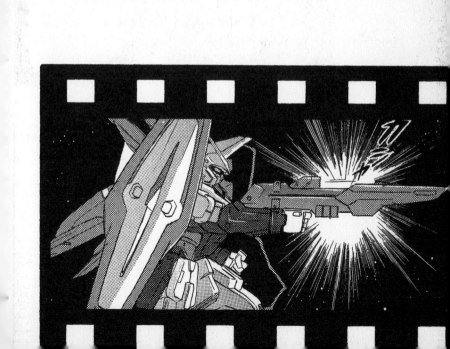

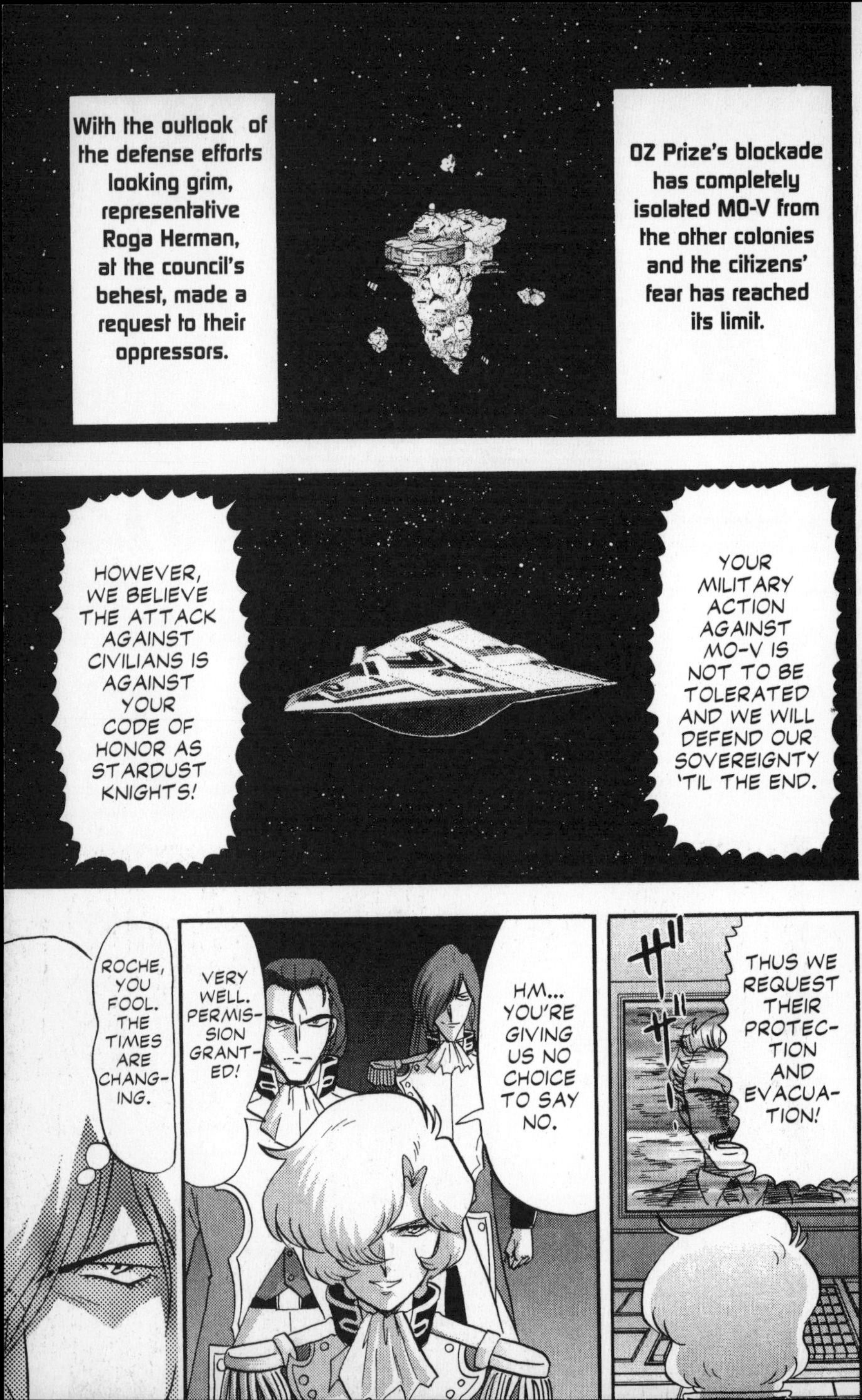
OZ Prize's blockade has completely isolated MO-V from the other colonies and the citizens' fear has reached its limit.
With the outlook of the defense efforts looking grim, representative Roga Herman, at the council's behest, made a request to their oppressors.
YOUR MILITARY ACTION AGAINST MO-V IS NOT TO BE TOLERATED AND WE WILL DEFEND OUR SOVEREIGNTY 'TIL THE END.
HOWEVER, WE BELIEVE THE ATTACK AGAINST CIVILIANS IS AGAINST YOUR CODE OF HONOR AS STARDUST KNIGHTS!
THUS WE REQUEST THEIR PROTECTION AND EVACUATION!
HM... YOU'RE GIVING US NO CHOICE TO SAY NO.
VERY WELL. PERMISSION GRANTED!
ROCHE, YOU FOOL. THE TIMES ARE CHANGING.

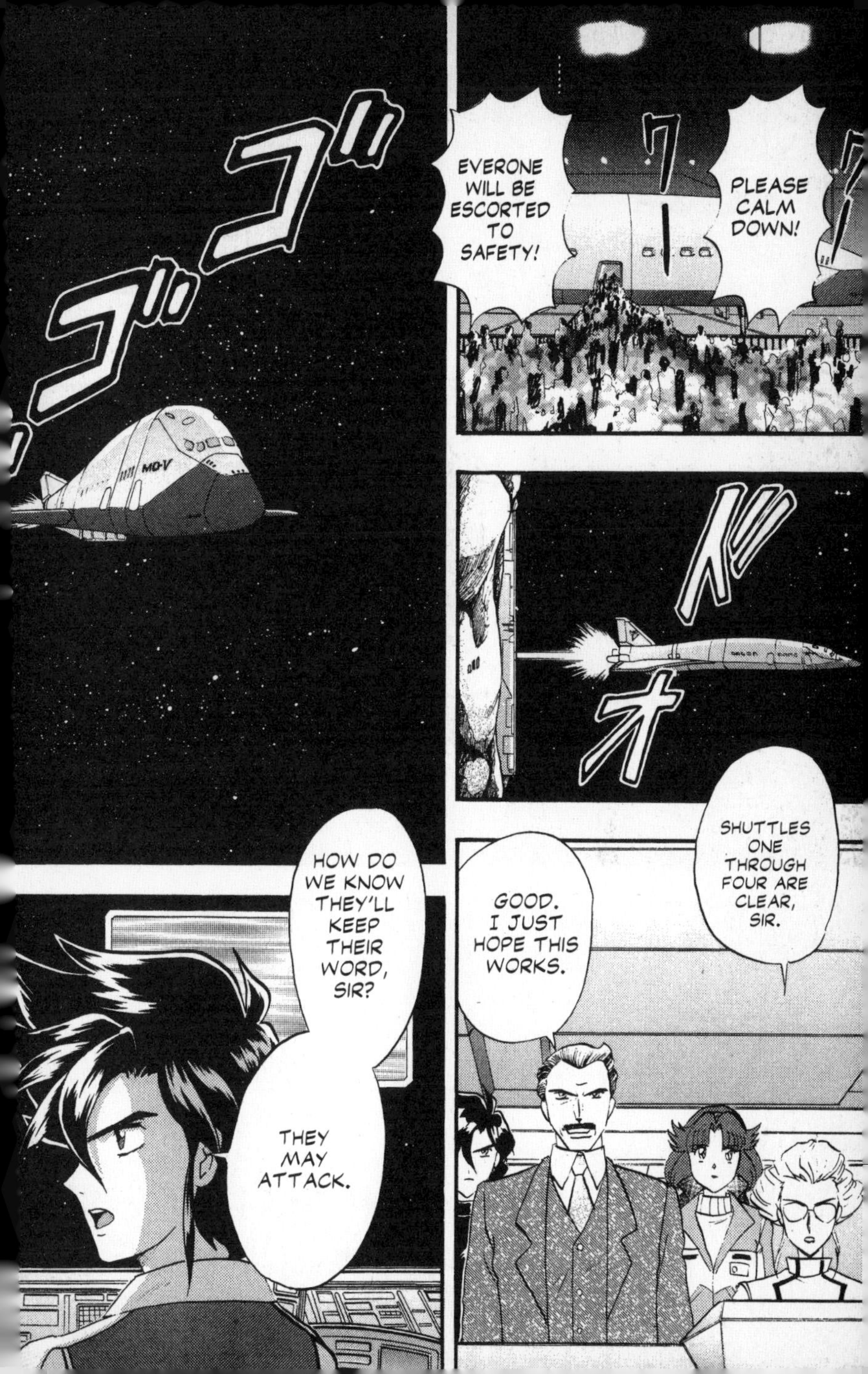
PLEASE CALM DOWN!
EVERONE WILL BE ESCORTED TO SAFETY!
SHUTTLES ONE THROUGH FOUR ARE CLEAR, SIR.
GOOD. I JUST HOPE THIS WORKS.
HOW DO WE KNOW THEY'LL KEEP THEIR WORD, SIR?
THEY MAY ATTACK.

#6 Dark General of Destruction

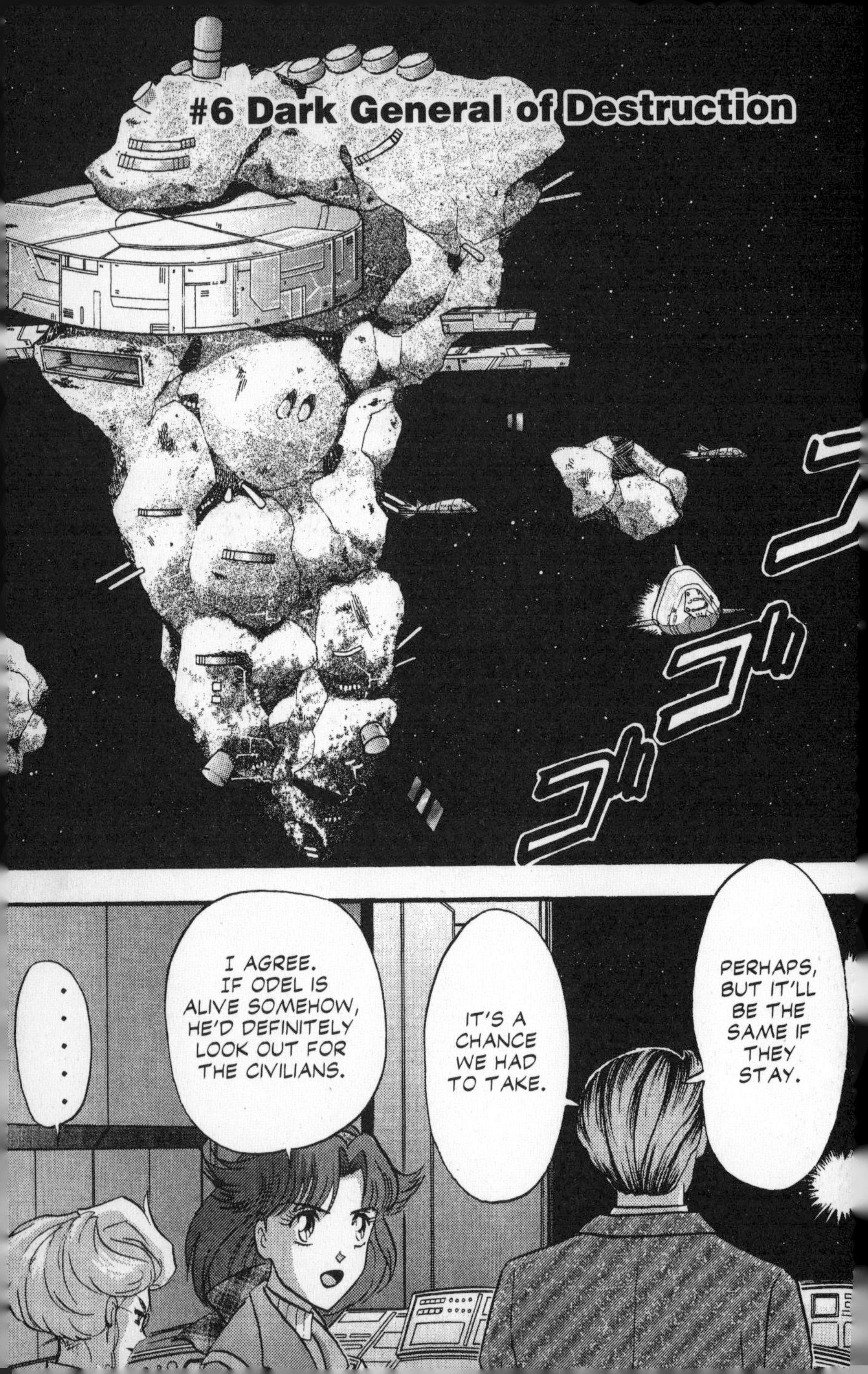
PERHAPS, BUT IT'LL BE THE SAME IF THEY STAY.
IT'S A CHANCE WE HAD TO TAKE.
I AGREE. IF ODEL IS ALIVE SOMEHOW, HE'D DEFINITELY LOOK OUT FOR THE CIVILIANS.
......

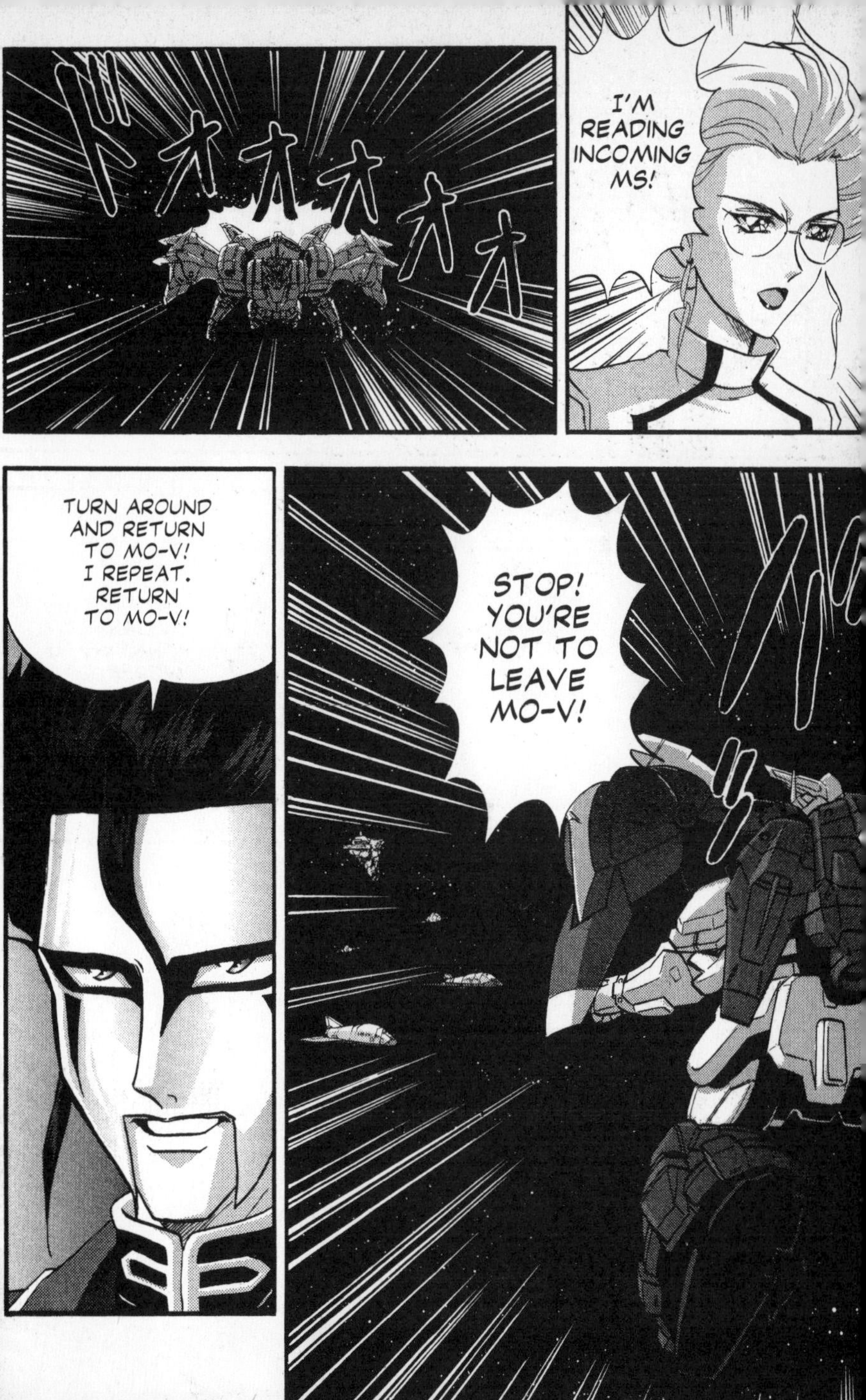
I'M READING INCOMING MS!
STOP! YOU'RE NOT TO LEAVE MO-V!
TURN AROUND AND RETURN TO MO-V! I REPEAT. RETURN TO MO-V!

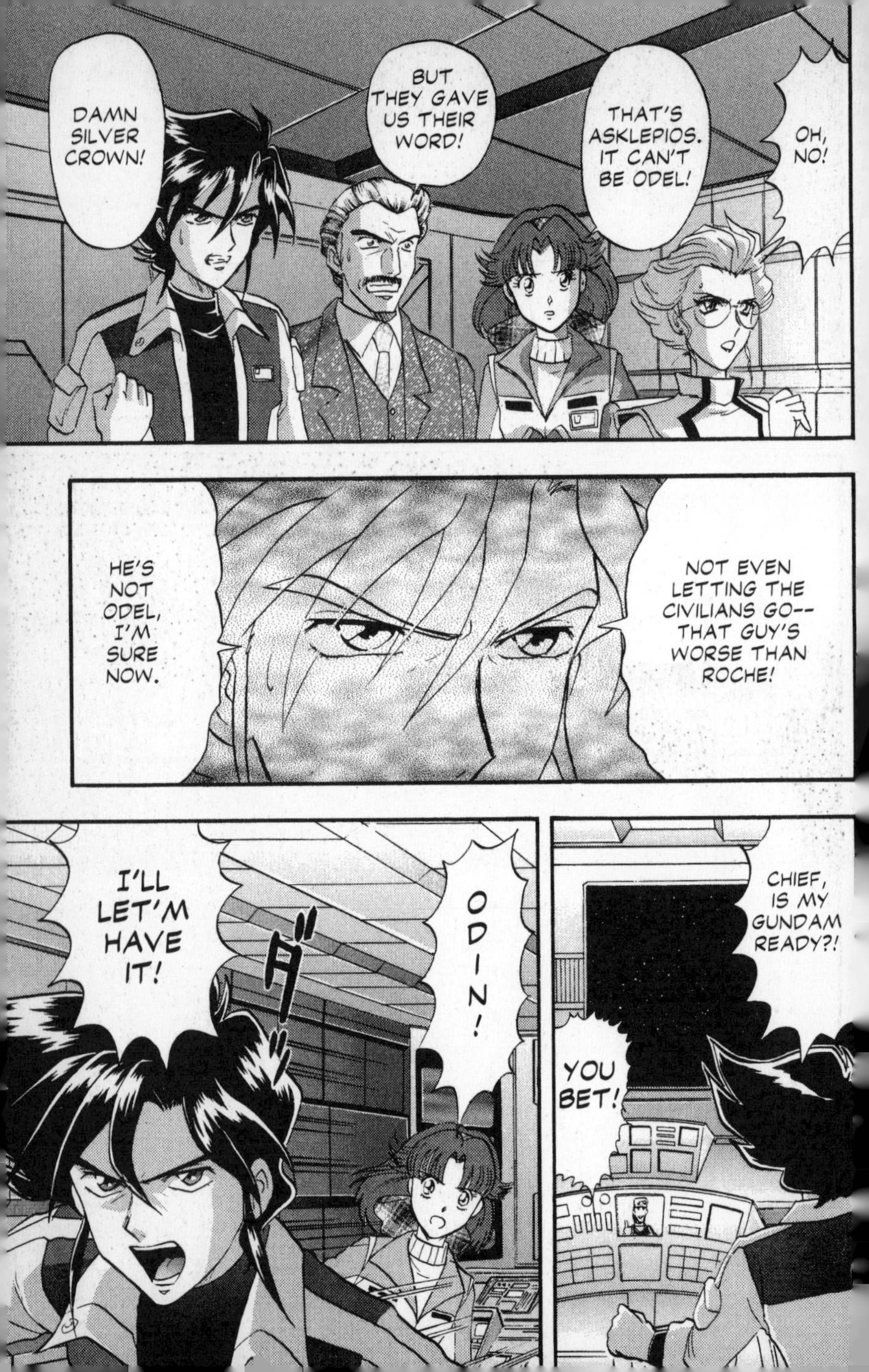
OH, NO!
THAT'S ASKLEPIOS. IT CAN'T BE ODEL!
BUT THEY GAVE US THEIR WORD!
DAMN SILVER CROWN!
NOT EVEN LETTING THE CIVILIANS GO-- THAT GUY'S WORSE THAN ROCHE!
HE'S NOT ODEL, I'M SURE NOW.
CHIEF, IS MY GUNDAM READY?!
YOU BET!
ODIN!
ガッ
I'LL LET'M HAVE IT!

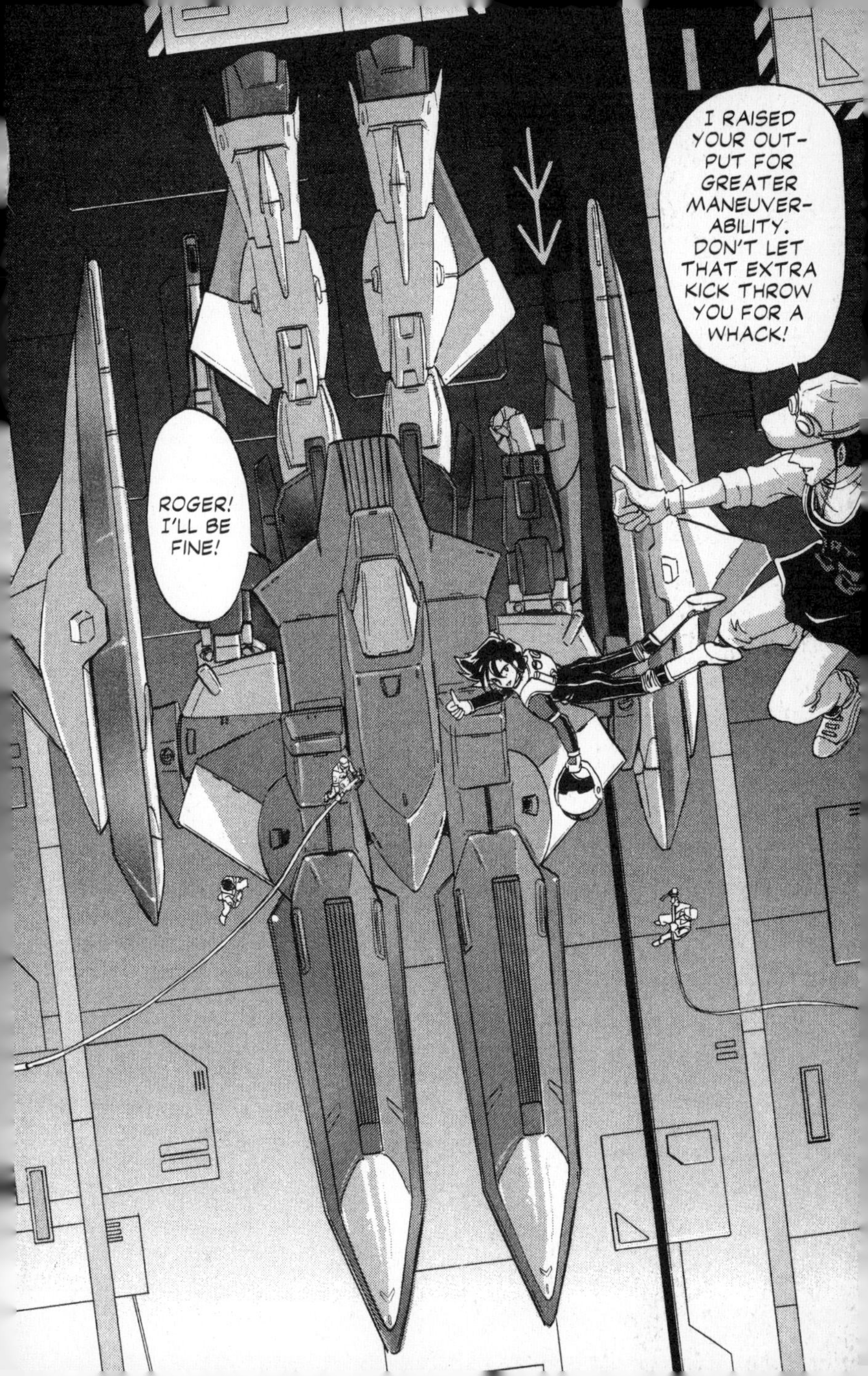
I RAISED YOUR OUT-PUT FOR GREATER MANEUVER-ABILITY. DON'T LET THAT EXTRA KICK THROW YOU FOR A WHACK!
ROGER! I'LL BE FINE!

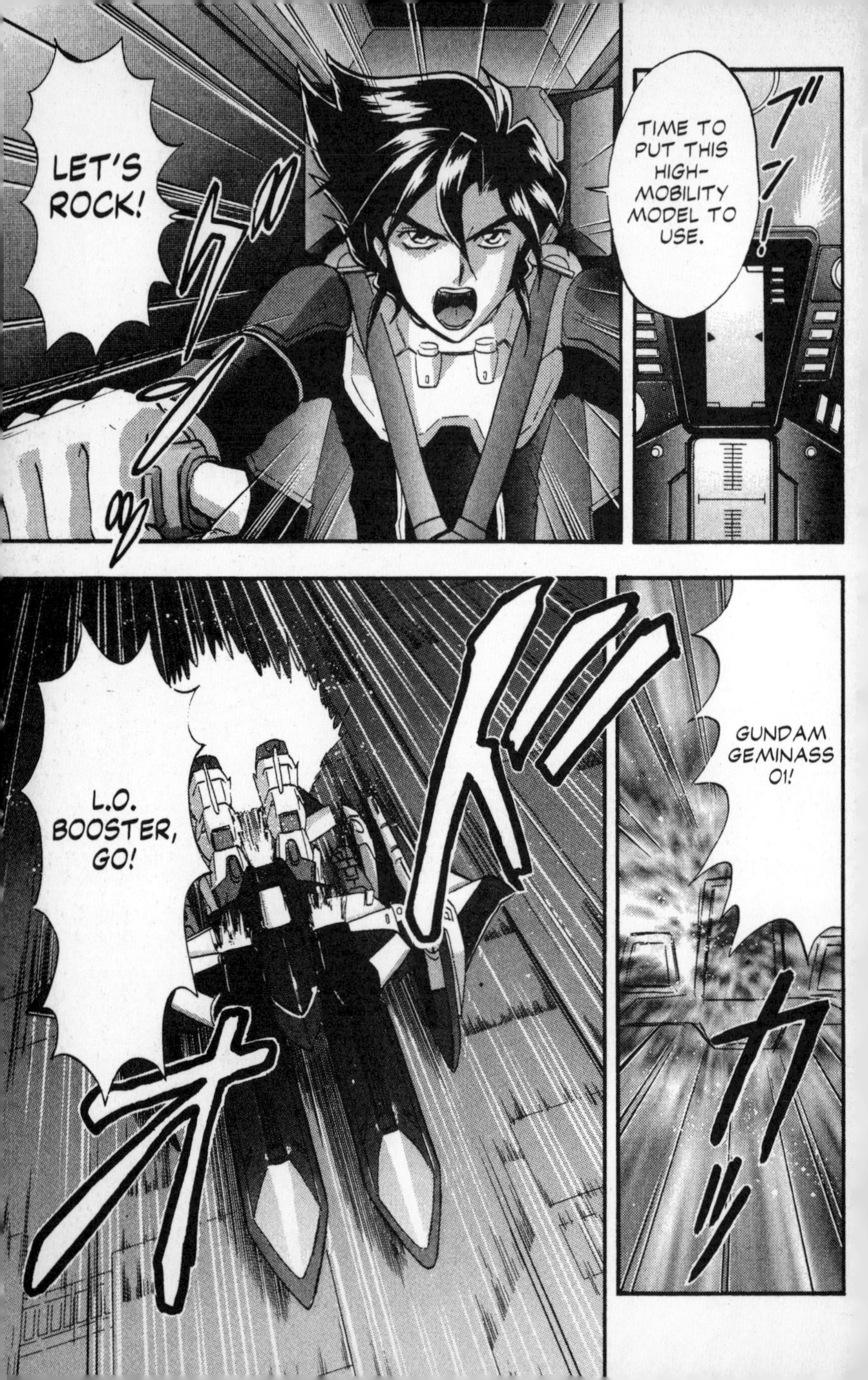
TIME TO PUT THIS HIGH-MOBILITY MODEL TO USE.
LET'S ROCK!
GUNDAM GEMINASS 01!
L.O. BOOSTER, GO!

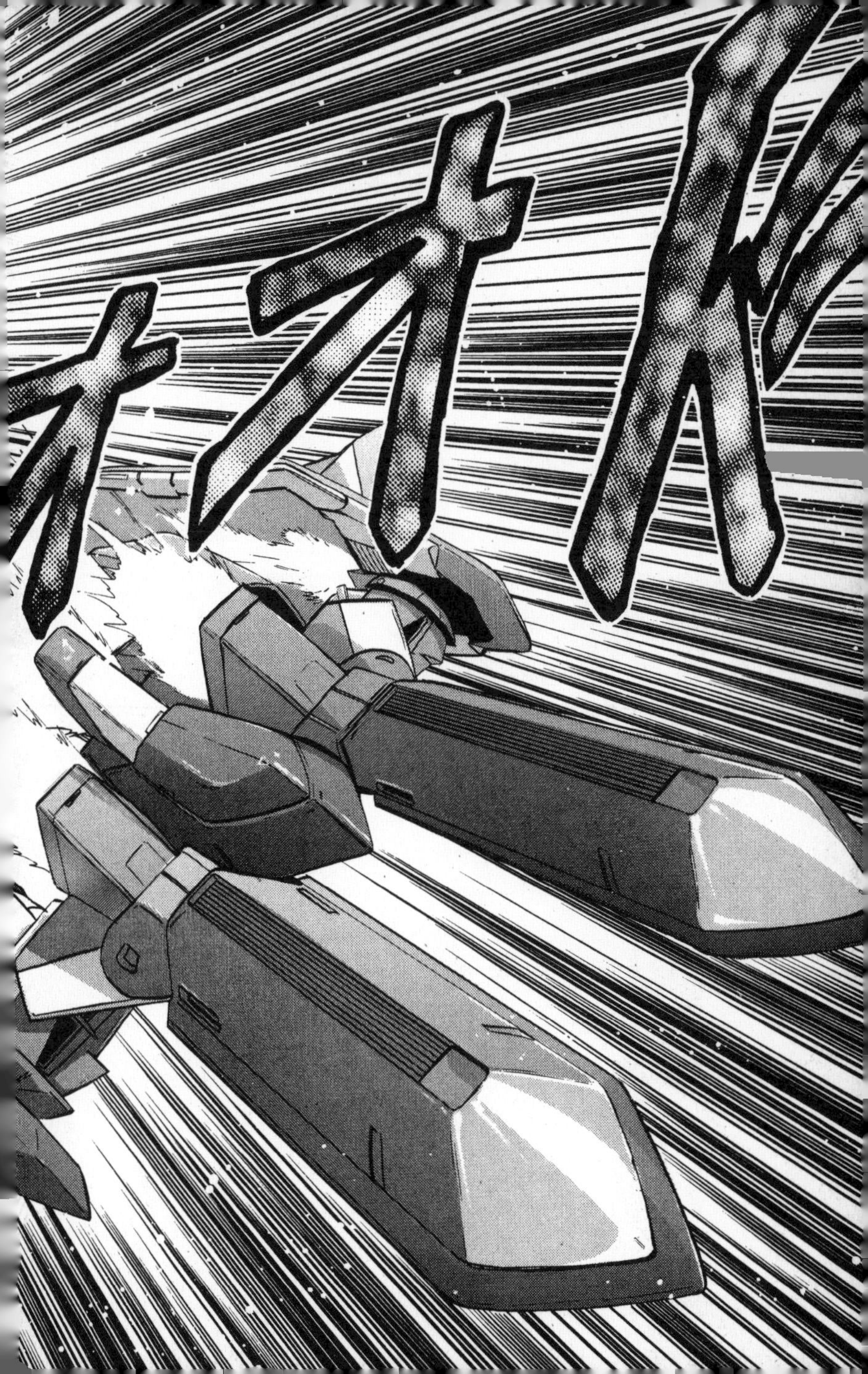
オオ

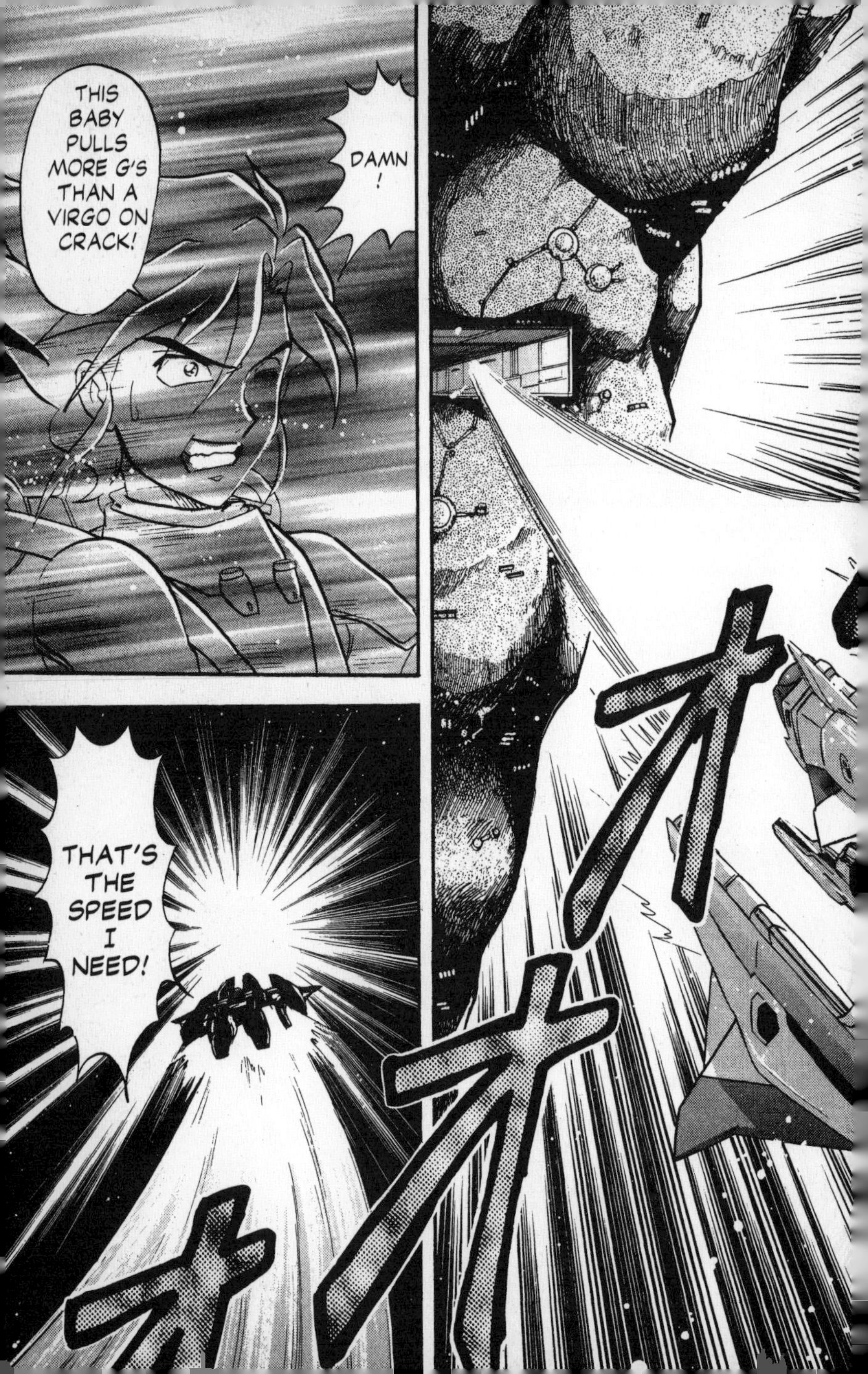
DAMN!
THIS BABY PULLS MORE G'S THAN A VIRGO ON CRACK!
THAT'S THE SPEED I NEED!

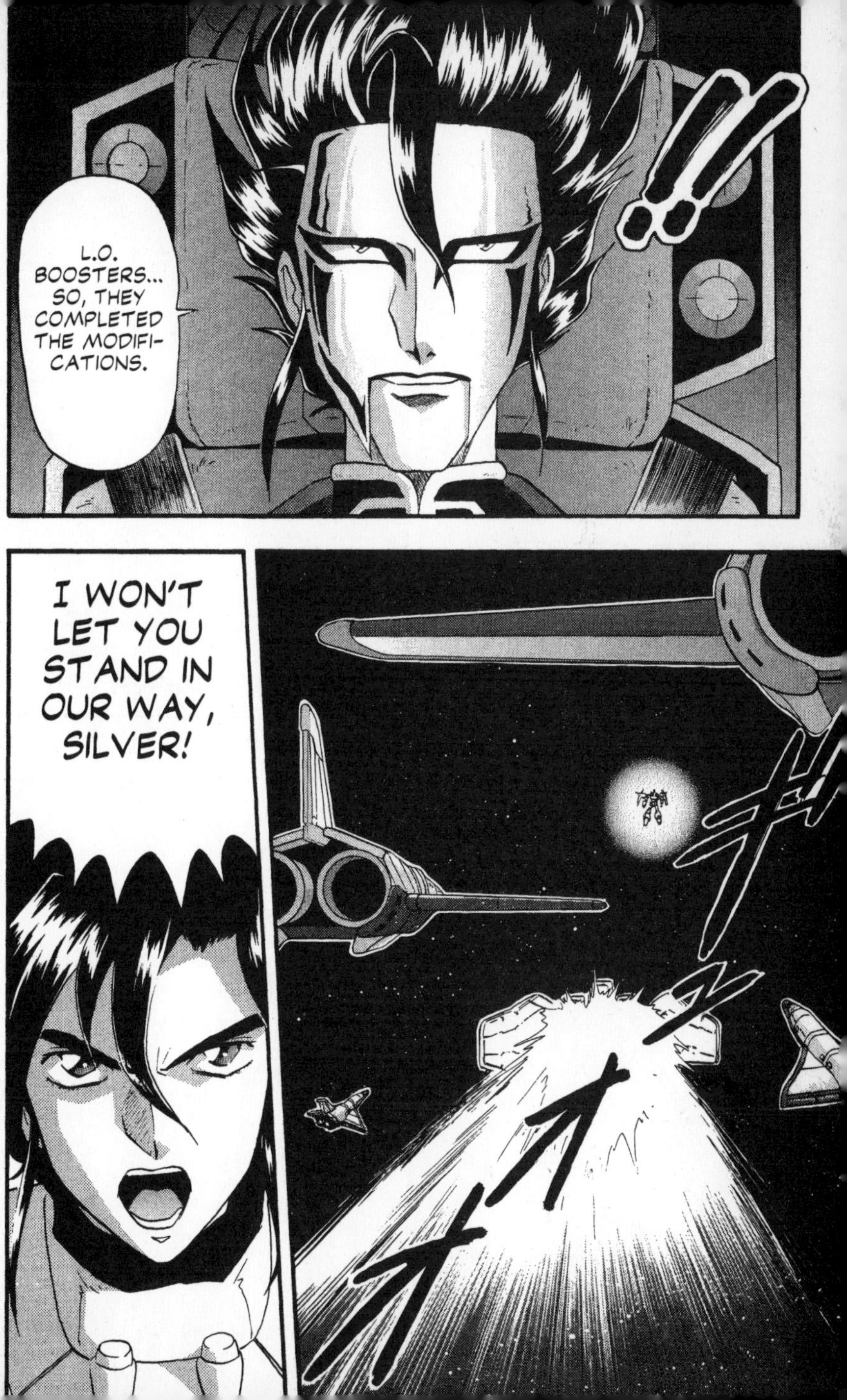
L.O. BOOSTERS... SO, THEY COMPLETED THE MODIFI-CATIONS.
!!
I WON'T LET YOU STAND IN OUR WAY, SILVER!

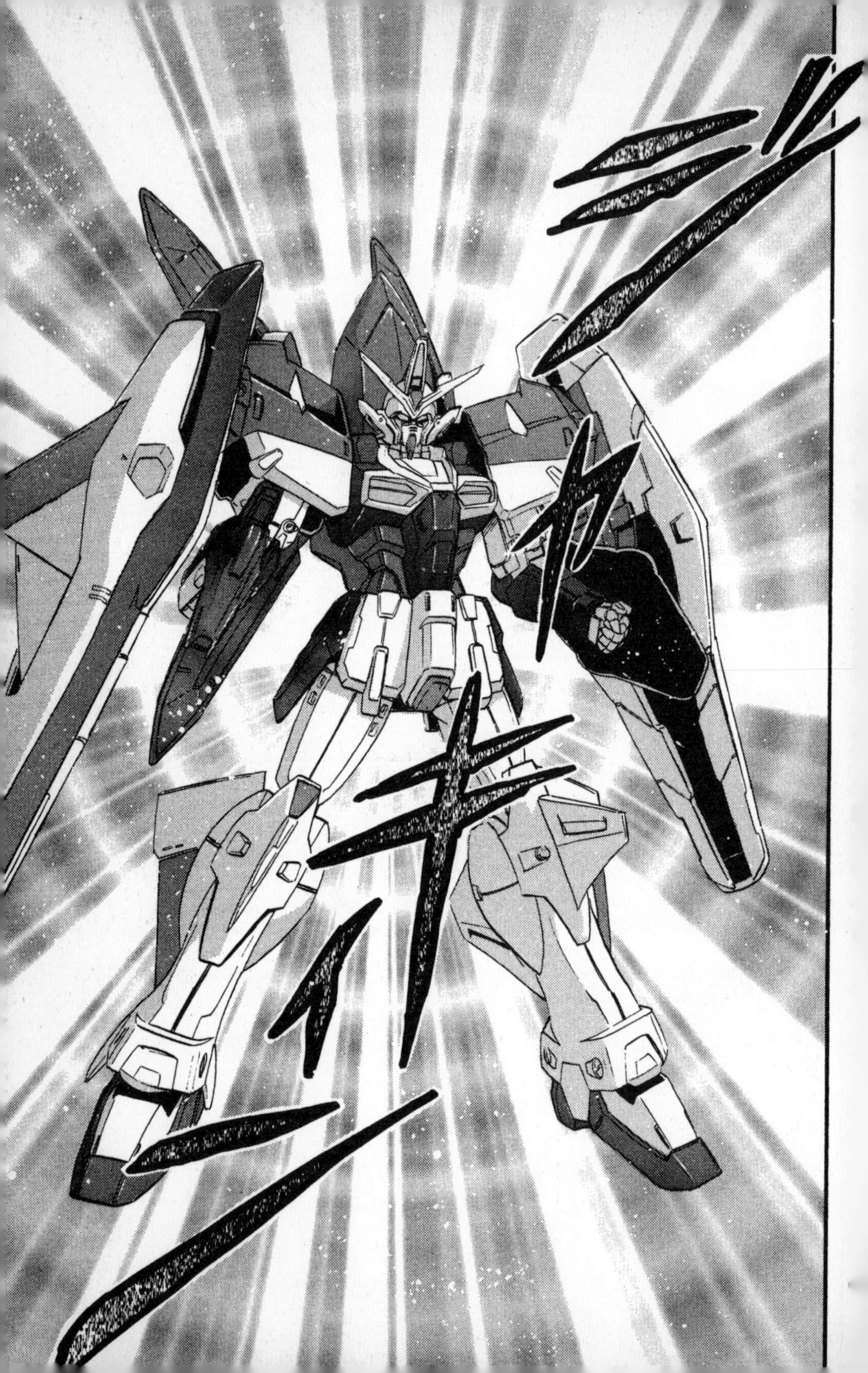

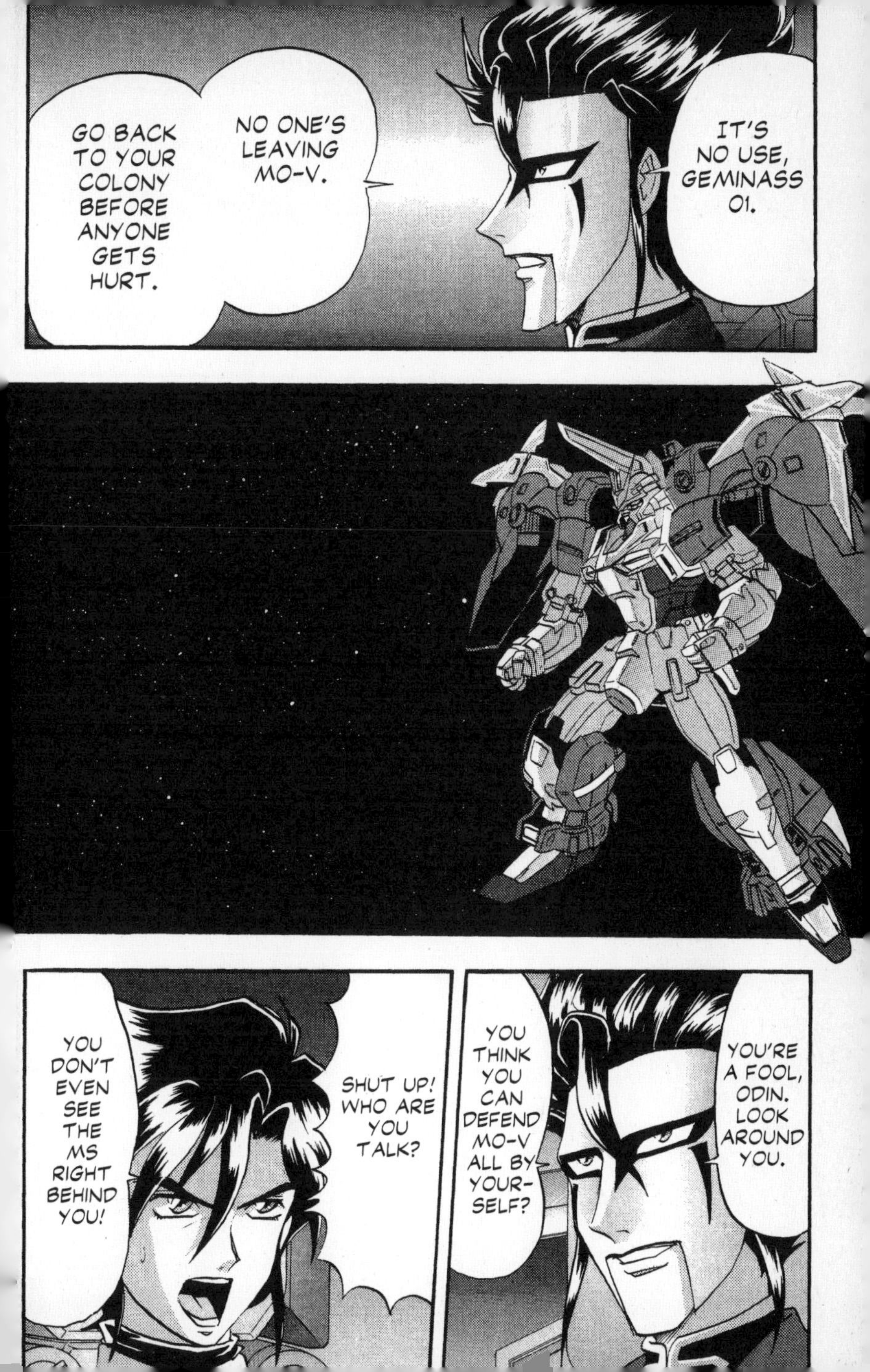
IT'S NO USE, GEMINASS 01.
NO ONE'S LEAVING MO-V.
GO BACK TO YOUR COLONY BEFORE ANYONE GETS HURT.
YOU'RE A FOOL, ODIN. LOOK AROUND YOU.
YOU THINK YOU CAN DEFEND MO-V ALL BY YOUR-SELF?
SHUT UP! WHO ARE YOU TALK?
YOU DON'T EVEN SEE THE MS RIGHT BEHIND YOU!

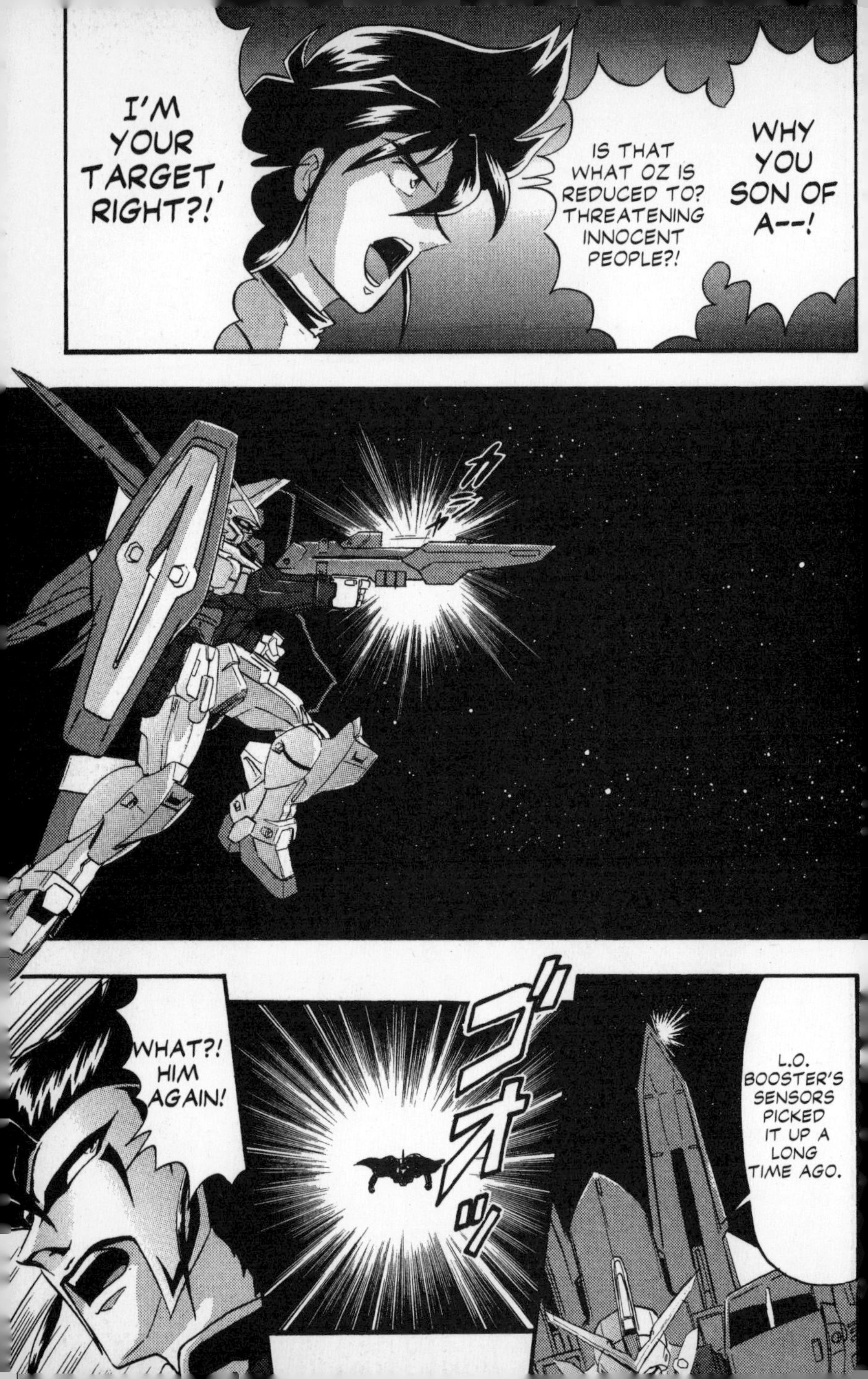
WHY YOU SON OF A--!
IS THAT WHAT OZ IS REDUCED TO? THREATENING INNOCENT PEOPLE?!
I'M YOUR TARGET, RIGHT?!
L.O. BOOSTER'S SENSORS PICKED IT UP A LONG TIME AGO.
WHAT?! HIM AGAIN!

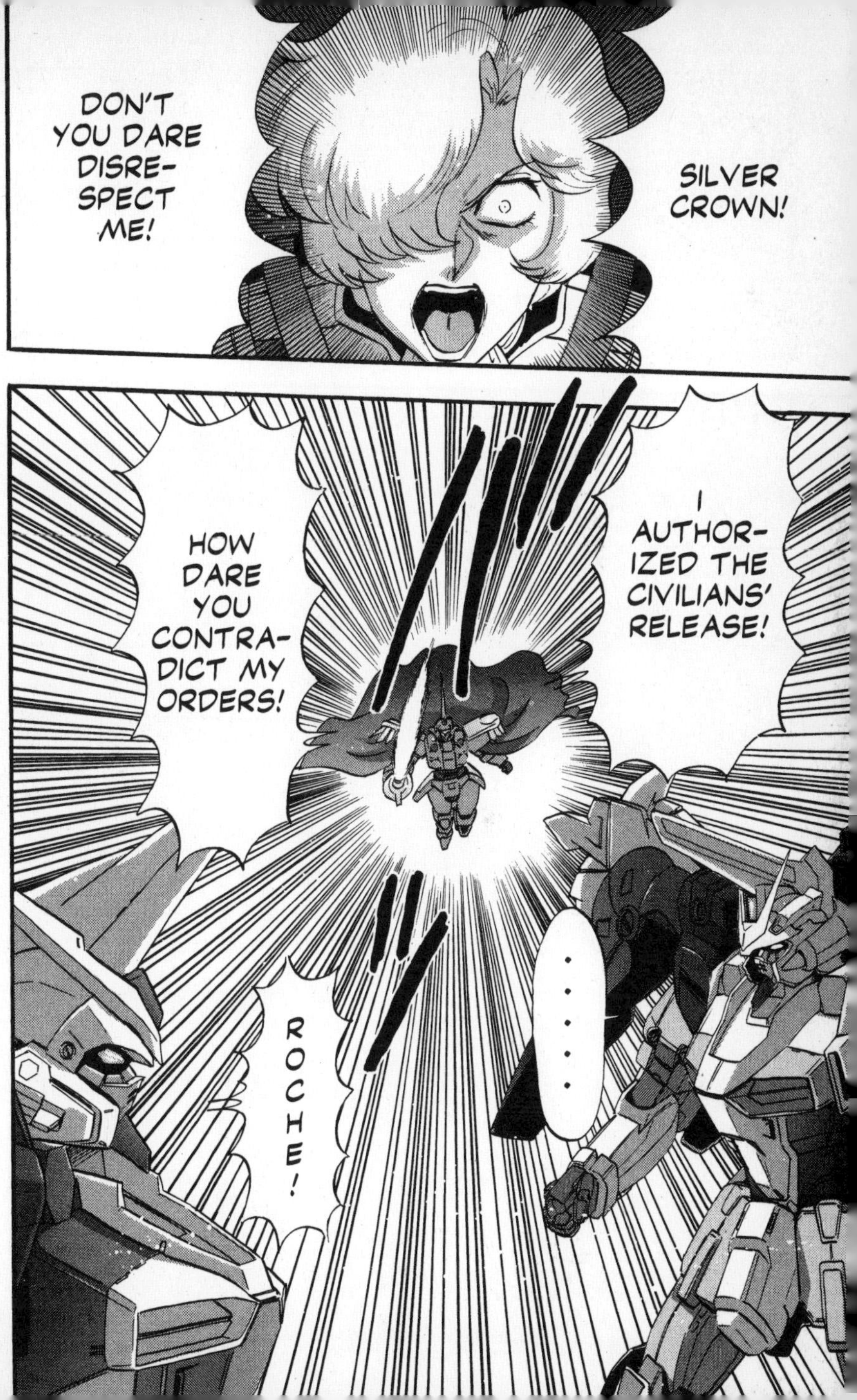
SILVER CROWN!
DON'T YOU DARE DISRE-SPECT ME!
I AUTHOR-IZED THE CIVILIANS' RELEASE!
HOW DARE YOU CONTRA-DICT MY ORDERS!
.....
ROCHE!

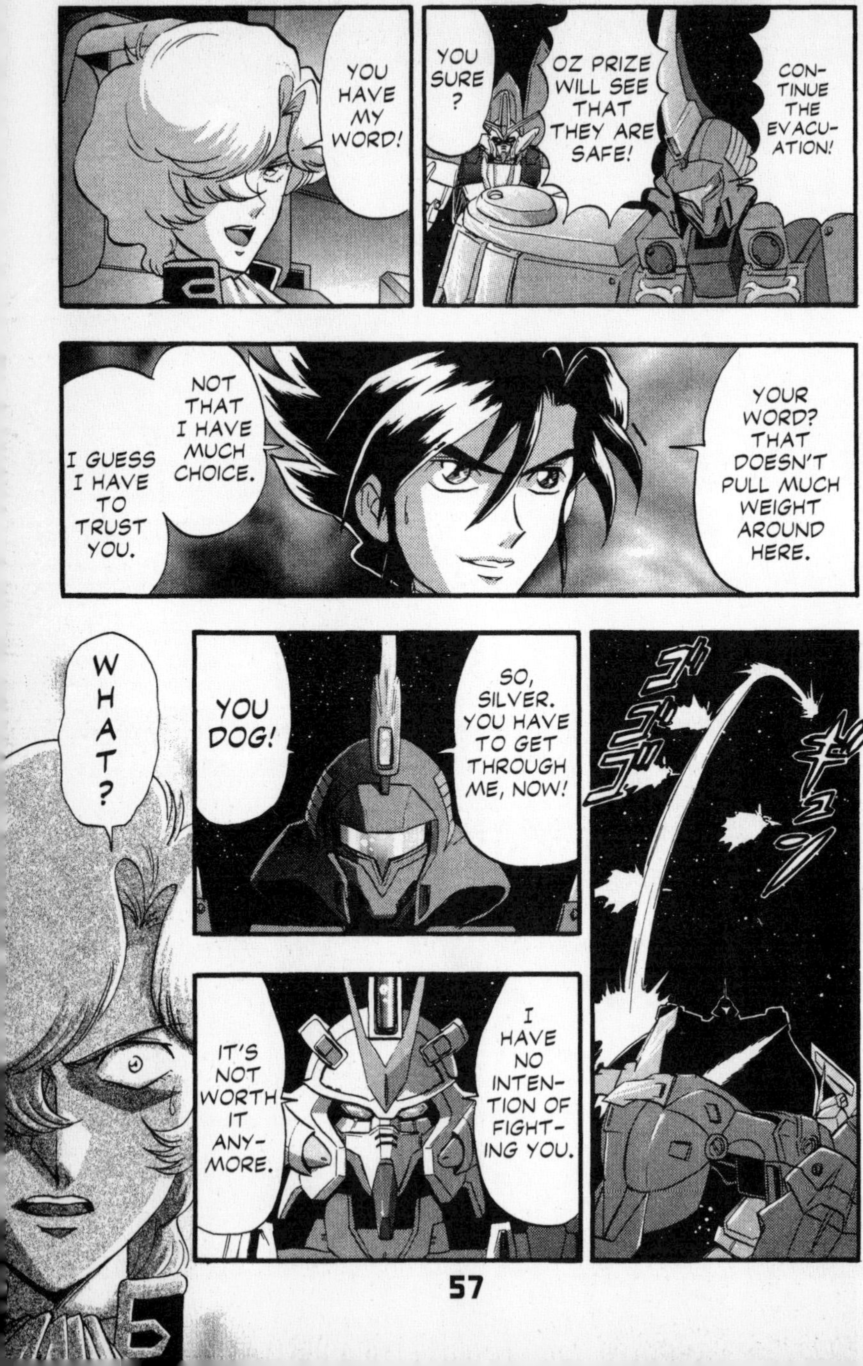
CON-TINUE THE EVACU-ATION!
OZ PRIZE WILL SEE THAT THEY ARE SAFE!
YOU SURE?
YOU HAVE MY WORD!
YOUR WORD? THAT DOESN'T PULL MUCH WEIGHT AROUND HERE.
NOT THAT I HAVE MUCH CHOICE.
I GUESS I HAVE TO TRUST YOU.
SO, SILVER. YOU HAVE TO GET THROUGH ME, NOW!
YOU DOG!
I HAVE NO INTEN-TION OF FIGHT-ING YOU.
IT'S NOT WORTH IT ANY-MORE.
WHAT?

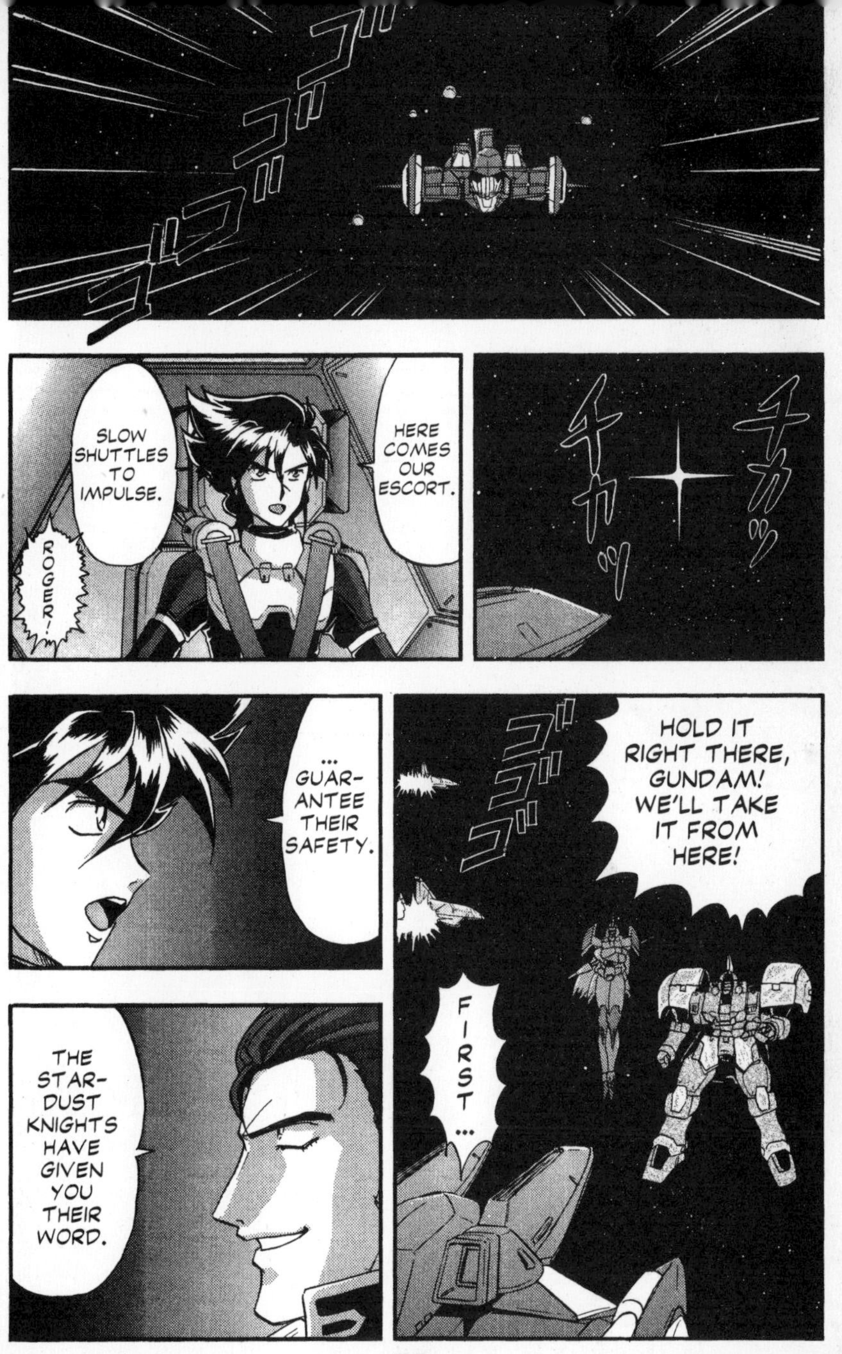
ゴゴゴゴ
チカッ
チカッ
HERE COMES OUR ESCORT.
SLOW SHUTTLES TO IMPULSE.
ROGER!
HOLD IT RIGHT THERE, GUNDAM! WE'LL TAKE IT FROM HERE!
ゴゴゴ
FIRST...
...GUARANTEE THEIR SAFETY.
THE STARDUST KNIGHTS HAVE GIVEN YOU THEIR WORD.

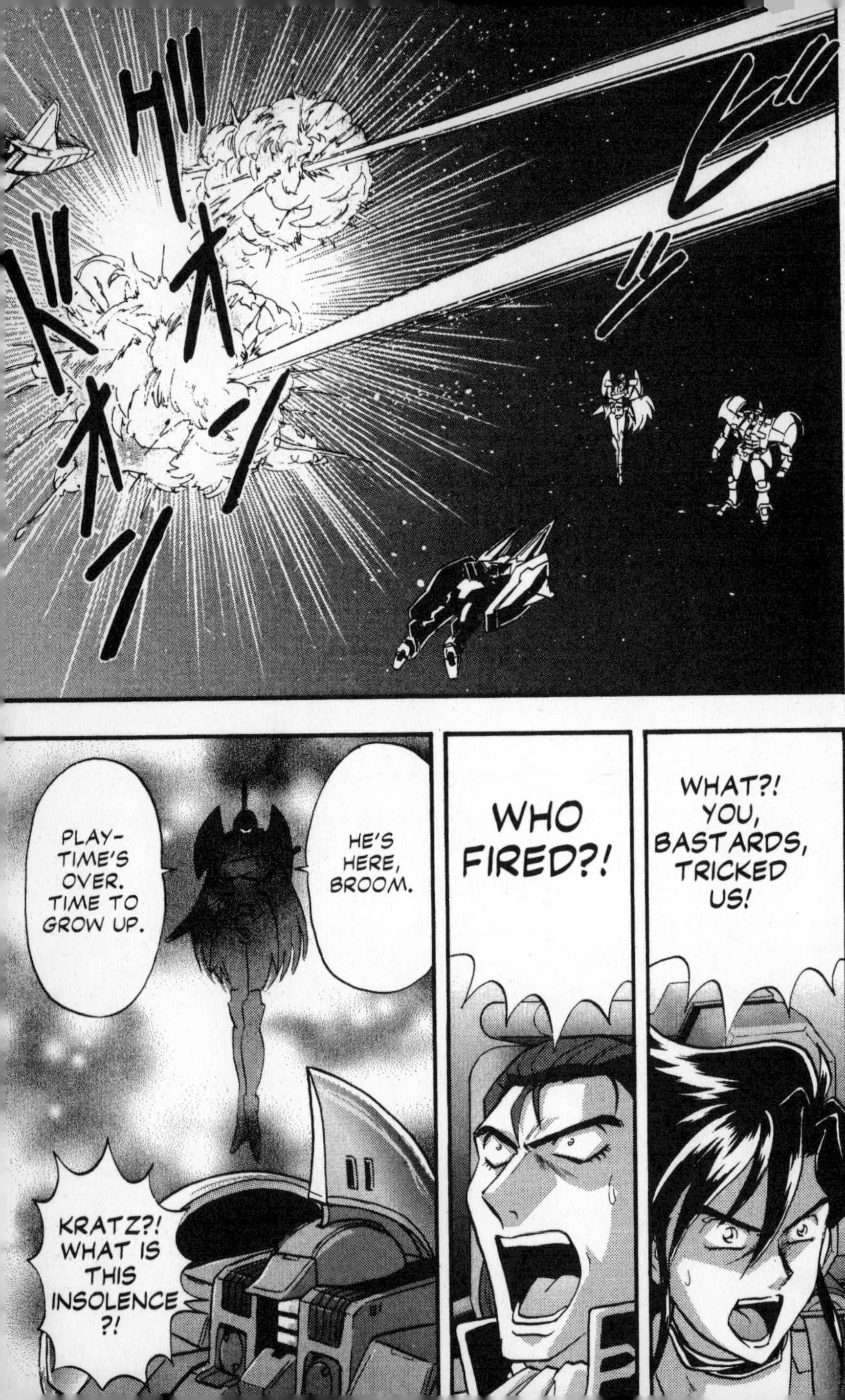
WHAT?! YOU, BASTARDS, TRICKED US!
WHO FIRED?!
HE'S HERE, BROOM.
PLAY-TIME'S OVER. TIME TO GROW UP.
KRATZ?! WHAT IS THIS INSOLENCE ?!

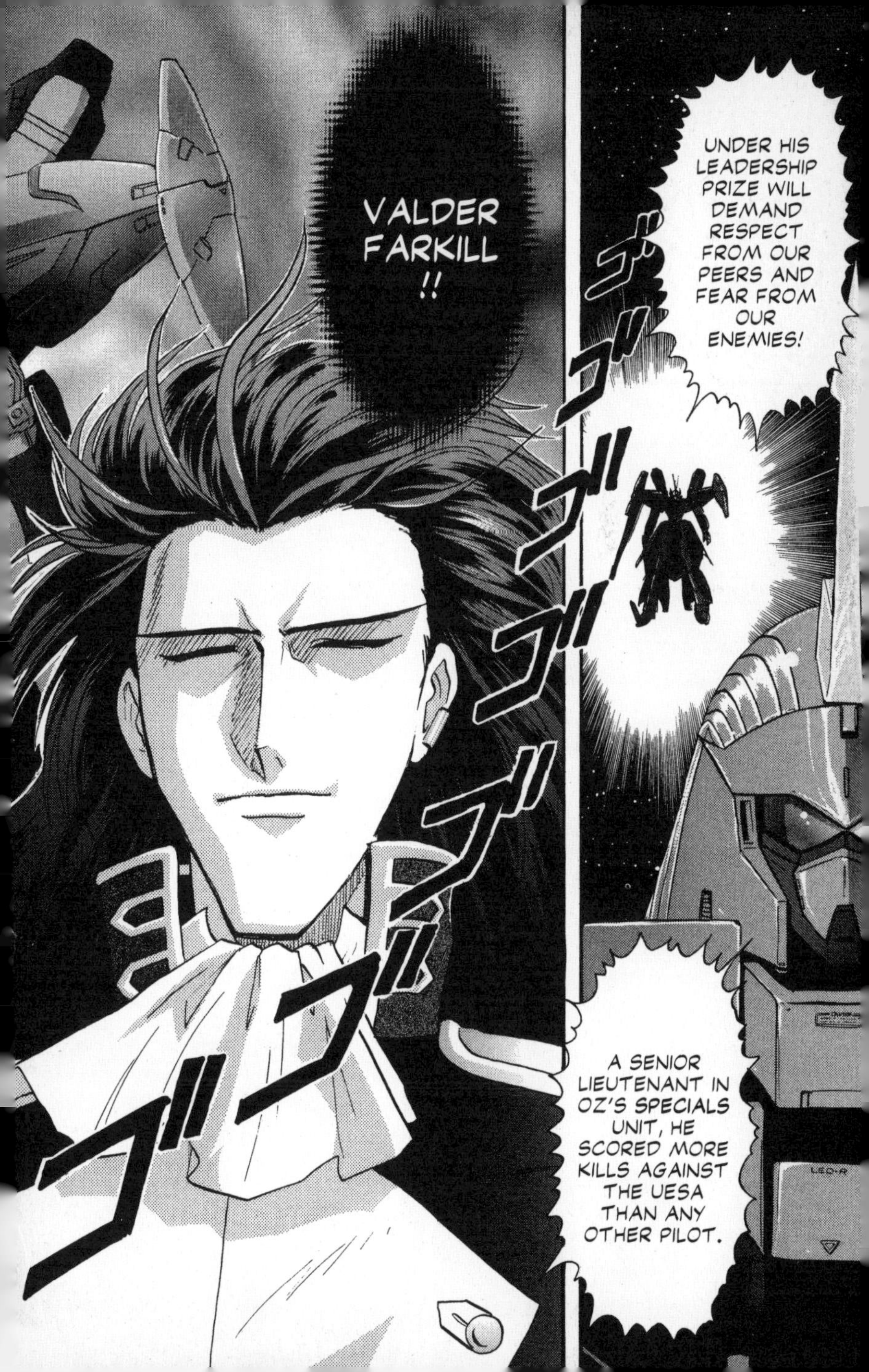
UNDER HIS LEADERSHIP PRIZE WILL DEMAND RESPECT FROM OUR PEERS AND FEAR FROM OUR ENEMIES!
A SENIOR LIEUTENANT IN OZ'S SPECIALS UNIT, HE SCORED MORE KILLS AGAINST THE UESA THAN ANY OTHER PILOT.
VALDER FARKILL !!

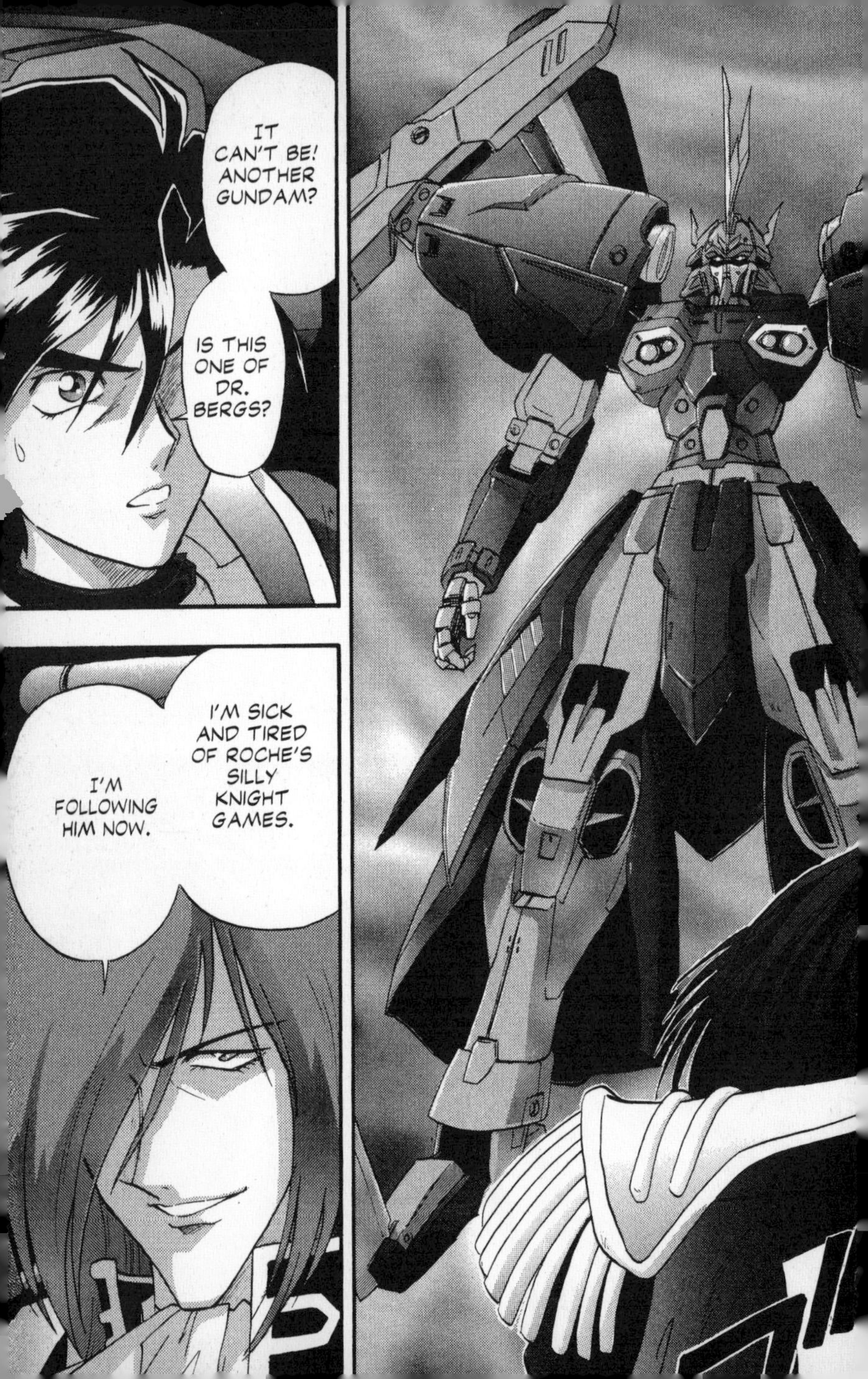
IT CAN'T BE! ANOTHER GUNDAM?
IS THIS ONE OF DR. BERGS?
I'M SICK AND TIRED OF ROCHE'S SILLY KNIGHT GAMES.
I'M FOLLOWING HIM NOW.

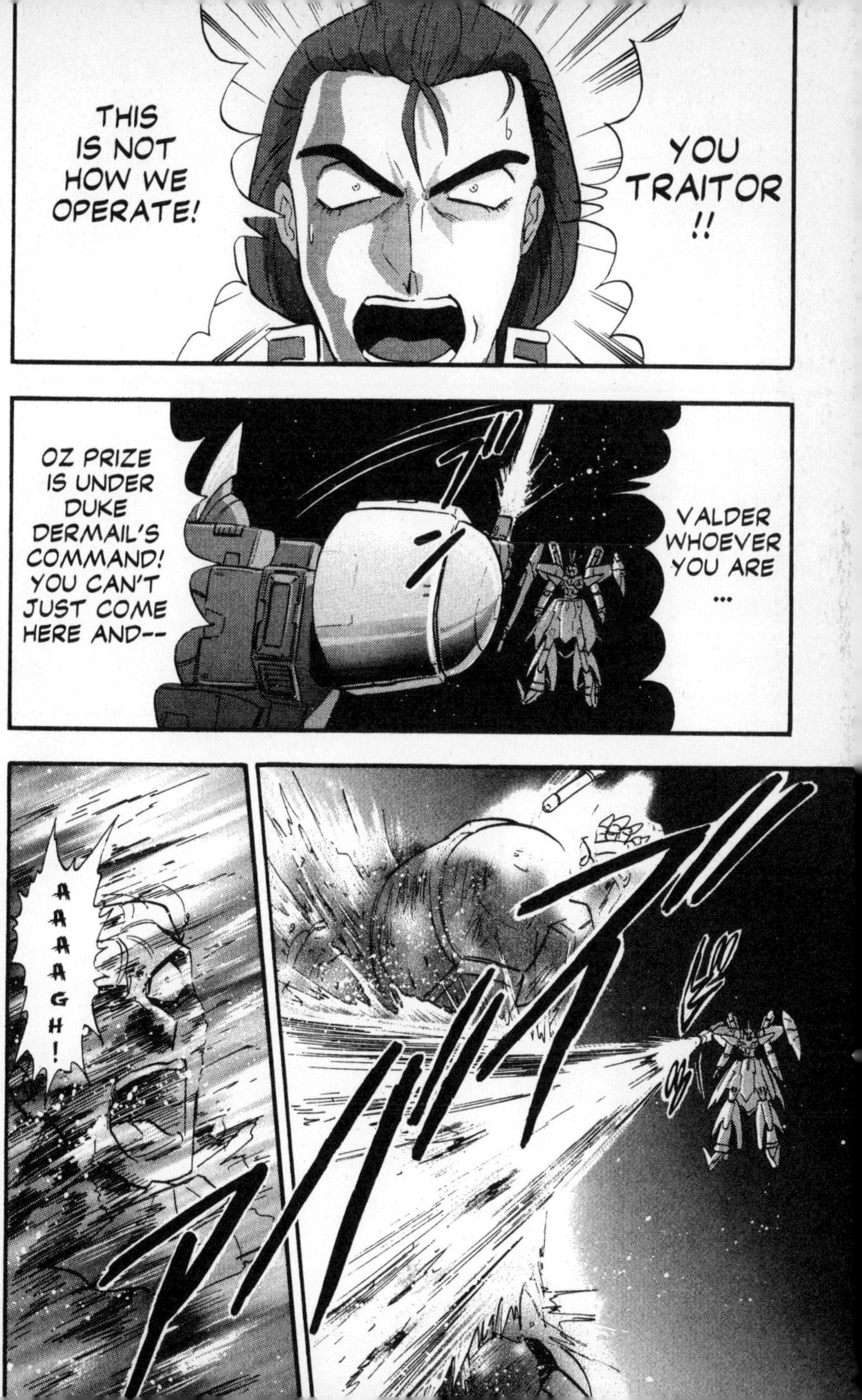
YOU TRAITOR !!
THIS IS NOT HOW WE OPERATE!
VALDER WHOEVER YOU ARE ...
OZ PRIZE IS UNDER DUKE DERMAIL'S COMMAND! YOU CAN'T JUST COME HERE AND--
AAAAAGH!

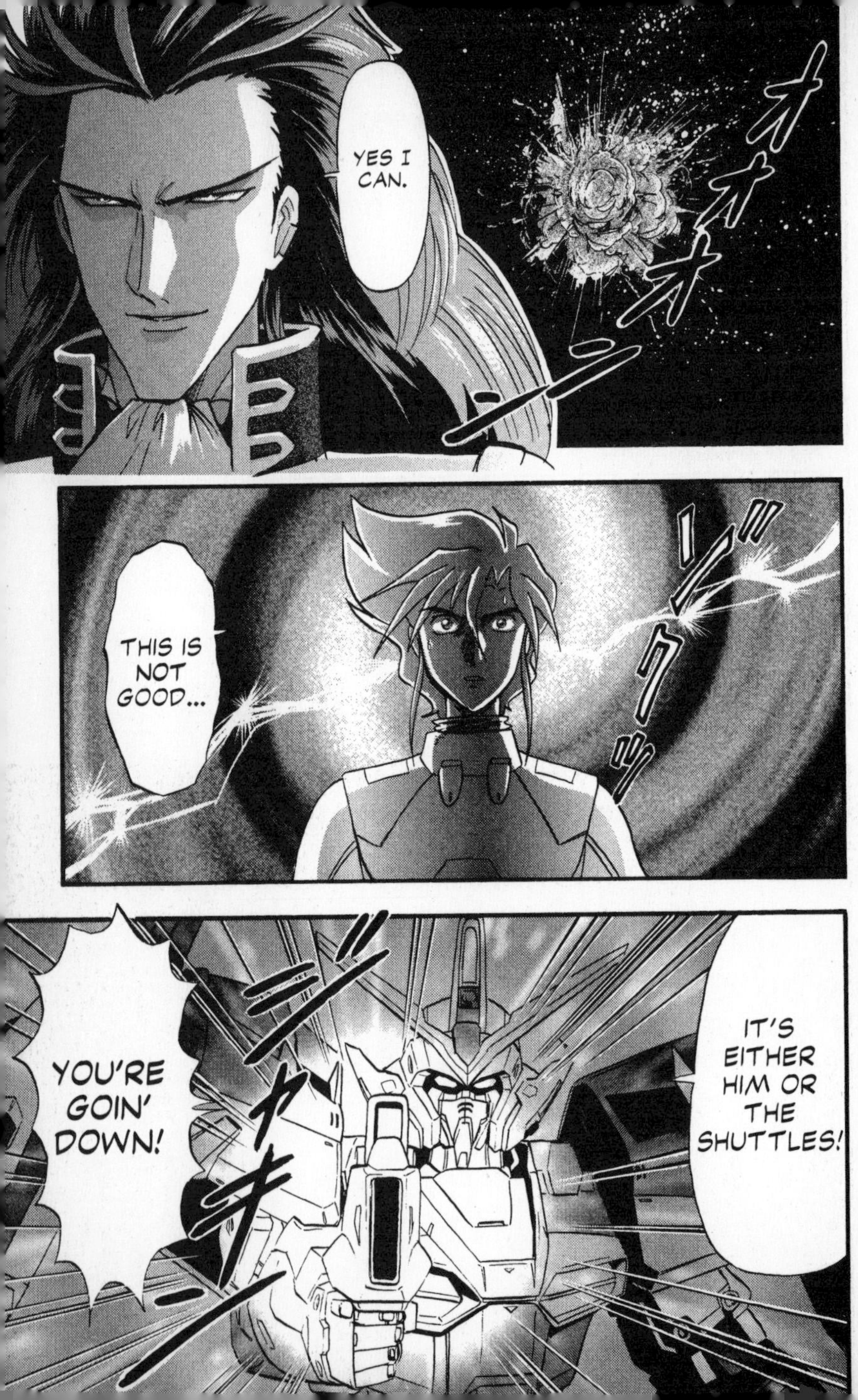
YES I CAN.
THIS IS NOT GOOD...
IT'S EITHER HIM OR THE SHUTTLES!
YOU'RE GOIN' DOWN!

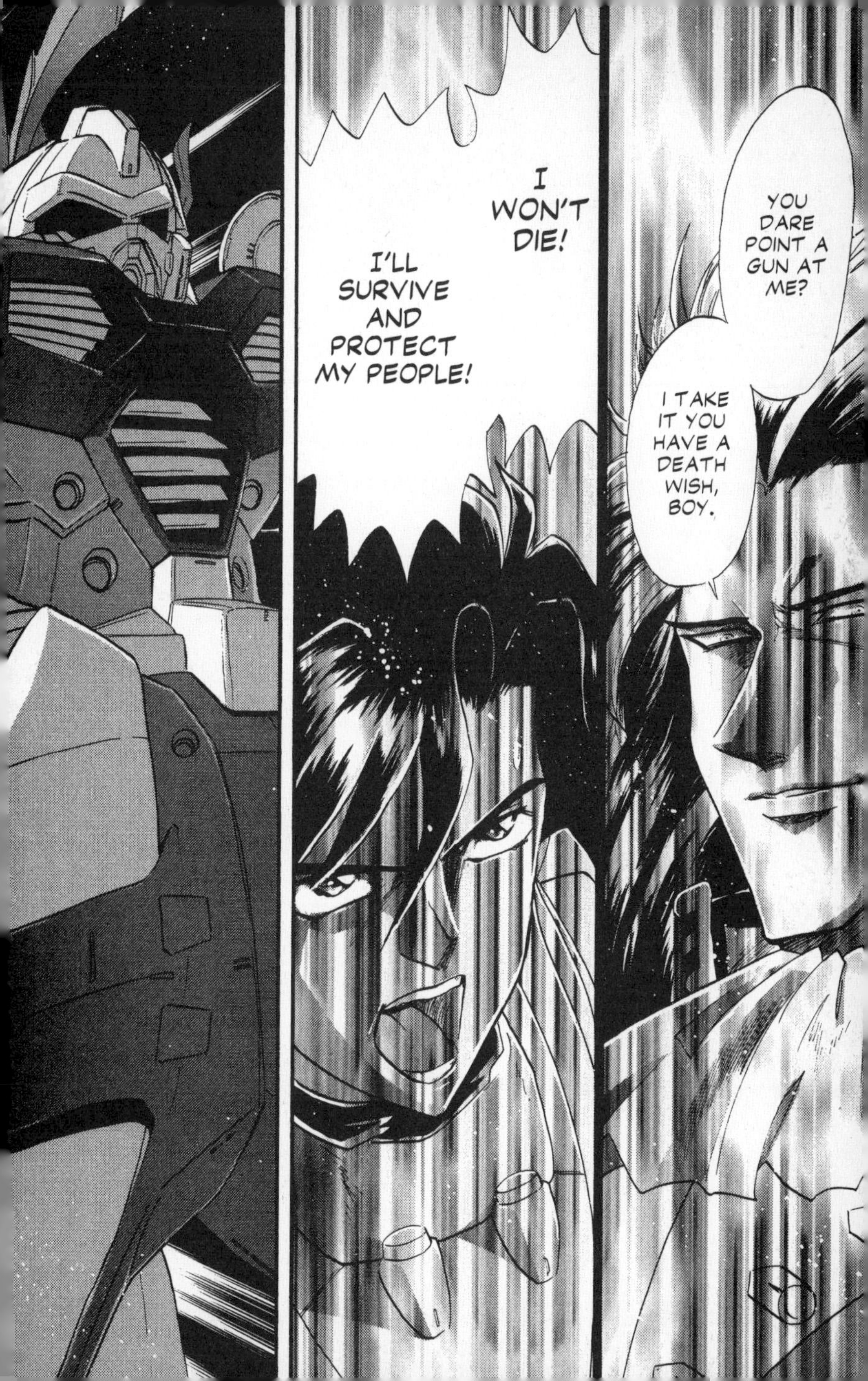
YOU DARE POINT A GUN AT ME?
I TAKE IT YOU HAVE A DEATH WISH, BOY.
I WON'T DIE!
I'LL SURVIVE AND PROTECT MY PEOPLE!

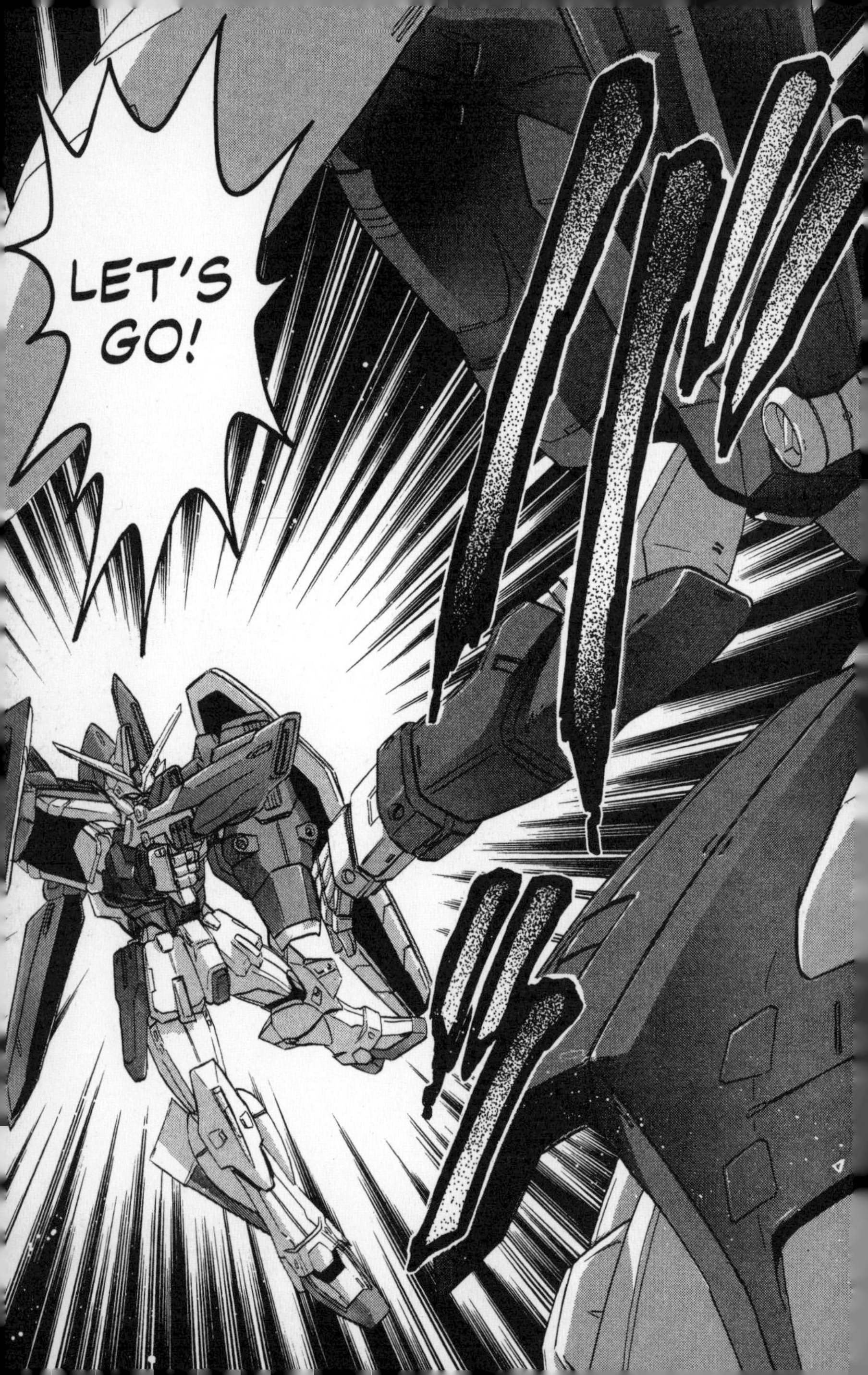
LET'S GO!

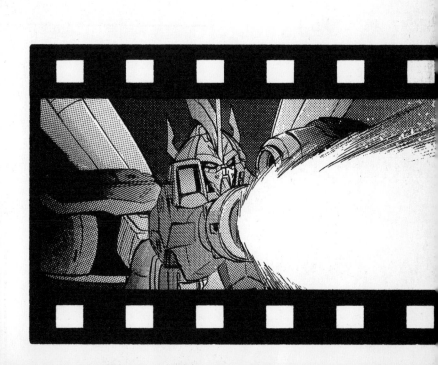

#7 Operation "Pandora"

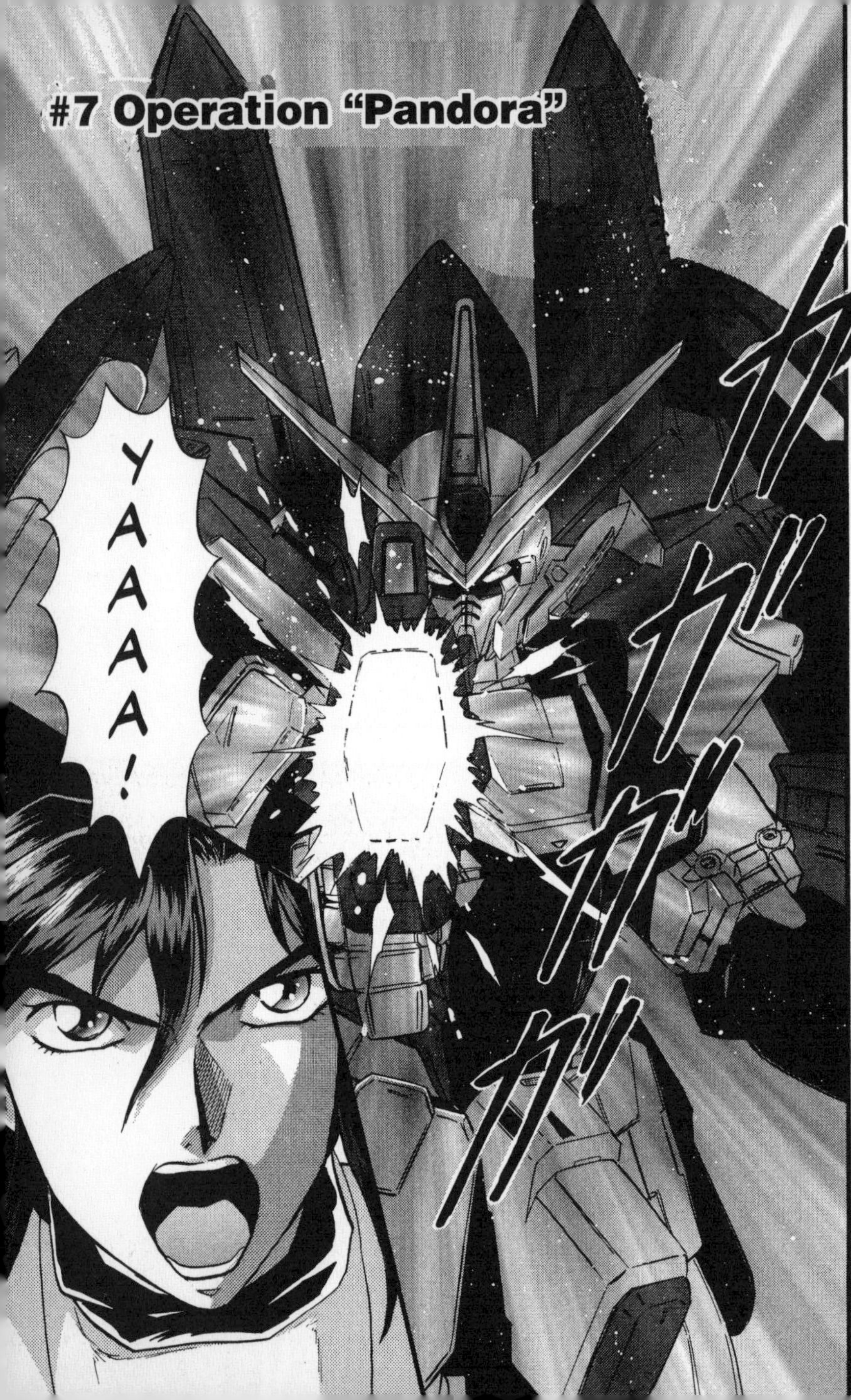
YAAAA!
ガガガガ

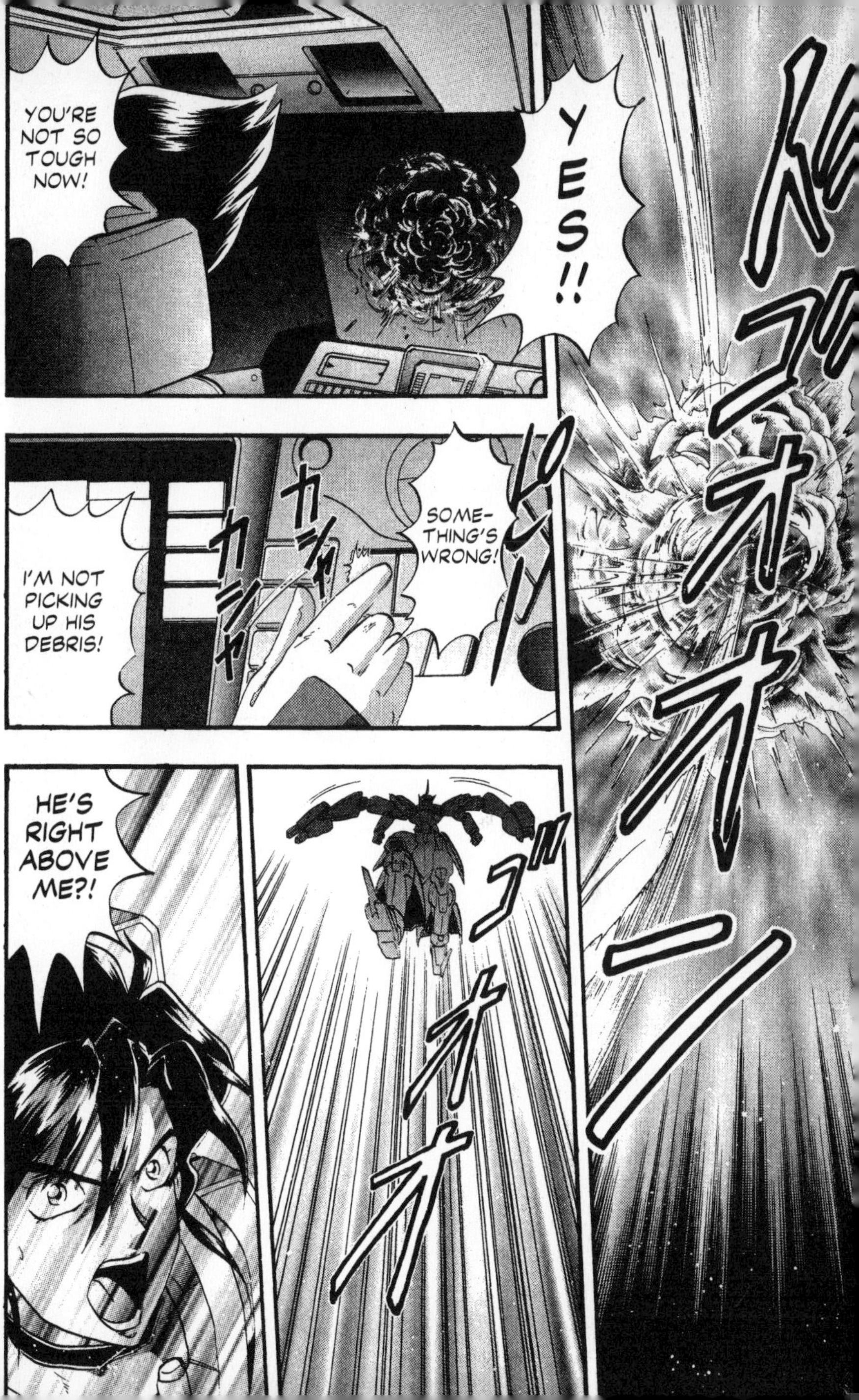
YES!!
YOU'RE NOT SO TOUGH NOW!
SOME-THING'S WRONG!
カシャ カシャ
I'M NOT PICKING UP HIS DEBRIS!
ゴオオオ
HE'S RIGHT ABOVE ME?!

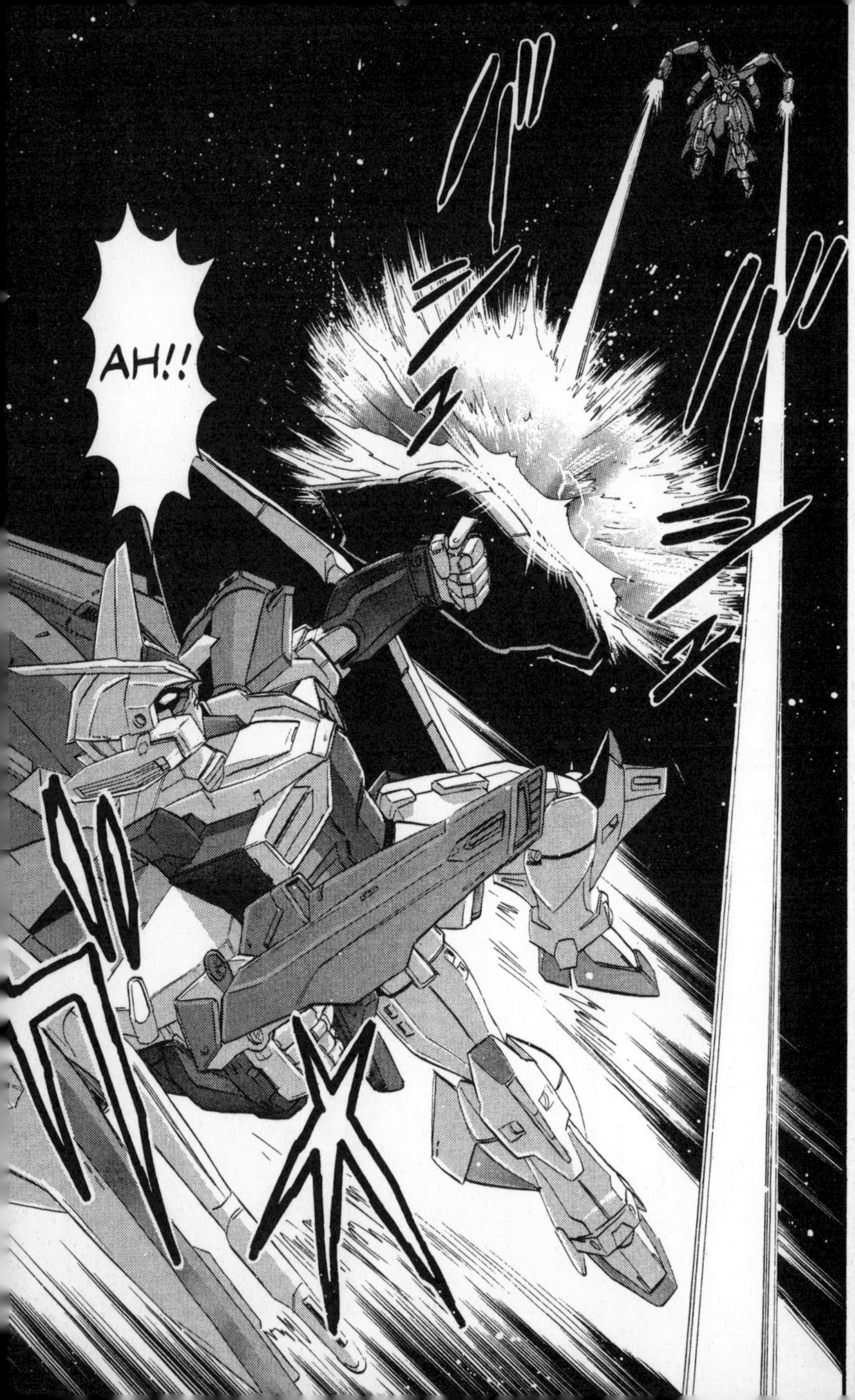
AH!!

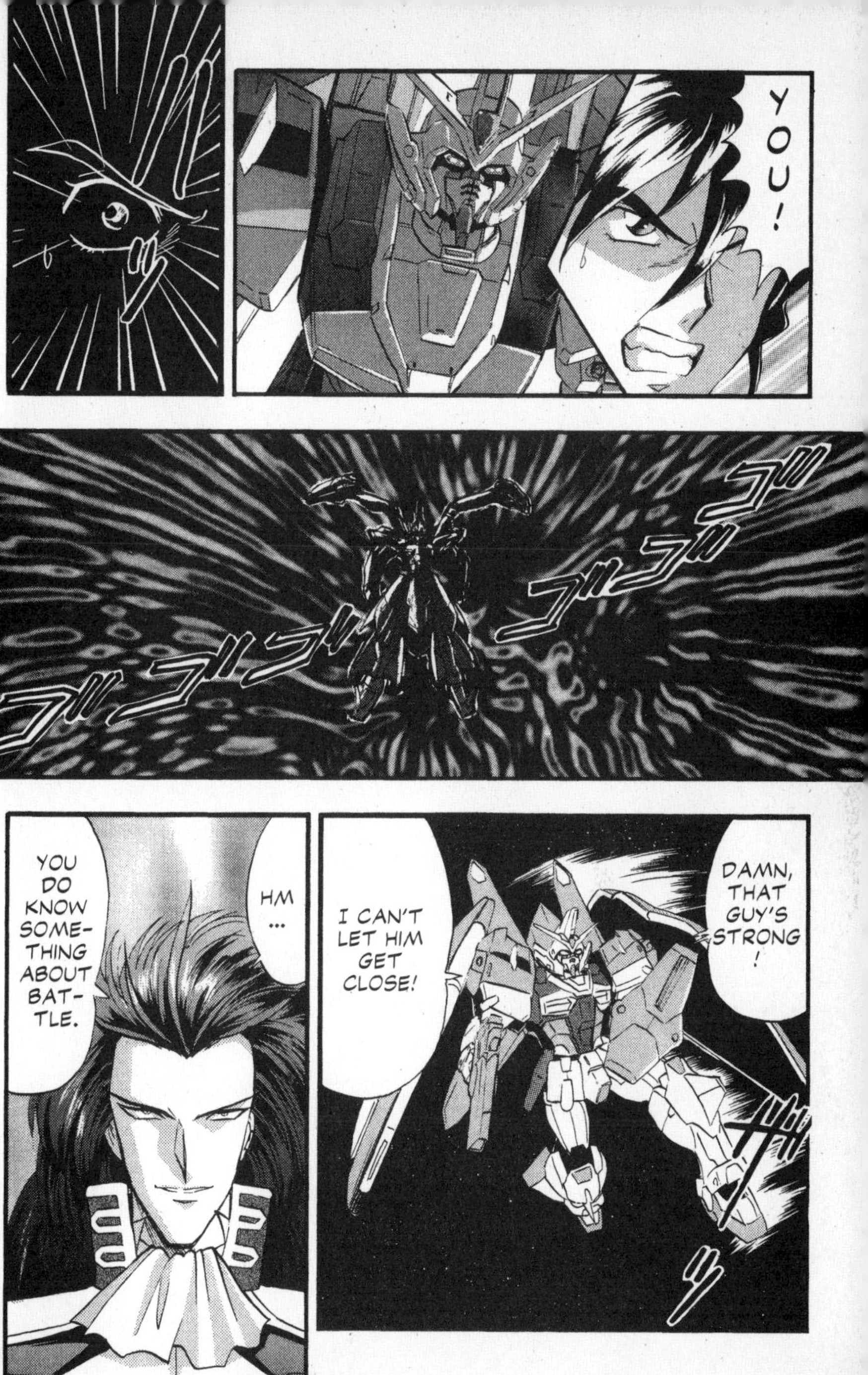
YOU!
DAMN, THAT GUY'S STRONG!
I CAN'T LET HIM GET CLOSE!
HM ...
YOU DO KNOW SOME-THING ABOUT BAT-TLE.

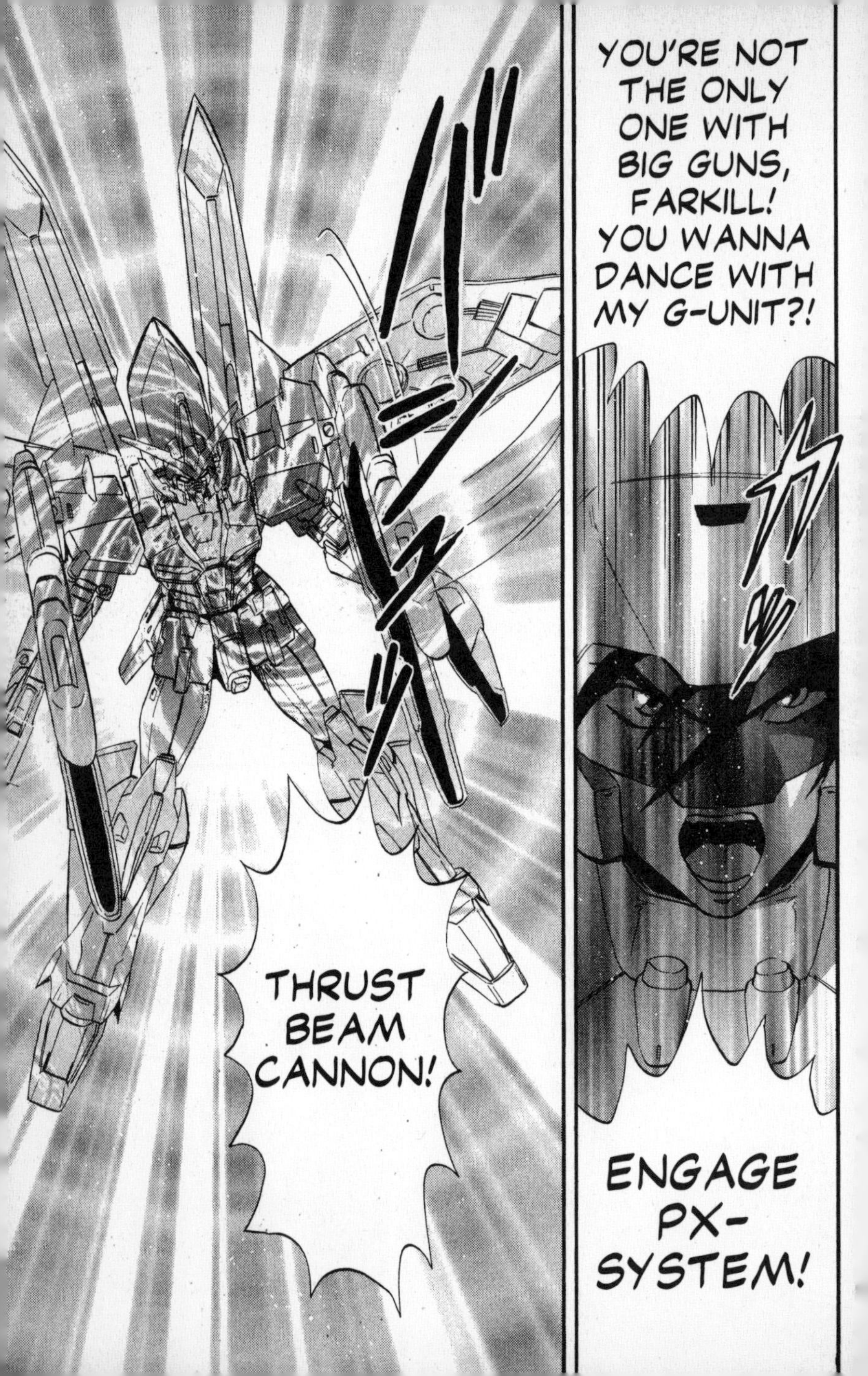
YOU'RE NOT THE ONLY ONE WITH BIG GUNS, FARKILL! YOU WANNA DANCE WITH MY G-UNIT?!
ENGAGE PX-SYSTEM!
THRUST BEAM CANNON!

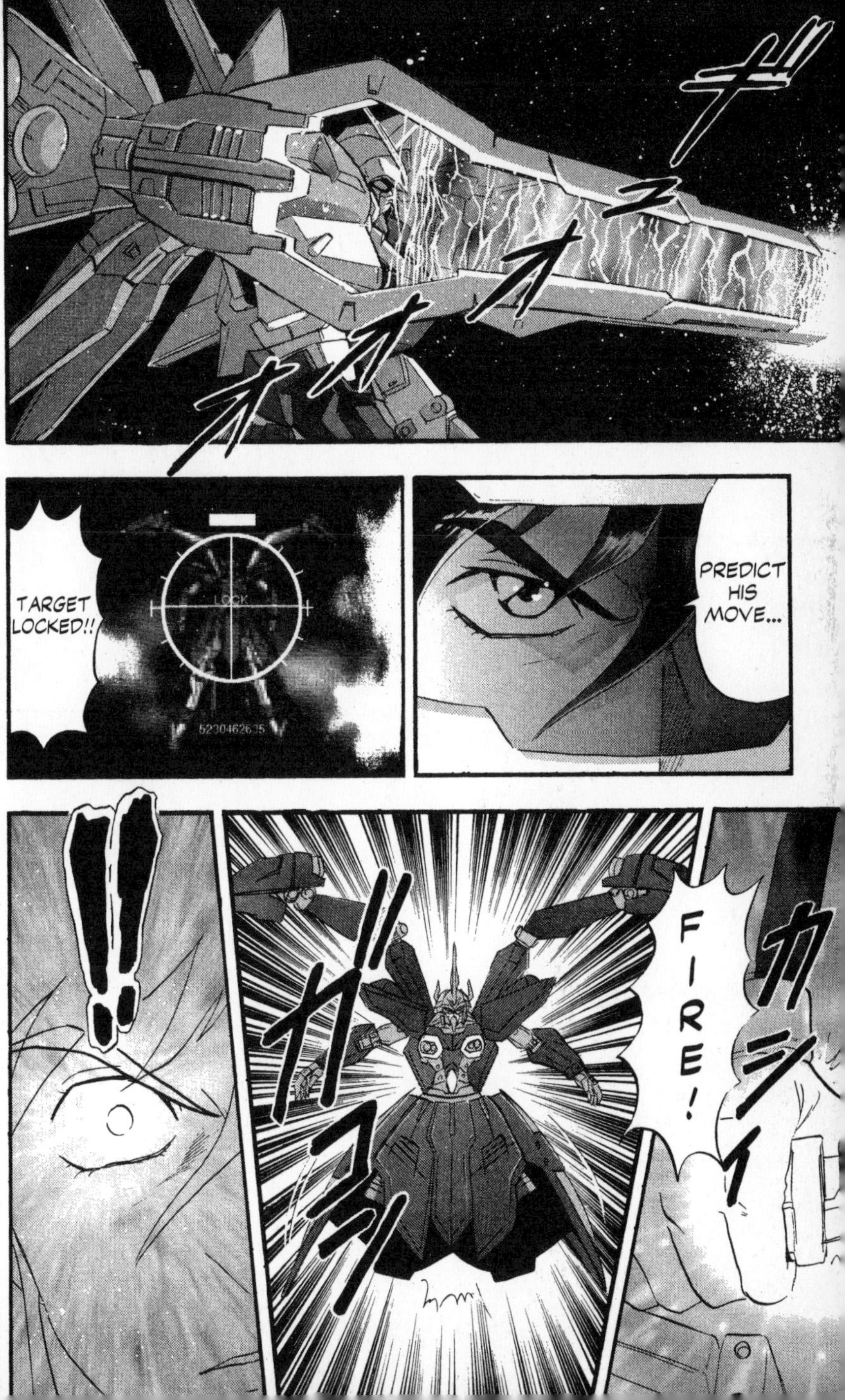
PREDICT HIS MOVE...
TARGET LOCKED!!
LOCK
FIRE!
!!

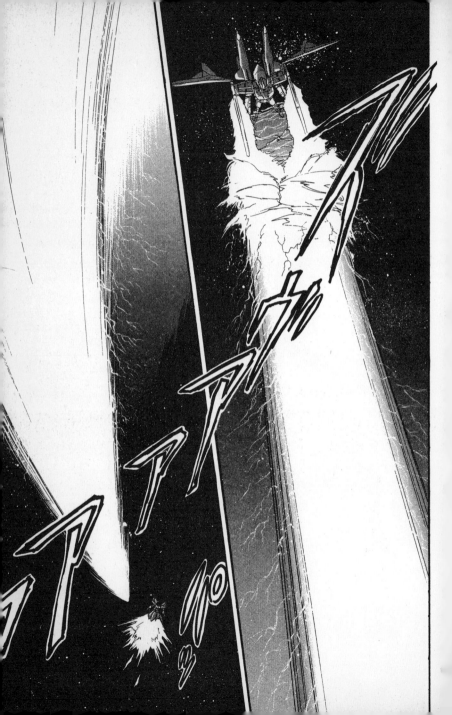

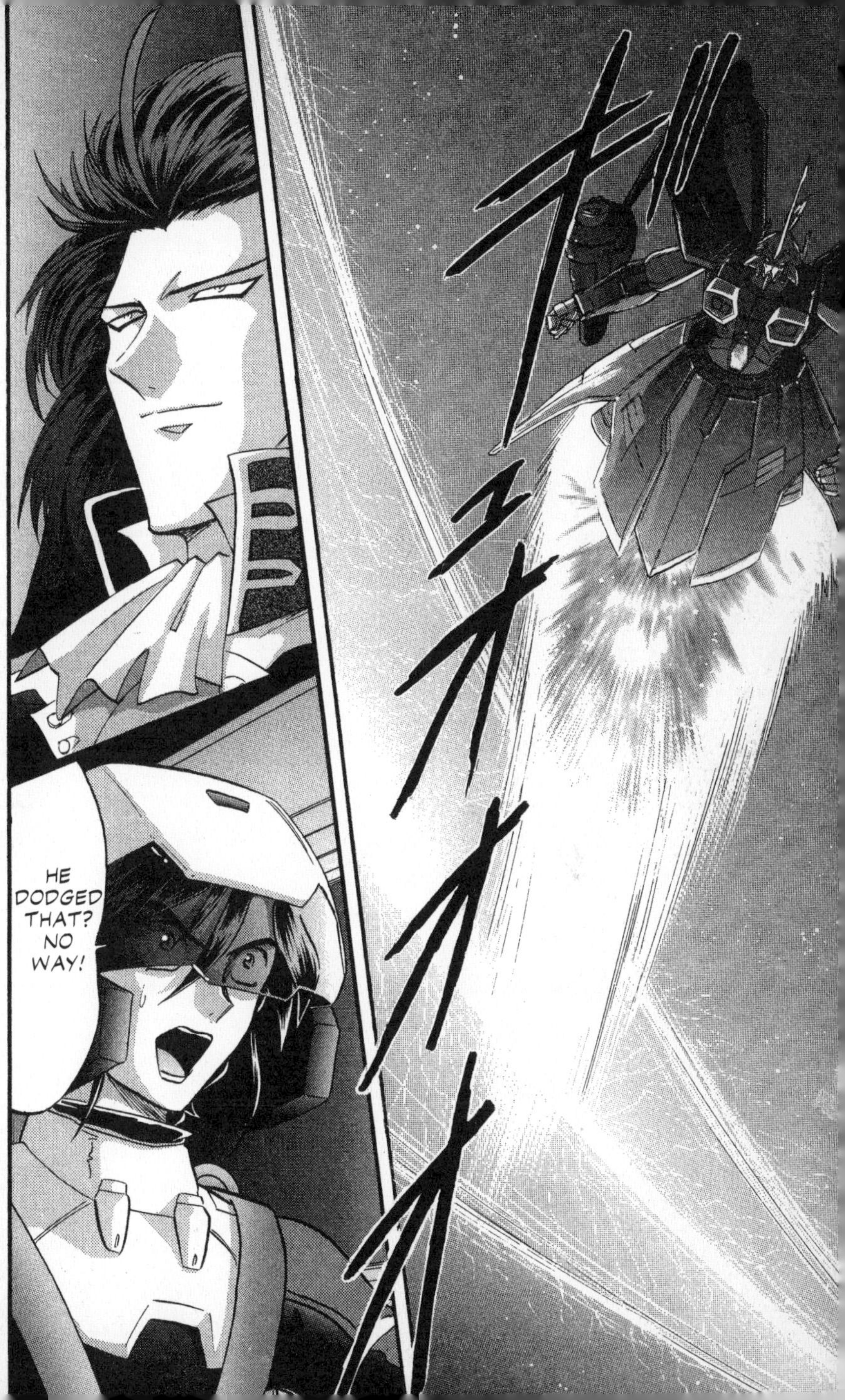
HE DODGED THAT? NO WAY!

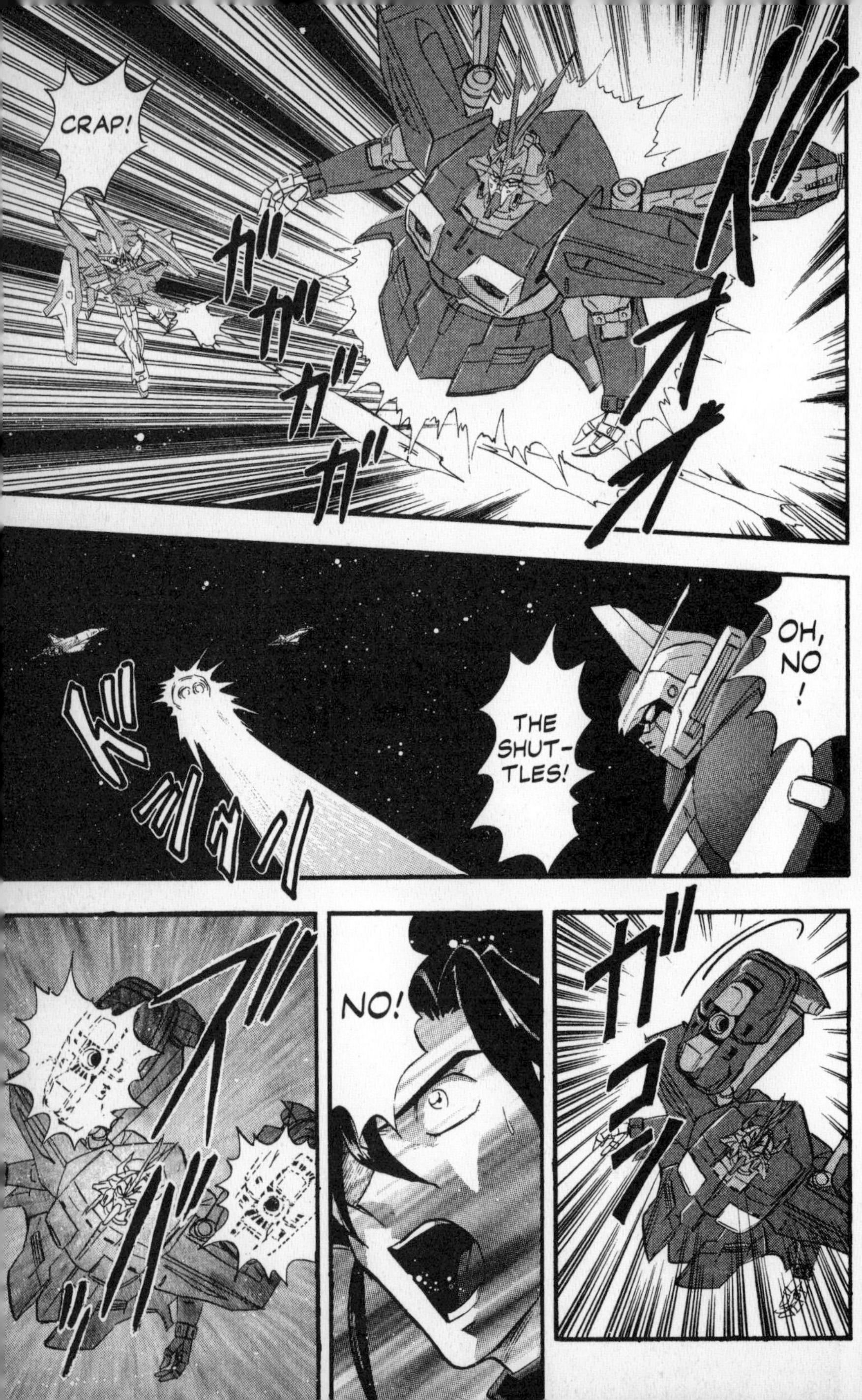

ガガガガ
CRAP!
OH, NO!
THE SHUTTLES!
NO!

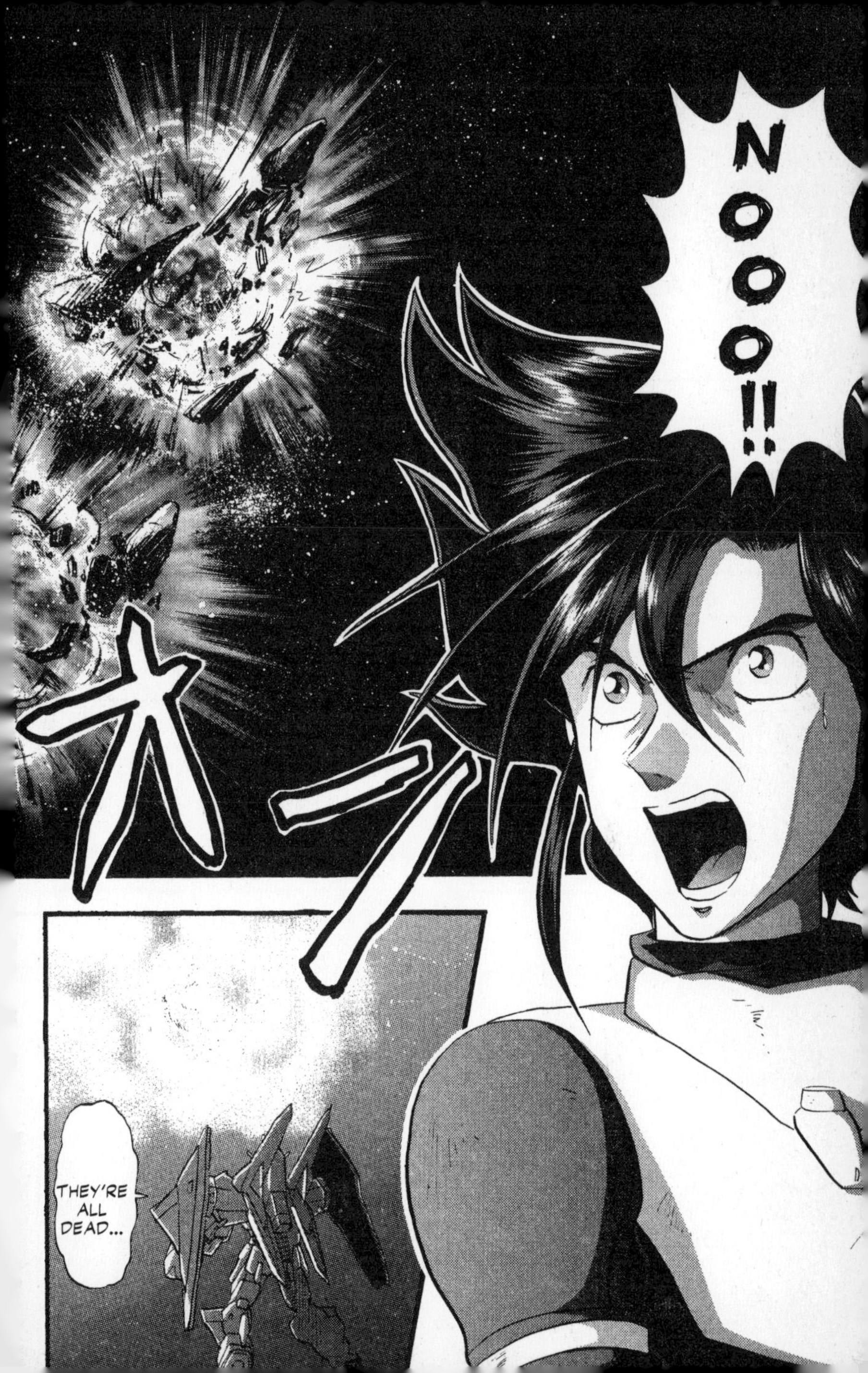
NOOOO!!
THEY'RE ALL DEAD...

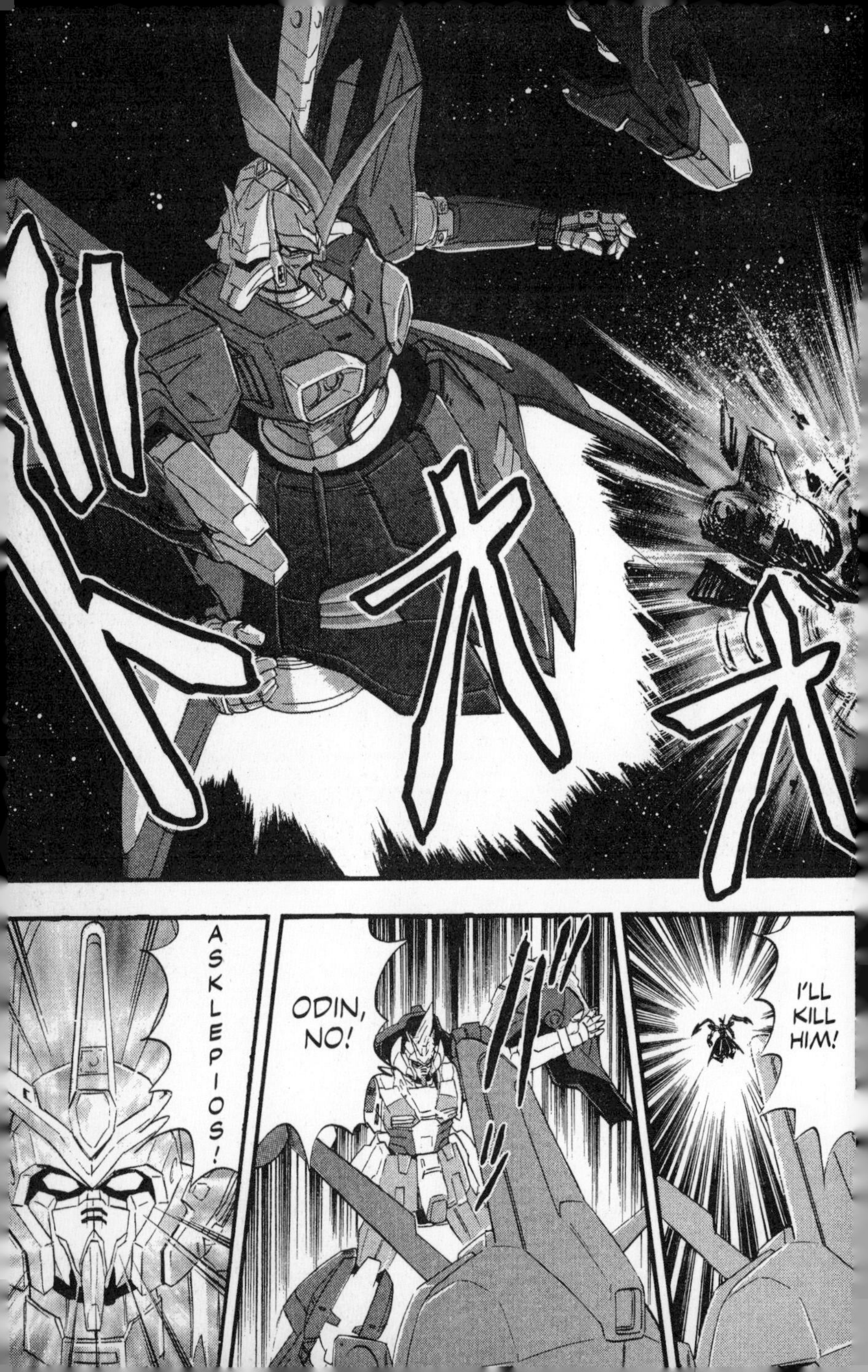
I'LL KILL HIM!
ODIN, NO!
ASKLEPIOS!

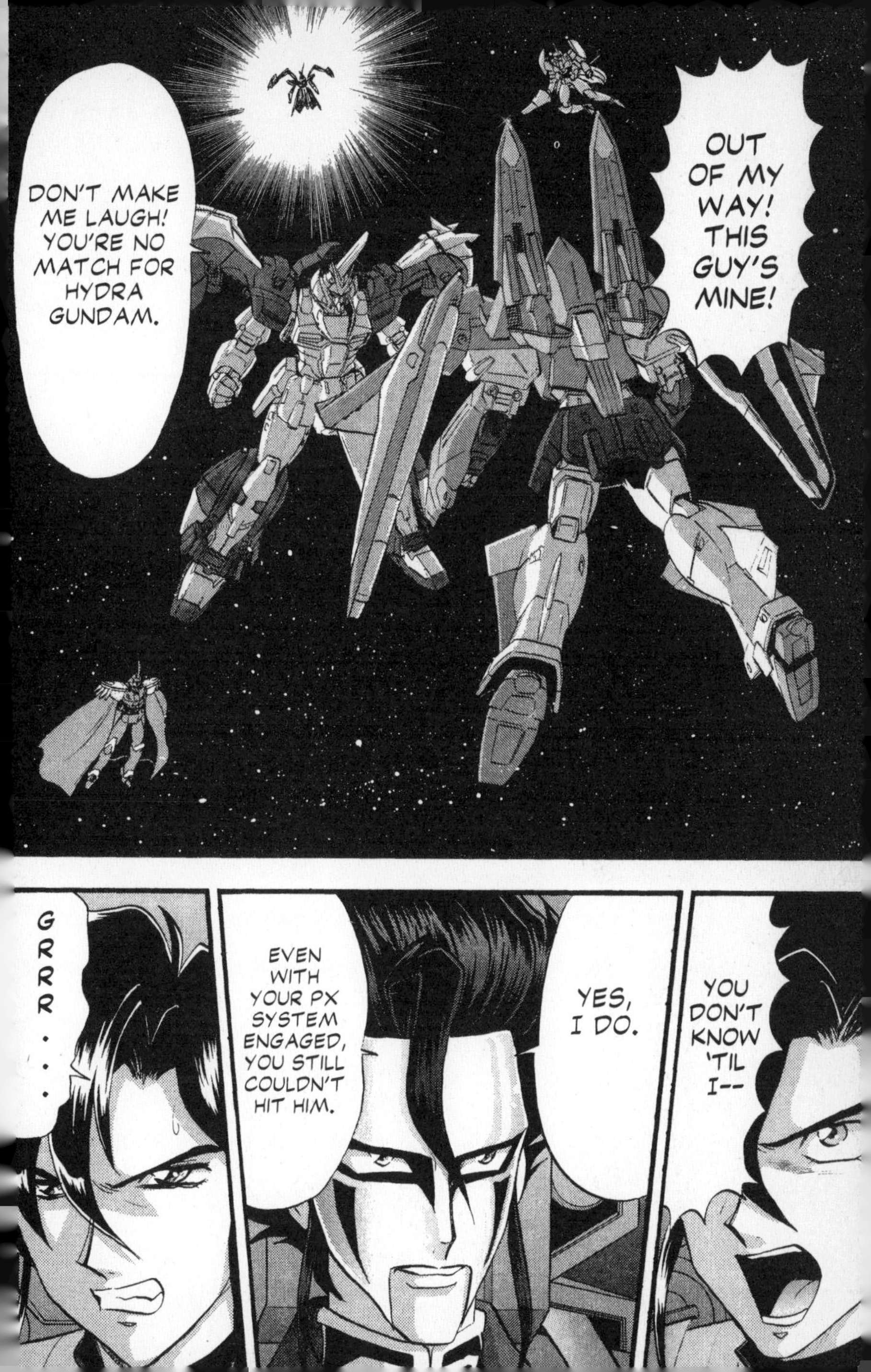
OUT OF MY WAY! THIS GUY'S MINE!
DON'T MAKE ME LAUGH! YOU'RE NO MATCH FOR HYDRA GUNDAM.
YOU DON'T KNOW 'TIL I--
YES, I DO.
EVEN WITH YOUR PX SYSTEM ENGAGED, YOU STILL COULDN'T HIT HIM.
GRRR . . .

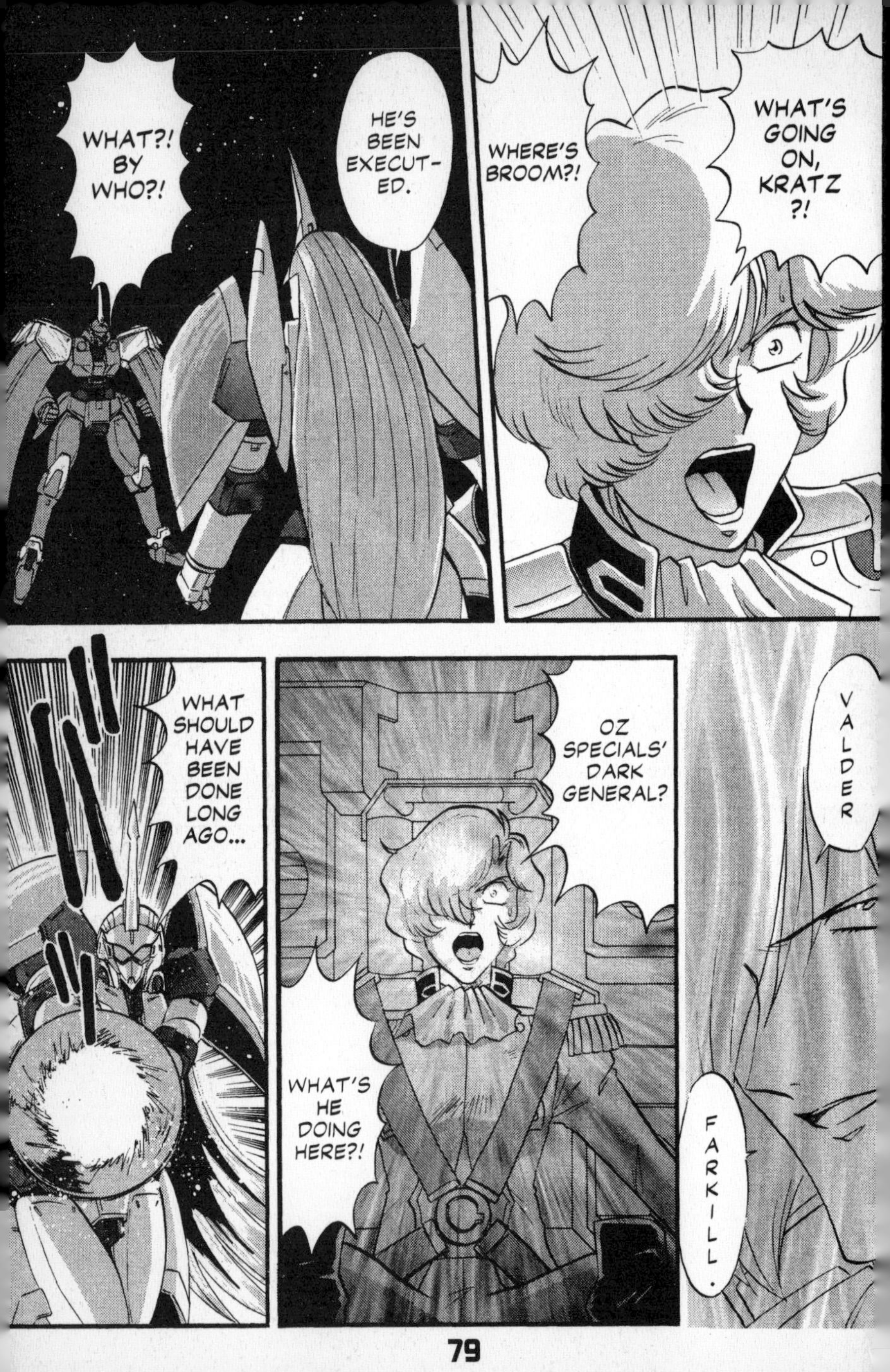
WHAT'S GOING ON, KRATZ?!
WHERE'S BROOM?!
HE'S BEEN EXECUT-ED.
WHAT?! BY WHO?!
VALDER FARKILL.
OZ SPECIALS' DARK GENERAL?
WHAT'S HE DOING HERE?!
WHAT SHOULD HAVE BEEN DONE LONG AGO...

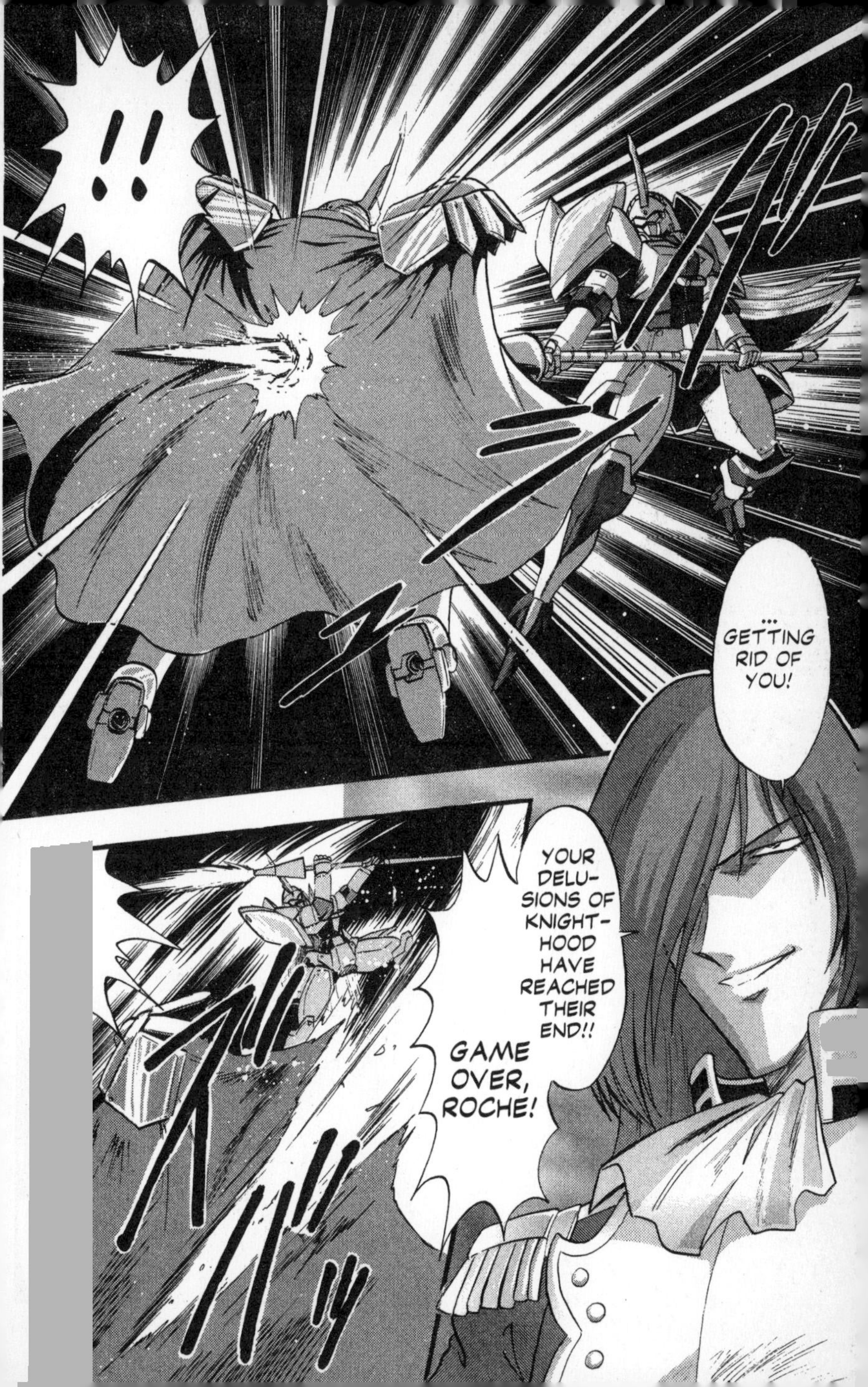
!!
...GETTING RID OF YOU!
YOUR DELUSIONS OF KNIGHTHOOD HAVE REACHED THEIR END!!
GAME OVER, ROCHE!

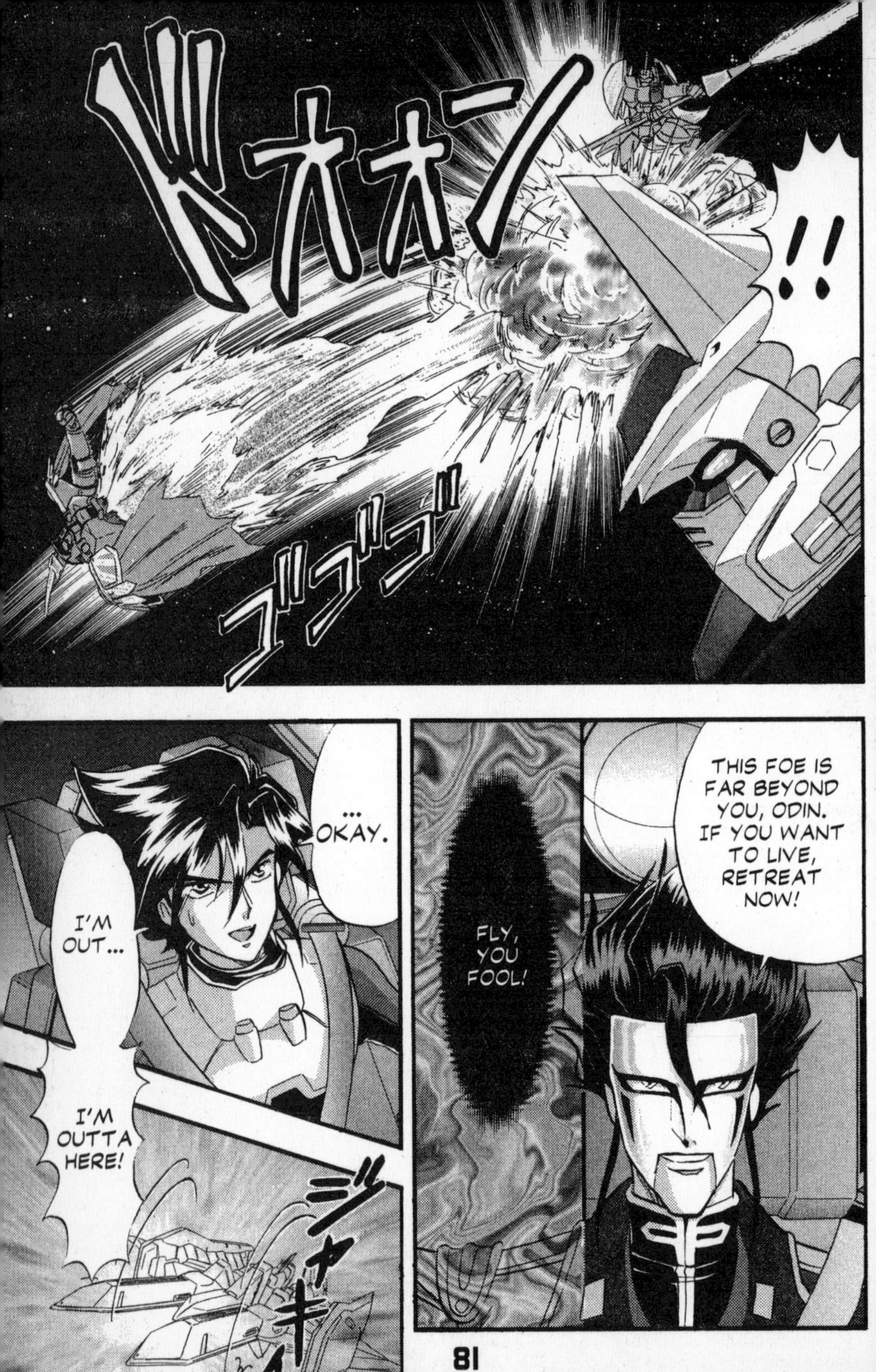
ドオオーン
!!
ゴゴゴ
THIS FOE IS FAR BEYOND YOU, ODIN. IF YOU WANT TO LIVE, RETREAT NOW!
FLY, YOU FOOL!
... OKAY.
I'M OUT...
I'M OUTTA HERE!
ジャキイ

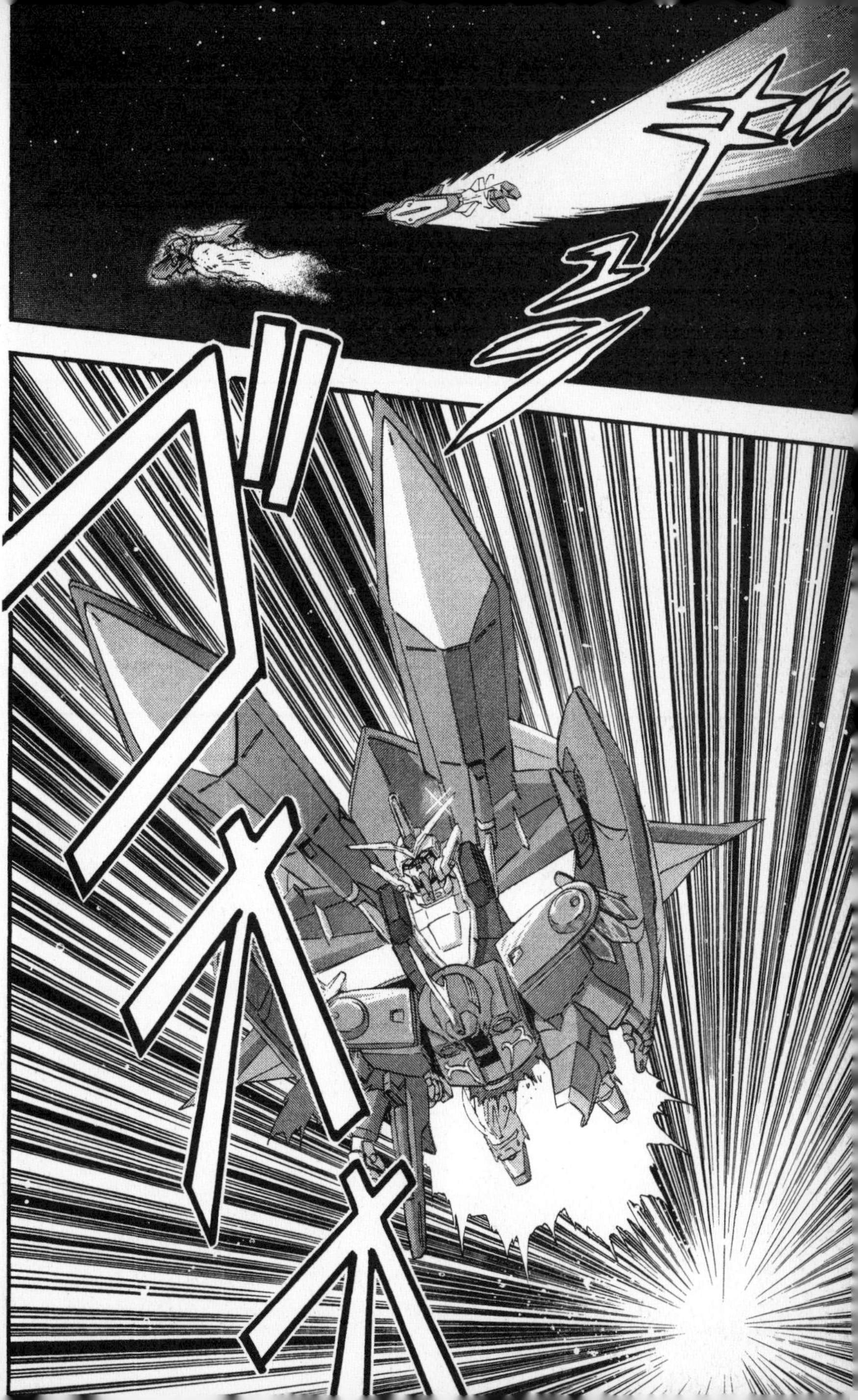

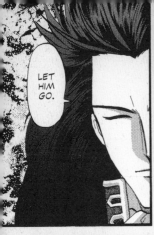

LET HIM GO.

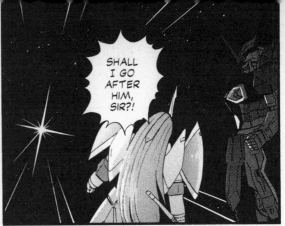

SHALL I GO AFTER HIM, SIR?!

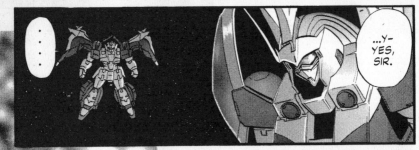

...Y- YES, SIR.

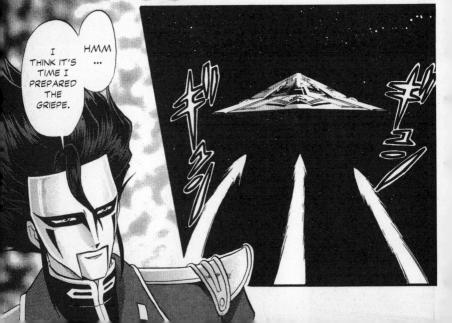

HMM...

I THINK IT'S TIME I PREPARED THE GRIEPE.

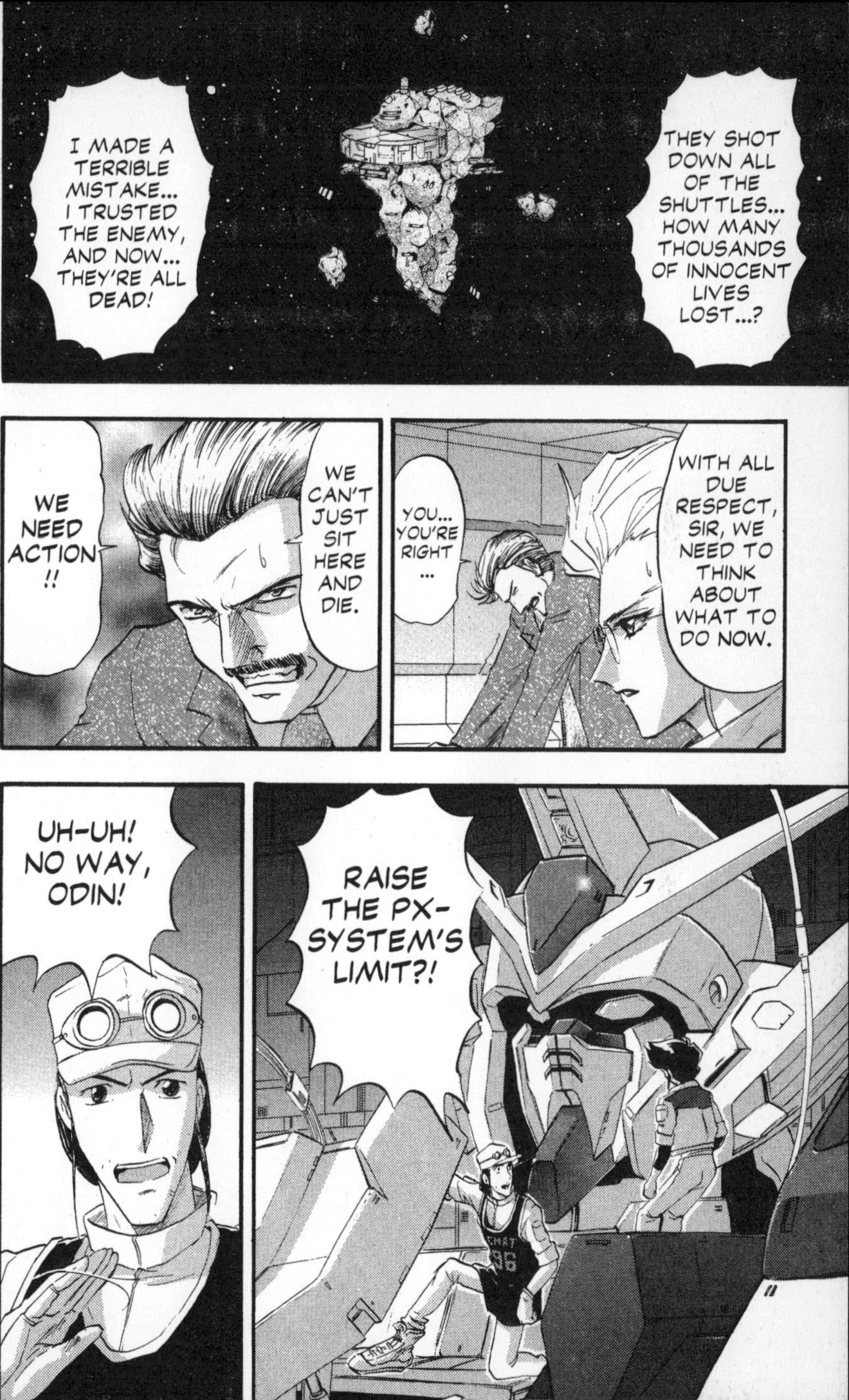

THEY SHOT DOWN ALL OF THE SHUTTLES... HOW MANY THOUSANDS OF INNOCENT LIVES LOST...?
I MADE A TERRIBLE MISTAKE... I TRUSTED THE ENEMY, AND NOW... THEY'RE ALL DEAD!
WITH ALL DUE RESPECT, SIR, WE NEED TO THINK ABOUT WHAT TO DO NOW.
YOU... YOU'RE RIGHT ...
WE CAN'T JUST SIT HERE AND DIE.
WE NEED ACTION !!
RAISE THE PX-SYSTEM'S LIMIT?!
UH-UH! NO WAY, ODIN!

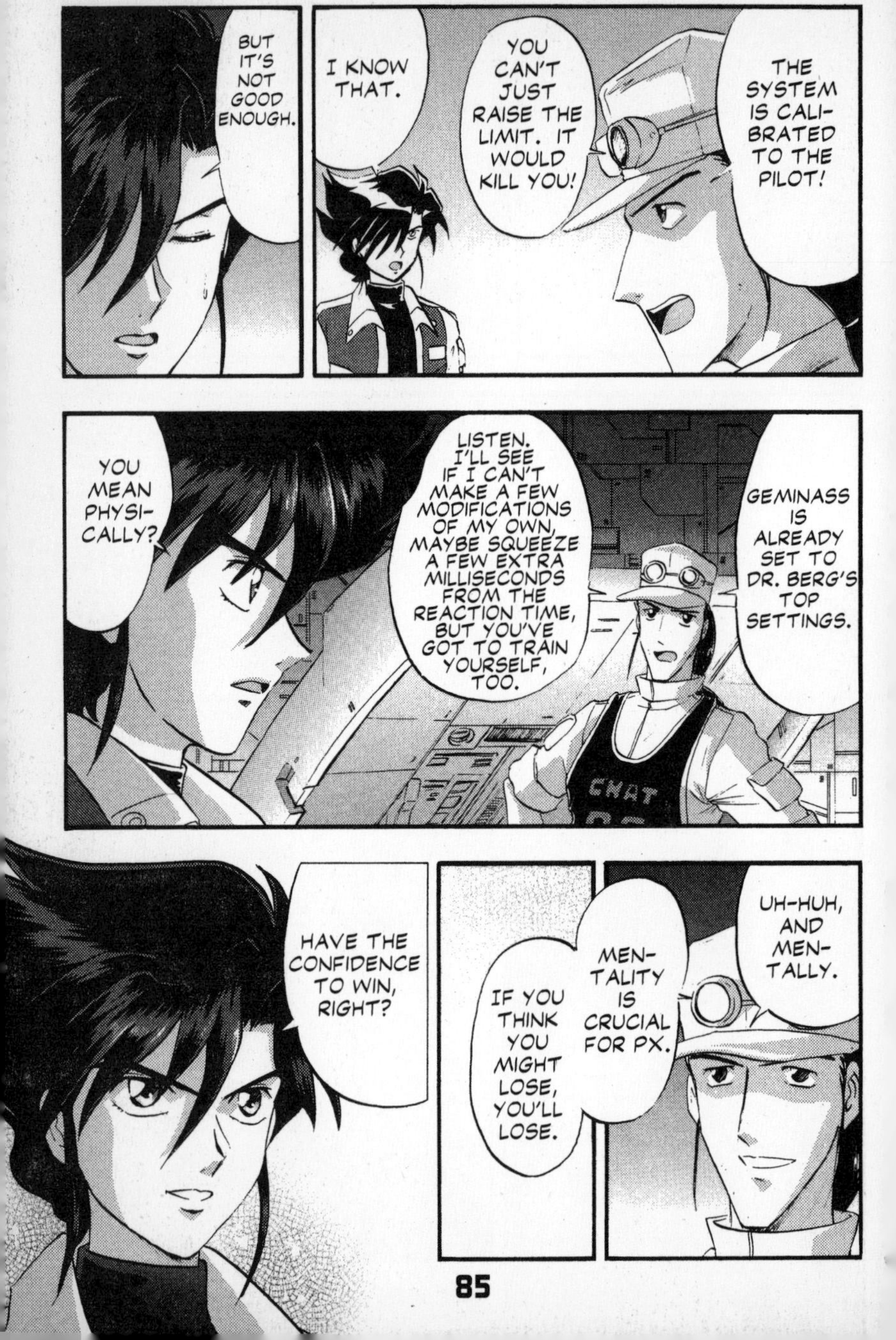
THE SYSTEM IS CALI-BRATED TO THE PILOT!
YOU CAN'T JUST RAISE THE LIMIT. IT WOULD KILL YOU!
I KNOW THAT.
BUT IT'S NOT GOOD ENOUGH.
GEMINASS IS ALREADY SET TO DR. BERG'S TOP SETTINGS.
LISTEN. I'LL SEE IF I CAN'T MAKE A FEW MODIFICATIONS OF MY OWN, MAYBE SQUEEZE A FEW EXTRA MILLISECONDS FROM THE REACTION TIME, BUT YOU'VE GOT TO TRAIN YOURSELF, TOO.
YOU MEAN PHYSI-CALLY?
UH-HUH, AND MEN-TALLY.
MEN-TALITY IS CRUCIAL FOR PX.
IF YOU THINK YOU MIGHT LOSE, YOU'LL LOSE.
HAVE THE CONFIDENCE TO WIN, RIGHT?

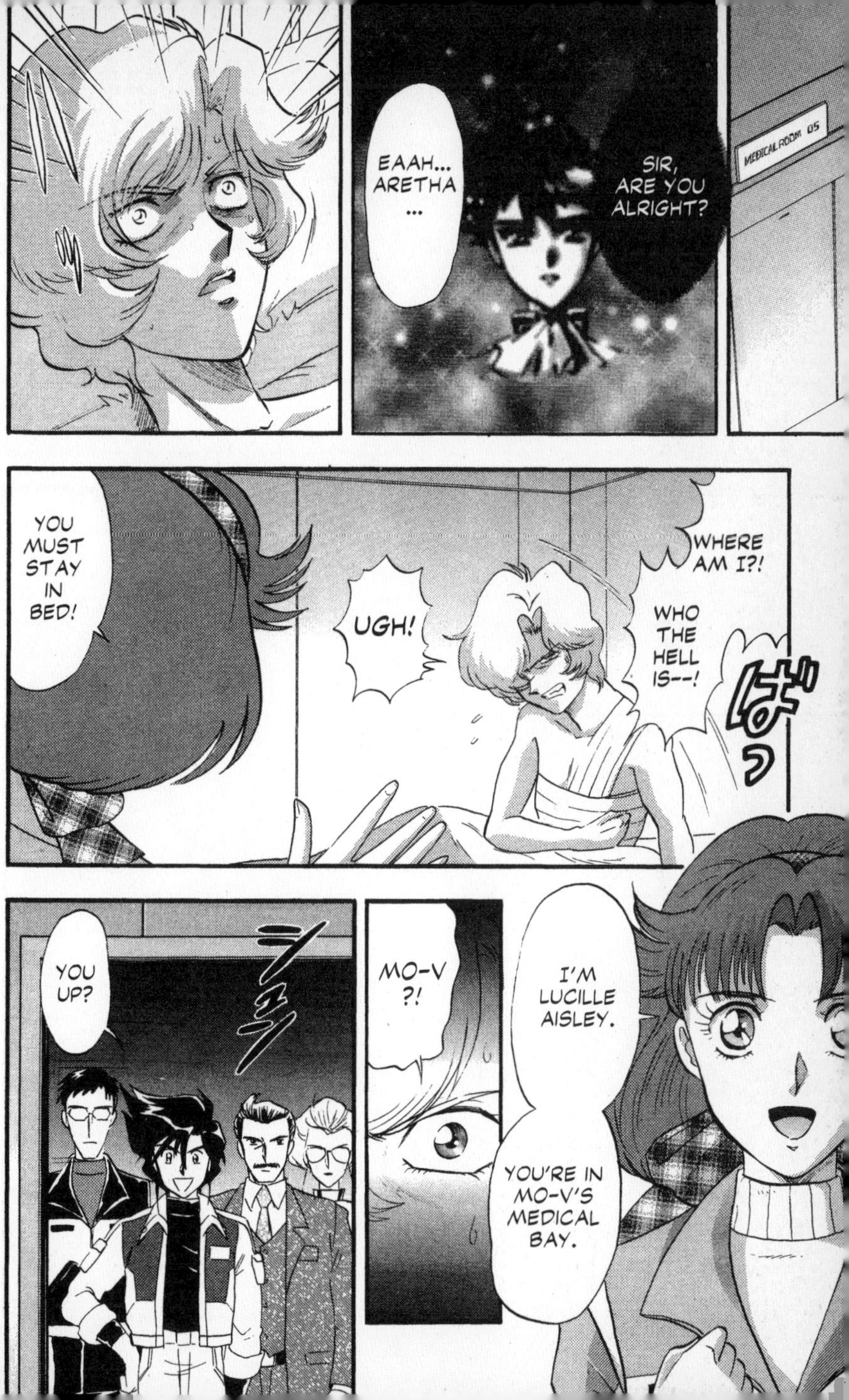
MEDICAL ROOM 05
SIR, ARE YOU ALRIGHT?
EAAH... ARETHA ...
WHERE AM I?!
WHO THE HELL IS--!
ばっ
UGH!
YOU MUST STAY IN BED!
I'M LUCILLE AISLEY.
YOU'RE IN MO-V'S MEDICAL BAY.
MO-V ?!
YOU UP?

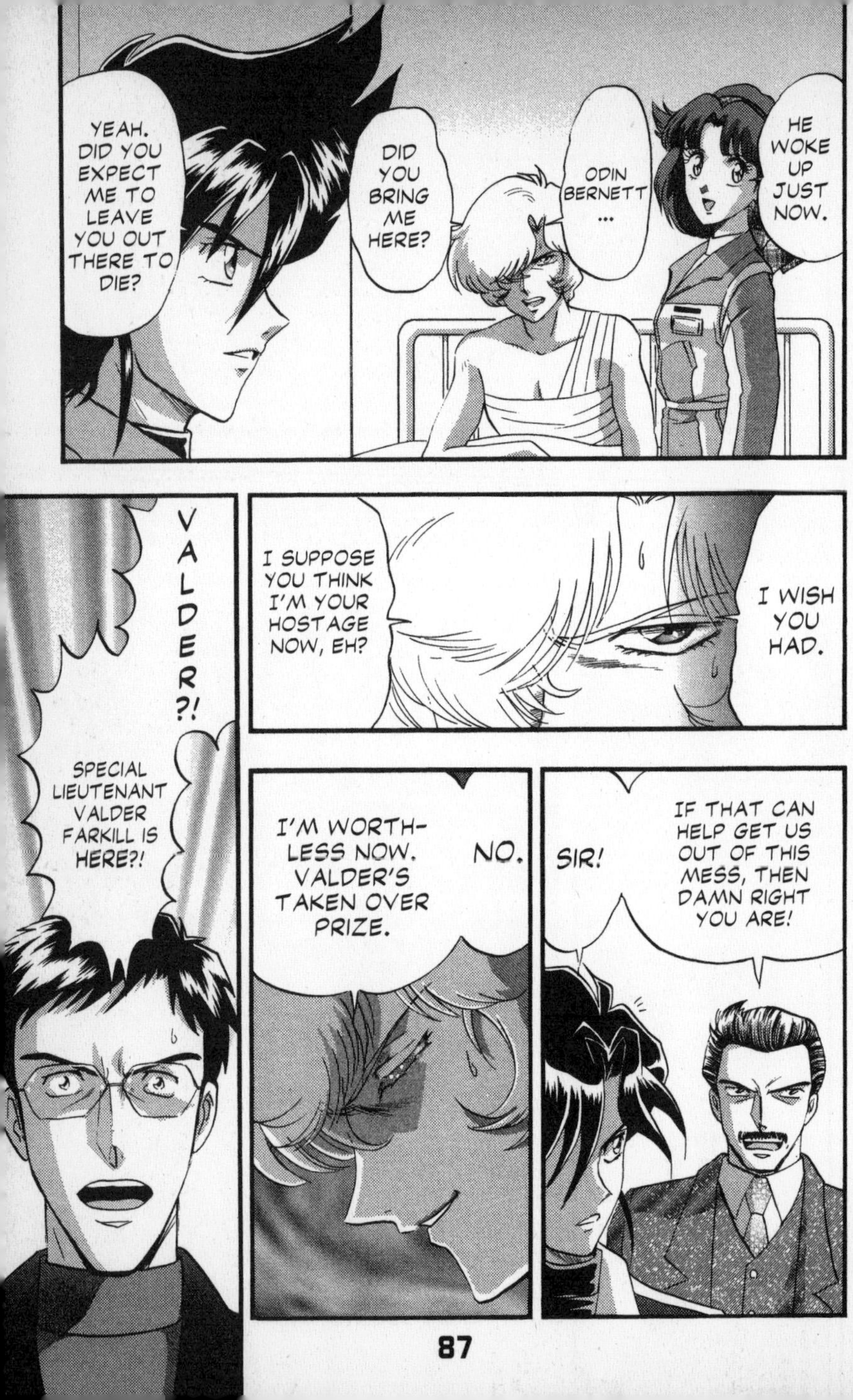
HE WOKE UP JUST NOW.
ODIN BERNETT ...
DID YOU BRING ME HERE?
YEAH. DID YOU EXPECT ME TO LEAVE YOU OUT THERE TO DIE?
I WISH YOU HAD.
I SUPPOSE YOU THINK I'M YOUR HOSTAGE NOW, EH?
IF THAT CAN HELP GET US OUT OF THIS MESS, THEN DAMN RIGHT YOU ARE!
SIR!
NO.
I'M WORTH-LESS NOW. VALDER'S TAKEN OVER PRIZE.
VALDER?!
SPECIAL LIEUTENANT VALDER FARKILL IS HERE?!

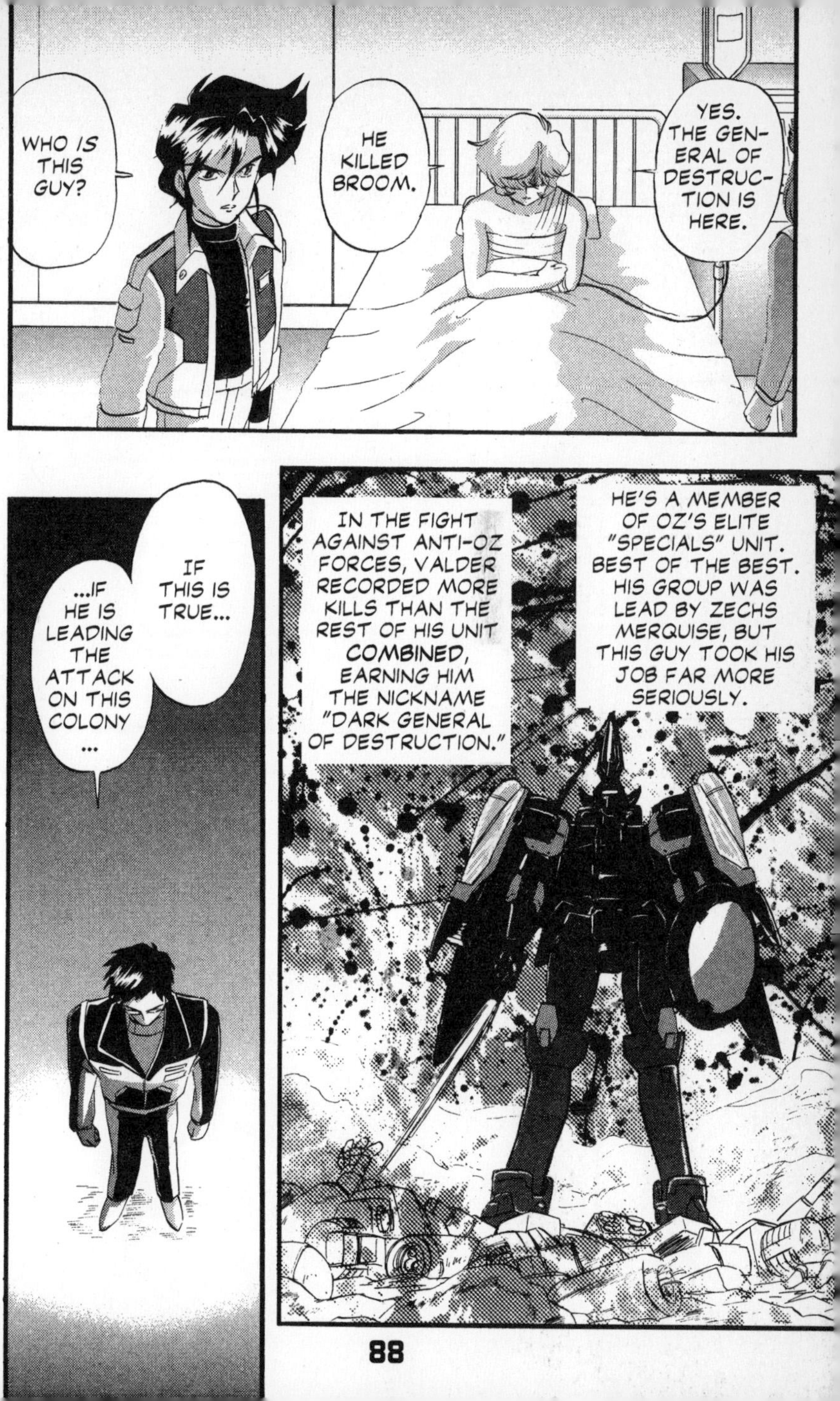
YES. THE GEN-ERAL OF DESTRUC-TION IS HERE.
HE KILLED BROOM.
WHO IS THIS GUY?
HE'S A MEMBER OF OZ'S ELITE "SPECIALS" UNIT. BEST OF THE BEST. HIS GROUP WAS LEAD BY ZECHS MERQUISE, BUT THIS GUY TOOK HIS JOB FAR MORE SERIOUSLY.
IN THE FIGHT AGAINST ANTI-OZ FORCES, VALDER RECORDED MORE KILLS THAN THE REST OF HIS UNIT COMBINED, EARNING HIM THE NICKNAME "DARK GENERAL OF DESTRUCTION."
IF THIS IS TRUE...
...IF HE IS LEADING THE ATTACK ON THIS COLONY ...

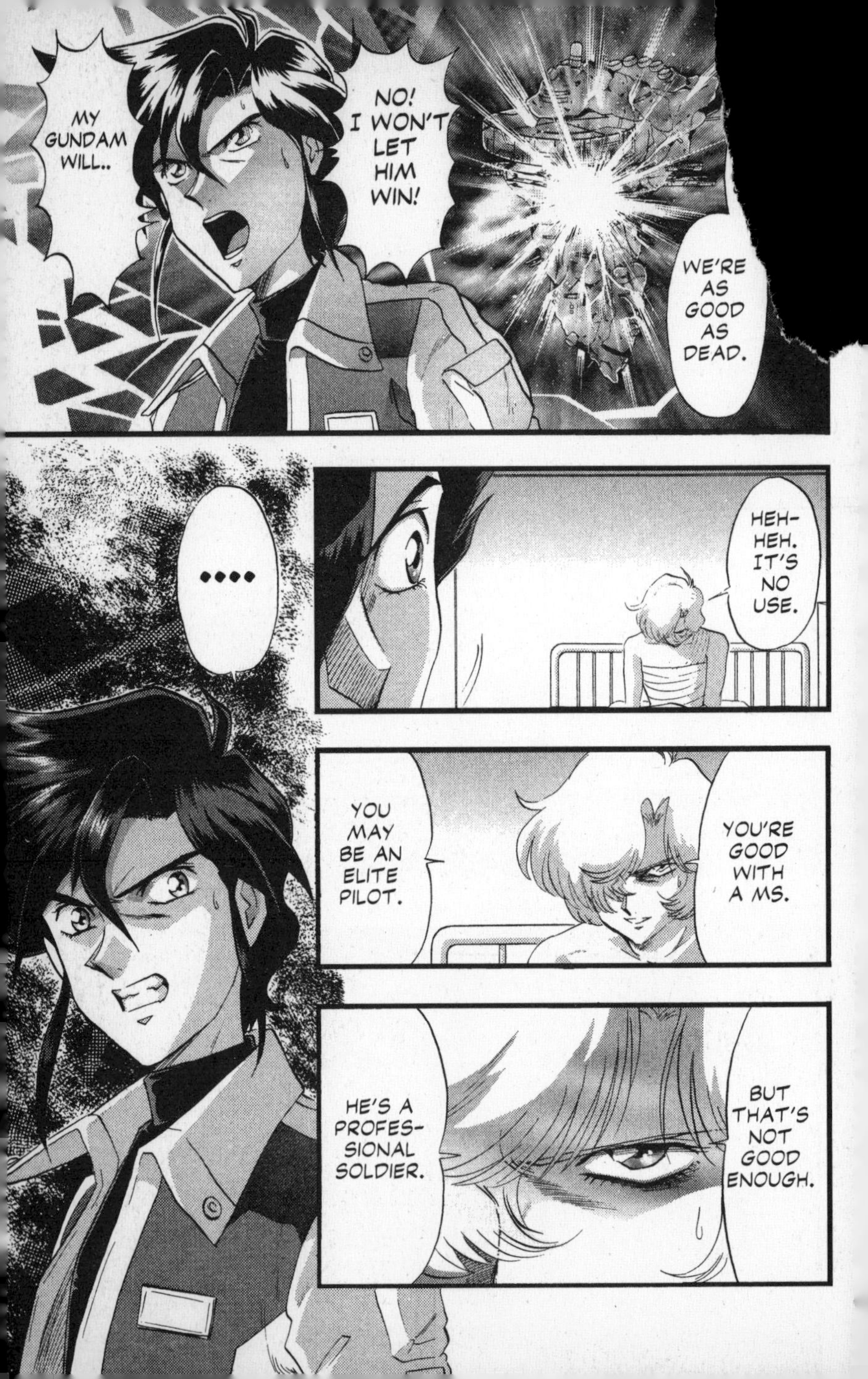
WE'RE AS GOOD AS DEAD.
NO! I WON'T LET HIM WIN!
MY GUNDAM WILL..
HEH-HEH. IT'S NO USE.
YOU'RE GOOD WITH A MS.
YOU MAY BE AN ELITE PILOT.
BUT THAT'S NOT GOOD ENOUGH.
HE'S A PROFES-SIONAL SOLDIER.
....

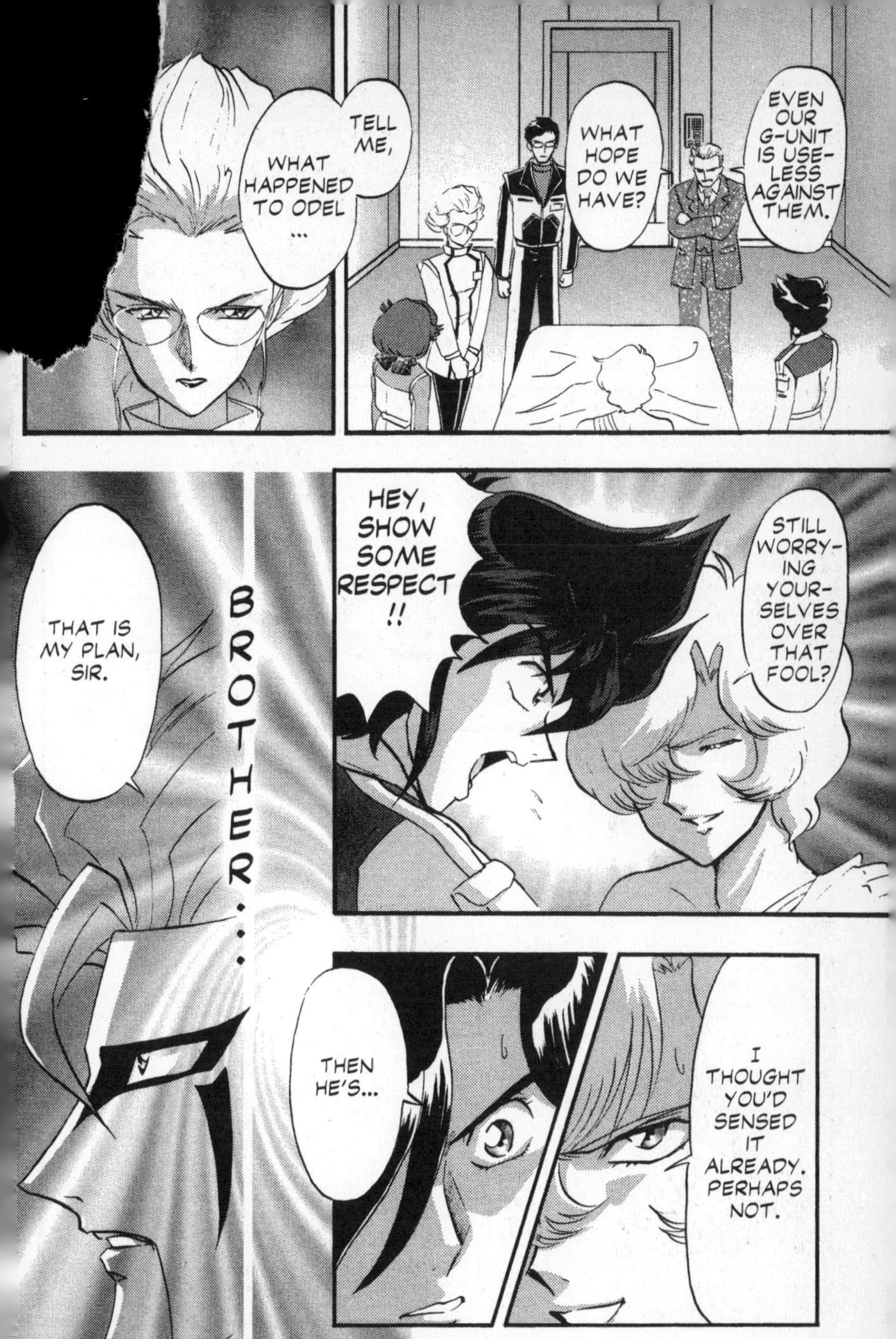
EVEN OUR G-UNIT IS USELESS AGAINST THEM.
WHAT HOPE DO WE HAVE?
TELL ME,
WHAT HAPPENED TO ODEL ...
STILL WORRYING YOURSELVES OVER THAT FOOL?
HEY, SHOW SOME RESPECT !!
I THOUGHT YOU'D SENSED IT ALREADY. PERHAPS NOT.
THEN HE'S...
THAT IS MY PLAN, SIR.
BROTHER...

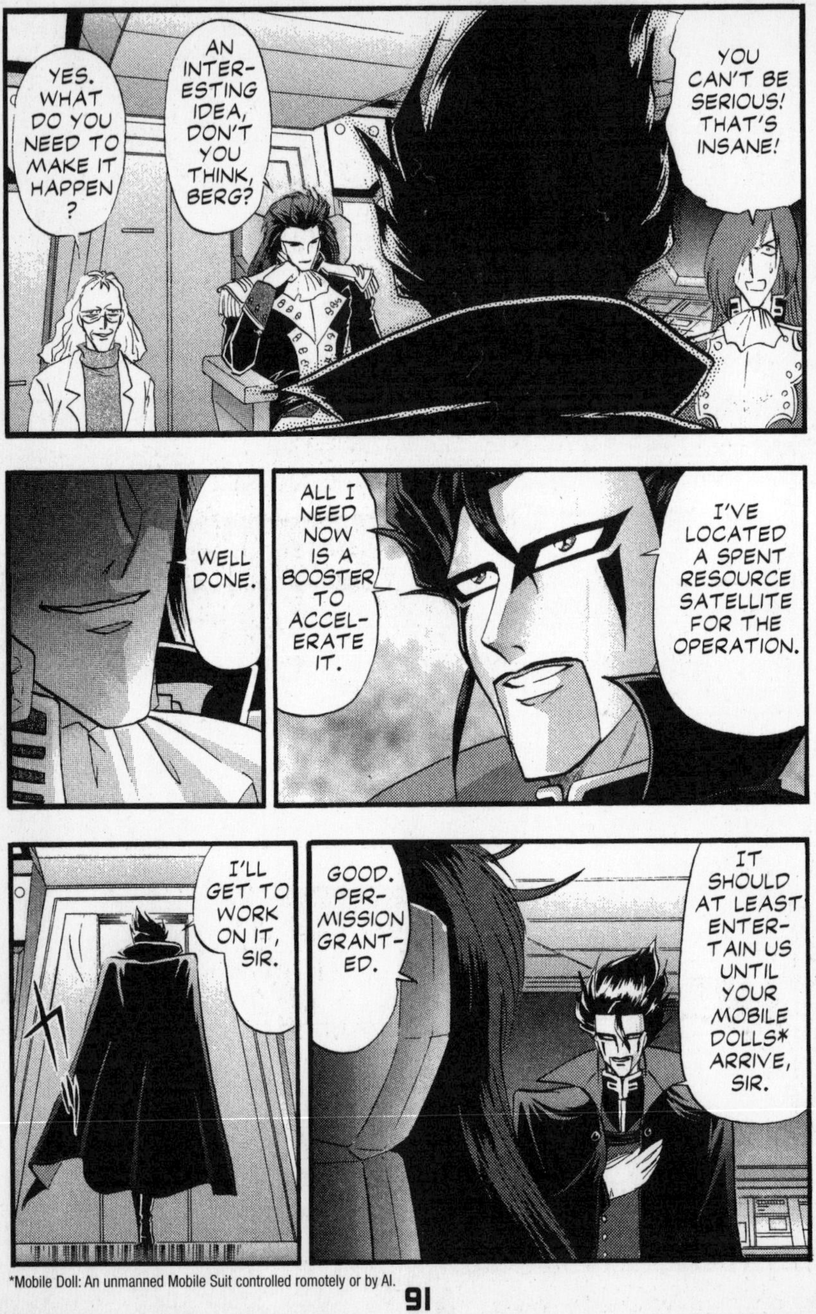
YOU CAN'T BE SERIOUS! THAT'S INSANE!
AN INTERESTING IDEA, DON'T YOU THINK, BERG?
YES. WHAT DO YOU NEED TO MAKE IT HAPPEN?
I'VE LOCATED A SPENT RESOURCE SATELLITE FOR THE OPERATION.
ALL I NEED NOW IS A BOOSTER TO ACCELERATE IT.
WELL DONE.
IT SHOULD AT LEAST ENTERTAIN US UNTIL YOUR MOBILE DOLLS* ARRIVE, SIR.
GOOD. PERMISSION GRANTED.
I'LL GET TO WORK ON IT, SIR.

*Mobile Doll: An unmanned Mobile Suit controlled romotely or by AI.

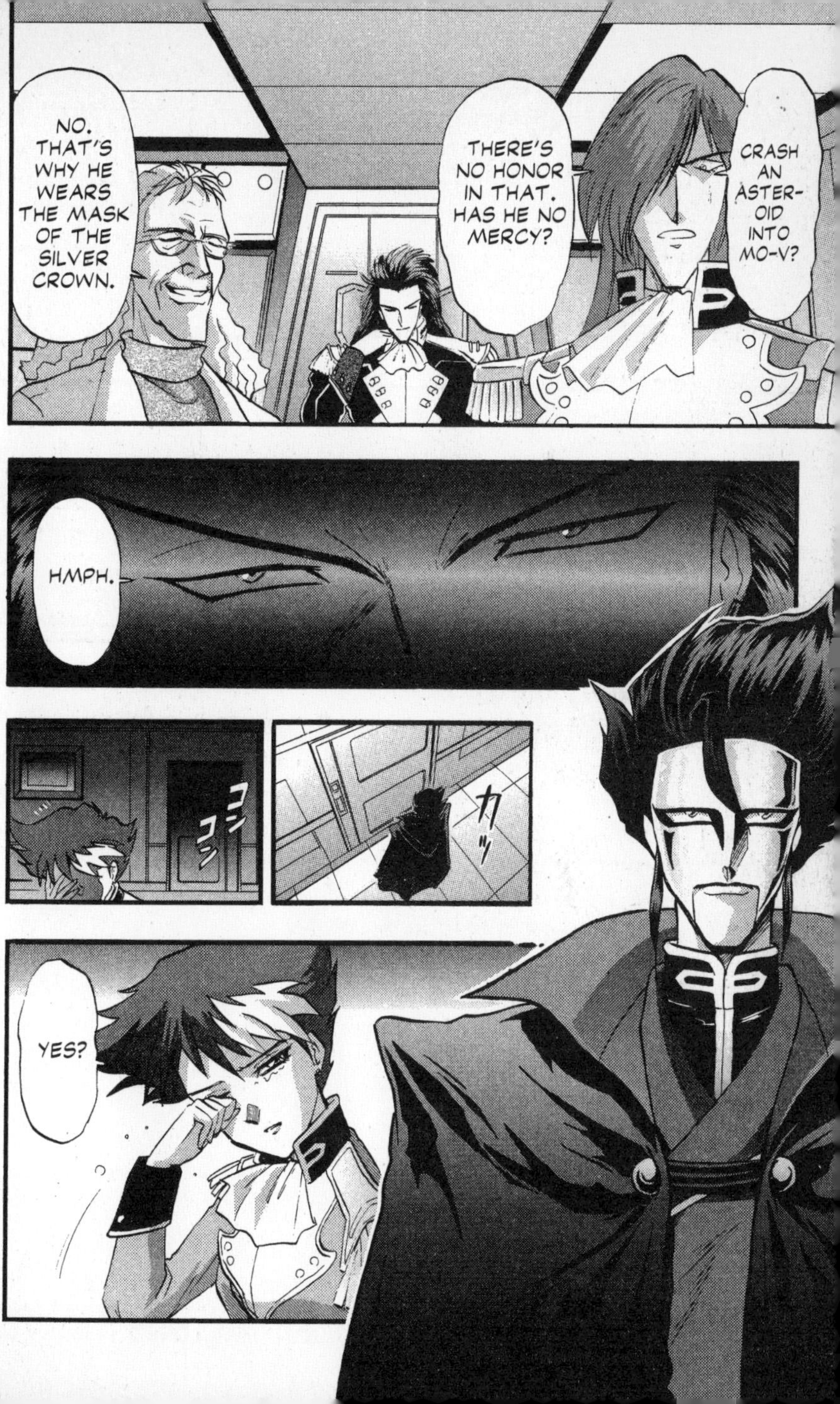
CRASH AN ASTER-OID INTO MO-V?
THERE'S NO HONOR IN THAT. HAS HE NO MERCY?
NO. THAT'S WHY HE WEARS THE MASK OF THE SILVER CROWN.
HMPH.
カッ
コン コン
YES?

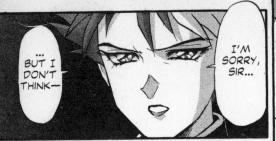

... BUT I DON'T THINK—

I'M SORRY, SIR...

LIEU- TENANT, YOU'LL ASSIST MY OPERA- TION.

SILVER CROWN?!

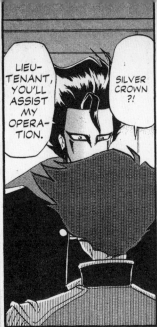

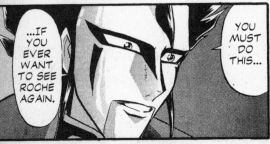

...IF YOU EVER WANT TO SEE ROCHE AGAIN.

YOU MUST DO THIS...

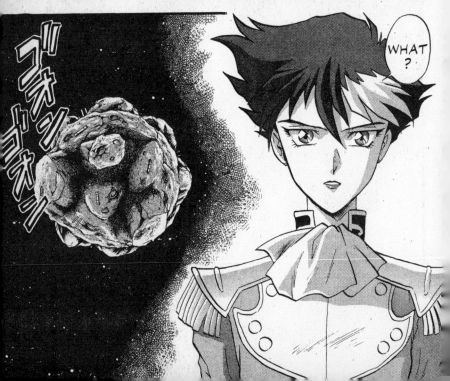

WHAT?

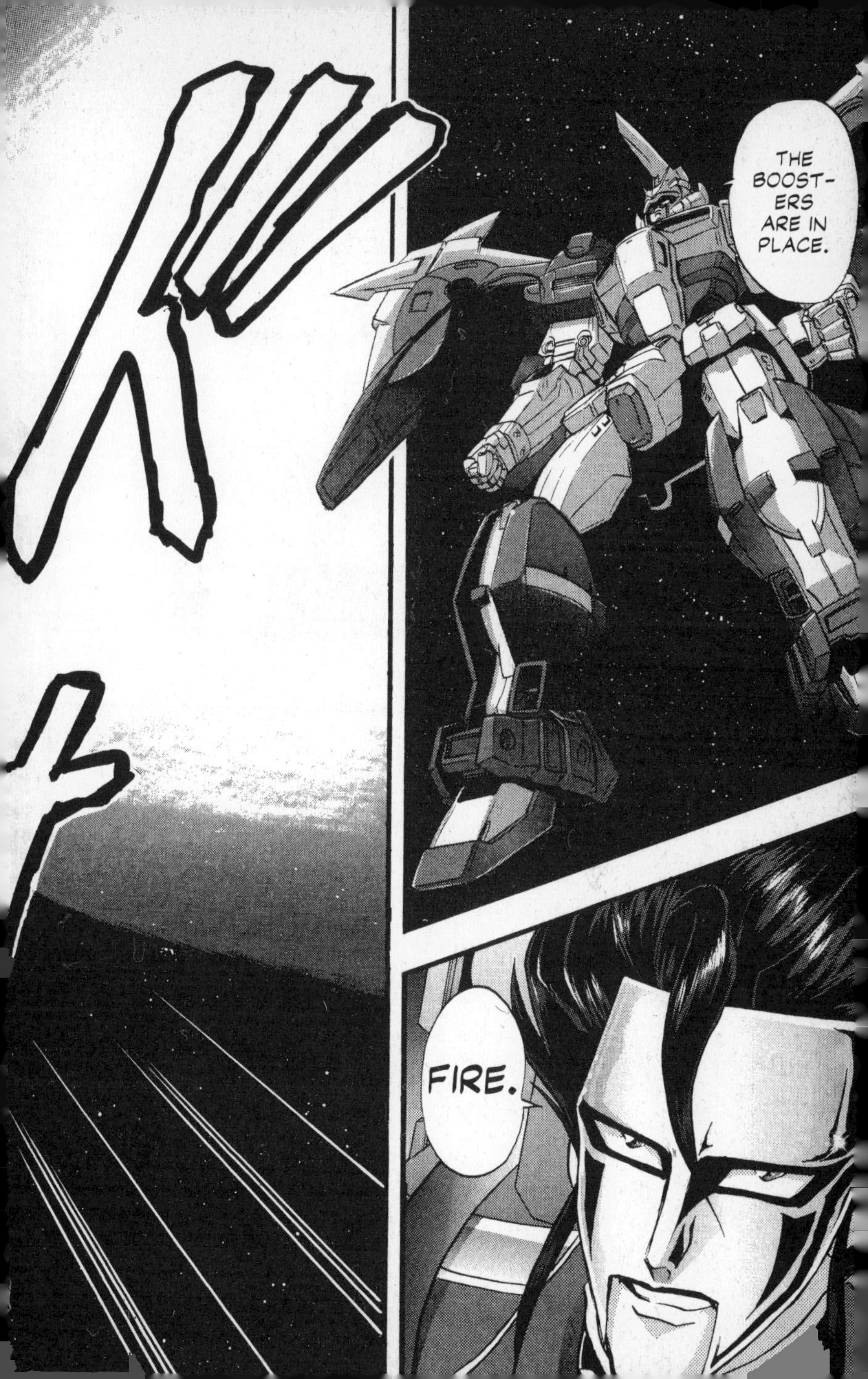
THE BOOSTERS ARE IN PLACE.
FIRE.

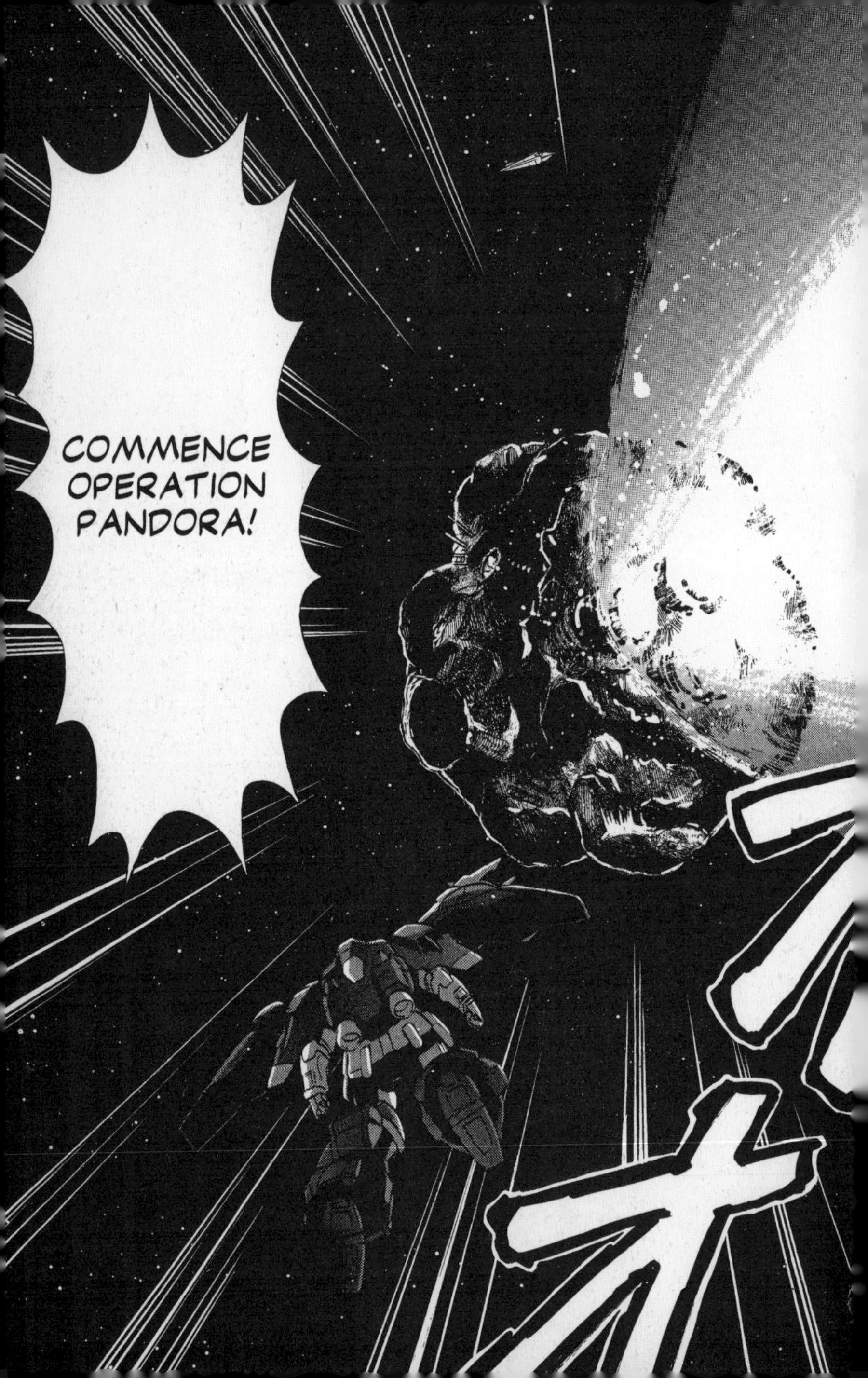
COMMENCE OPERATION PANDORA!

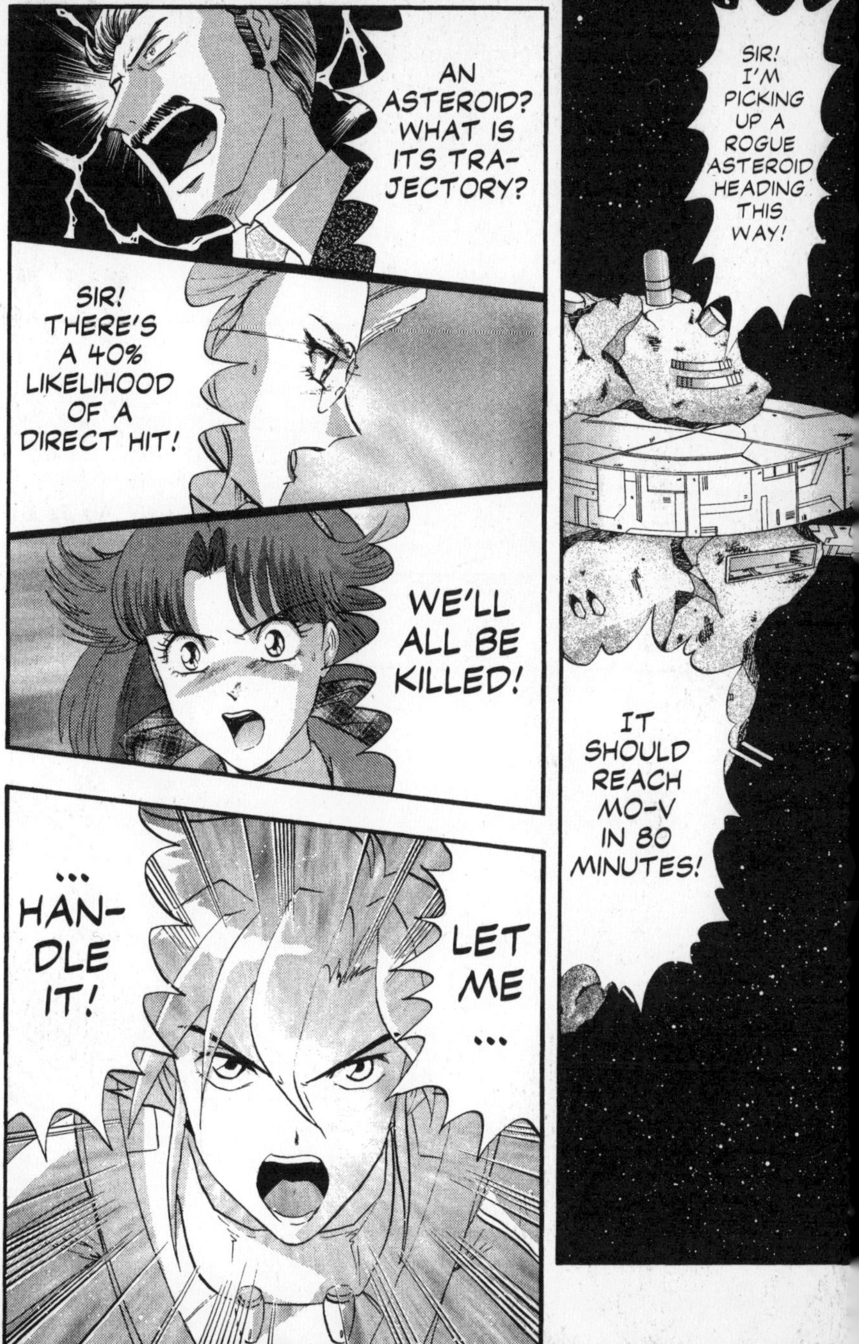
SIR! I'M PICKING UP A ROGUE ASTEROID HEADING THIS WAY!
IT SHOULD REACH MO-V IN 80 MINUTES!
AN ASTEROID? WHAT IS ITS TRA-JECTORY?
SIR! THERE'S A 40% LIKELIHOOD OF A DIRECT HIT!
WE'LL ALL BE KILLED!
LET ME ...
... HÄN-DLE IT!

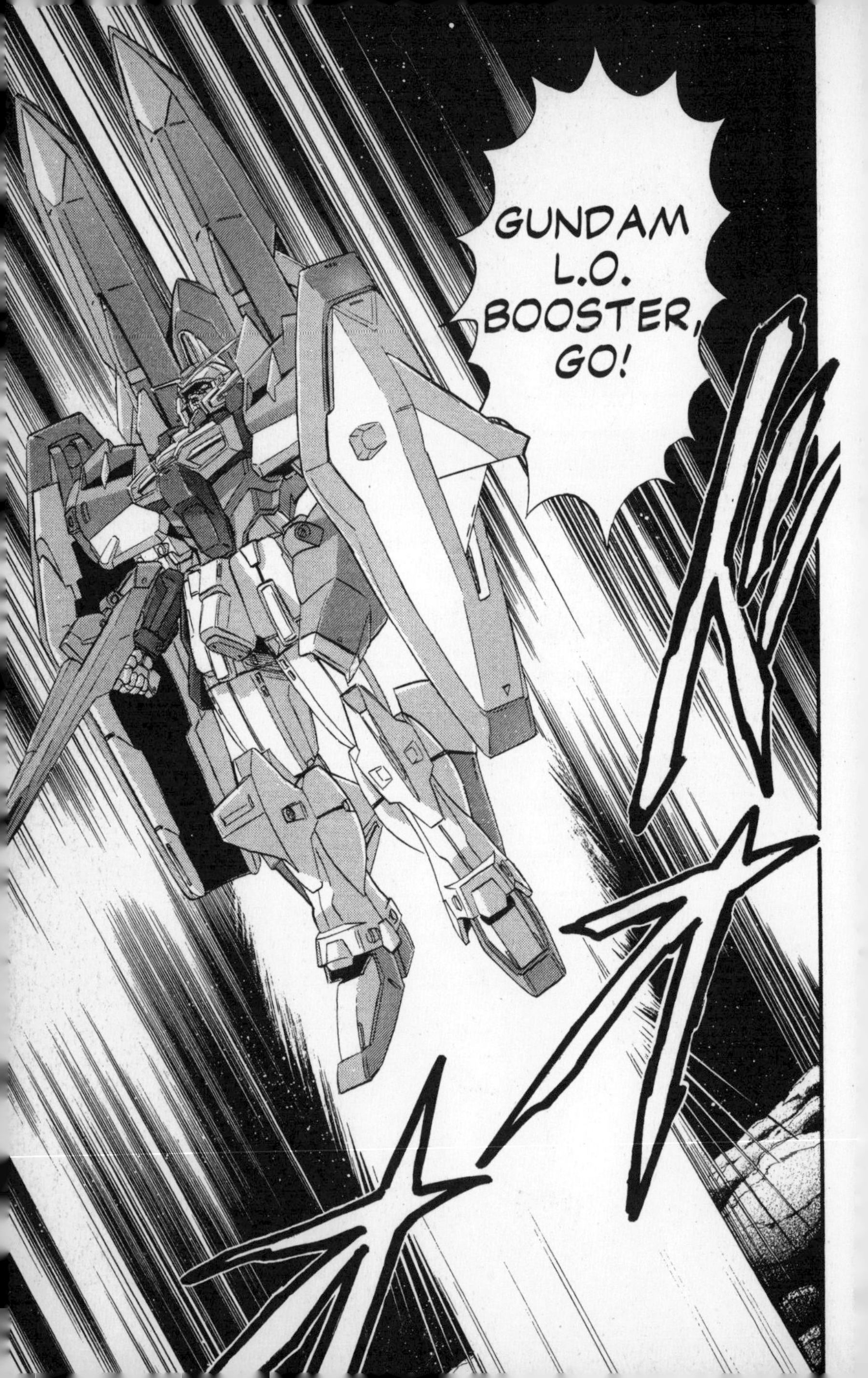
GUNDAM L.O. BOOSTER, GO!

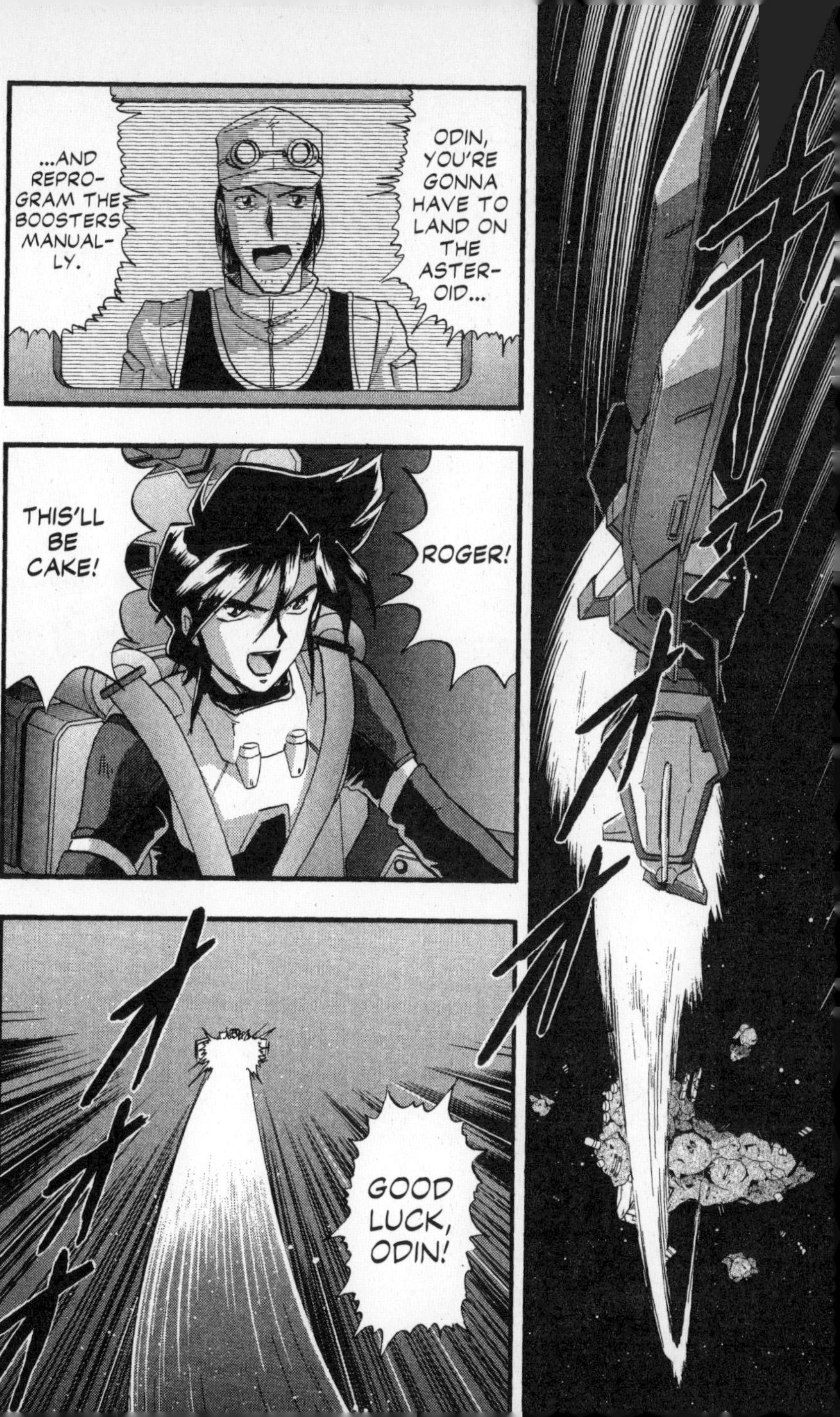
ODIN, YOU'RE GONNA HAVE TO LAND ON THE ASTEROID...
...AND REPROGRAM THE BOOSTERS MANUALLY.
ROGER!
THIS'LL BE CAKE!
GOOD LUCK, ODIN!

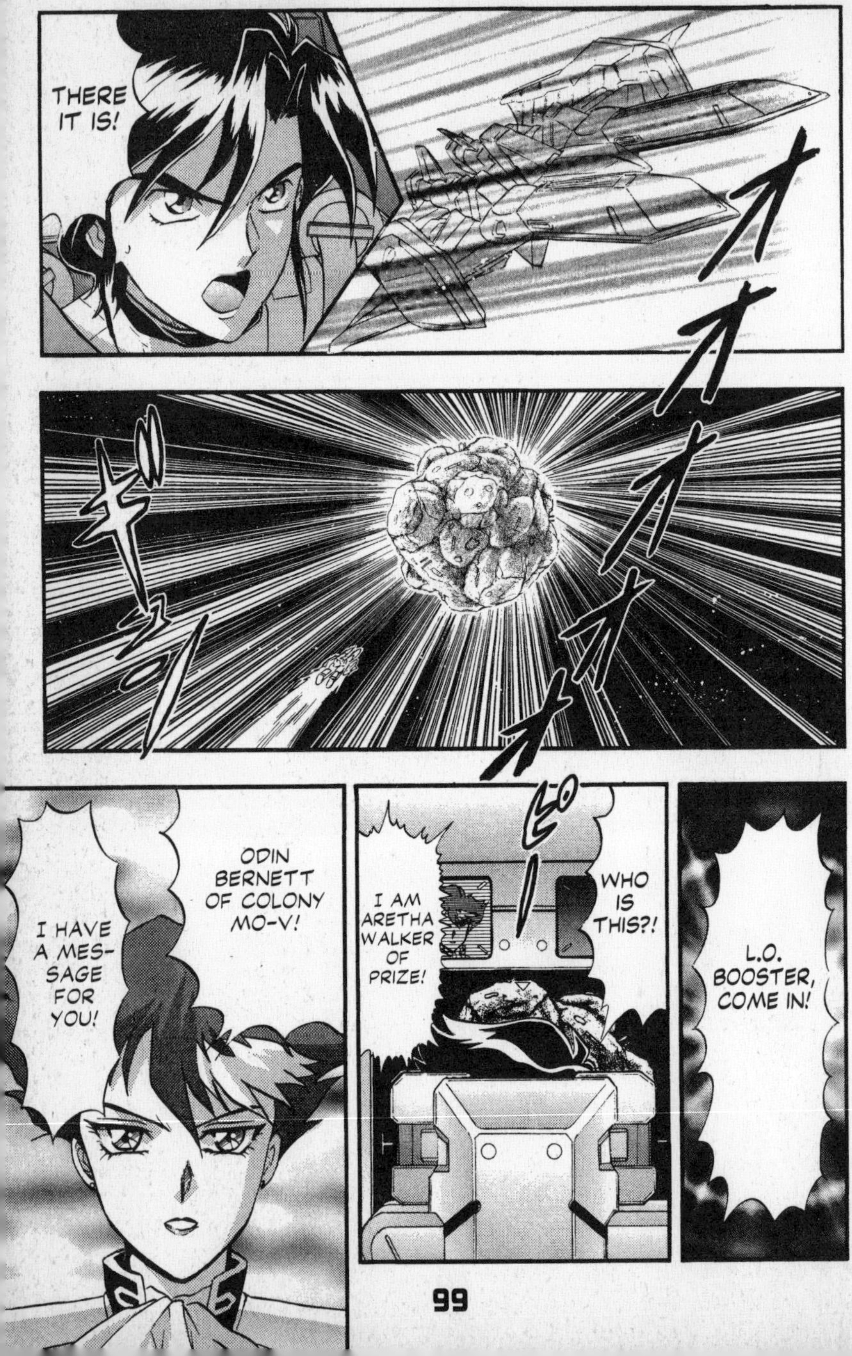
THERE IT IS!
L.O. BOOSTER, COME IN!
WHO IS THIS?!
I AM ARETHA WALKER OF PRIZE!
ODIN BERNETT OF COLONY MO-V!
I HAVE A MESSAGE FOR YOU!

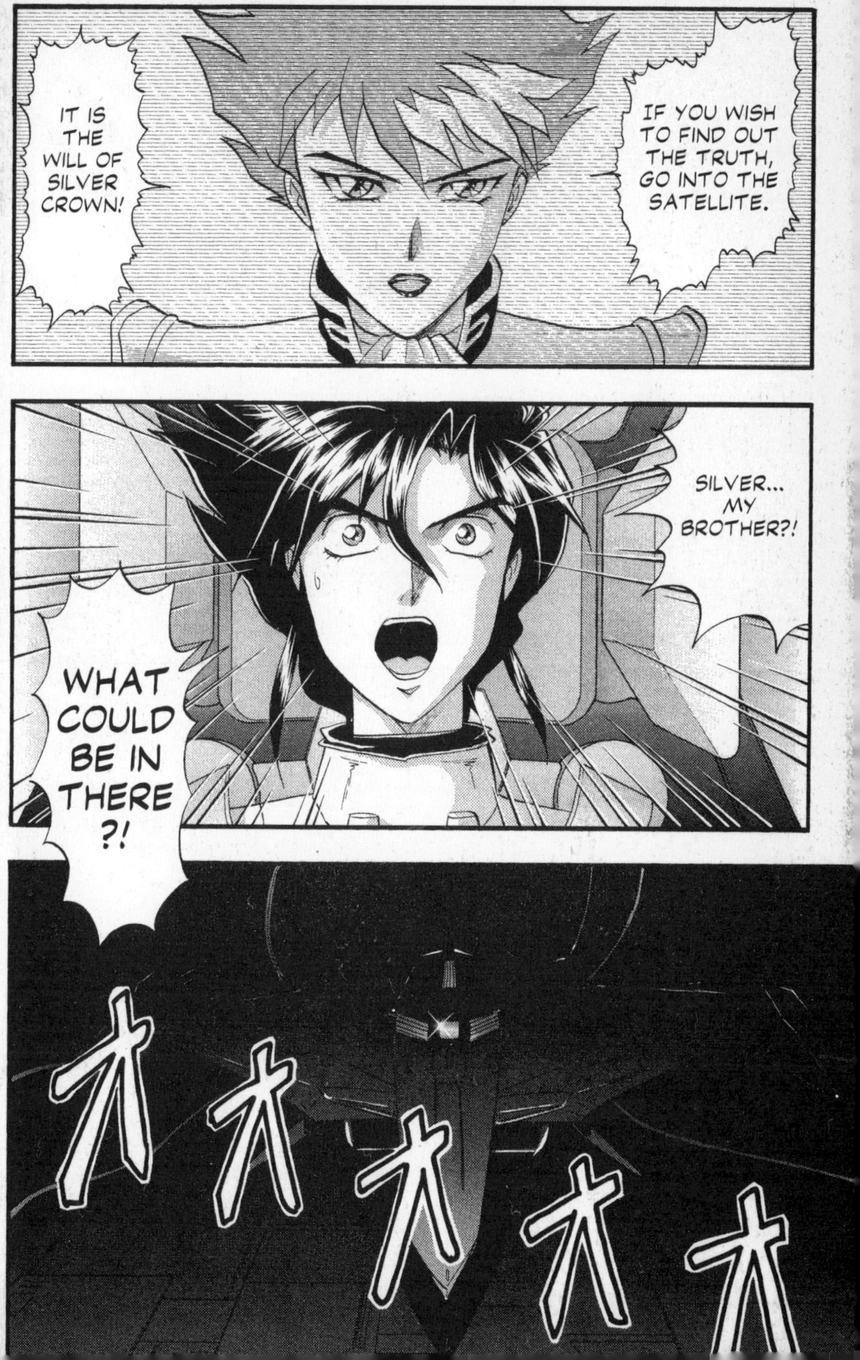
IF YOU WISH TO FIND OUT THE TRUTH, GO INTO THE SATELLITE.
IT IS THE WILL OF SILVER CROWN!
SILVER... MY BROTHER?!
WHAT COULD BE IN THERE ?!
オオオオオ

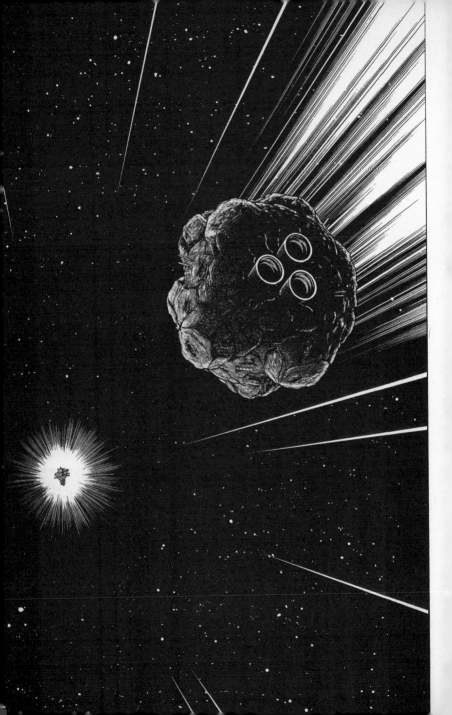

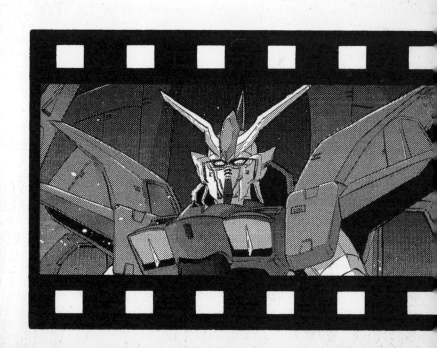

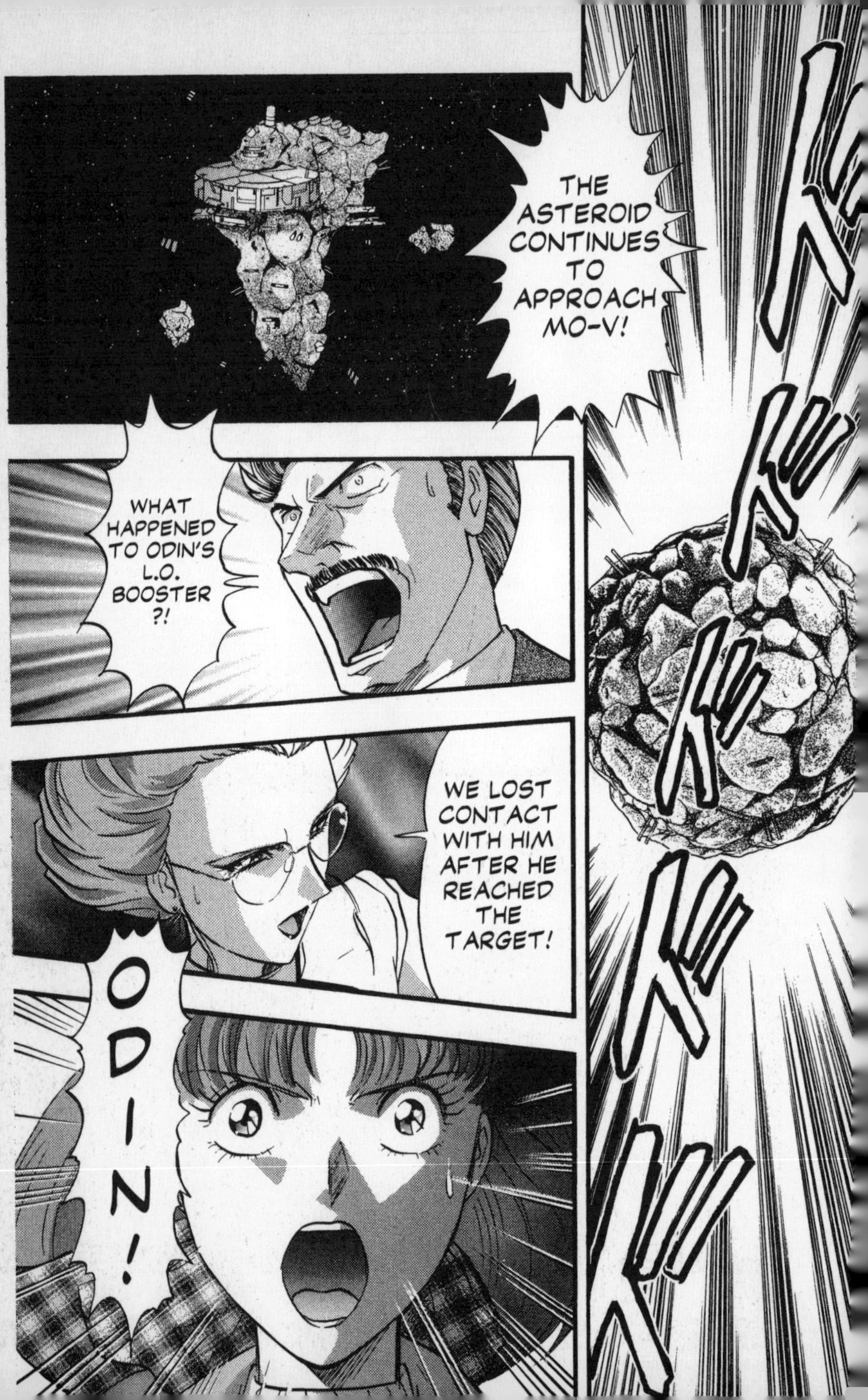
THE ASTEROID CONTINUES TO APPROACH MO-V!
WHAT HAPPENED TO ODIN'S L.O. BOOSTER ?!
WE LOST CONTACT WITH HIM AFTER HE REACHED THE TARGET!
ODIN!

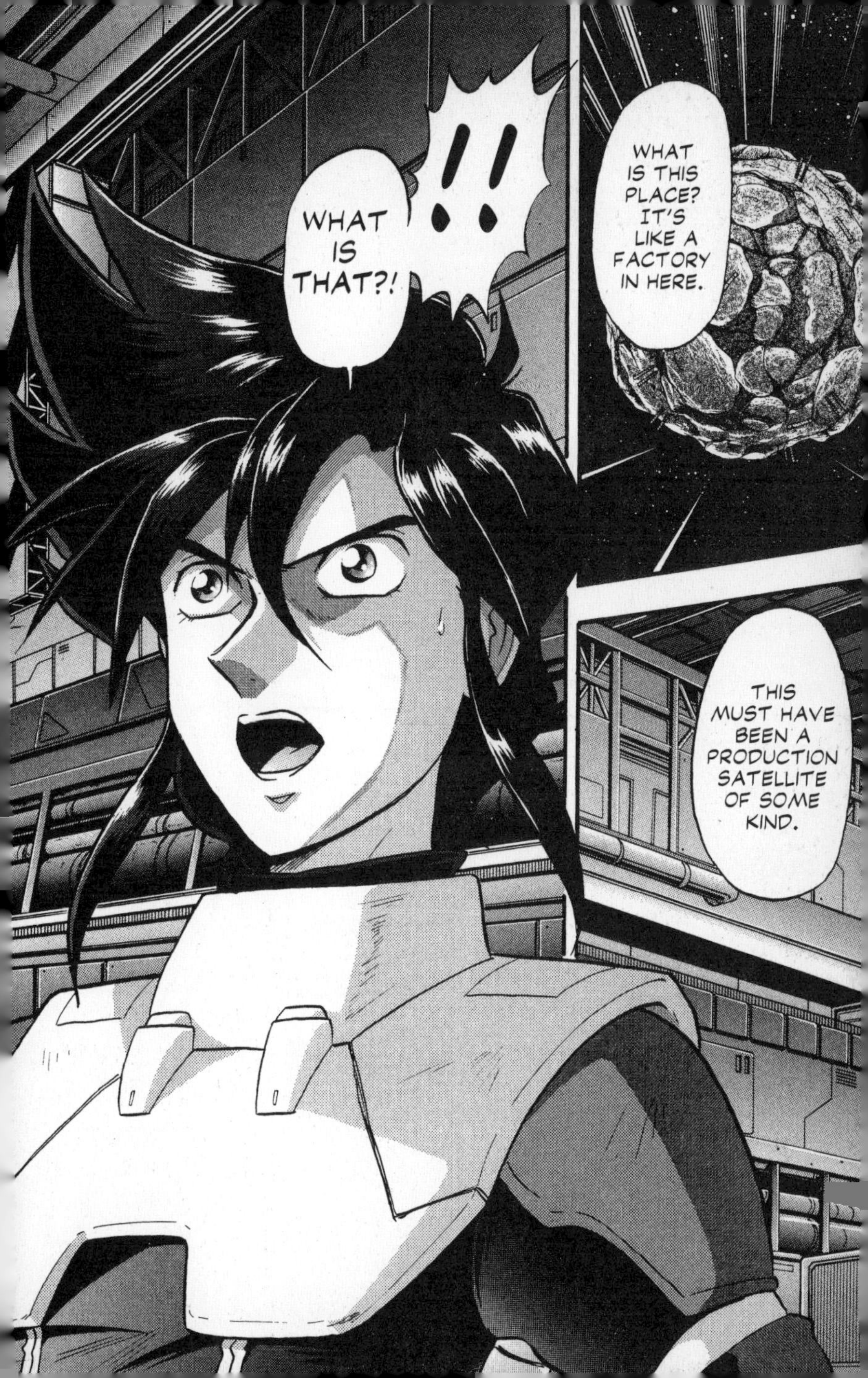
WHAT IS THIS PLACE? IT'S LIKE A FACTORY IN HERE.
THIS MUST HAVE BEEN A PRODUCTION SATELLITE OF SOME KIND.
!!
WHAT IS THAT?!

#8 Engage, Griepe!

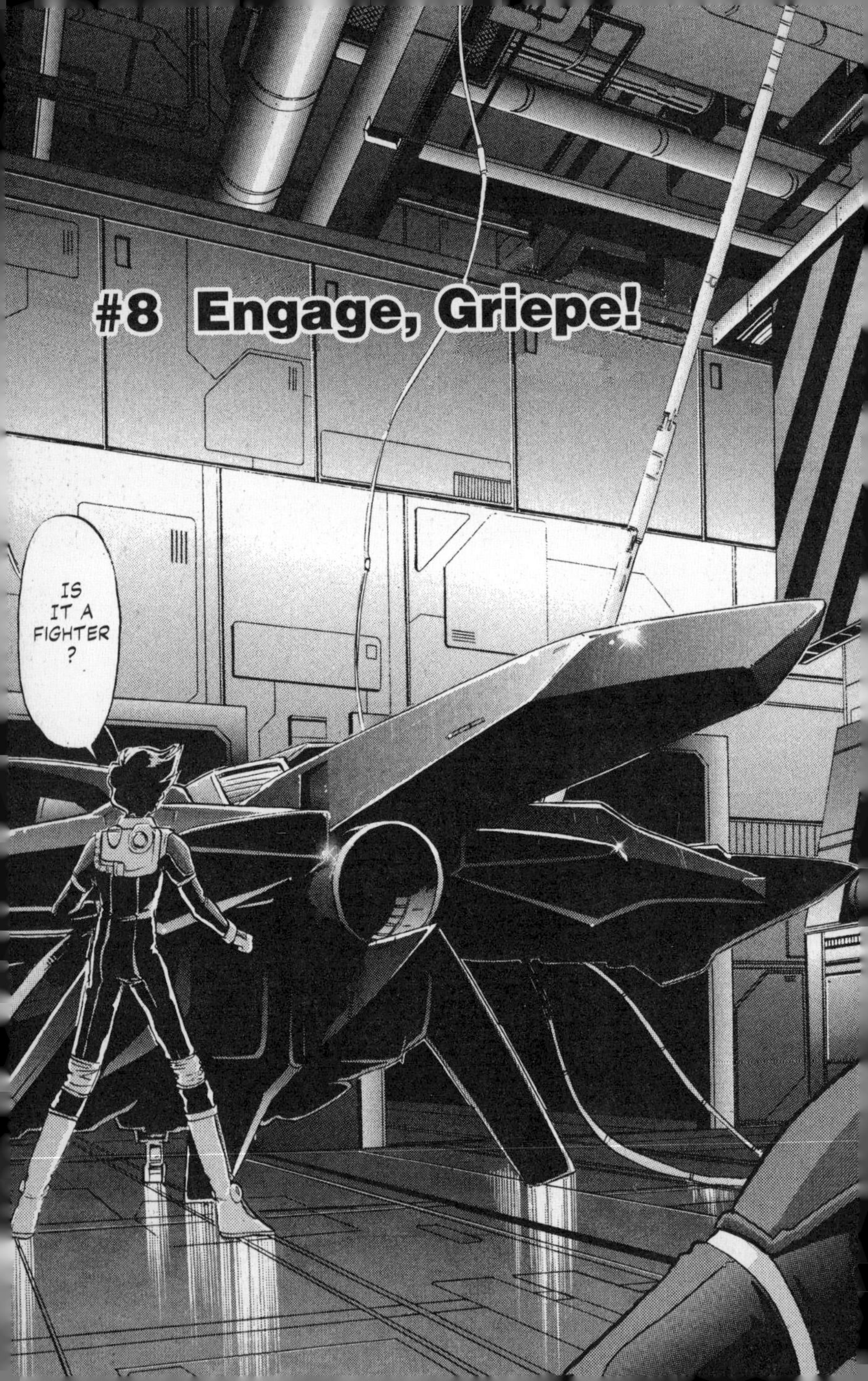
IS IT A FIGHTER?

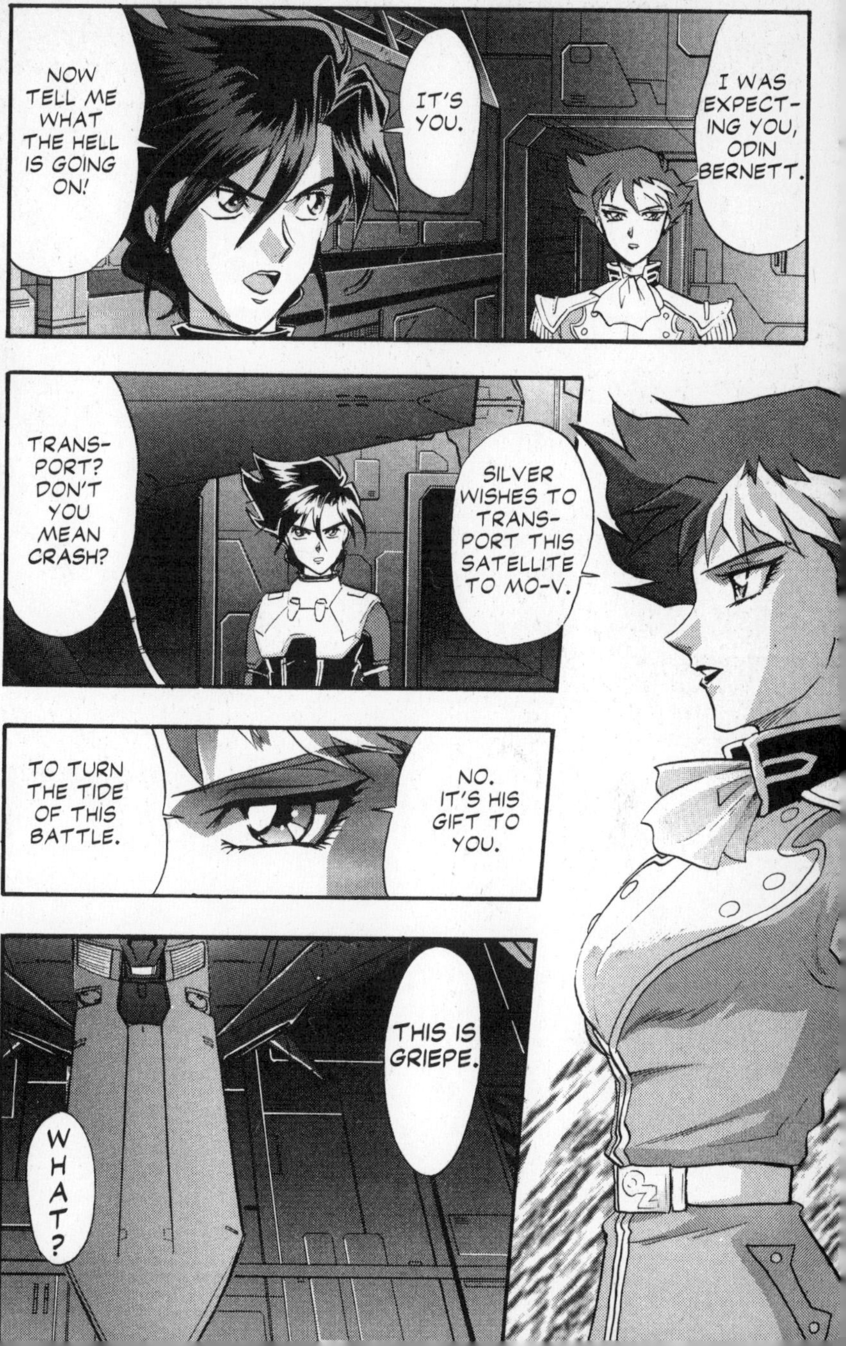
I WAS EXPECTING YOU, ODIN BERNETT.
IT'S YOU.
NOW TELL ME WHAT THE HELL IS GOING ON!
SILVER WISHES TO TRANSPORT THIS SATELLITE TO MO-V.
TRANSPORT? DON'T YOU MEAN CRASH?
NO. IT'S HIS GIFT TO YOU.
TO TURN THE TIDE OF THIS BATTLE.
THIS IS GRIEPE.
WHAT?

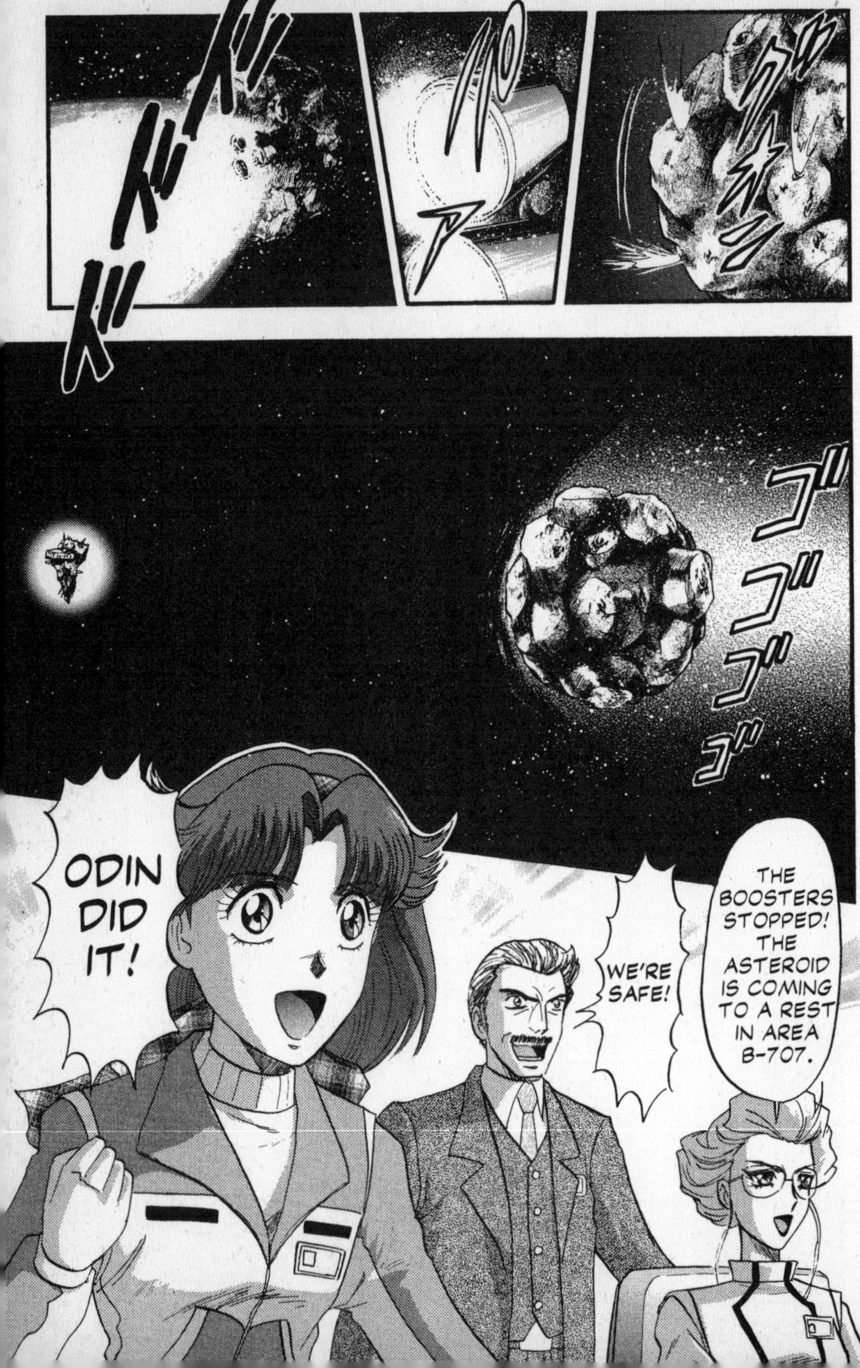
THE BOOSTERS STOPPED! THE ASTEROID IS COMING TO A REST IN AREA B-707.
WE'RE SAFE!
ODIN DID IT!

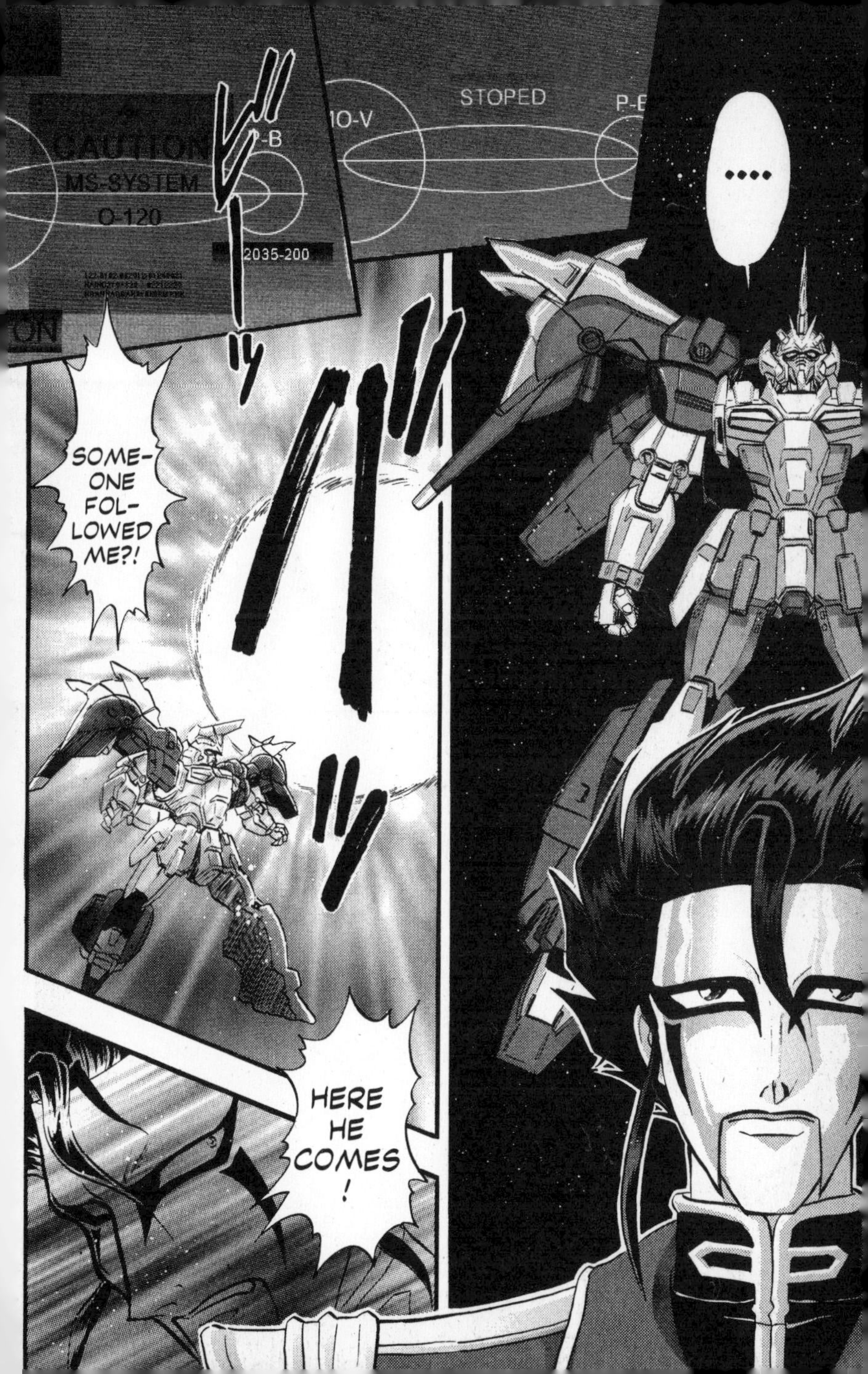

....
STOPED
10-V
P-B
CAUTION
MS-SYSTEM
O-120
P-B
2035-200
ON
SOME-ONE FOL-LOWED ME?!
HERE HE COMES!

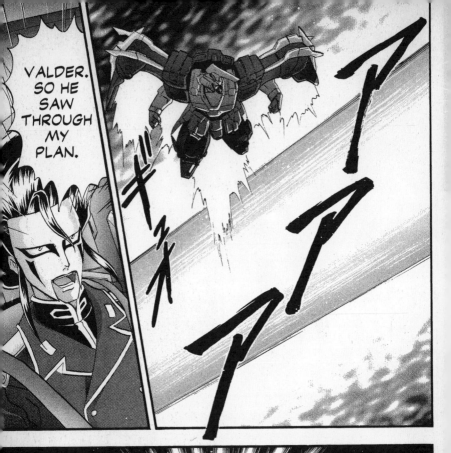

VALDER. SO HE SAW THROUGH MY PLAN.

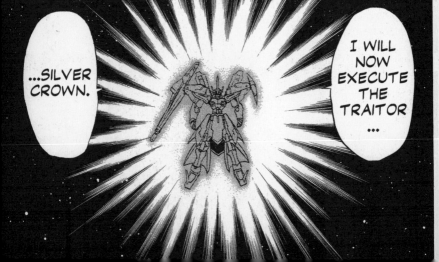

...SILVER CROWN.

I WILL NOW EXECUTE THE TRAITOR...

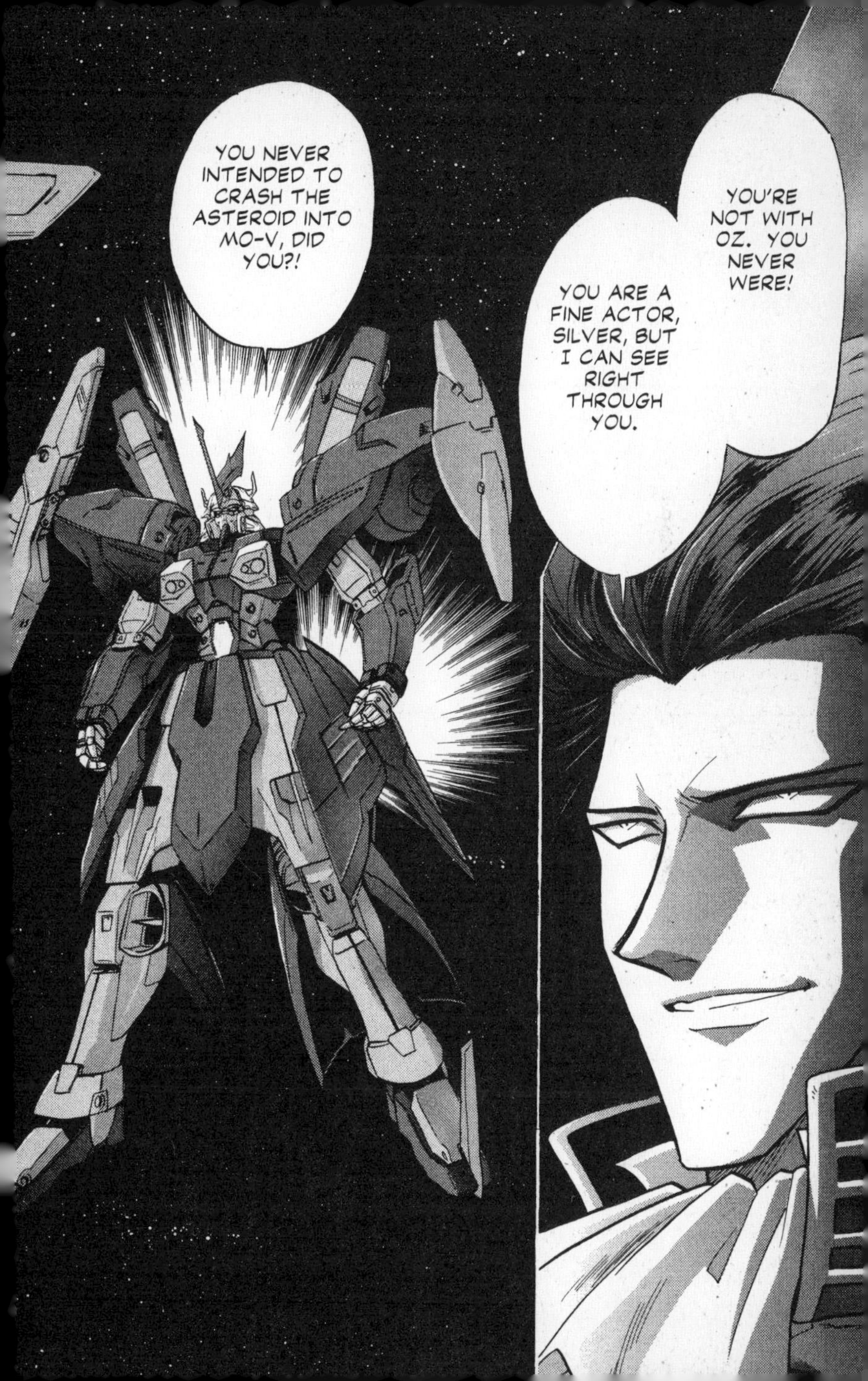
YOU'RE NOT WITH OZ. YOU NEVER WERE!
YOU ARE A FINE ACTOR, SILVER, BUT I CAN SEE RIGHT THROUGH YOU.
YOU NEVER INTENDED TO CRASH THE ASTEROID INTO MO-V, DID YOU?!

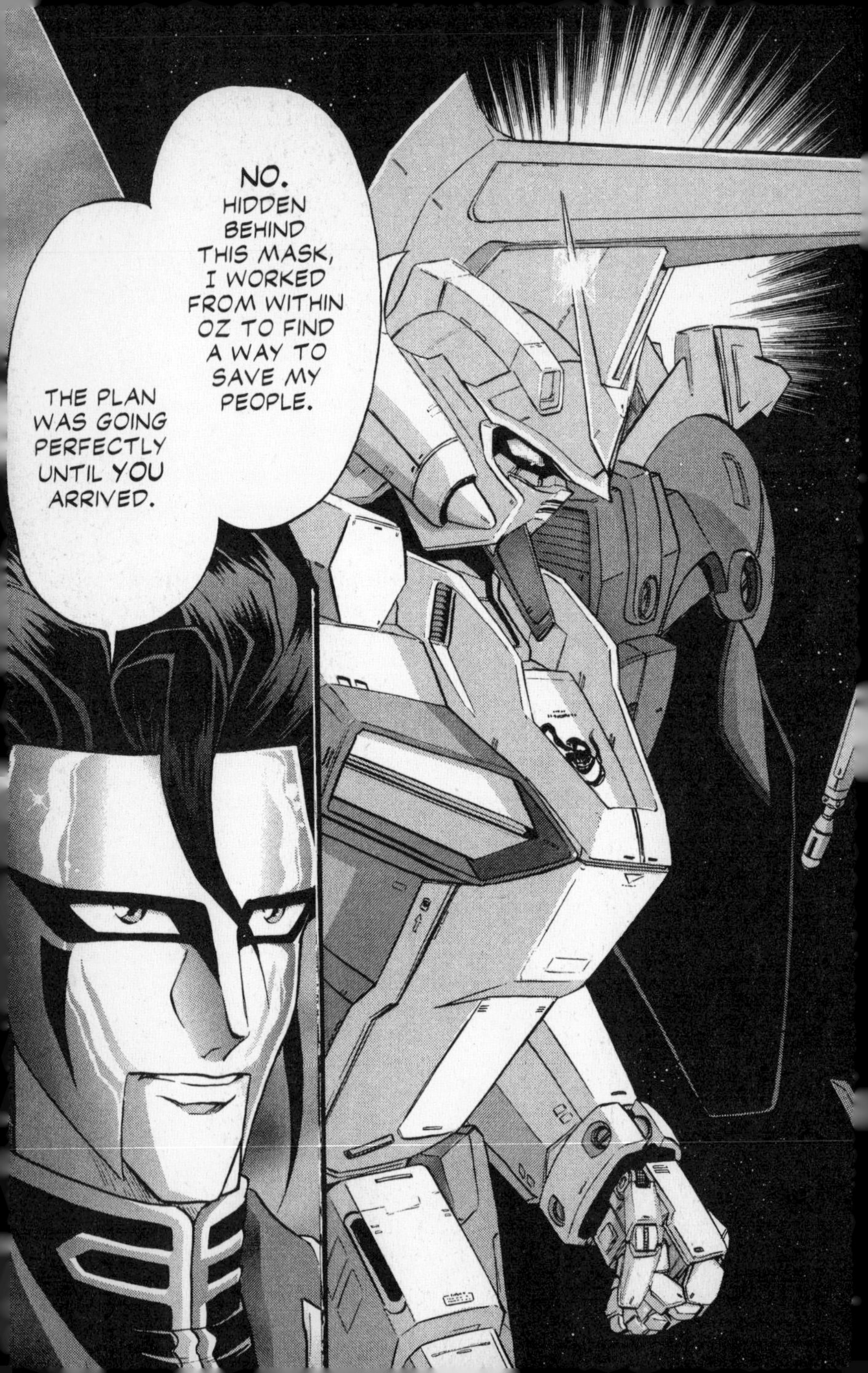
NO. HIDDEN BEHIND THIS MASK, I WORKED FROM WITHIN OZ TO FIND A WAY TO SAVE MY PEOPLE.
THE PLAN WAS GOING PERFECTLY UNTIL YOU ARRIVED.

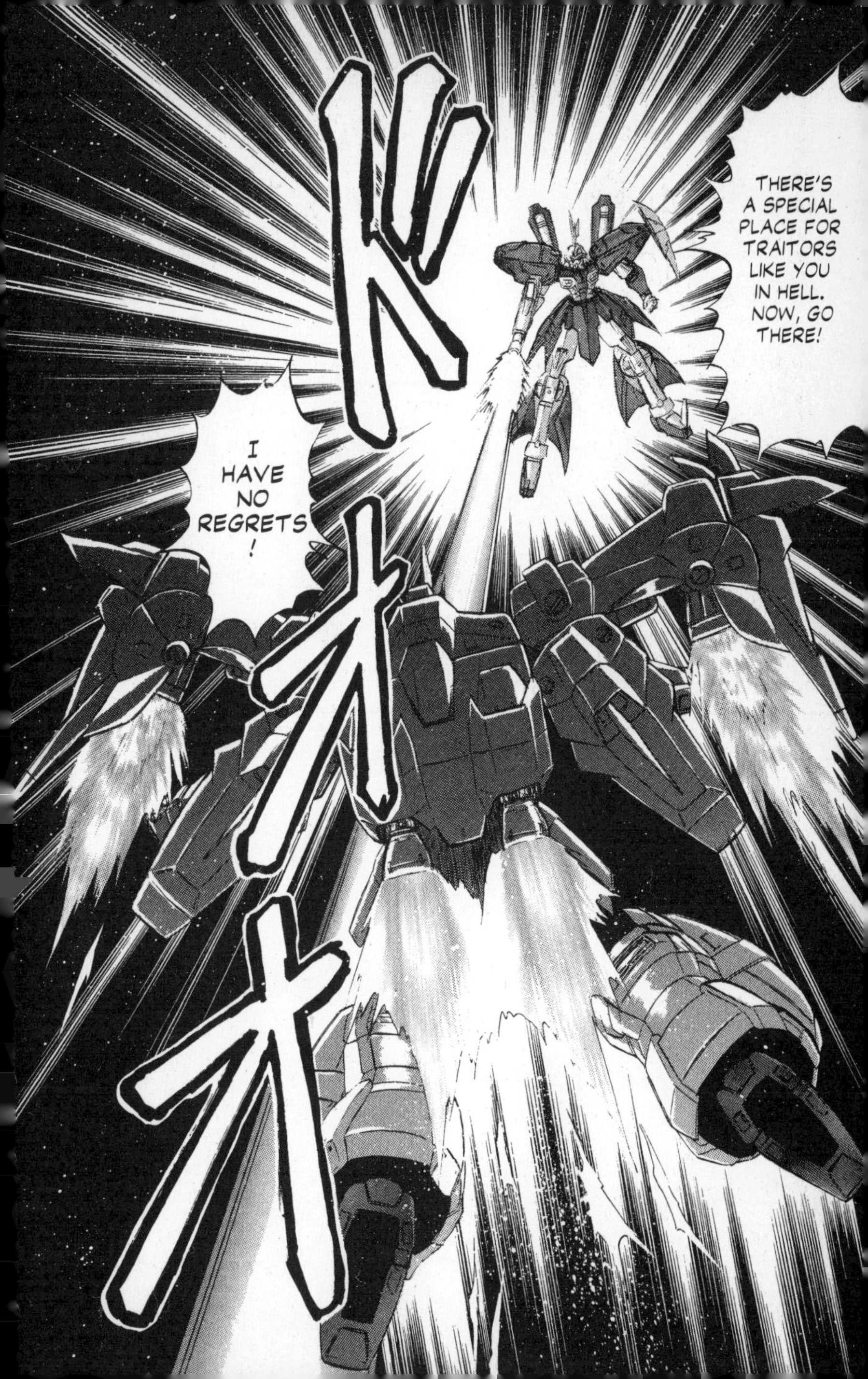
THERE'S A SPECIAL PLACE FOR TRAITORS LIKE YOU IN HELL. NOW, GO THERE!
I HAVE NO REGRETS!

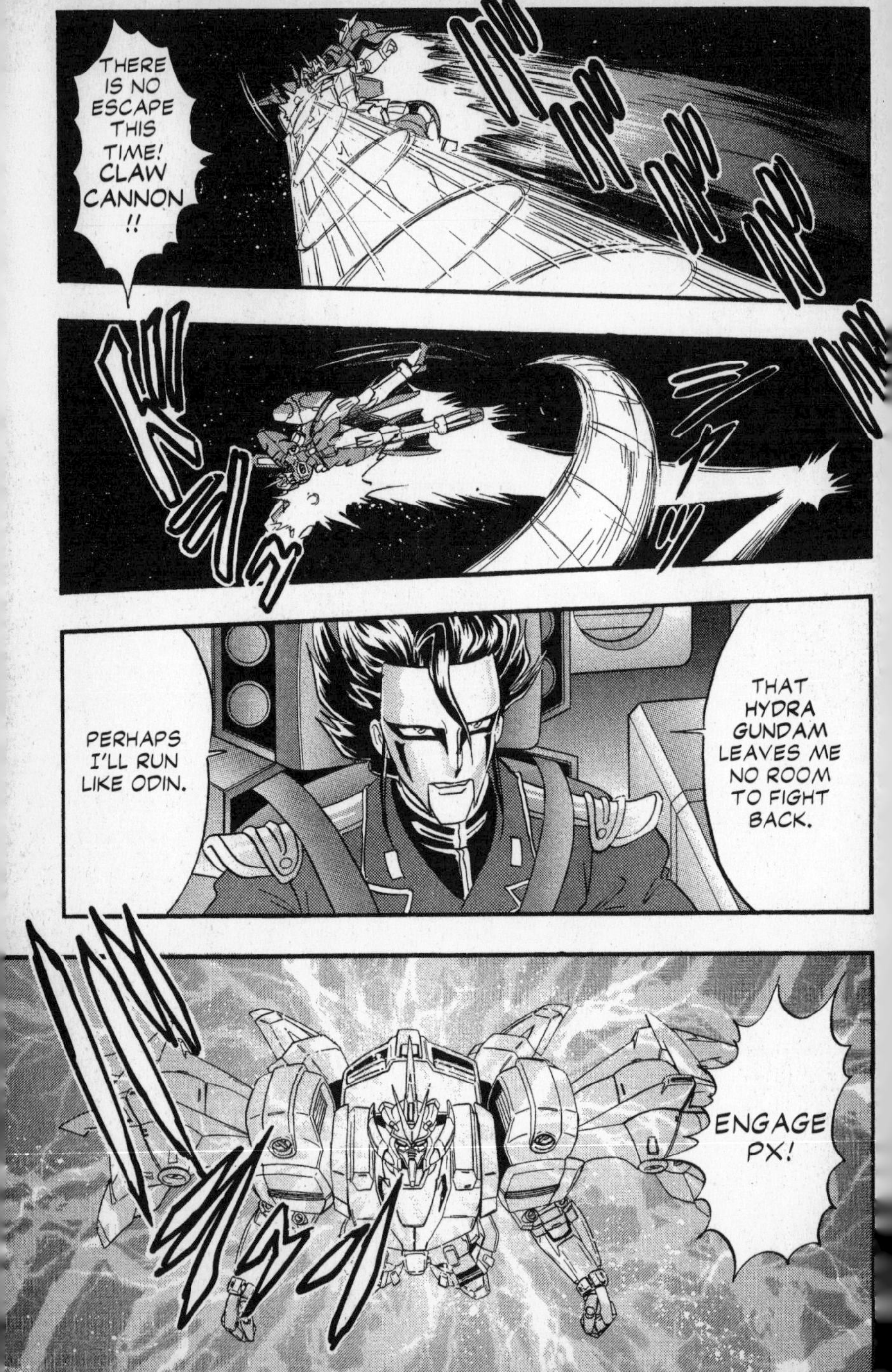
THERE IS NO ESCAPE THIS TIME! CLAW CANNON !!
THAT HYDRA GUNDAM LEAVES ME NO ROOM TO FIGHT BACK.
PERHAPS I'LL RUN LIKE ODIN.
ENGAGE PX!

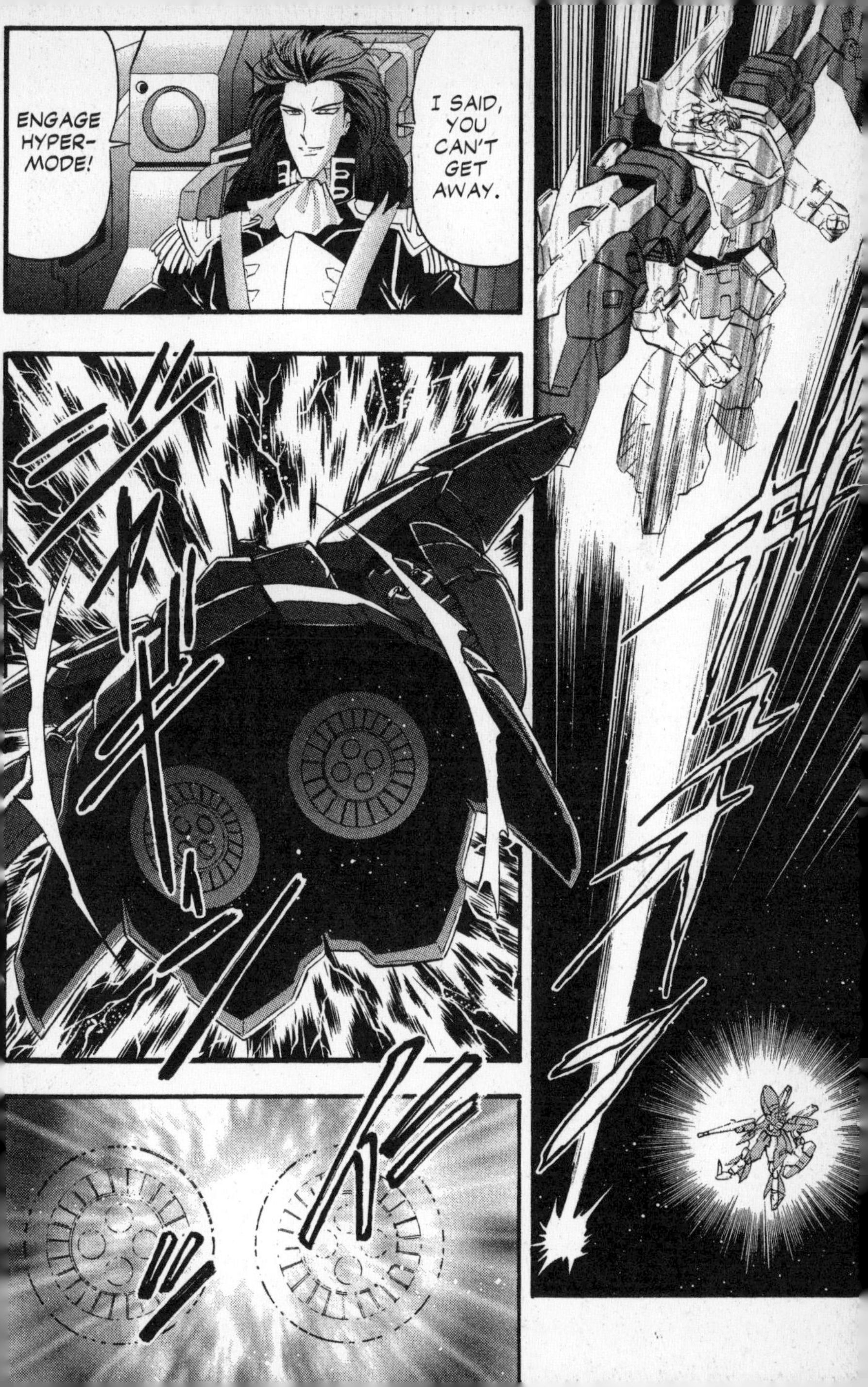
I SAID, YOU CAN'T GET AWAY.
ENGAGE HYPER-MODE!

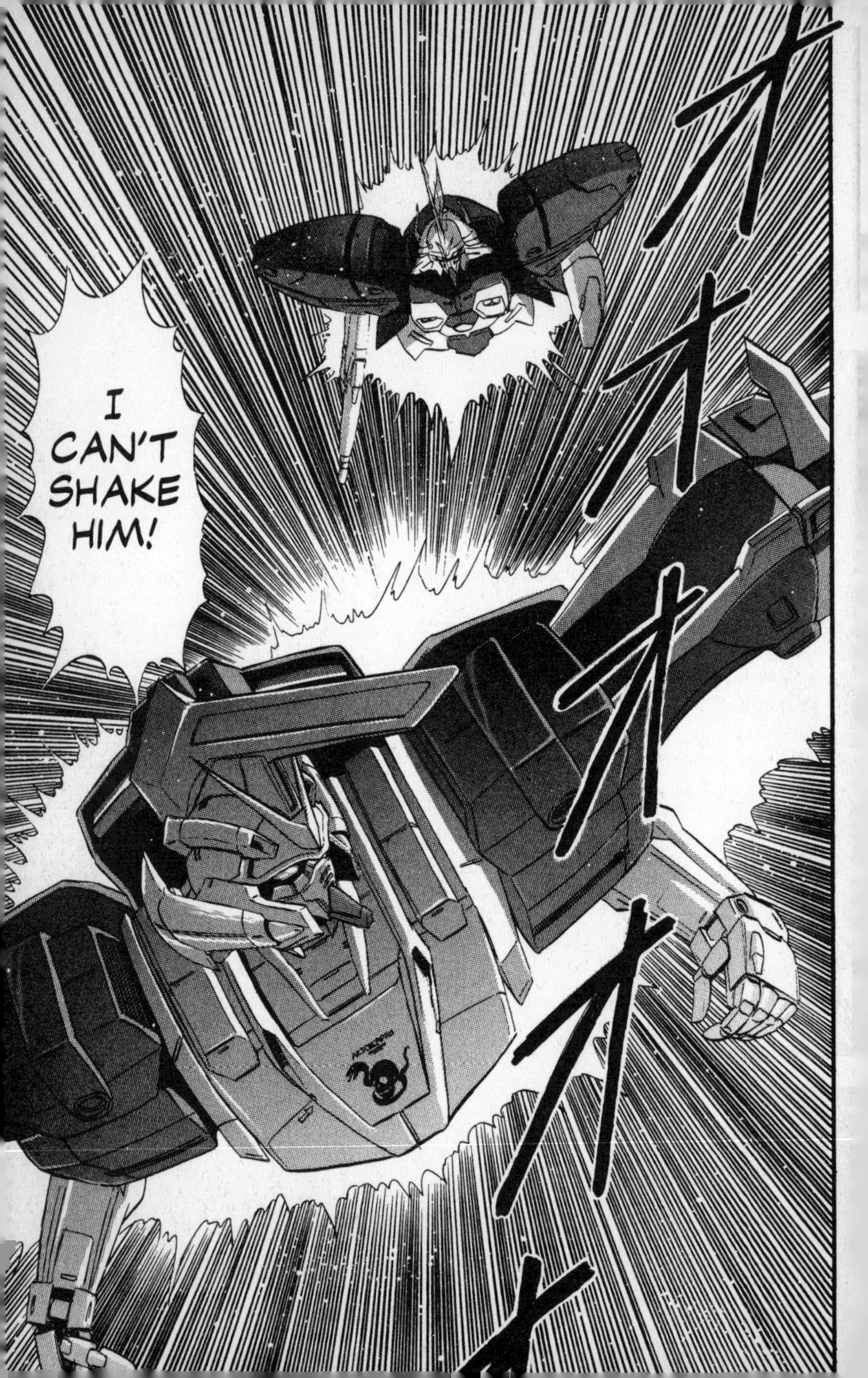
I CAN'T SHAKE HIM!

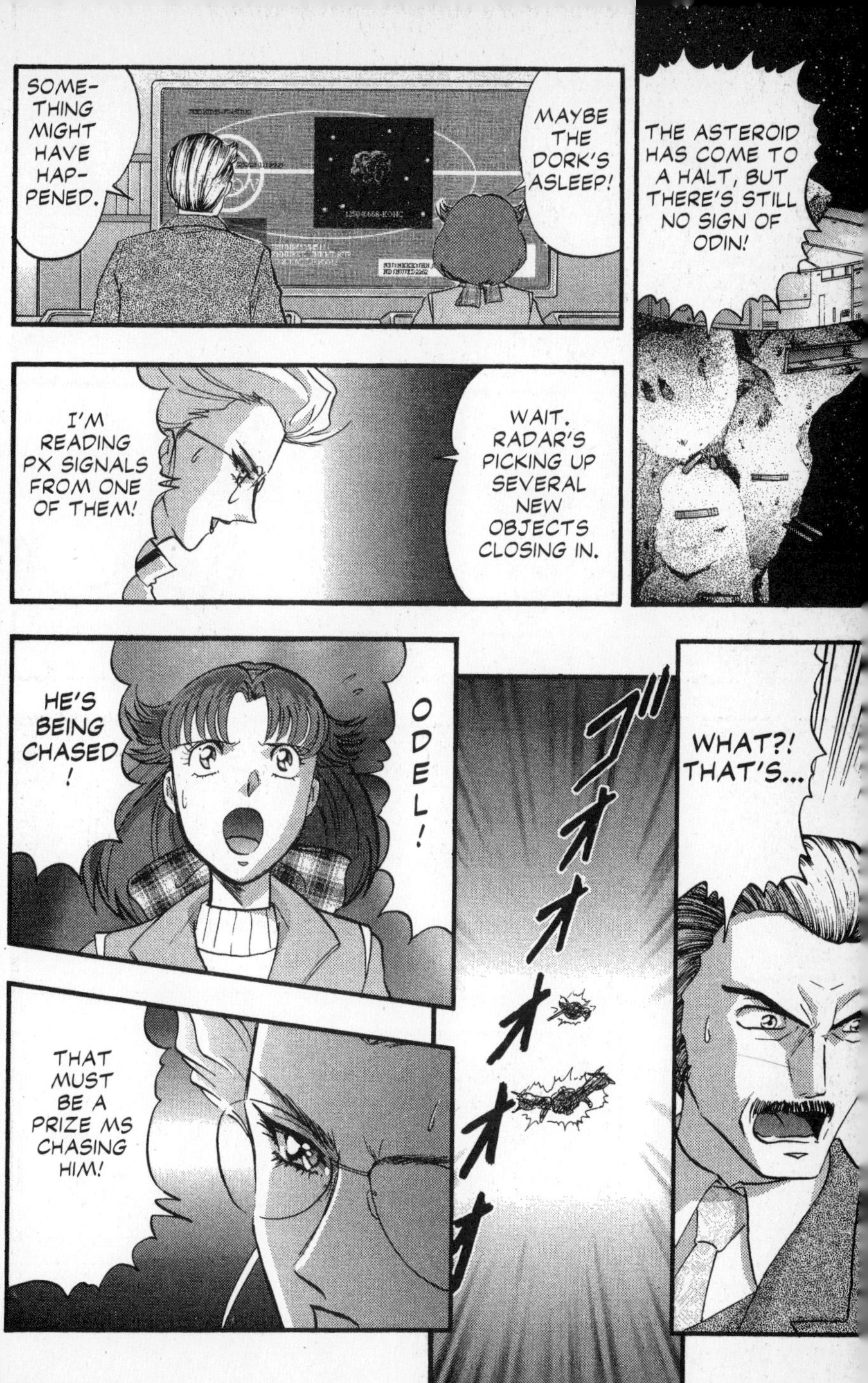
THE ASTEROID HAS COME TO A HALT, BUT THERE'S STILL NO SIGN OF ODIN!
MAYBE THE DORK'S ASLEEP!
SOMETHING MIGHT HAVE HAPPENED.
WAIT. RADAR'S PICKING UP SEVERAL NEW OBJECTS CLOSING IN.
I'M READING PX SIGNALS FROM ONE OF THEM!
WHAT?! THAT'S...
ゴオオオオオ
ODEL!
HE'S BEING CHASED!
THAT MUST BE A PRIZE MS CHASING HIM!

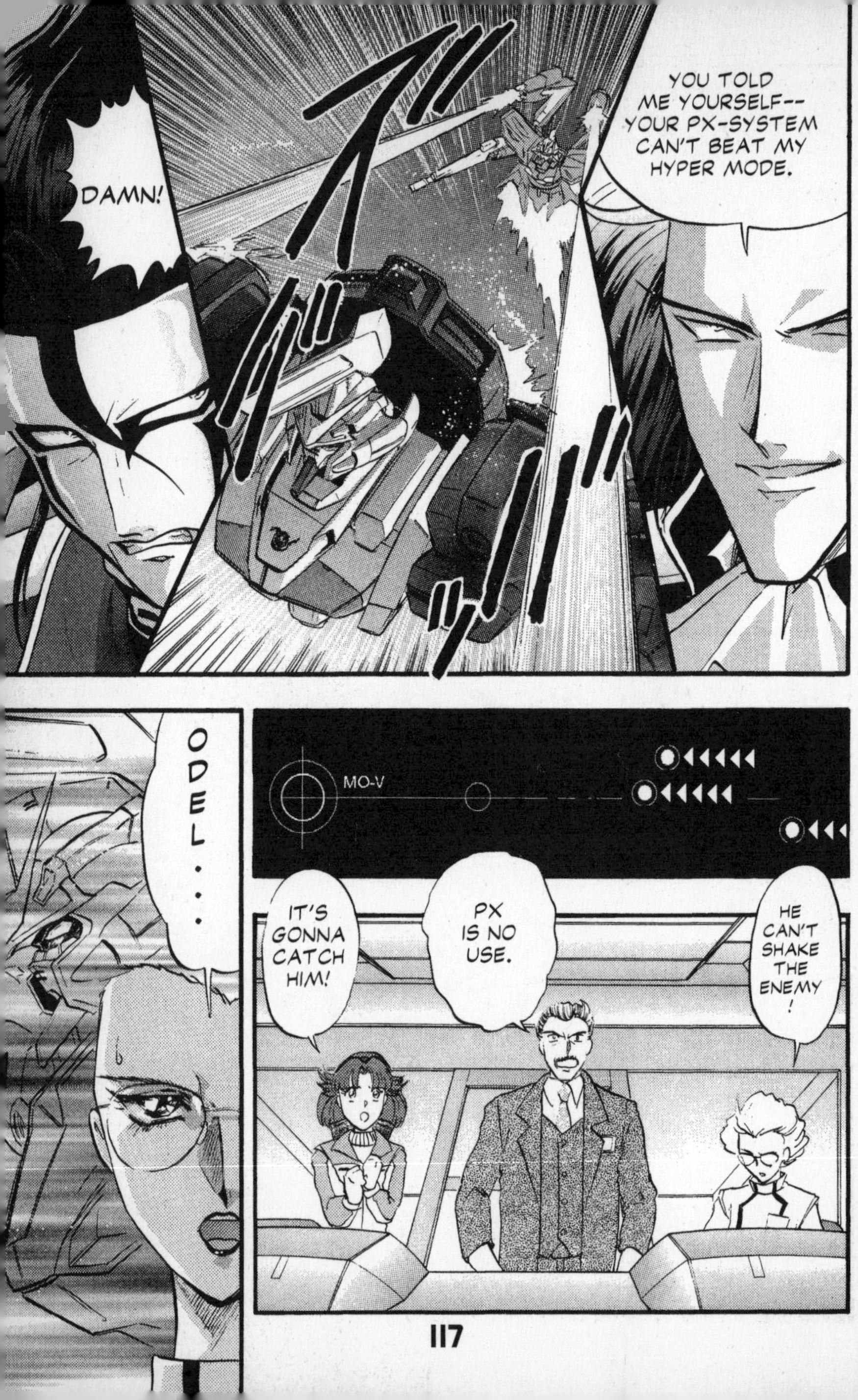
YOU TOLD ME YOURSELF--YOUR PX-SYSTEM CAN'T BEAT MY HYPER MODE.
DAMN!
MO-V
HE CAN'T SHAKE THE ENEMY!
PX IS NO USE.
IT'S GONNA CATCH HIM!
ODEL...

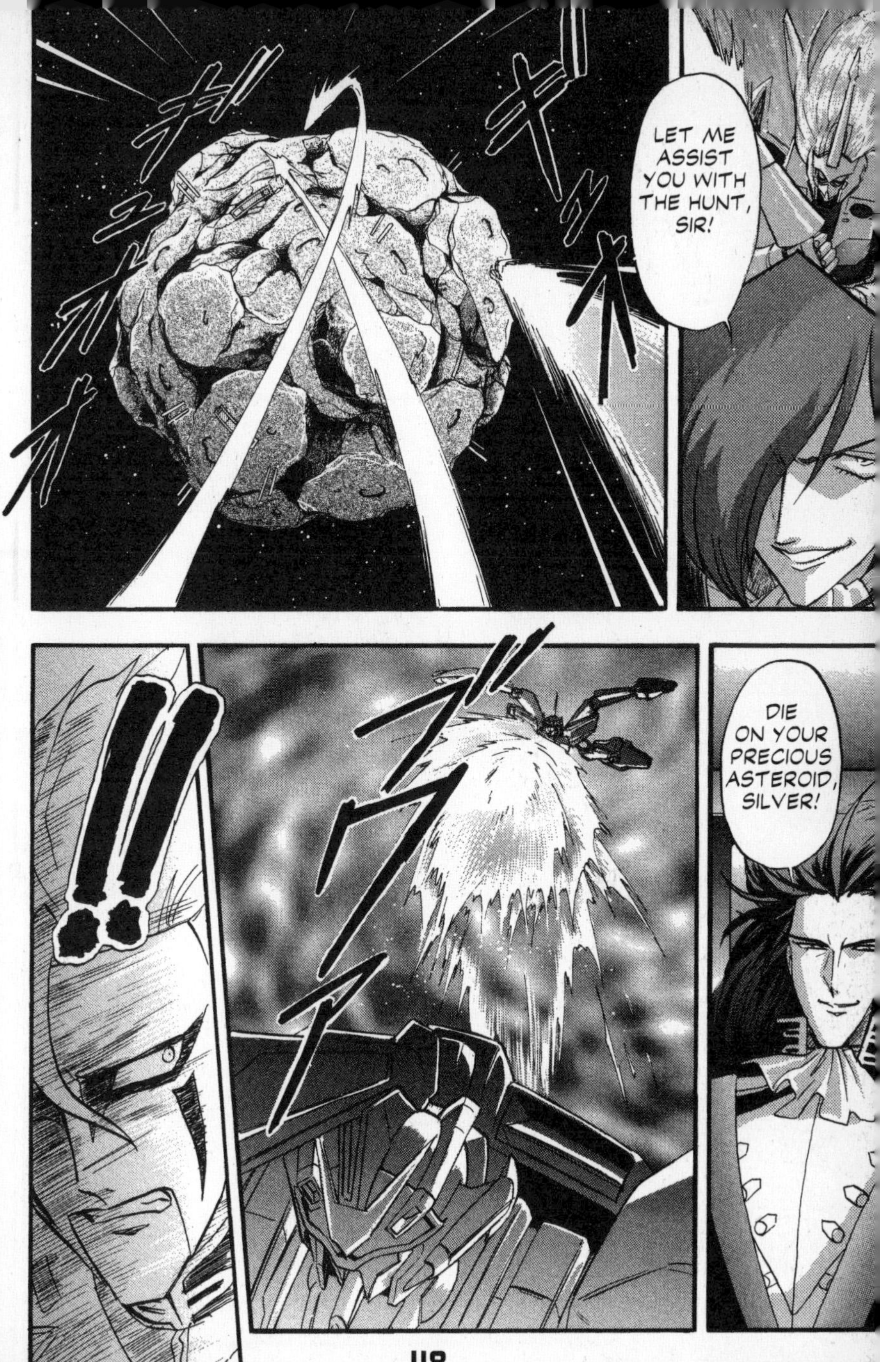
LET ME ASSIST YOU WITH THE HUNT, SIR!
DIE ON YOUR PRECIOUS ASTEROID, SILVER!

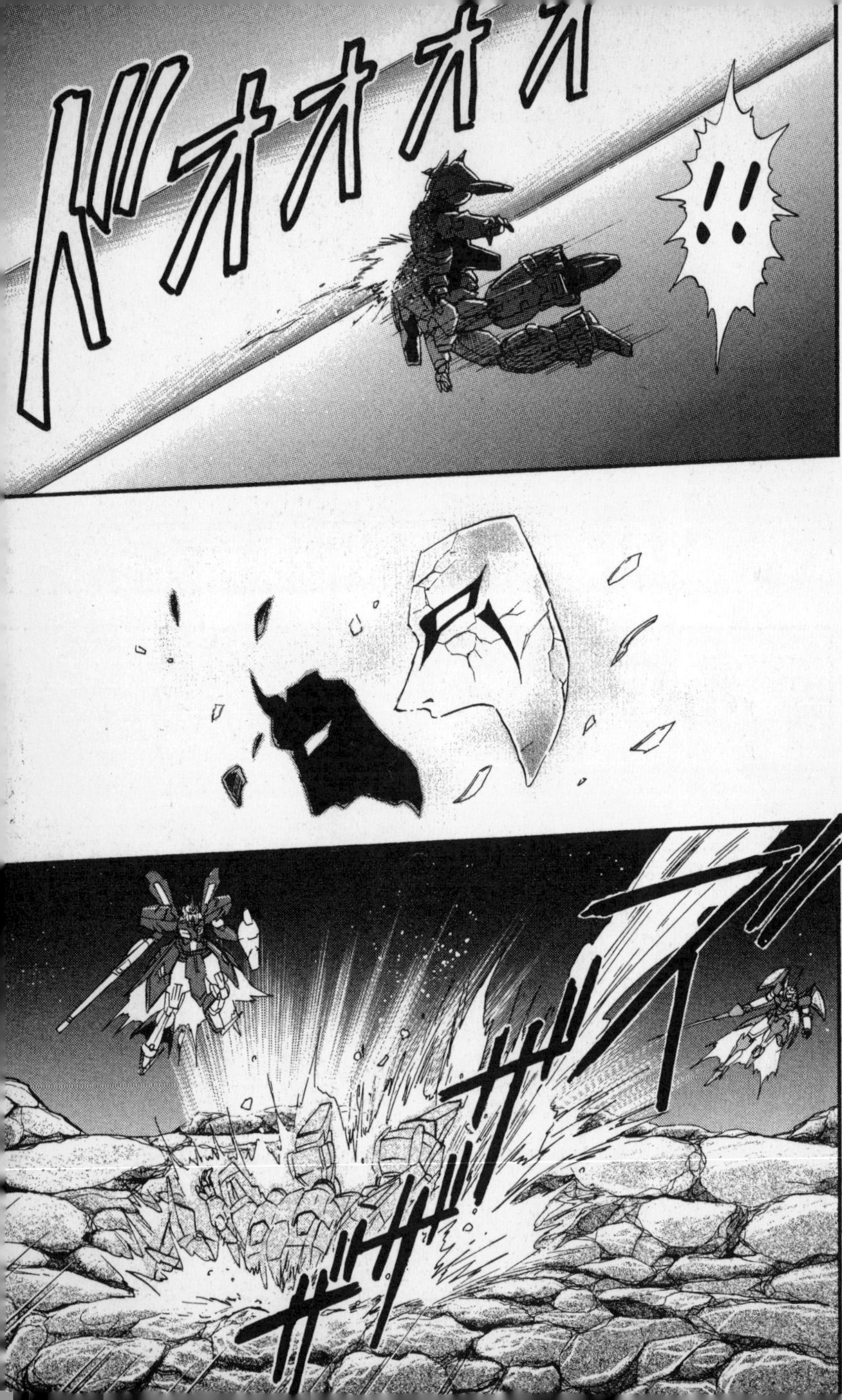
ドオオオン
!!

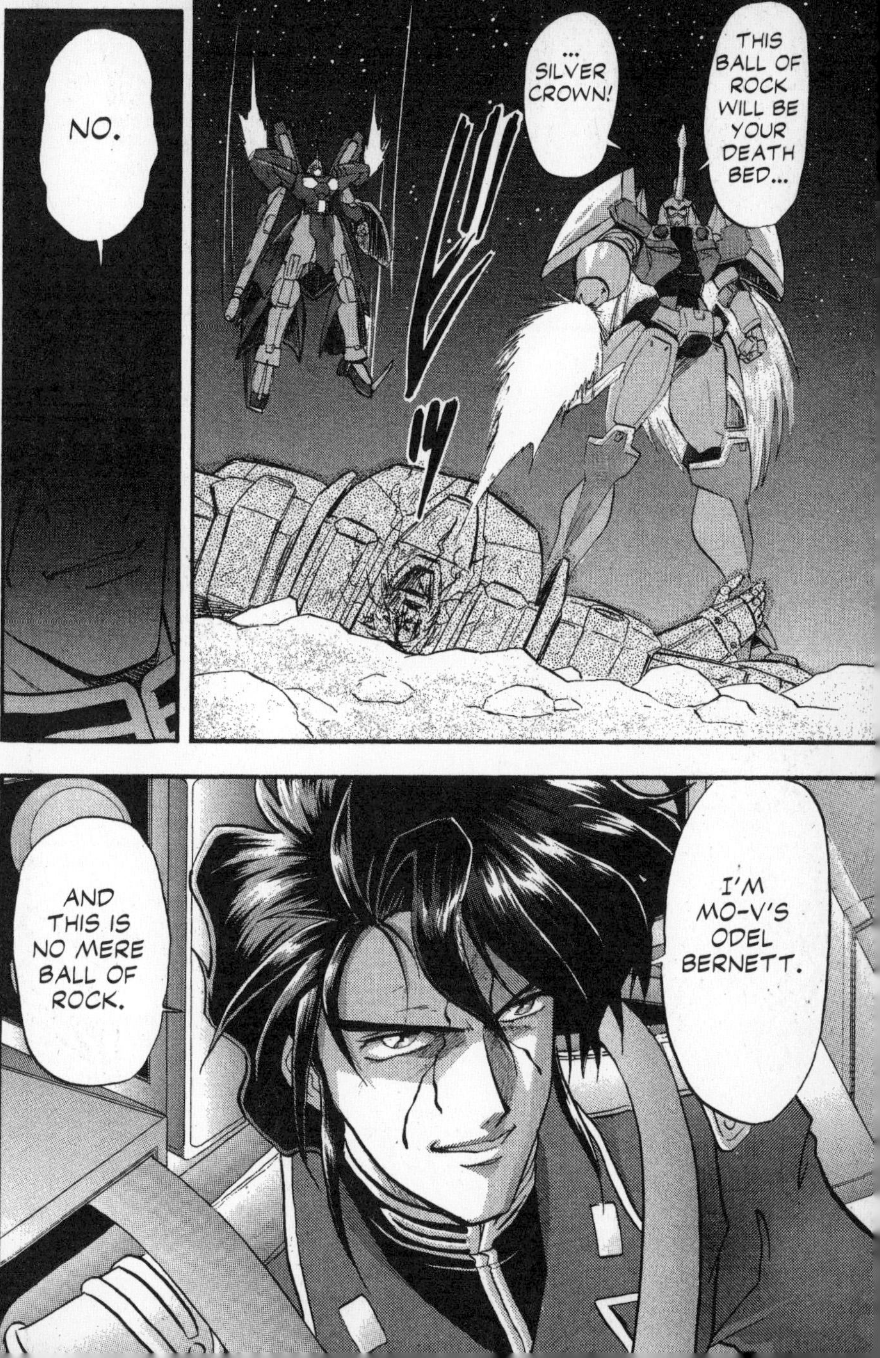
THIS BALL OF ROCK WILL BE YOUR DEATH BED...
... SILVER CROWN!
NO.
I'M MO-V'S ODEL BERNETT.
AND THIS IS NO MERE BALL OF ROCK.

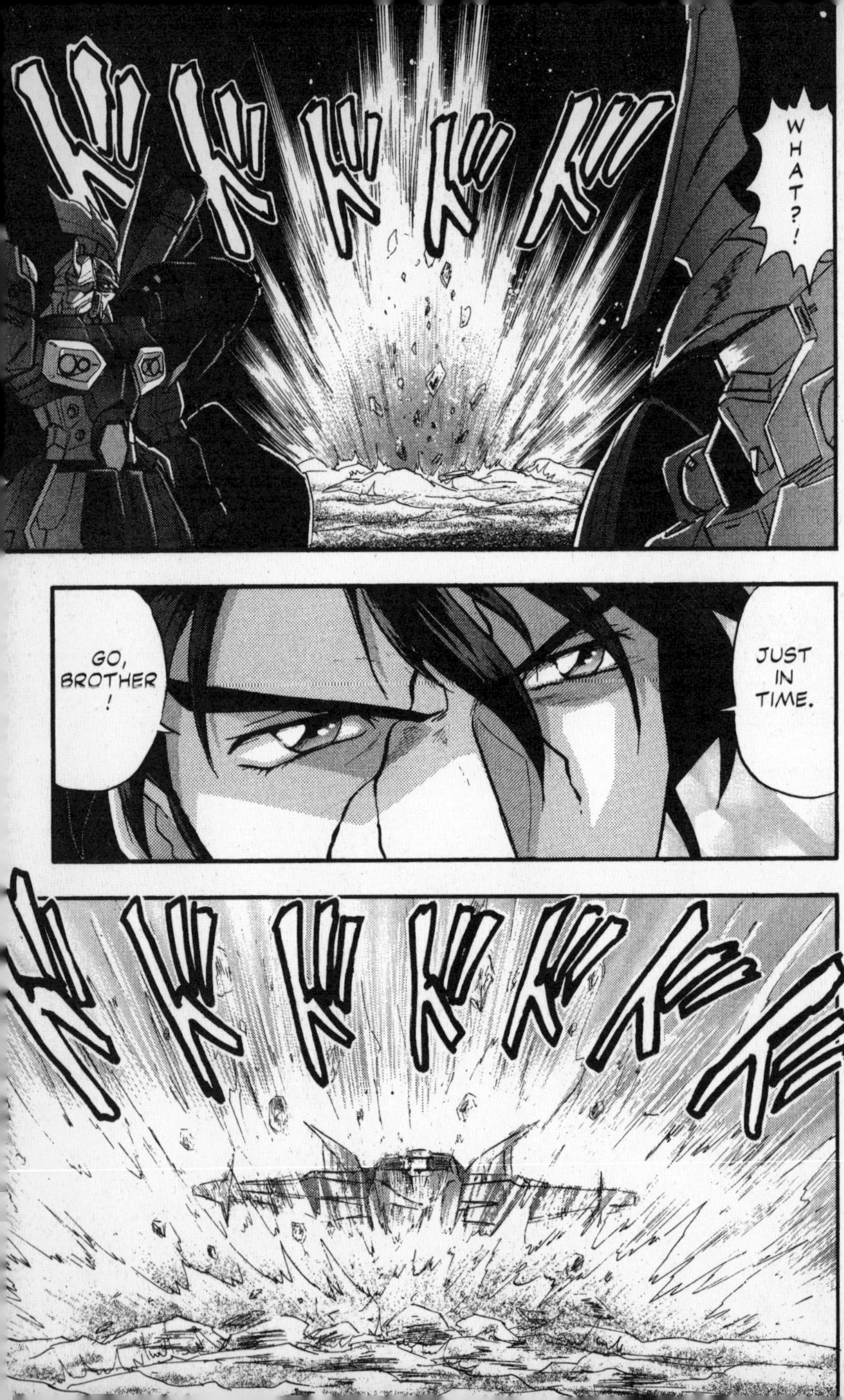
WHAT?!
JUST IN TIME.
GO, BROTHER!

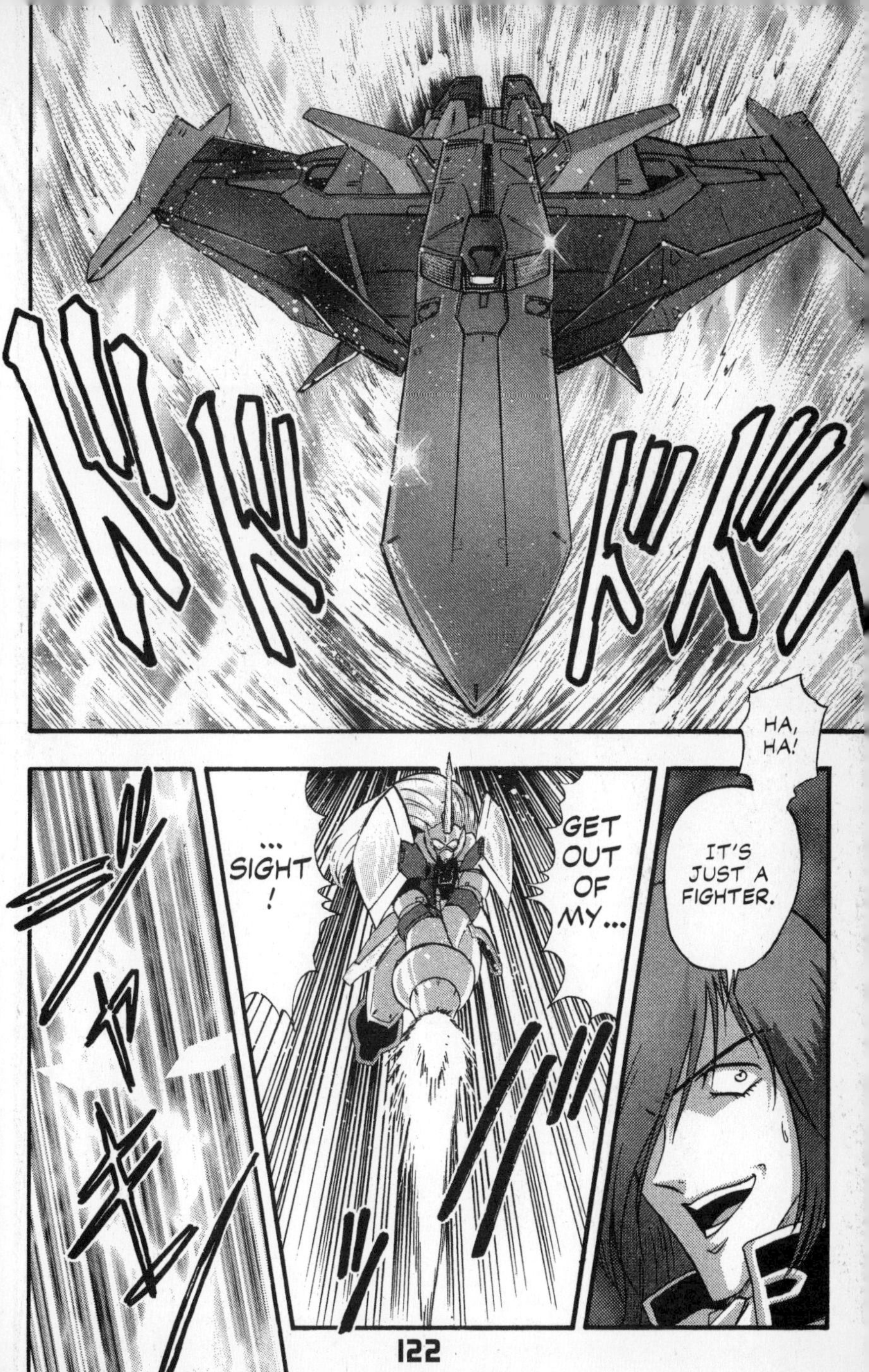
HA, HA!
IT'S JUST A FIGHTER.
GET OUT OF MY...
... SIGHT!

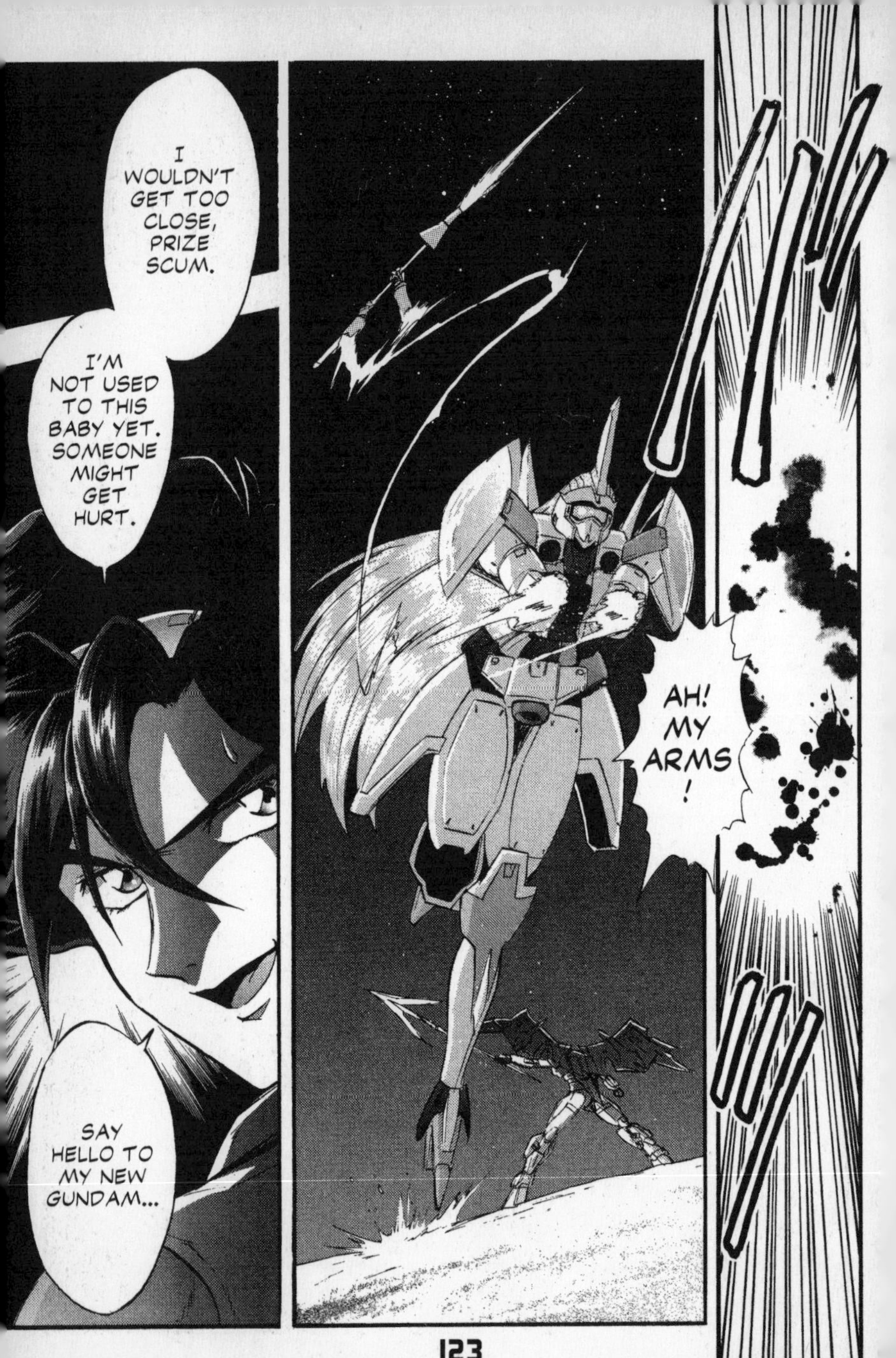
AH! MY ARMS!
I WOULDN'T GET TOO CLOSE, PRIZE SCUM.
I'M NOT USED TO THIS BABY YET. SOMEONE MIGHT GET HURT.
SAY HELLO TO MY NEW GUNDAM...

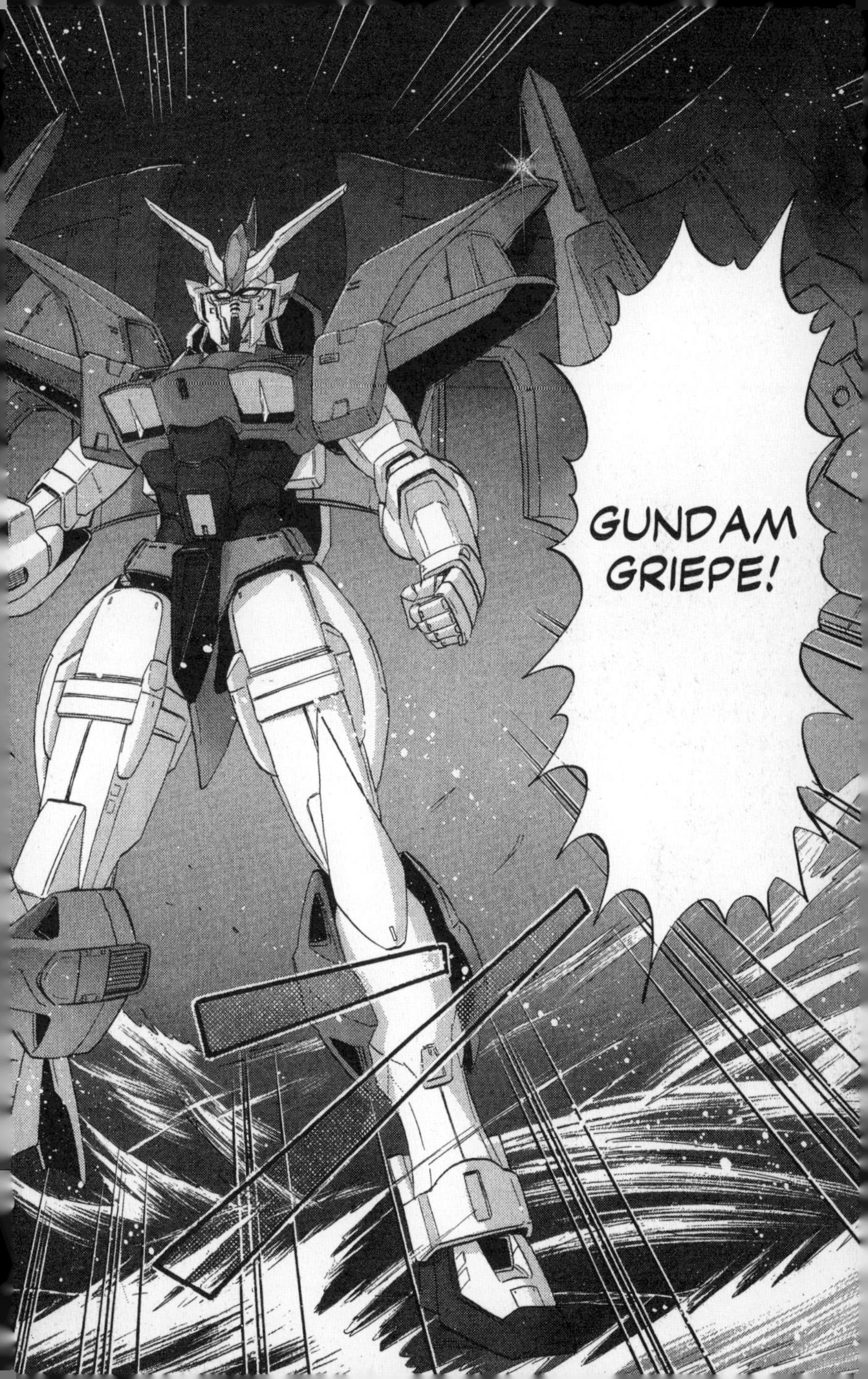
GUNDAM GRIEPE!

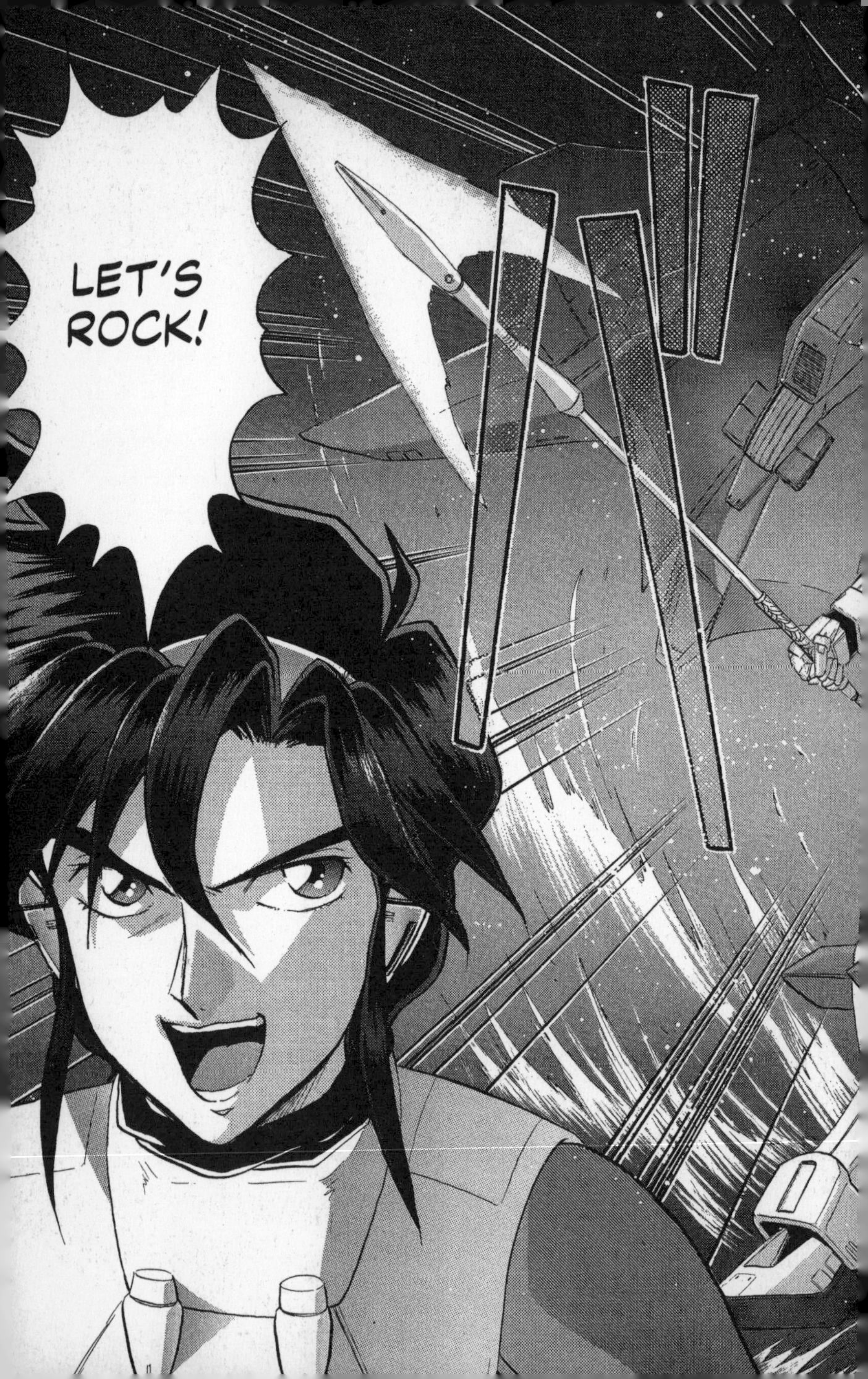
LET'S ROCK!

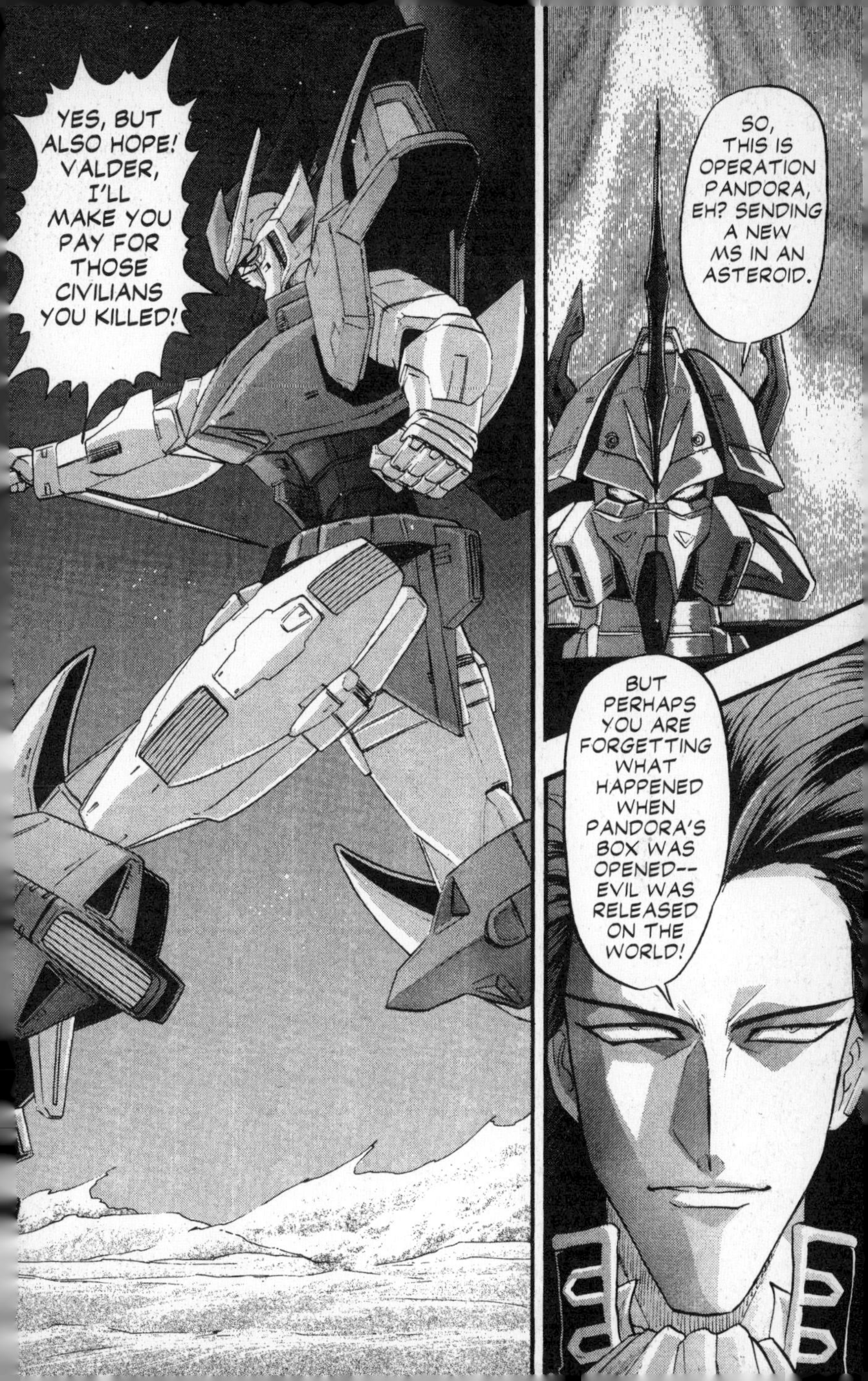
SO, THIS IS OPERATION PANDORA, EH? SENDING A NEW MS IN AN ASTEROID.
BUT PERHAPS YOU ARE FORGETTING WHAT HAPPENED WHEN PANDORA'S BOX WAS OPENED-- EVIL WAS RELEASED ON THE WORLD!
YES, BUT ALSO HOPE! VALDER, I'LL MAKE YOU PAY FOR THOSE CIVILIANS YOU KILLED!

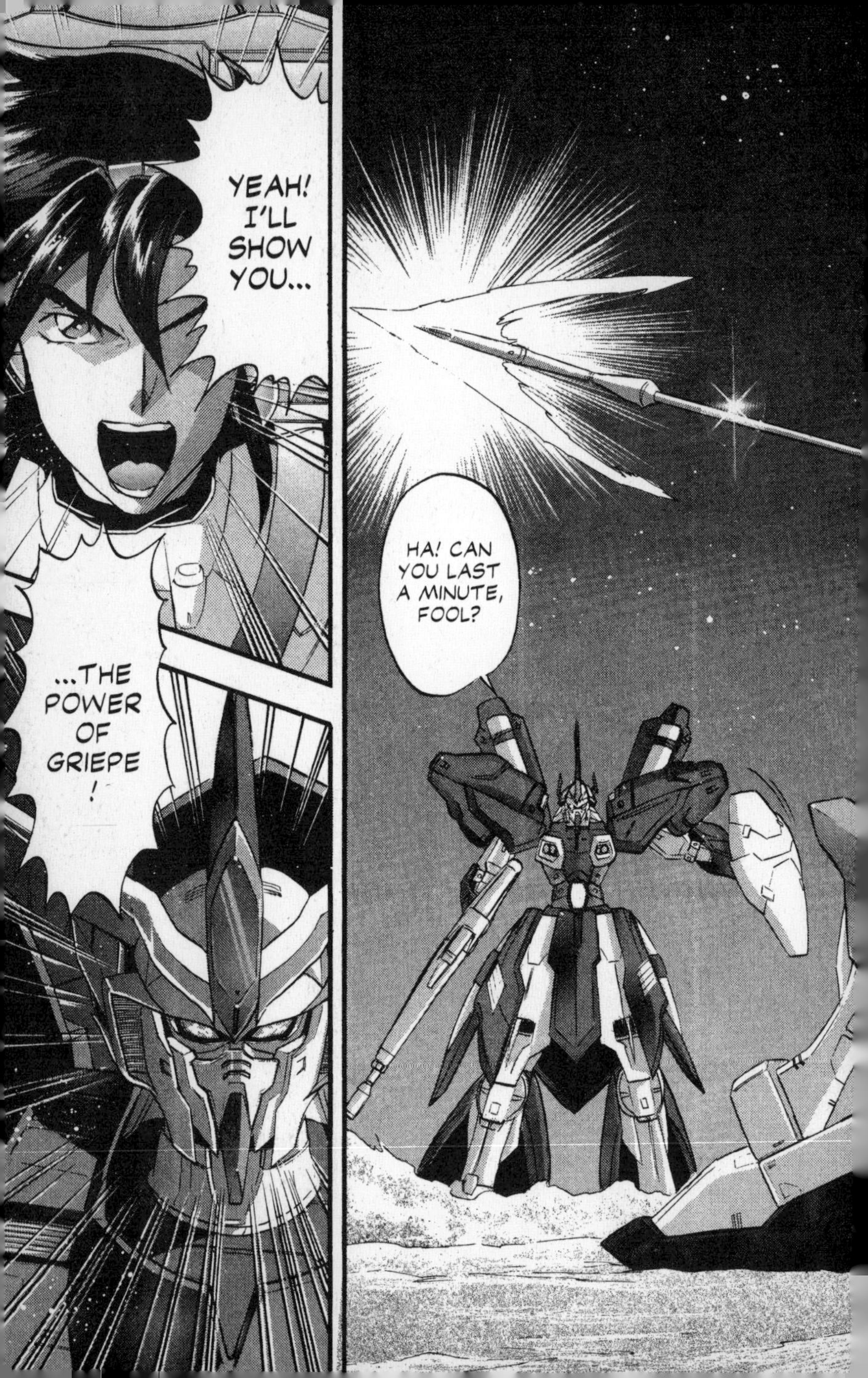
HA! CAN YOU LAST A MINUTE, FOOL?
YEAH! I'LL SHOW YOU...
...THE POWER OF GRIEPE!

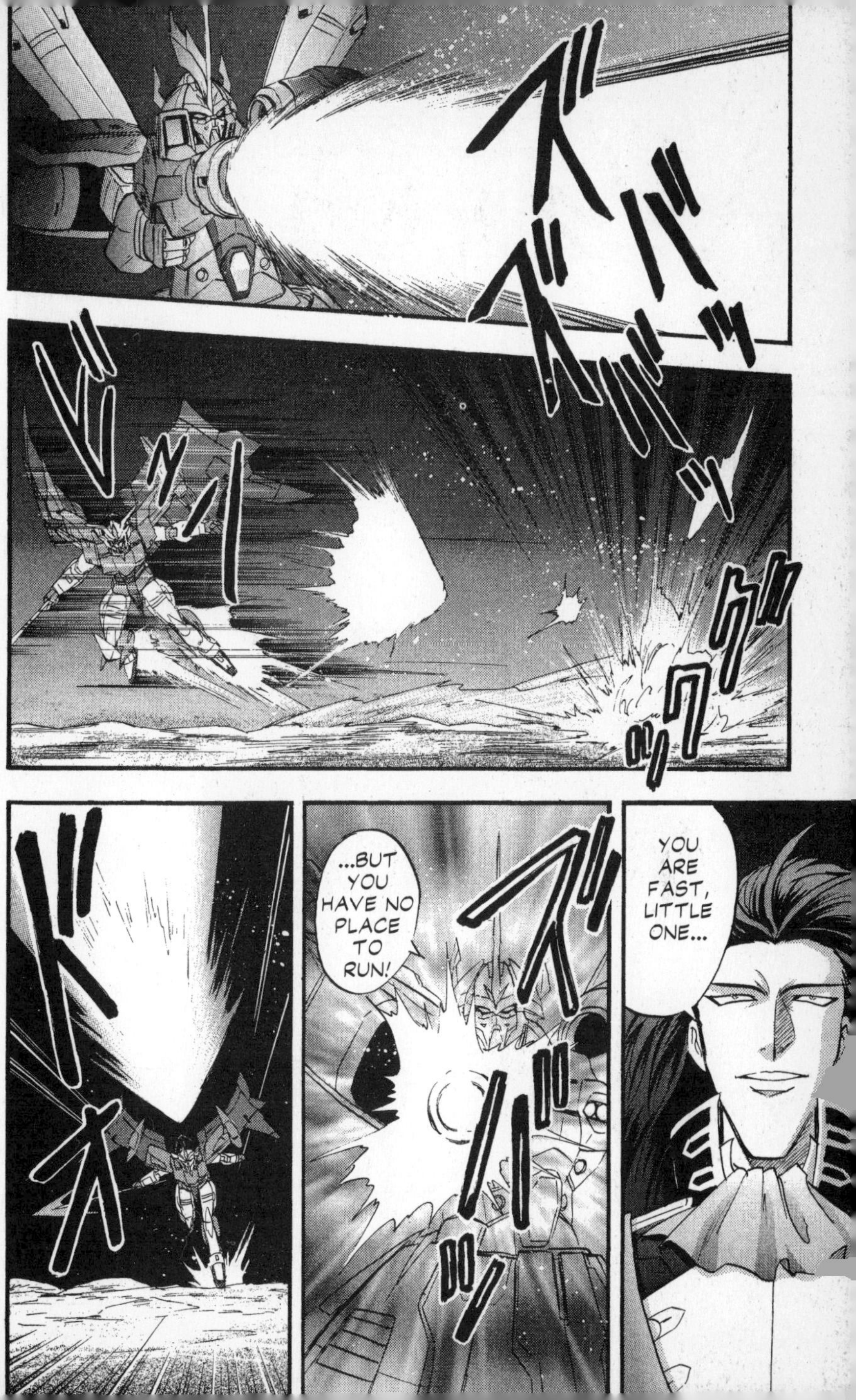
YOU ARE FAST, LITTLE ONE...
...BUT YOU HAVE NO PLACE TO RUN!

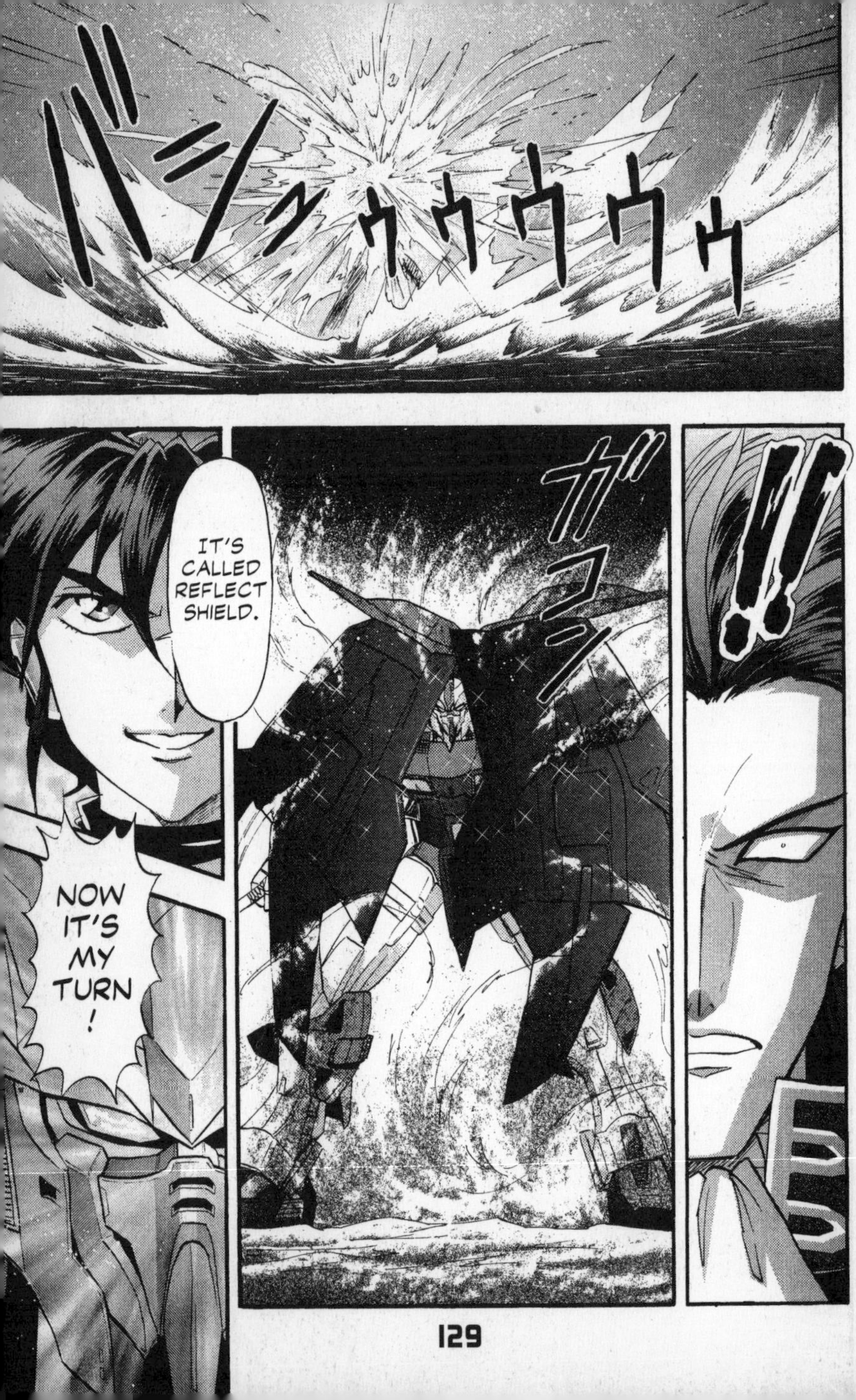
バシュゥウウウゥ
!!
ガコン
IT'S CALLED REFLECT SHIELD.
NOW IT'S MY TURN!

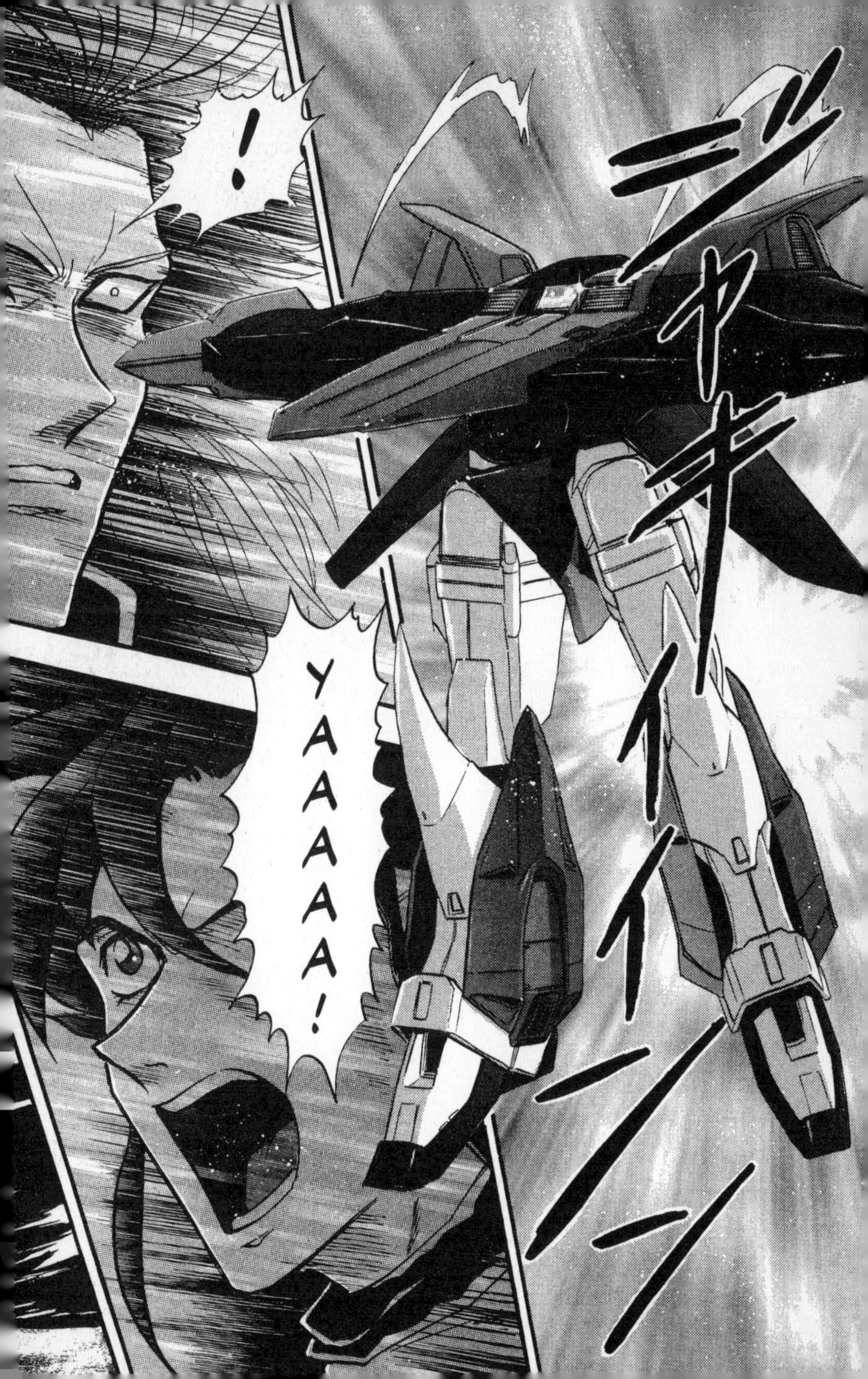
ジャキイイーン
!
YAAAAA!

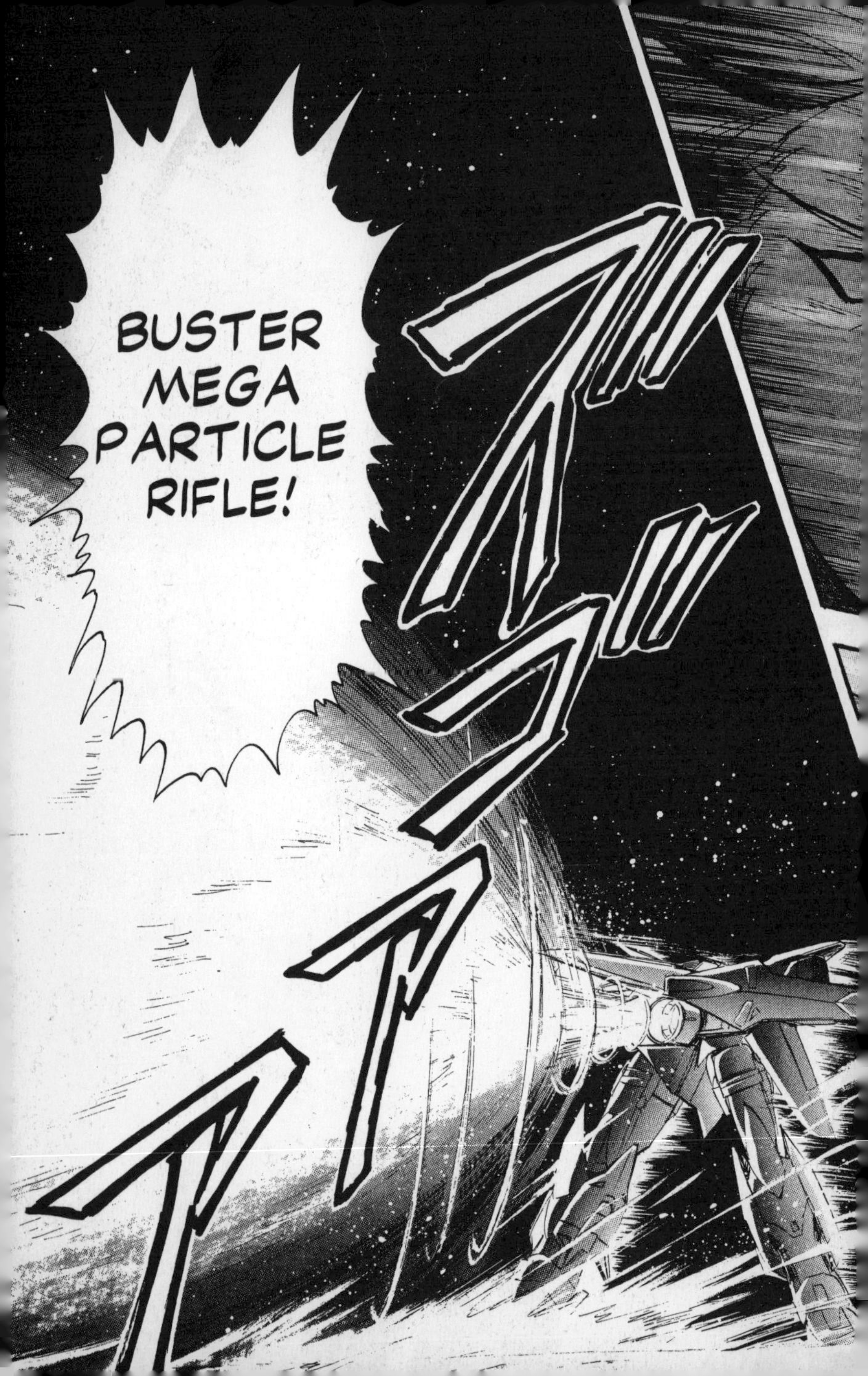
BUSTER MEGA PARTICLE RIFLE!

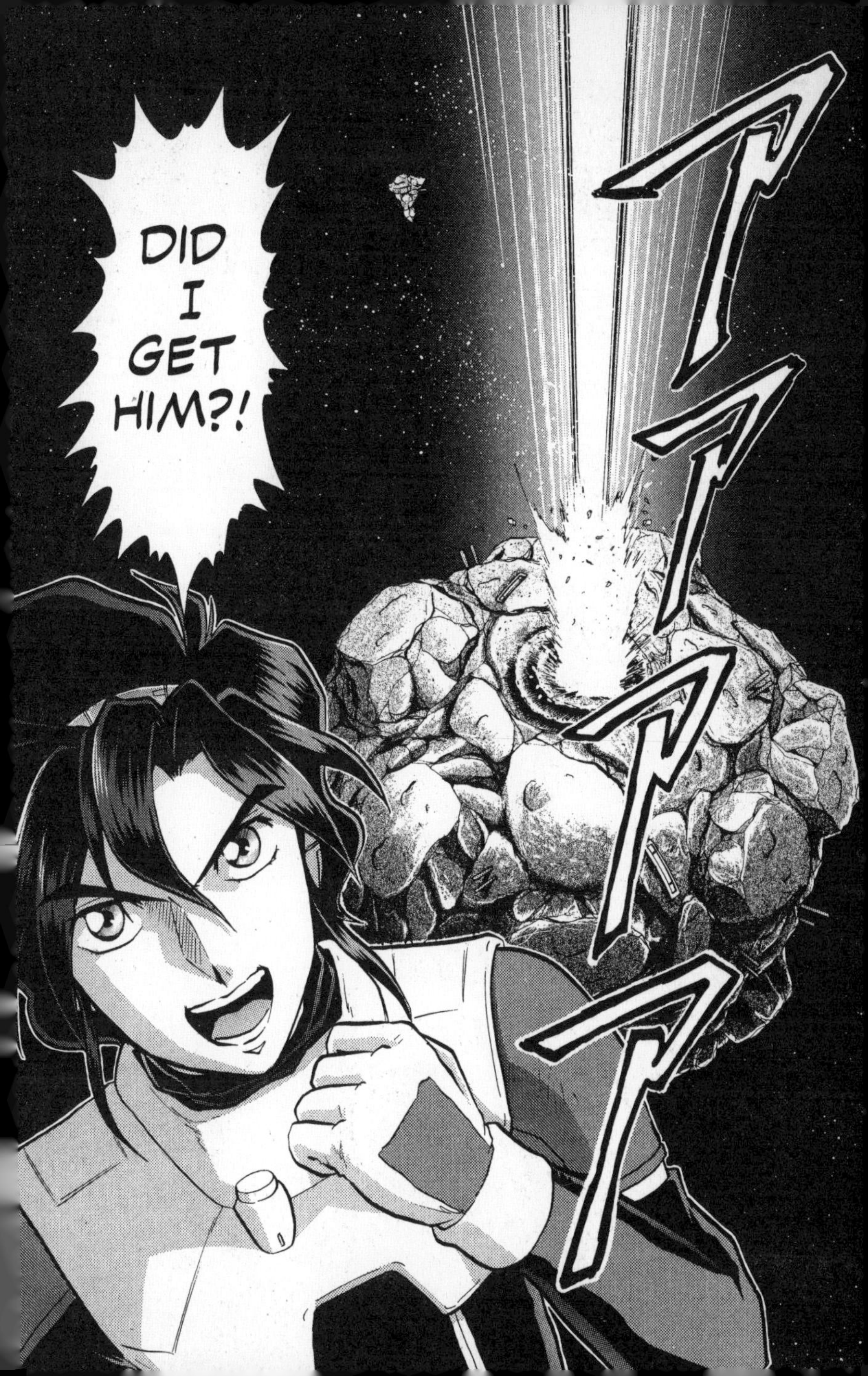
DID I GET HIM?!

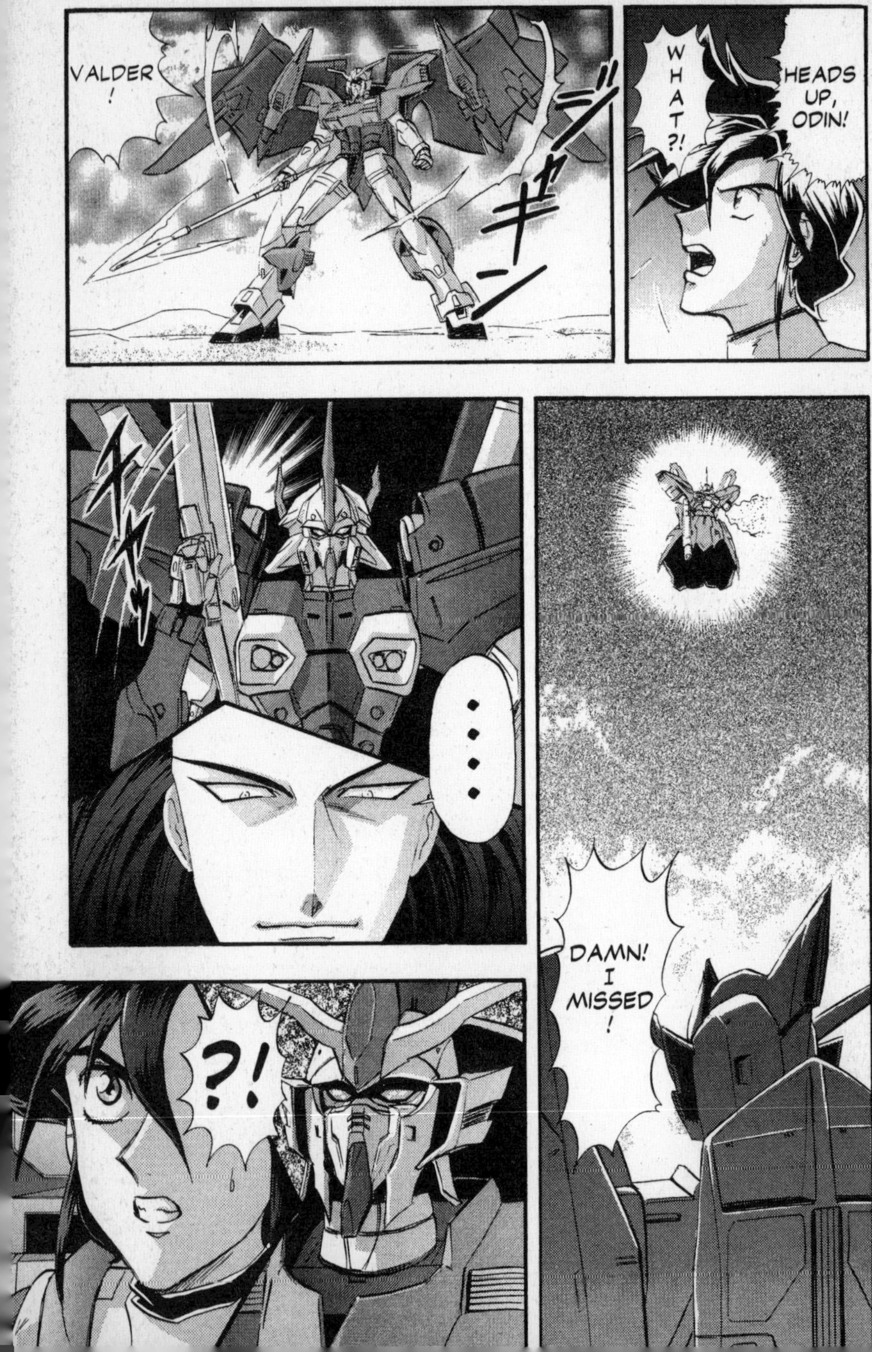
HEADS UP, ODIN!
WHAT?!
VALDER!
DAMN! I MISSED!
....
?!

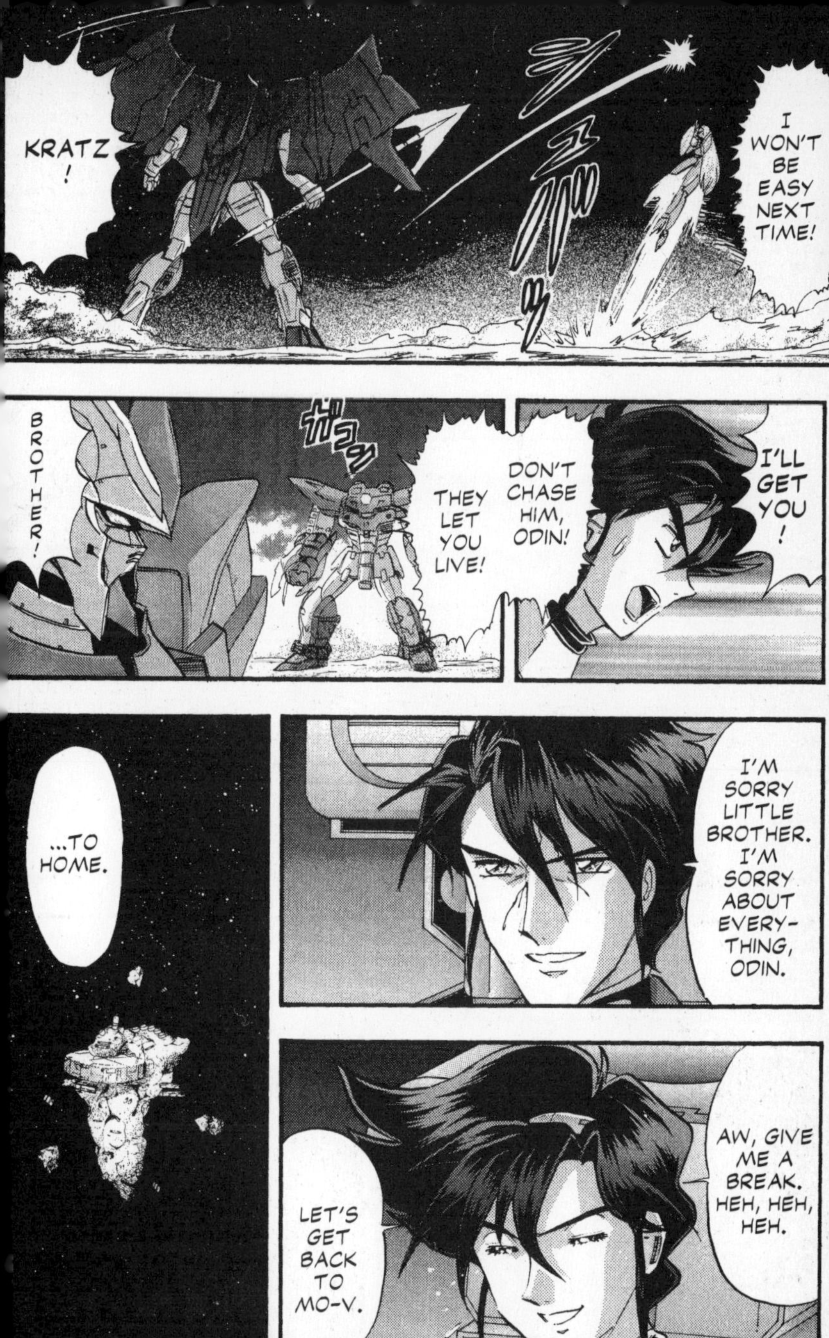
I WON'T BE EASY NEXT TIME!
KRATZ!
I'LL GET YOU!
DON'T CHASE HIM, ODIN!
THEY LET YOU LIVE!
BROTHER!
I'M SORRY LITTLE BROTHER. I'M SORRY ABOUT EVERYTHING, ODIN.
AW, GIVE ME A BREAK. HEH, HEH, HEH.
LET'S GET BACK TO MO-V.
...TO HOME.

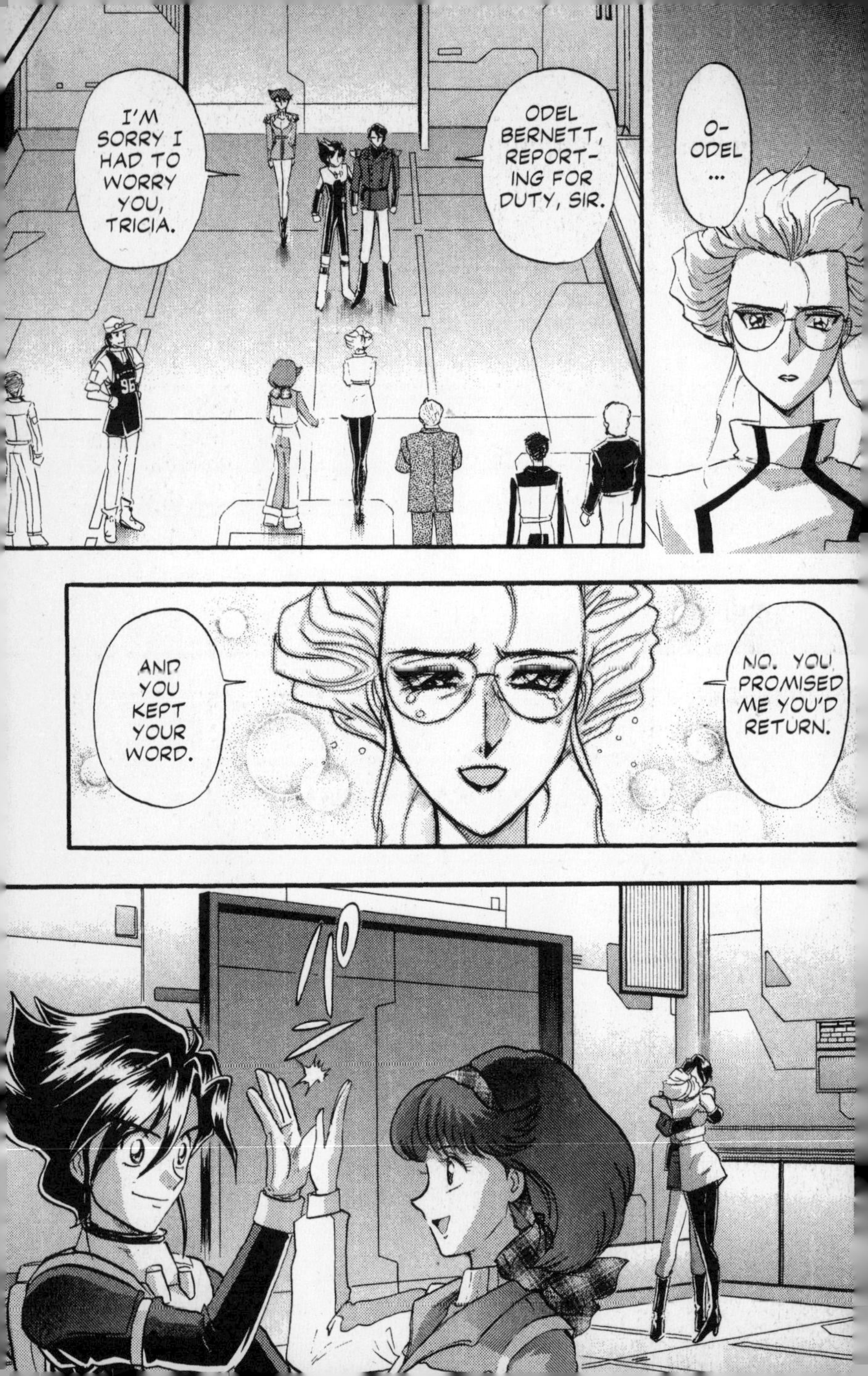
O-ODEL...
ODEL BERNETT, REPORTING FOR DUTY, SIR.
I'M SORRY I HAD TO WORRY YOU, TRICIA.
NO. YOU PROMISED ME YOU'D RETURN.
AND YOU KEPT YOUR WORD.

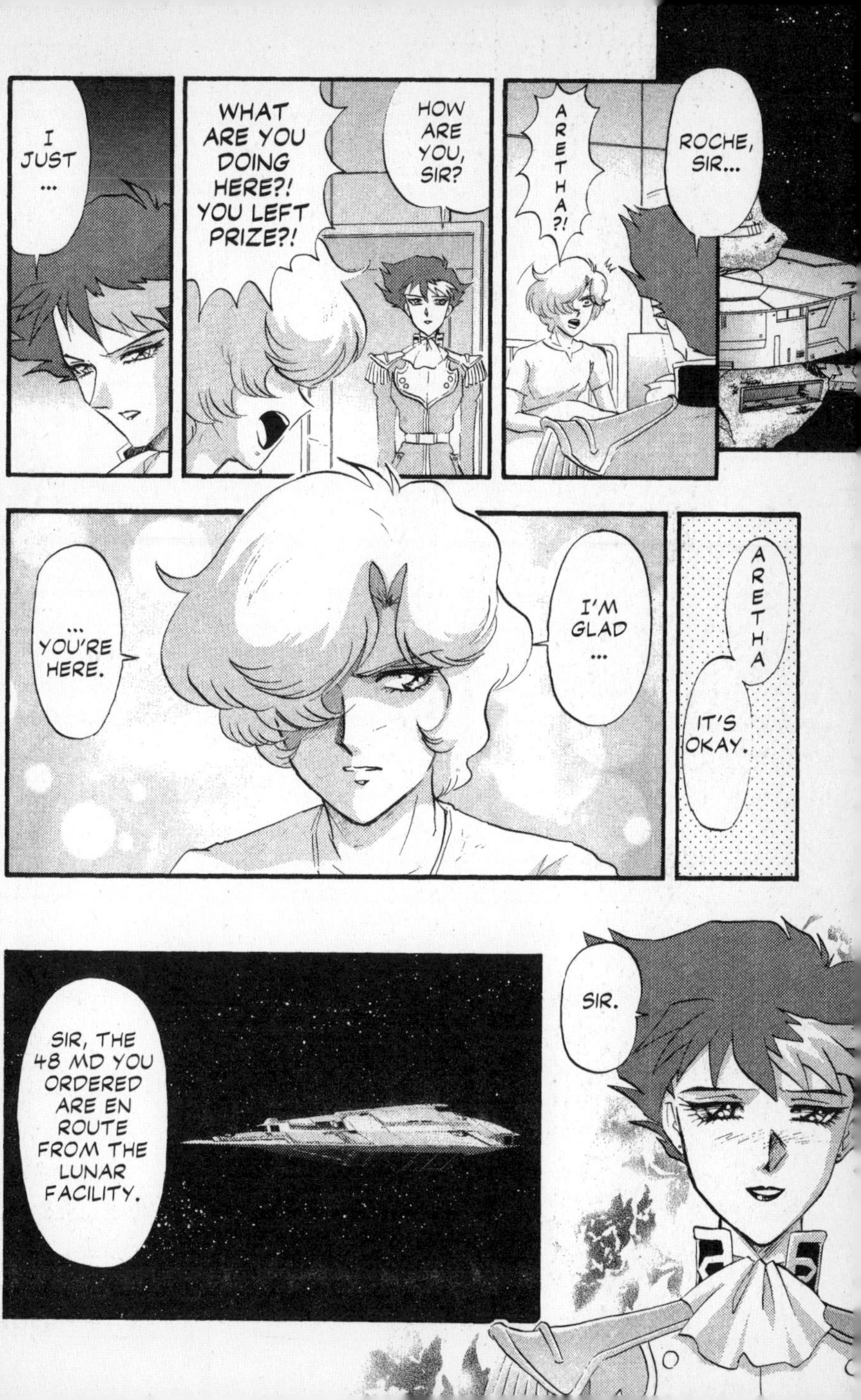

ROCHE, SIR...
ARETHA?!
HOW ARE YOU, SIR?
WHAT ARE YOU DOING HERE?! YOU LEFT PRIZE?!
I JUST ...
ARETHA
IT'S OKAY.
I'M GLAD ...
... YOU'RE HERE.
SIR.
SIR, THE 48 MD YOU ORDERED ARE EN ROUTE FROM THE LUNAR FACILITY.

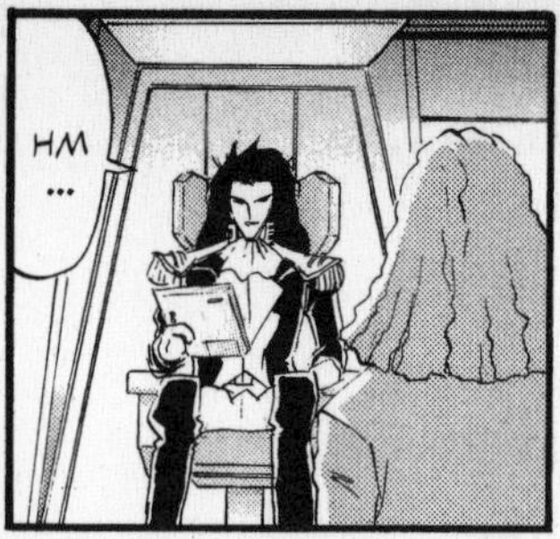
HM
...

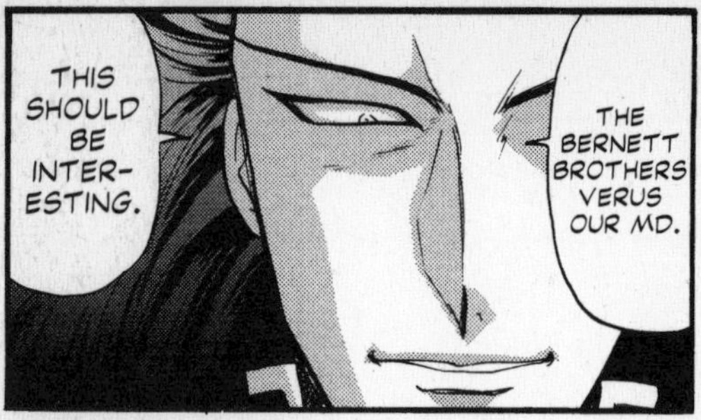
THE BERNETT BROTHERS VERUS OUR MD.
THIS SHOULD BE INTER-ESTING.

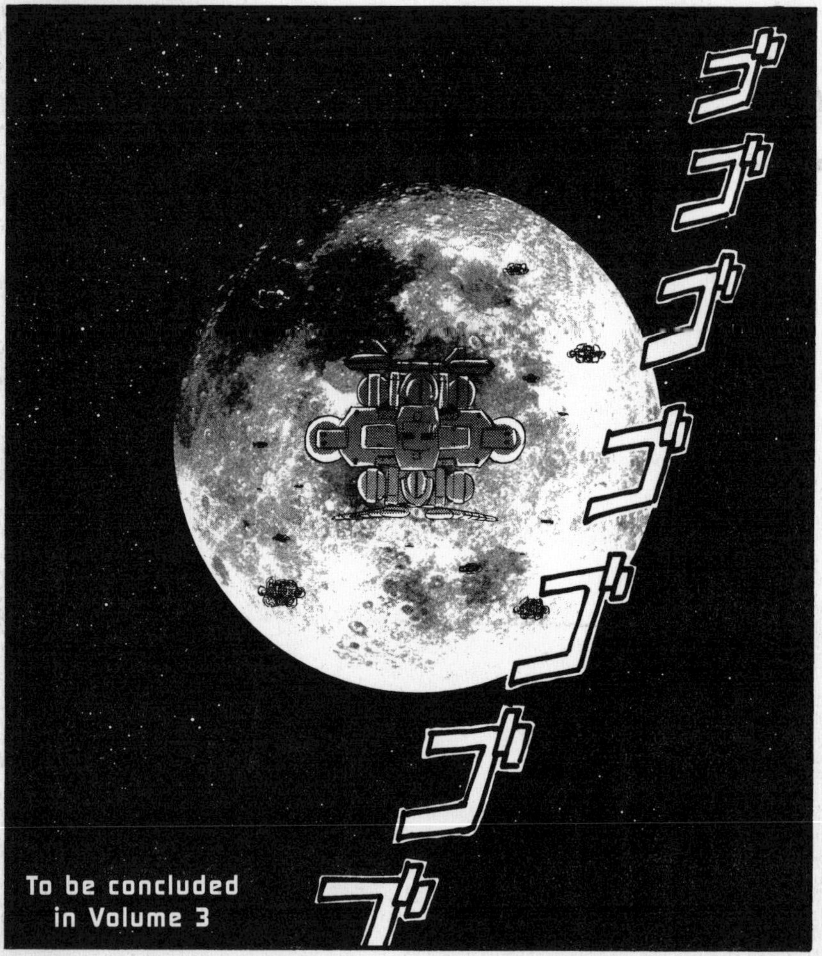
To be concluded in Volume 3

The Bernett brothers are reunited,
but the outlook is worse than ever.
With an army of Mobile Dolls en route
to MO-V, the two pilots search for a
way to save their home.

The Battle for MO-V will be concluded in
Gundam: The Last Outpost Volume 3.
Available April 2003.

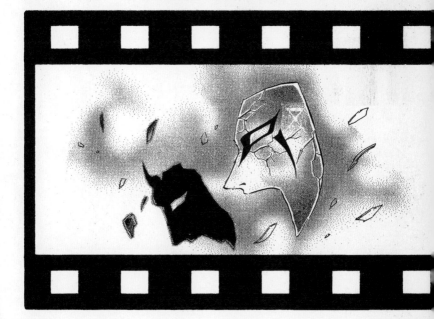

GO FOR IT, DOMON!
-GUNDAM PARTY-

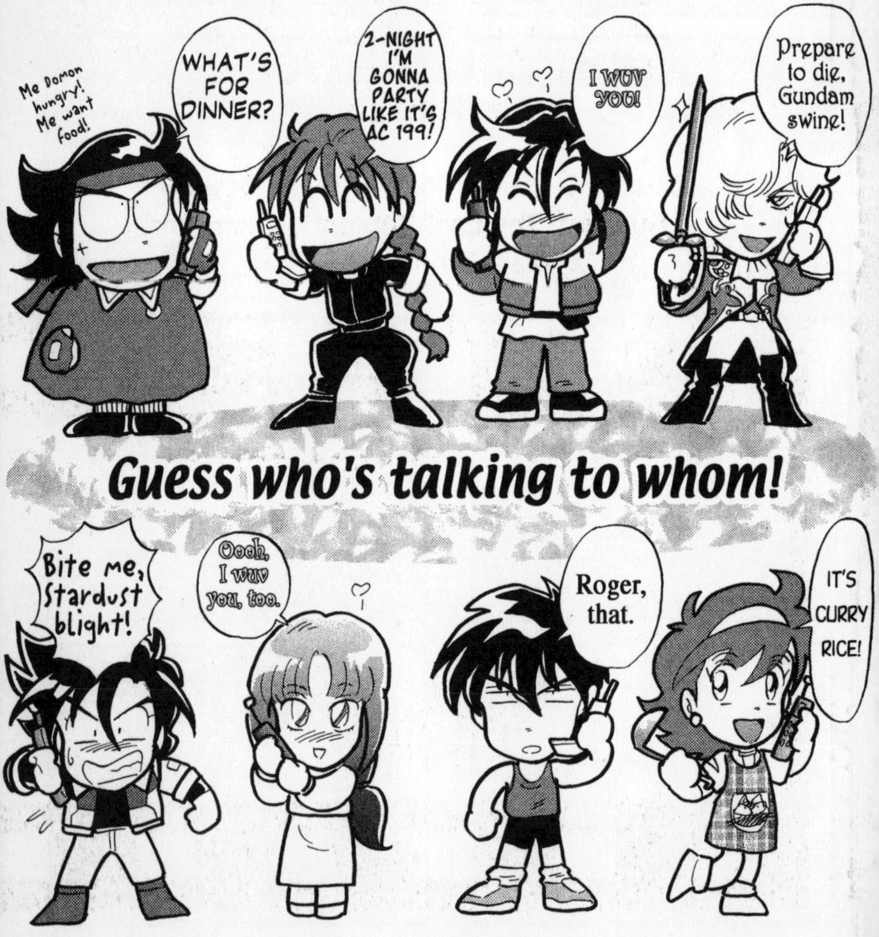
Prepare to die, Gundam swine!
I WUV YOU!
2-NIGHT I'M GONNA PARTY LIKE IT'S AC 199!
WHAT'S FOR DINNER?
Me Domon hungry! Me want food!
Guess who's talking to whom!
IT'S CURRY RICE!
Roger, that.
Oooh, I wuv you, too.
Bite me, Stardust blight!

Introducing Silver Clown

AW, SNAP! IT'S THAT NEW PILOT!
THAT MASK!
ばっ
ha! ha! ha!
...... DOH!

Casting Call Closed

Heh, heh, heh! On to stage two!
Time to unveil my great actor!
Did somebody call for great actors?
No one's cooler than the FROST Bros!
ばん
I'm ready for my close up, Mr. Berg!
Golden Globes, here I come!
ぼん
Wrong series!
Girl, Don't you point that finger at me!
I'm your man!
Me too!
NOT AGAIN!

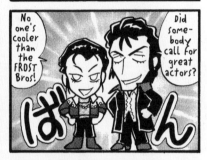

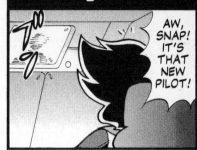

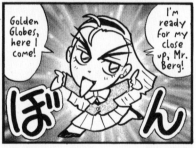

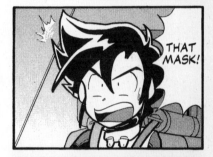

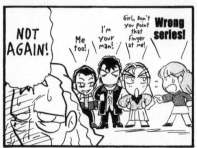

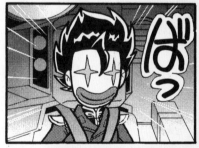

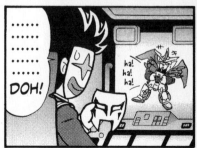

Outta-Sync

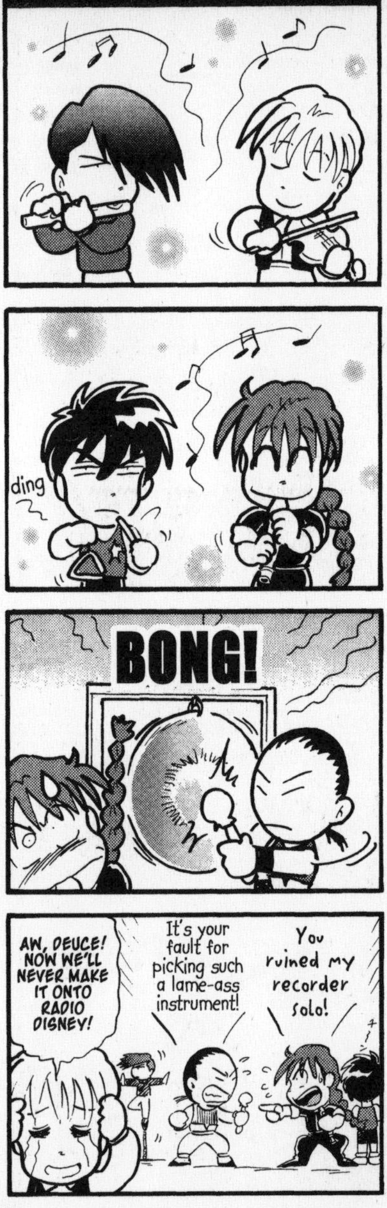
ding
BONG!
You ruined my recorder solo!
It's your fault for picking such a lame-ass instrument!
AW, DEUCE! NOW WE'LL NEVER MAKE IT ONTO RADIO DISNEY!

Domon vs. the Stray Cat

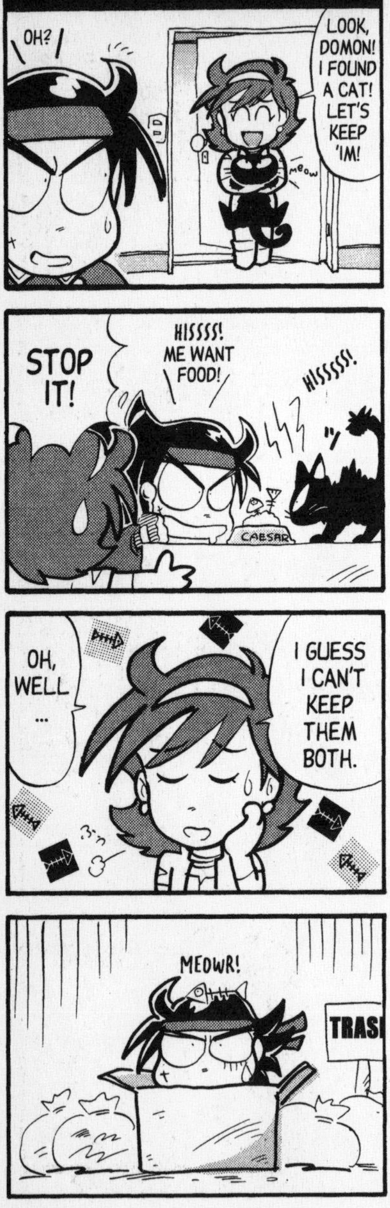
LOOK, DOMON! I FOUND A CAT! LET'S KEEP 'IM!
MEOW
OH?
HISSSSS!
HISSSSS! ME WANT FOOD!
STOP IT!
CAESAR
I GUESS I CAN'T KEEP THEM BOTH.
OH, WELL ...
TRAS
MEOWR!

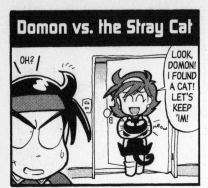

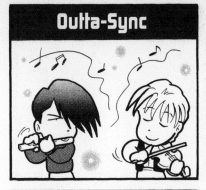

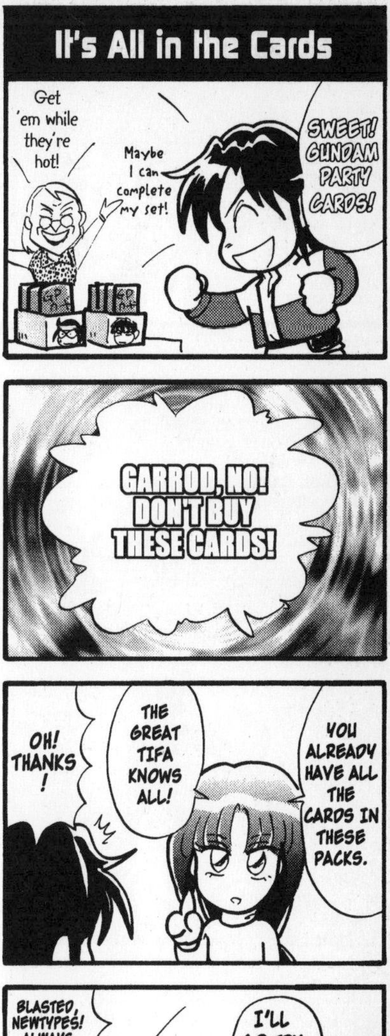
It's All in the Cards
SWEET! GUNDAM PARTY CARDS!
Get 'em while they're hot!
Maybe I can complete my set!
GARROD, NO! DON'T BUY THESE CARDS!
YOU ALREADY HAVE ALL THE CARDS IN THESE PACKS.
THE GREAT TIFA KNOWS ALL!
OH! THANKS!
I'LL GO TRY THE NEXT PLACE!
I hate psychics!
BLASTED, NEWTYPES! ALWAYS KILLING BUSINESS!

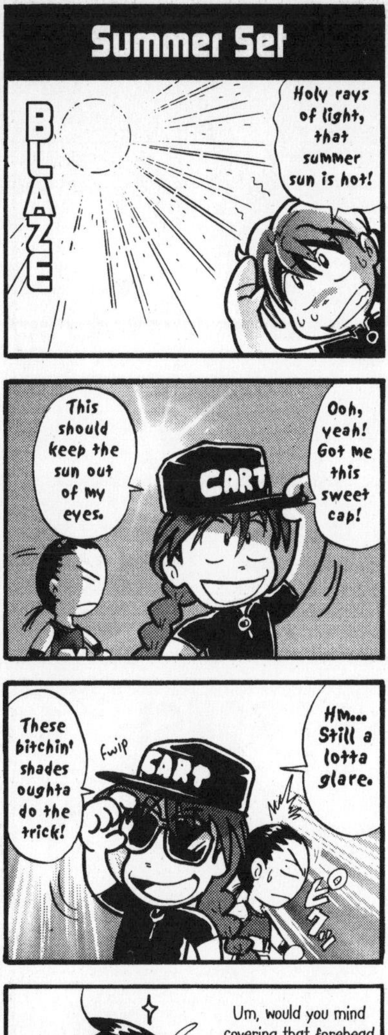
Summer Set
Holy rays of light, that summer sun is hot!
BLAZE
Ooh, yeah! Got me this sweet cap!
CART
This should keep the sun out of my eyes.
Hm... Still a lotta glare.
CART
Fwip
These bitchin' shades oughta do the trick!
Um, would you mind covering that forehead of yours. The glare is blinding us all the way back in Neo-Japan.
QUIET, YOU!

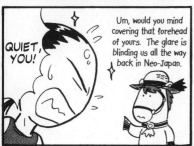

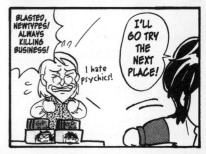

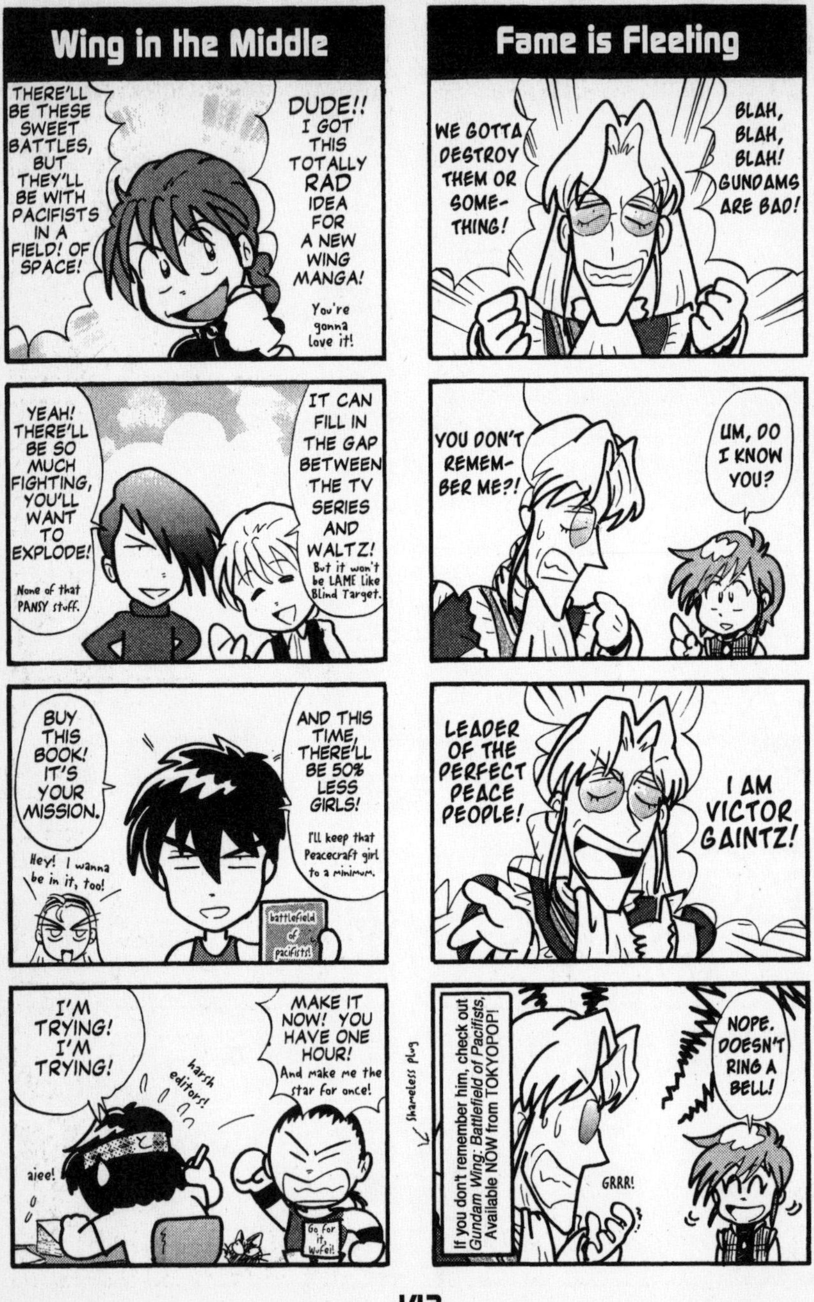
Fame is Fleeting
BLAH, BLAH, BLAH! GUNDAMS ARE BAD!
WE GOTTA DESTROY THEM OR SOMETHING!
UM, DO I KNOW YOU?
YOU DON'T REMEMBER ME?!
I AM VICTOR GAINTZ!
LEADER OF THE PERFECT PEACE PEOPLE!
NOPE. DOESN'T RING A BELL!
GRRR!
If you don't remember him, check out Gundam Wing: Battlefield of Pacifists, Available NOW from TOKYOPOP!
Shameless plug
Wing in the Middle
DUDE!! I GOT THIS TOTALLY RAD IDEA FOR A NEW WING MANGA!
You're gonna love it!
THERE'LL BE THESE SWEET BATTLES, BUT THEY'LL BE WITH PACIFISTS IN A FIELD! OF SPACE!
IT CAN FILL IN THE GAP BETWEEN THE TV SERIES AND WALTZ!
But it won't be LAME like Blind Target.
YEAH! THERE'LL BE SO MUCH FIGHTING, YOU'LL WANT TO EXPLODE!
None of that PANSY stuff.
AND THIS TIME, THERE'LL BE 50% LESS GIRLS!
I'll keep that Peacecraft girl to a minimum.
BUY THIS BOOK! IT'S YOUR MISSION.
battlefield of pacifists!
Hey! I wanna be in it, too!
MAKE IT NOW! YOU HAVE ONE HOUR!
And make me the star for once!
I'M TRYING! I'M TRYING!
harsh editors!
aiee!
Go for it, Wufei!

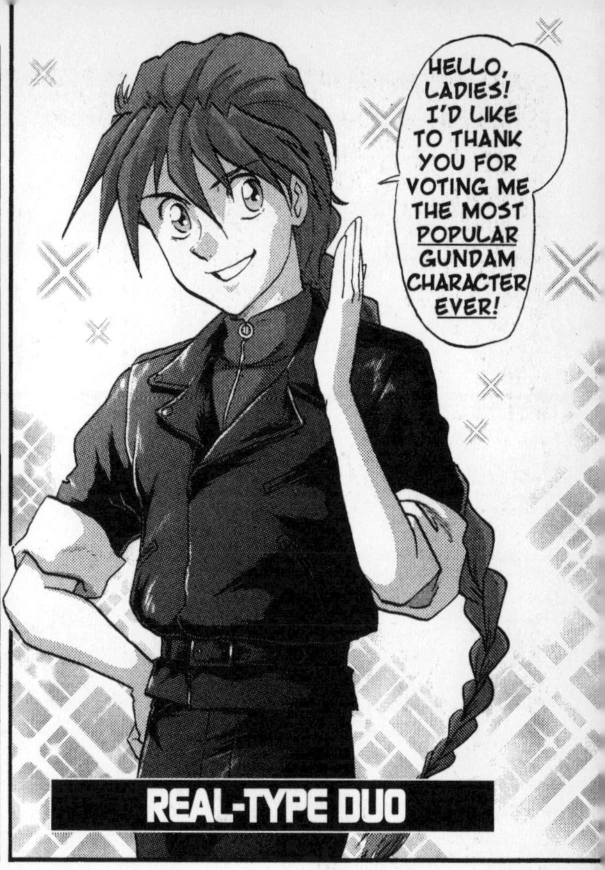
HELLO, LADIES! I'D LIKE TO THANK YOU FOR VOTING ME THE MOST POPULAR GUNDAM CHARACTER EVER!
REAL-TYPE DUO

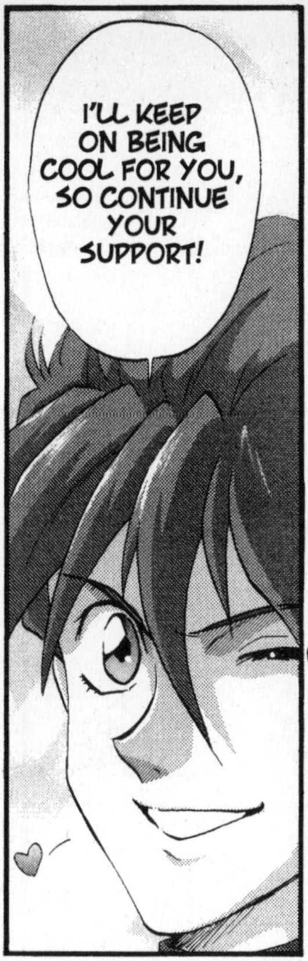
I'LL KEEP ON BEING COOL FOR YOU, SO CONTINUE YOUR SUPPORT!

GO FOR IT, DOMON!
-GUNDAM PARTY-

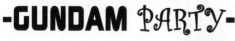

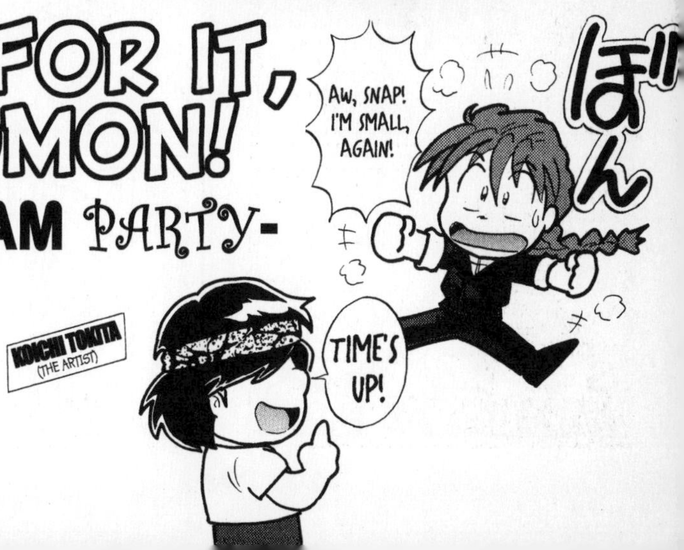
ぼん
AW, SNAP! I'M SMALL, AGAIN!
TIME'S UP!
KOICHI TOKITA (THE ARTIST)

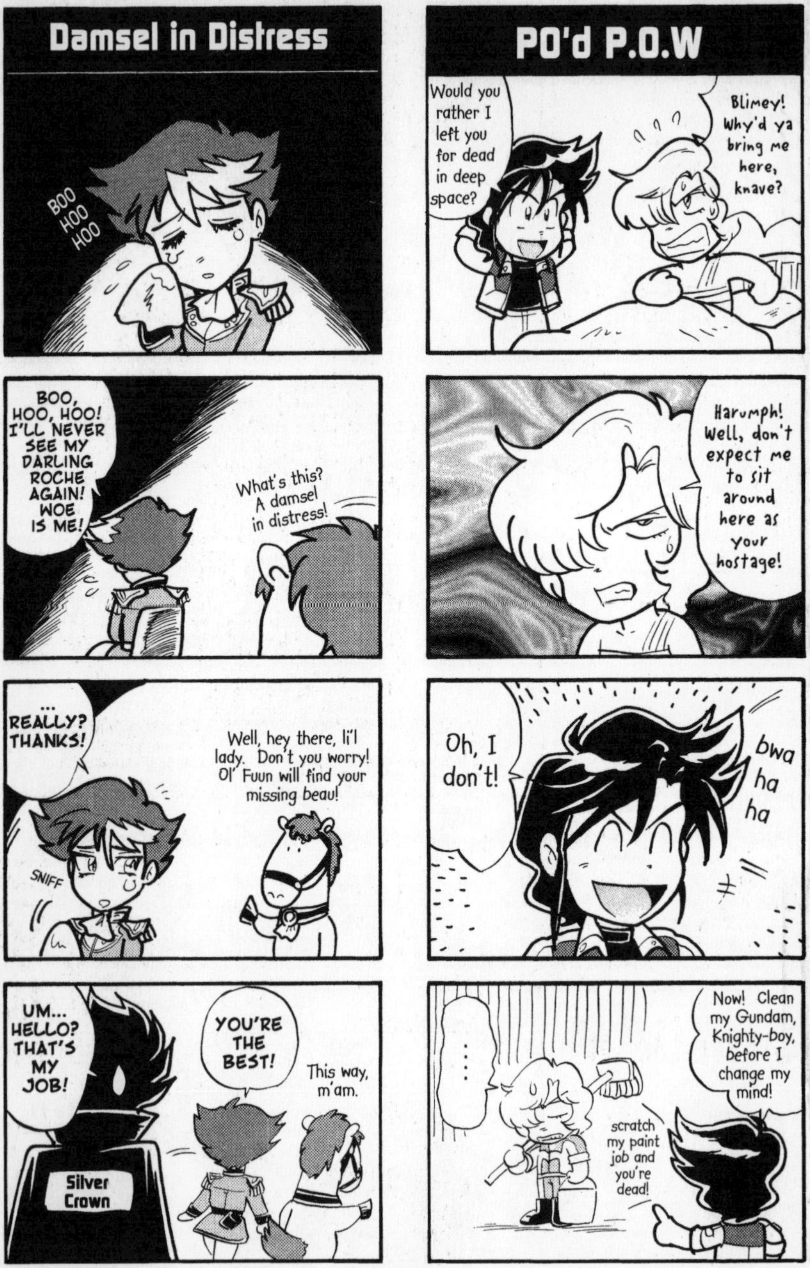
PO'd P.O.W
Blimey! Why'd ya bring me here, knave?
Would you rather I left you for dead in deep space?
Harumph! Well, don't expect me to sit around here as your hostage!
bwa ha ha
Oh, I don't!
Now! Clean my Gundam, Knighty-boy, before I change my mind!
scratch my paint job and you're dead!
....
Damsel in Distress
BOO HOO HOO
What's this? A damsel in distress!
BOO, HOO, HOO! I'LL NEVER SEE MY DARLING ROCHE AGAIN! WOE IS ME!
Well, hey there, li'l lady. Don't you worry! Ol' Fuun will find your missing beau!
... REALLY? THANKS!
SNIFF
This way, m'am.
YOU'RE THE BEST!
UM... HELLO? THAT'S MY JOB!
Silver Crown

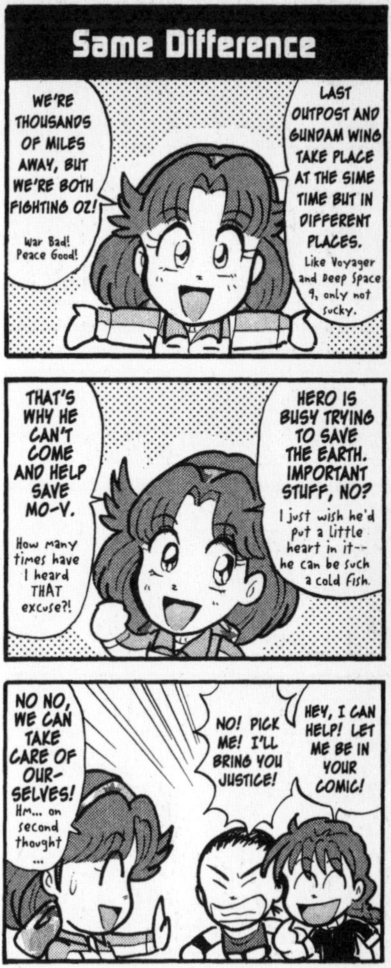
Same Difference
LAST OUTPOST AND GUNDAM WING TAKE PLACE AT THE SIME TIME BUT IN DIFFERENT PLACES.
Like Voyager and Deep Space 9, only not sucky.
WE'RE THOUSANDS OF MILES AWAY, BUT WE'RE BOTH FIGHTING OZ!
War Bad! Peace Good!
HERO IS BUSY TRYING TO SAVE THE EARTH. IMPORTANT STUFF, NO?
I just wish he'd put a little heart in it--he can be such a cold fish.
THAT'S WHY HE CAN'T COME AND HELP SAVE MO-V.
How many times have I heard THAT excuse?!
HEY, I CAN HELP! LET ME BE IN YOUR COMIC!
NO! PICK ME! I'LL BRING YOU JUSTICE!
NO NO, WE CAN TAKE CARE OF OUR-SELVES!
Hm... on second thought ...
HEY, BABY! HOW'D YOU LIKE A LI'L HELP...
...FROM THE FROST BROS!
NO THANKS!
Wrong series, Lame-brains!
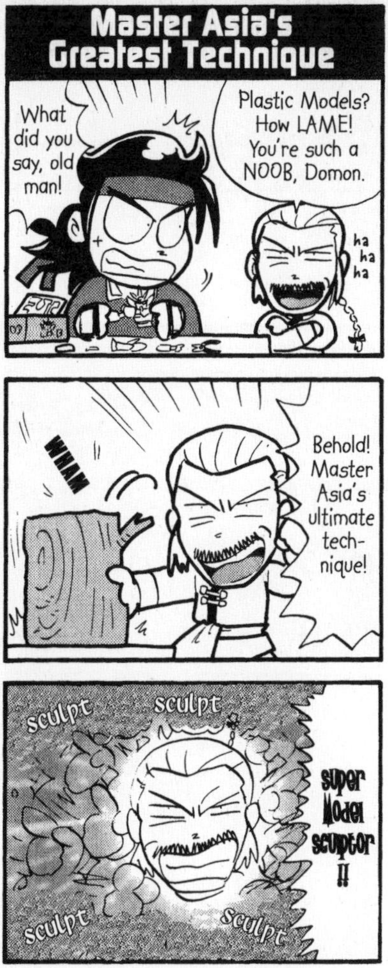
Master Asia's Greatest Technique
Plastic Models? How LAME! You're such a NOOB, Domon.
What did you say, old man!
ha ha ha
Behold! Master Asia's ultimate tech-nique!
WHAM
Super Model Sculptor !!
sculpt
sculpt
sculpt
sculpt
Eat this, puny pupil!
1/4 scale TIFA
Teach me, master!

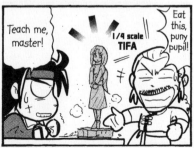

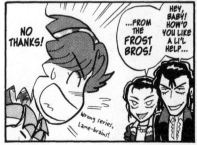

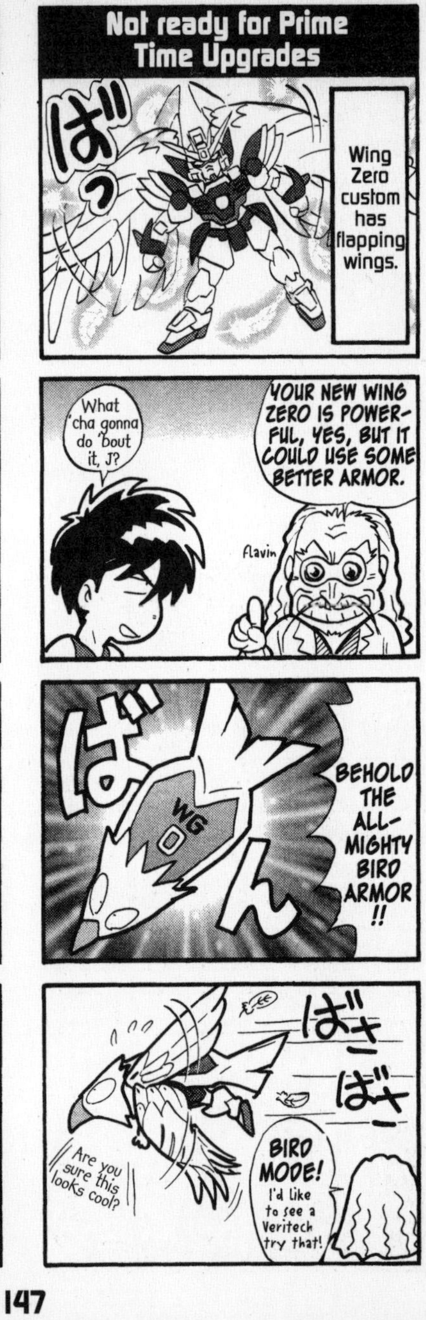
Not ready for Prime Time Upgrades
Wing Zero custom has flapping wings.
ばっ
YOUR NEW WING ZERO IS POWER-FUL, YES, BUT IT COULD USE SOME BETTER ARMOR.
What 'cha gonna do 'bout it, J?
Flavin
BEHOLD THE ALL-MIGHTY BIRD ARMOR!!
ばん
ばさばさ
BIRD MODE!
I'd like to see a Veritech try that!
Are you sure this looks cool?

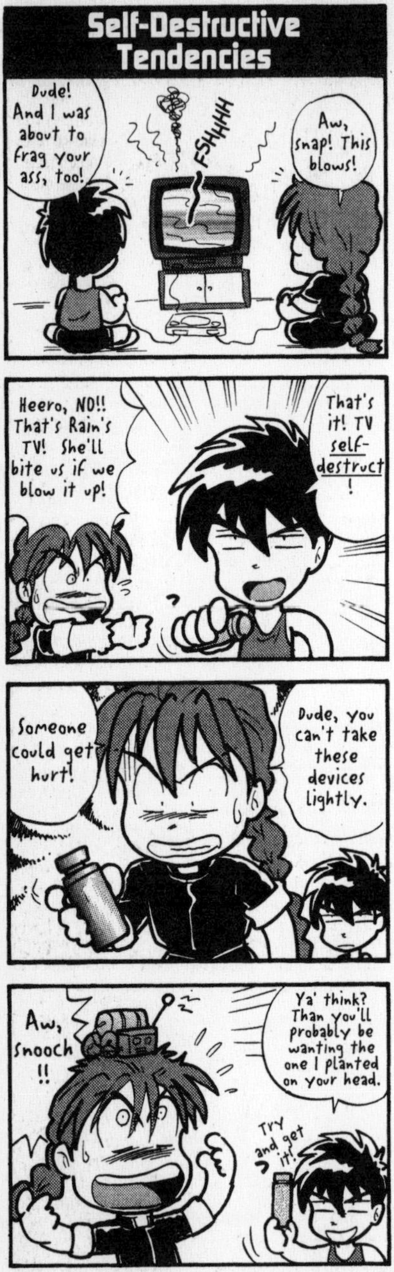
Self-Destructive Tendencies
Aw, snap! This blows!
FSHHHH
Dude! And I was about to frag your ass, too!
That's it! TV self-destruct!
Heero, NO!! That's Rain's TV! She'll bite us if we blow it up!
Dude, you can't take these devices lightly.
Someone could get hurt!
Ya' think? Than you'll probably be wanting the one I planted on your head.
Try and get it!
Aw, snooch!!

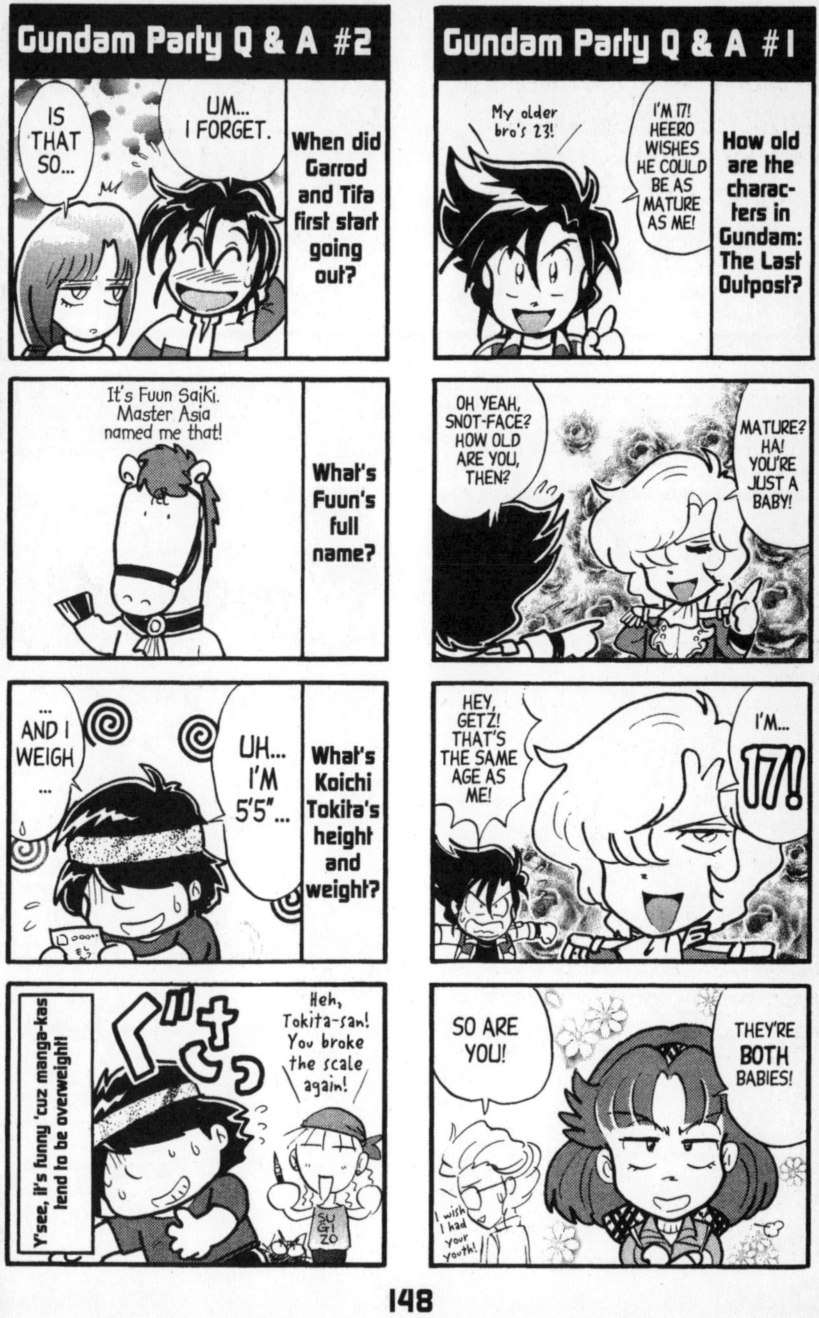
Gundam Party Q & A #1
How old are the characters in Gundam: The Last Outpost?
I'M 17! HEERO WISHES HE COULD BE AS MATURE AS ME!
My older bro's 23!
MATURE? HA! YOU'RE JUST A BABY!
OH YEAH, SNOT-FACE? HOW OLD ARE YOU, THEN?
I'M... 17!
HEY, GETZ! THAT'S THE SAME AGE AS ME!
THEY'RE BOTH BABIES!
SO ARE YOU!
I wish I had your youth!
Gundam Party Q & A #2
When did Garrod and Tifa first start going out?
UM... I FORGET.
IS THAT SO...
What's Fuun's full name?
It's Fuun Saiki. Master Asia named me that!
What's Koichi Tokita's height and weight?
UH... I'M 5'5"...
... AND I WEIGH ...
Y'see, it's funny 'cuz manga-kas tend to be overweight!
Heh, Tokita-san! You broke the scale again!
SUGIZO

GO FOR IT, DOMON!

- ANPAN PARTY -

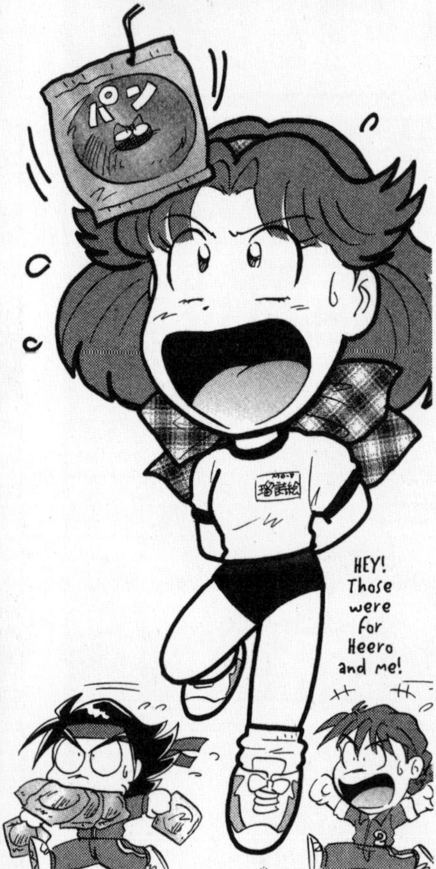
パン
HEY! Those were for Heero and me!

More than Meets the Eye!

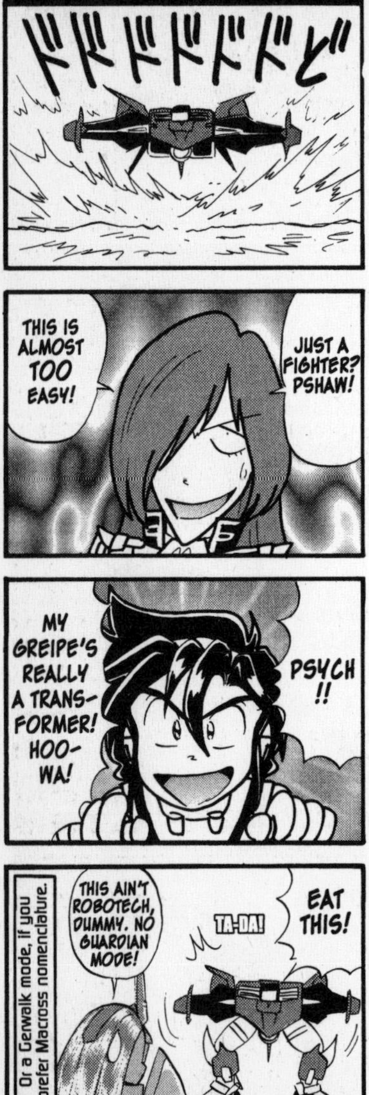
ドドドドドドど
JUST A FIGHTER? PSHAW!
THIS IS ALMOST TOO EASY!
PSYCH !!
MY GREIPE'S REALLY A TRANS-FORMER! HOO-WA!
EAT THIS!
TA-DA!
THIS AIN'T ROBOTECH, DUMMY. NO GUARDIAN MODE!
Or a Gerwalk mode, if you prefer Macross nomenclature.

People in Masks Cannot be Trusted

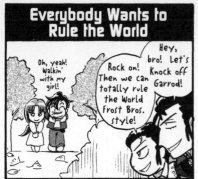

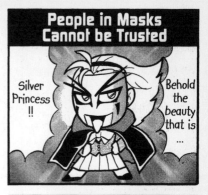

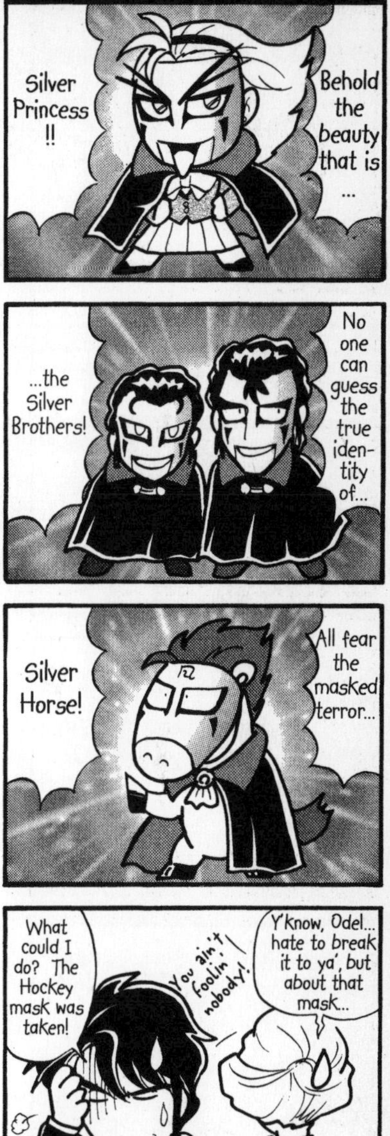
Behold the beauty that is ...
Silver Princess !!
No one can guess the true identity of...
...the Silver Brothers!
All fear the masked terror...
Silver Horse!
Y'know, Odel... hate to break it to ya', but about that mask...
You ain't foolin' nobody!
What could I do? The Hockey mask was taken!

Everybody Wants to Rule the World

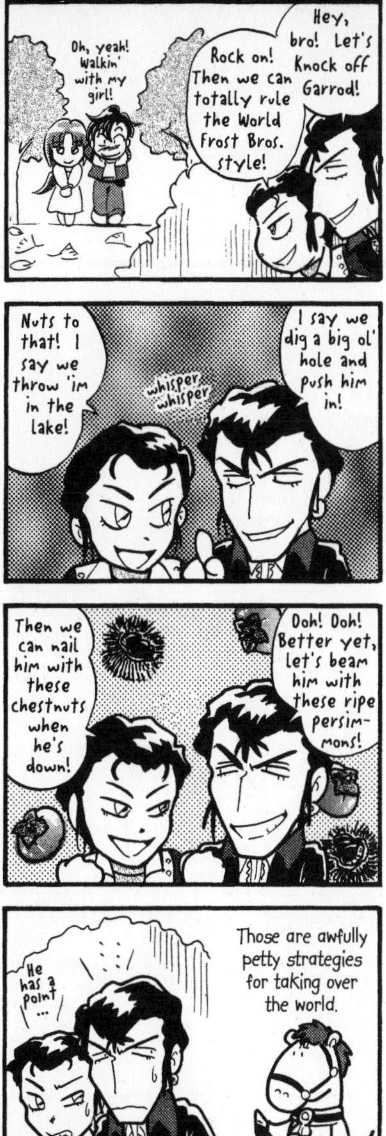
Hey, bro! Let's Knock off Garrod!
Rock on! Then we can totally rule the World Frost Bros. style!
Oh, yeah! Walkin' with my girl!
I say we dig a big ol' hole and push him in!
whisper whisper
Nuts to that! I say we throw 'im in the lake!
Ooh! Ooh! Better yet, let's beam him with these ripe persimmons!
Then we can nail him with these chestnuts when he's down!
Those are awfully petty strategies for taking over the world.
He has a point ...

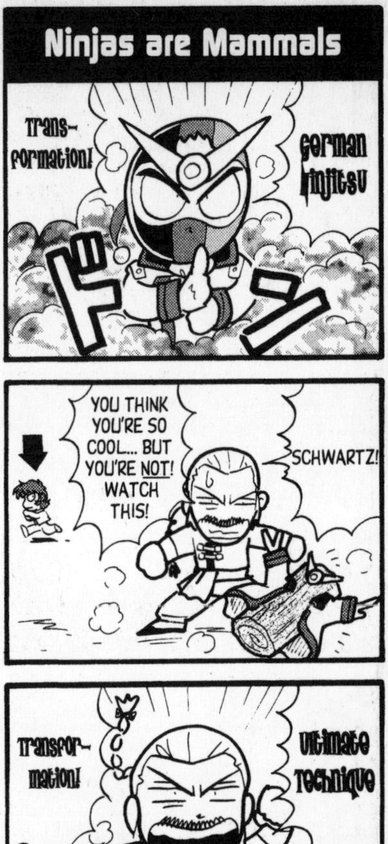
Ninjas are Mammals
German Ninjitsu
Trans-formation!
ドン
SCHWARTZ!
YOU THINK YOU'RE SO COOL... BUT YOU'RE NOT! WATCH THIS!
Ultimate Technique
Transfor-mation!
ボン
HEY!
Hay is for horses, now leave me alone!
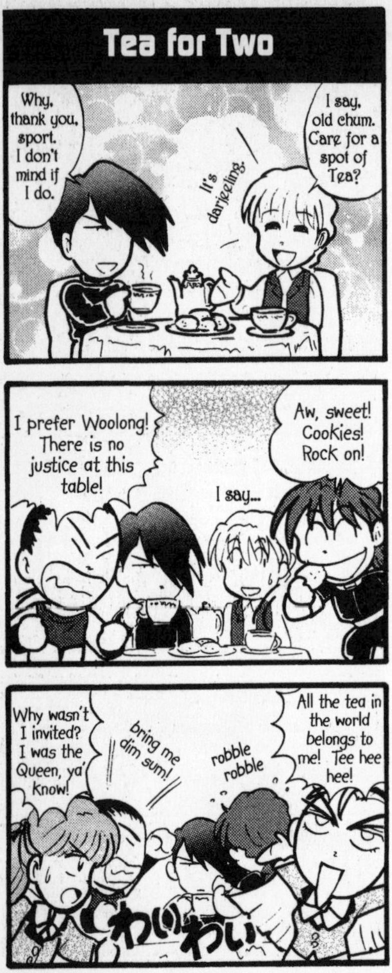
Tea for Two
I say, old chum. Care for a spot of Tea?
It's darjeeling.
Why, thank you, sport. I don't mind if I do.
Aw, sweet! Cookies! Rock on!
I say...
I prefer Woolong! There is no justice at this table!
All the tea in the world belongs to me! Tee hee hee!
robble robble
bring me dim sum!
Why wasn't I invited? I was the Queen, ya' know!
わいわい
MY TEA TIME...!
snarf snarf

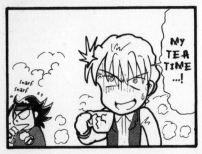

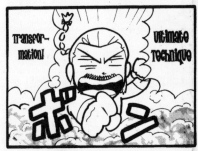

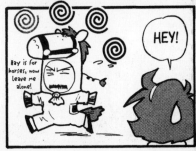

Reality Bites #1

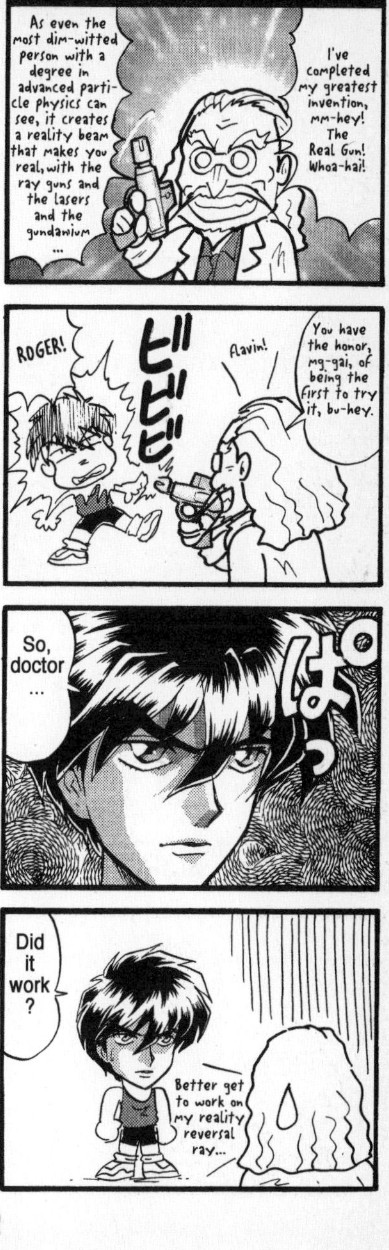
I've completed my greatest invention, mm-hey! The Real Gun! Whoa-hai!
As even the most dim-witted person with a degree in advanced particle physics can see, it creates a reality beam that makes you real, with the ray guns and the lasers and the gundanium ...
You have the honor, mg-gai, of being the first to try it, bu-hey.
Flavin!
ビビビビ
ROGER!
ぱっ
So, doctor ...
Did it work ?
Better get to work on my reality reversal ray...

Reality Bites #2

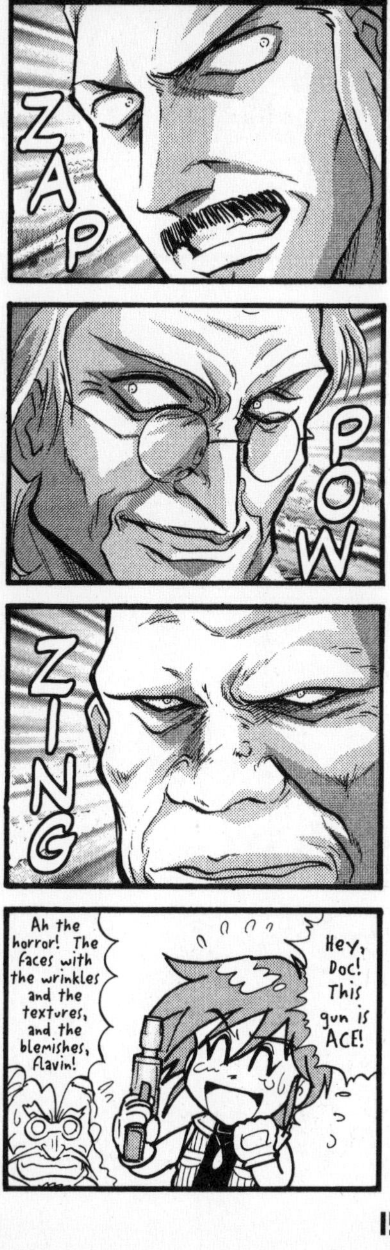
ZAP
POW
ZING
Hey, Doc! This gun is ACE!
Ah the horror! The faces with the wrinkles and the textures, and the blemishes, Flavin!

I Mastered the Ultimate Technique

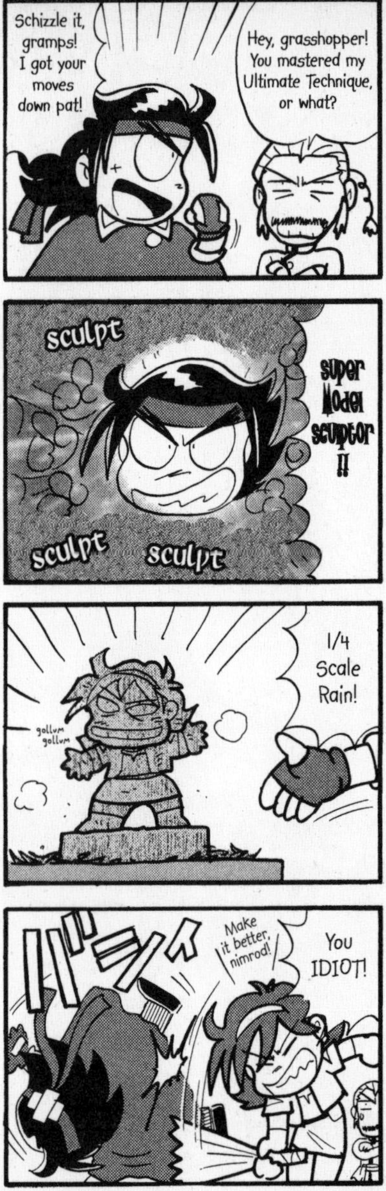
Hey, grasshopper! You mastered my Ultimate Technique, or what?
Schizzle it, gramps! I got your moves down pat!
Super Model Sculptor !!
sculpt
sculpt
sculpt
1/4 Scale Rain!
gollum gollum
You IDIOT!
Make it better, nimrod!

Spartacus

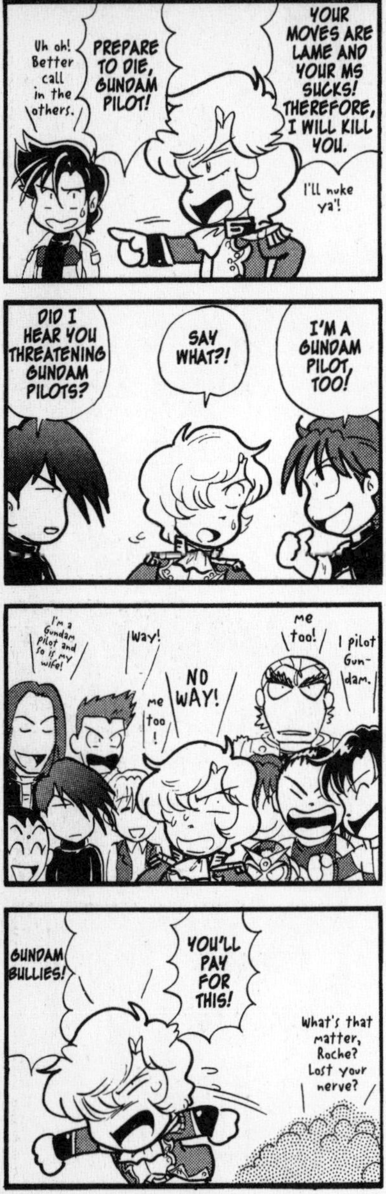
YOUR MOVES ARE LAME AND YOUR MS SUCKS! THEREFORE, I WILL KILL YOU.
I'll nuke ya'!
PREPARE TO DIE, GUNDAM PILOT!
Uh oh! Better call in the others.
I'M A GUNDAM PILOT, TOO!
SAY WHAT?!
DID I HEAR YOU THREATENING GUNDAM PILOTS?
I pilot Gun-dam.
me too!
NO WAY!
me too!
way!
I'm a Gundam pilot and so is my wife!
What's that matter, Roche? Lost your nerve?
YOU'LL PAY FOR THIS!
GUNDAM BULLIES!

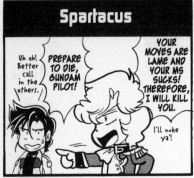

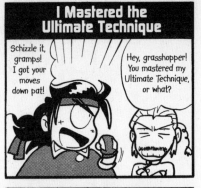

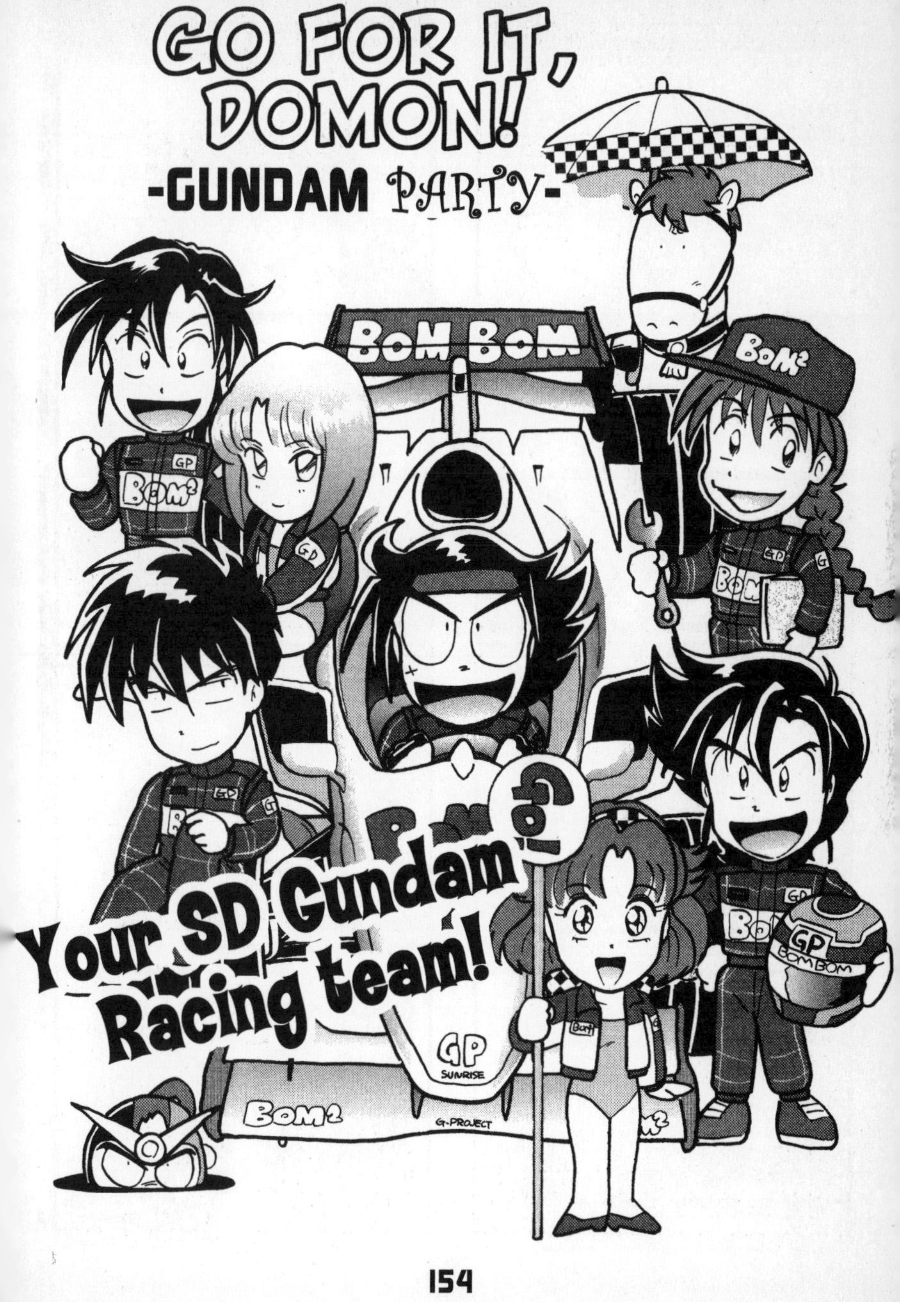
GO FOR IT, DOMON!
-GUNDAM PARTY-
BOM BOM
BOM²
GP
GD
G
Your SD Gundam Racing team!
GP
SUNRISE
G-PROJECT
GP
BOMBOM

Robots in Disguise

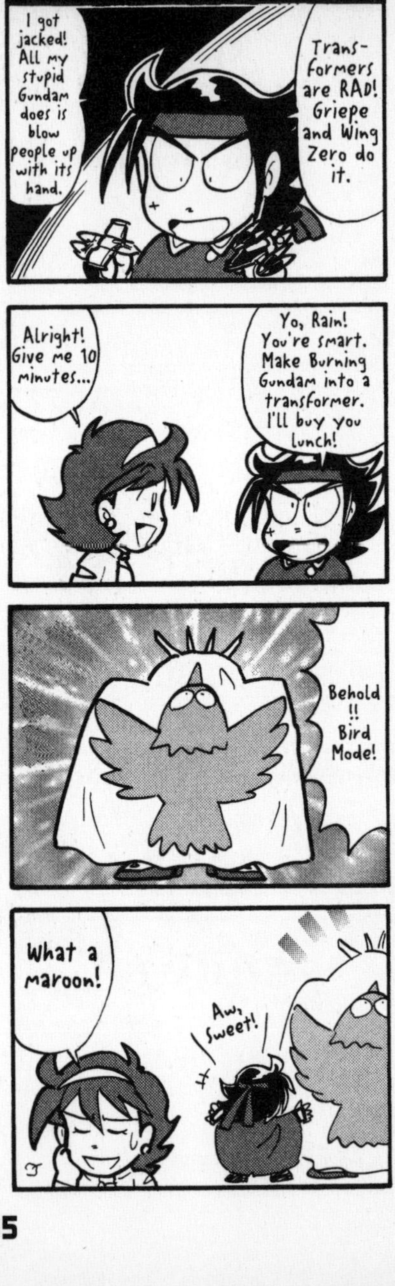
Trans-formers are RAD! Griepe and Wing Zero do it.
I got jacked! All my stupid Gundam does is blow people up with its hand.
Yo, Rain! You're smart. Make Burning Gundam into a transformer. I'll buy you lunch!
Alright! Give me 10 minutes...
Behold!! Bird Mode!
Aw, Sweet!
What a maroon!

Music Appreciation

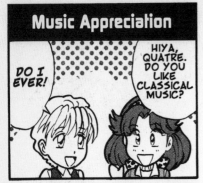

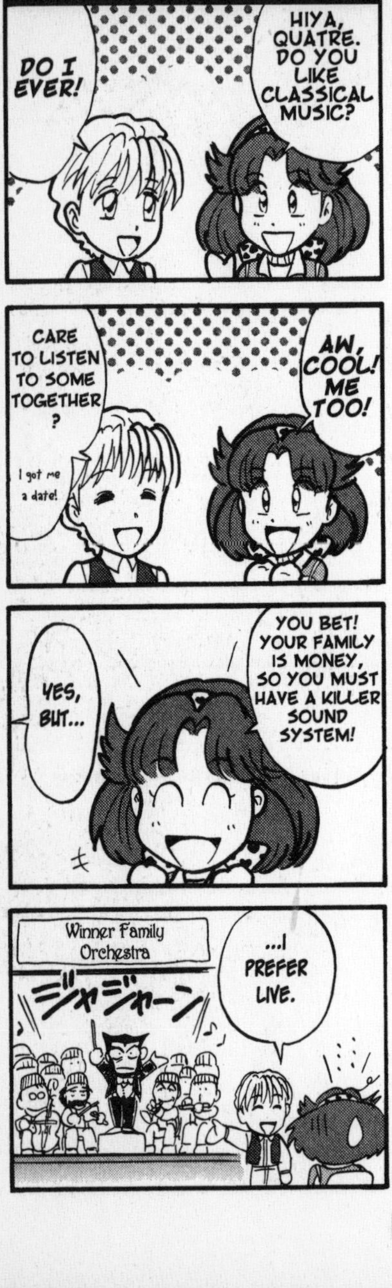
HIYA, QUATRE. DO YOU LIKE CLASSICAL MUSIC?
DO I EVER!
AW, COOL! ME TOO!
CARE TO LISTEN TO SOME TOGETHER?
I got me a date!
YOU BET! YOUR FAMILY IS MONEY, SO YOU MUST HAVE A KILLER SOUND SYSTEM!
YES, BUT...
...I PREFER LIVE.
Winner Family Orchestra
ジャジャーン

A Series of Unfortunate Events

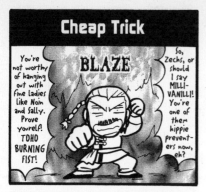

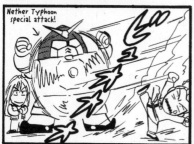

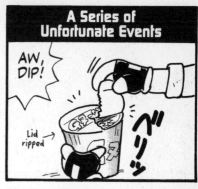

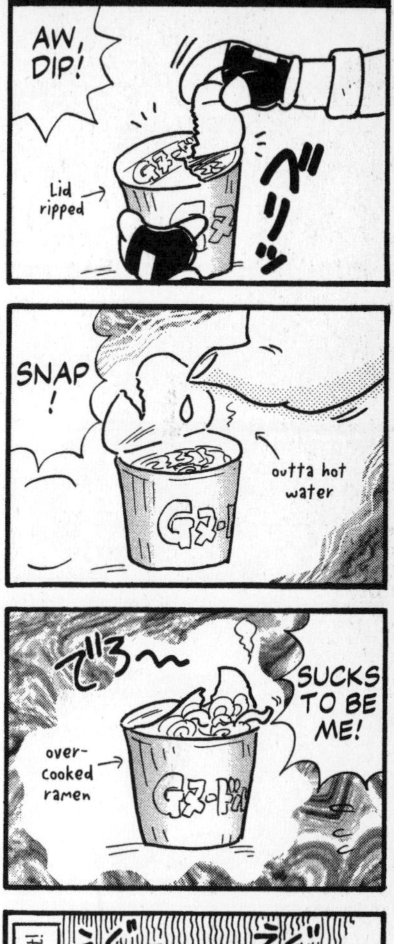
ベリッ
AW, DIP!
Lid ripped
SNAP!
outta hot water
SUCKS TO BE ME!
でろ〜
over-cooked ramen
chop-sticks didn't break right
えぐ えぐ
Beat That, Lemony Snicket!

Cheap Trick

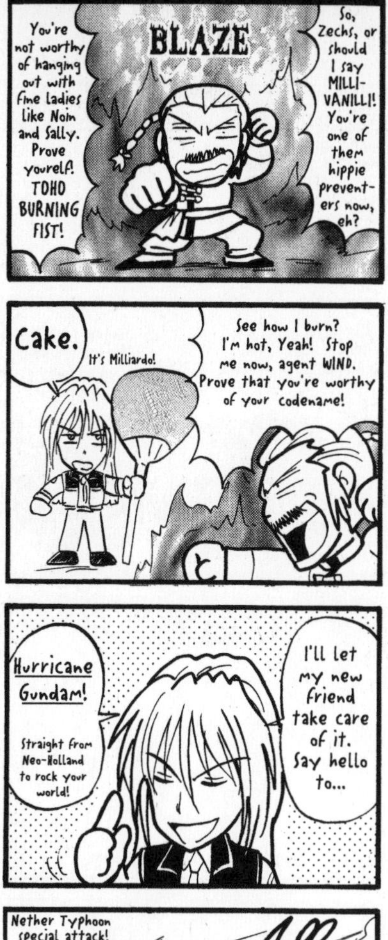
So, Zechs, or should I say MILLI-VANILLI! You're one of them hippie preventers now, eh?
BLAZE
You're not worthy of hanging out with fine ladies like Noin and Sally. Prove yourelf! TOHO BURNING FIST!
See how I burn? I'm hot, Yeah! Stop me now, agent WIND. Prove that you're worthy of your codename!
It's Milliardo!
Cake.
I'll let my new friend take care of it. Say hello to...
Hurricane Gundam!
Straight from Neo-Holland to rock your world!
Nether Typhoon special attack!

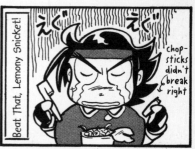

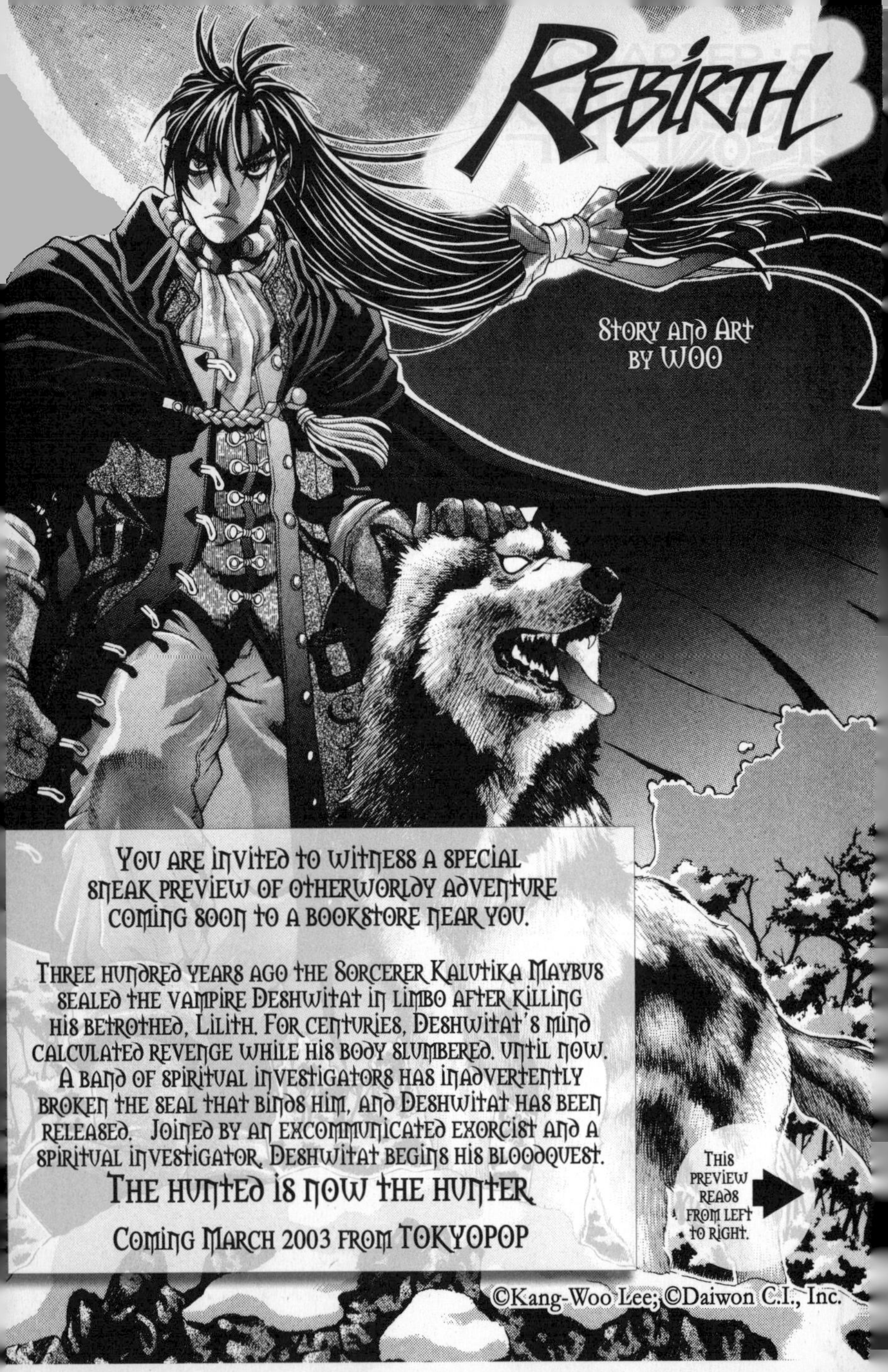
REBIRTH
Story and Art
by WOO
You are invited to witness a special sneak preview of otherworldy adventure coming soon to a bookstore near you.
Three hundred years ago the Sorcerer Kalutika Maybus sealed the vampire Deshwitat in limbo after killing his betrothed, Lilith. For centuries, Deshwitat's mind calculated revenge while his body slumbered. Until now. A band of spiritual investigators has inadvertently broken the seal that binds him, and Deshwitat has been released. Joined by an excommunicated exorcist and a spiritual investigator, Deshwitat begins his bloodquest.
THE HUNTED IS NOW THE HUNTER.
Coming March 2003 from TOKYOPOP
This preview reads from left to right.
©Kang-Woo Lee; ©Daiwon C.I., Inc.

FOUR-PANEL MADNESS
-GUNDAM PARADISE-

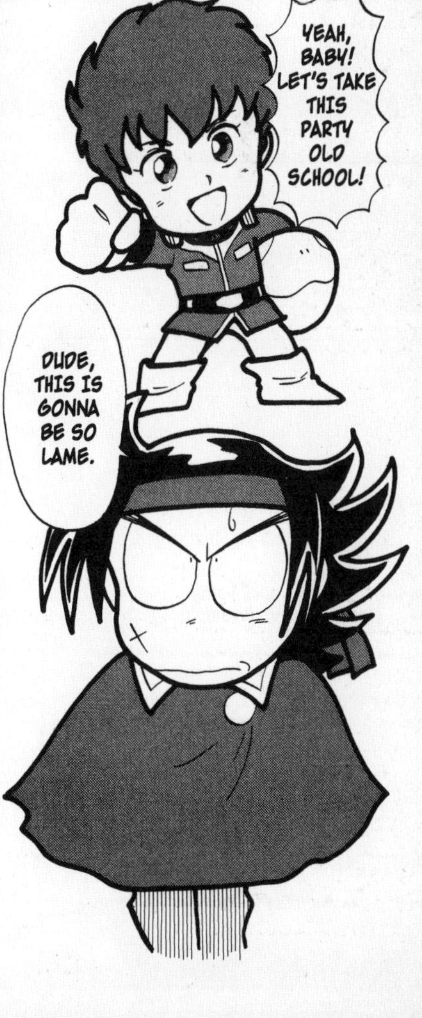
YEAH, BABY! LET'S TAKE THIS PARTY OLD SCHOOL!
DUDE, THIS IS GONNA BE SO LAME.

Little Ray Of Light

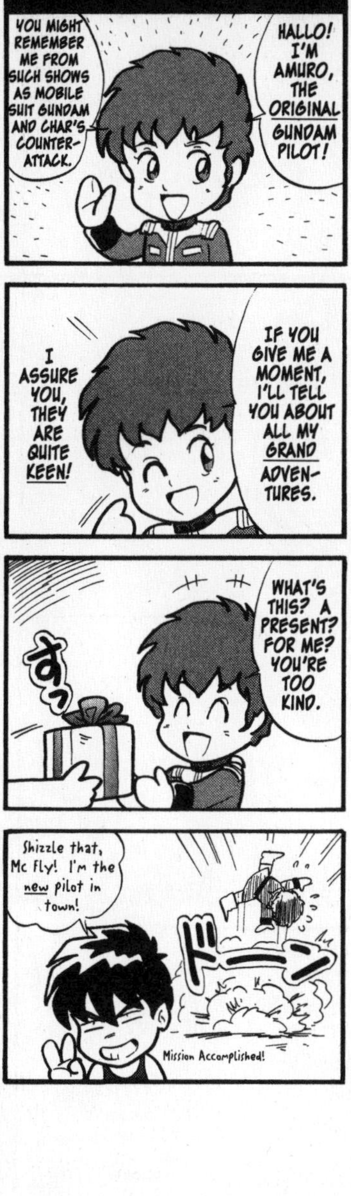
HALLO! I'M AMURO, THE ORIGINAL GUNDAM PILOT!
YOU MIGHT REMEMBER ME FROM SUCH SHOWS AS MOBILE SUIT GUNDAM AND CHAR'S COUNTER-ATTACK.
IF YOU GIVE ME A MOMENT, I'LL TELL YOU ABOUT ALL MY GRAND ADVENTURES.
I ASSURE YOU, THEY ARE QUITE KEEN!
WHAT'S THIS? A PRESENT? FOR ME? YOU'RE TOO KIND.
すっ
Shizzle that, Mc Fly! I'm the new pilot in town!
ドーン
Mission Accomplished!

Burns Me Up

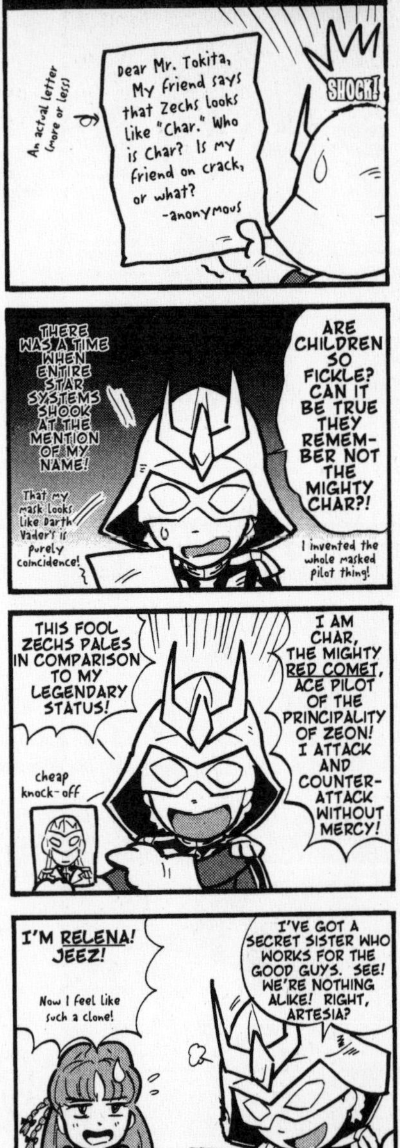
SHOCK!
Dear Mr. Tokita, My friend says that Zechs looks like "Char." Who is Char? Is my friend on crack, or what? -anonymous
An actual letter (more or less)
ARE CHILDREN SO FICKLE? CAN IT BE TRUE THEY REMEMBER NOT THE MIGHTY CHAR?!
I invented the whole masked pilot thing!
THERE WAS A TIME WHEN ENTIRE STAR SYSTEMS SHOOK AT THE MENTION OF MY NAME!
That my mask looks like Darth Vader's is purely coincidence!
I AM CHAR, THE MIGHTY RED COMET, ACE PILOT OF THE PRINCIPALITY OF ZEON! I ATTACK AND COUNTER-ATTACK WITHOUT MERCY!
THIS FOOL ZECHS PALES IN COMPARISON TO MY LEGENDARY STATUS!
cheap knock-off
I'VE GOT A SECRET SISTER WHO WORKS FOR THE GOOD GUYS. SEE! WE'RE NOTHING ALIKE! RIGHT, ARTESIA?
I'M RELENA! JEEZ!
Now I feel like such a clone!

Running Man

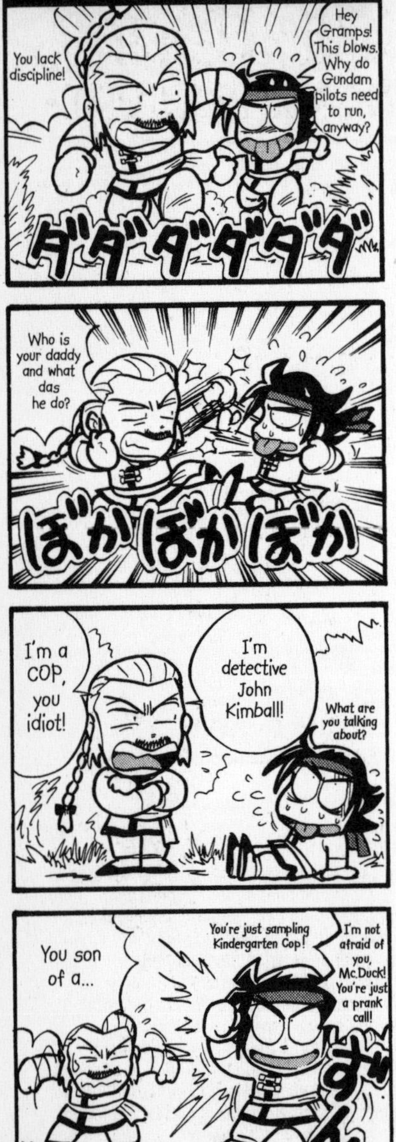
Hey Gramps! This blows. Why do Gundam pilots need to run, anyway?
You lack discipline!
ダダダダダダ
Who is your daddy and what das he do?
ぼかぼかぼか
What are you talking about?
I'm detective John Kimball!
I'm a COP, you idiot!
I'm not afraid of you, Mc.Duck! You're just a prank call!
You're just sampling Kindergarten Cop!
You son of a...
ずん

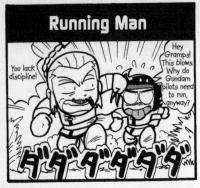

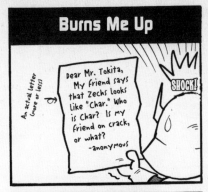

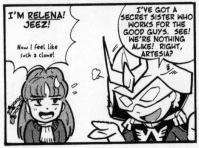

FOUR-PANEL MADNESS

-GUNDAM PARADISE-

-First Paradise-

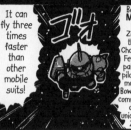

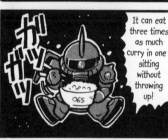

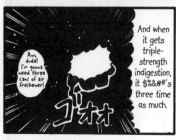

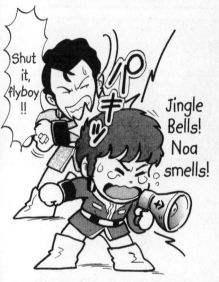

Jingle Bells! Noa smells!
Shut it, flyboy!!

Mobile Suit Gundam is...

...The first gundam series that originally aired back in 1979! In Universal Century 0079 a faction of colonists broke away from the Earth Federation to form the Principality of Zeon. This Federation fought the separatists, but Zeon scientists had created a new weapon which gave them a major edge in battle: the Mobile Suit! To counter this threat, the Federation creates a new weapon of their own, the Gundam. Before the Gundam can be properly tested, the ship which housed it, Side 7, is attacked, and a young man named Amuro Ray must pilot the MS to protect his home and stop Zeon's Forces.

More Isn't Always Better
Behold the MS-06s, custom Zaku II of the great Char Aznable! Fear its red paintjob, the pilot's trademark color! Bow before its communications antenna, unique among Zaukus!
ゴオ
It can fly three times faster than other mobile suits!
It can beat video games three times as fast without using cheat codes, yeah!
ピュンピュン
It can eat three times as much curry in one sitting without throwing up!
ガツガツ
And when it gets triple-strength indigestion, it $%&@#'s three time as much.
Aw, dude! I'm gonna need three cans of air freshener!
ゴオオ

A Very Goufy Strip

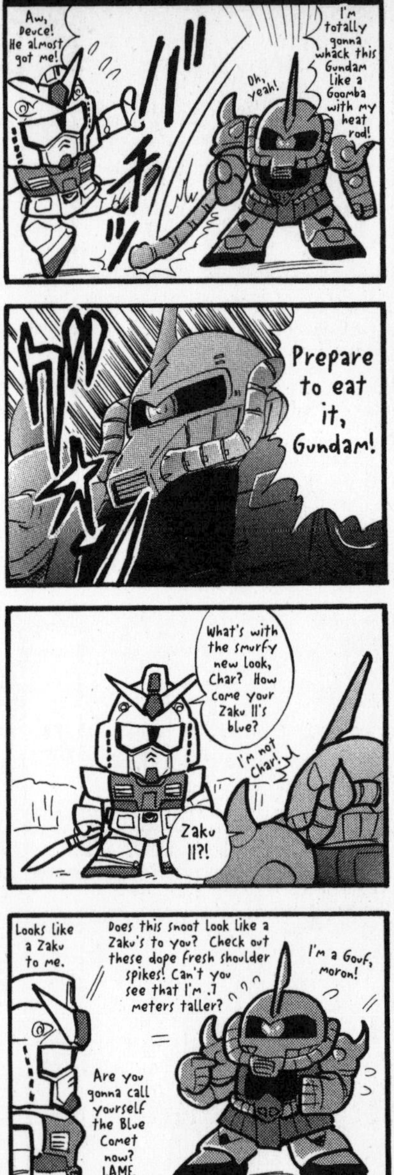
I'm totally gonna whack this Gundam like a Goomba with my heat rod!
Oh, yeah!
Aw, Deuce! He almost got me!
Prepare to eat it, Gundam!
What's with the smurfy new look, Char? How come your Zaku II's blue?
I'm not Char!
Zaku II?!
I'm a Gouf, moron!
Does this snoot look like a Zaku's to you? Check out these dope fresh shoulder spikes! Can't you see that I'm .7 meters taller?
Looks like a Zaku to me.
Are you gonna call yourself the Blue Comet now? LAME.

Bad Karma

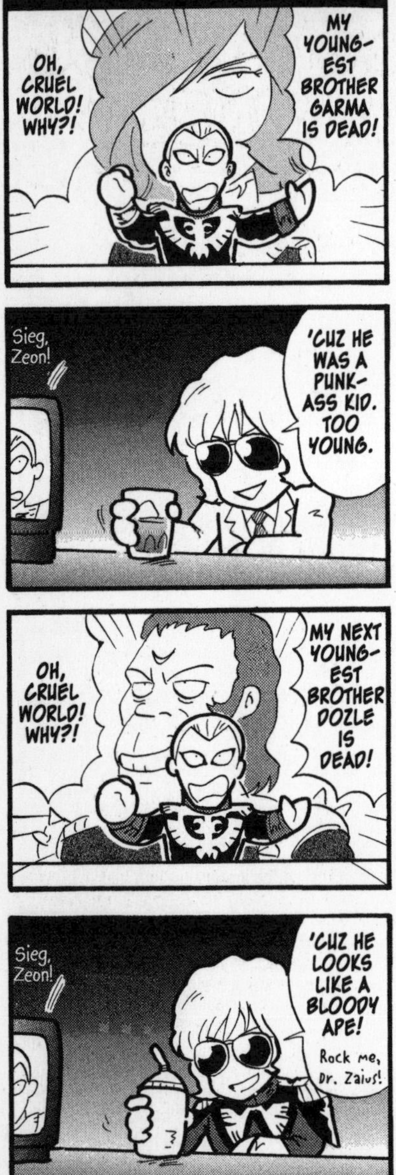
MY YOUNGEST BROTHER GARMA IS DEAD!
OH, CRUEL WORLD! WHY?!
'CUZ HE WAS A PUNK-ASS KID. TOO YOUNG.
Sieg, Zeon!
MY NEXT YOUNGEST BROTHER DOZLE IS DEAD!
OH, CRUEL WORLD! WHY?!
'CUZ HE LOOKS LIKE A BLOODY APE!
Rock me, Dr. Zaius!
Sieg, Zeon!

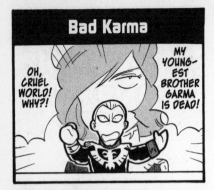

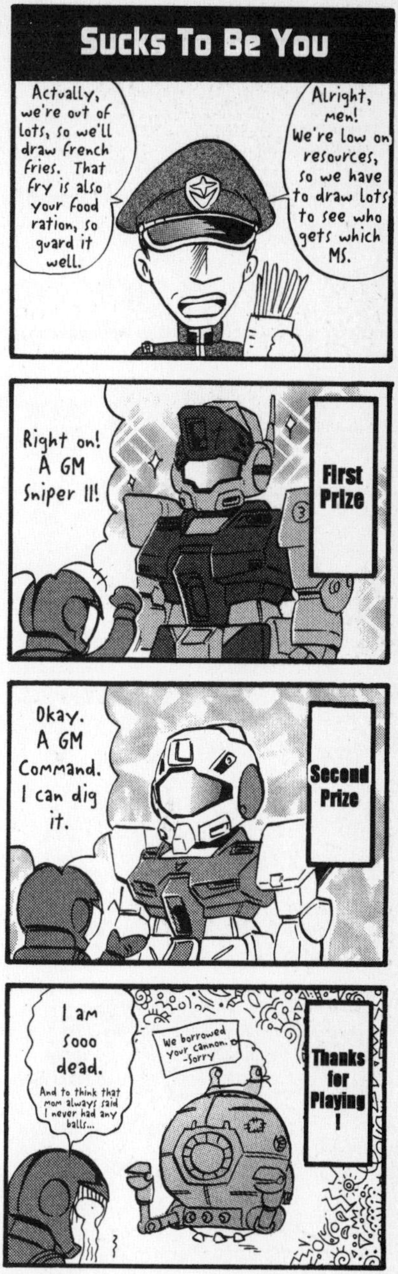
Sucks To Be You
Alright, men! We're low on resources, so we have to draw lots to see who gets which MS.
Actually, we're out of lots, so we'll draw french fries. That fry is also your food ration, so guard it well.
First Prize
Right on! A GM Sniper II!
Second Prize
Okay. A GM Command. I can dig it.
Thanks for Playing!
We borrowed your cannon. -Sorry
I am sooo dead.
And to think that mom always said I never had any balls...

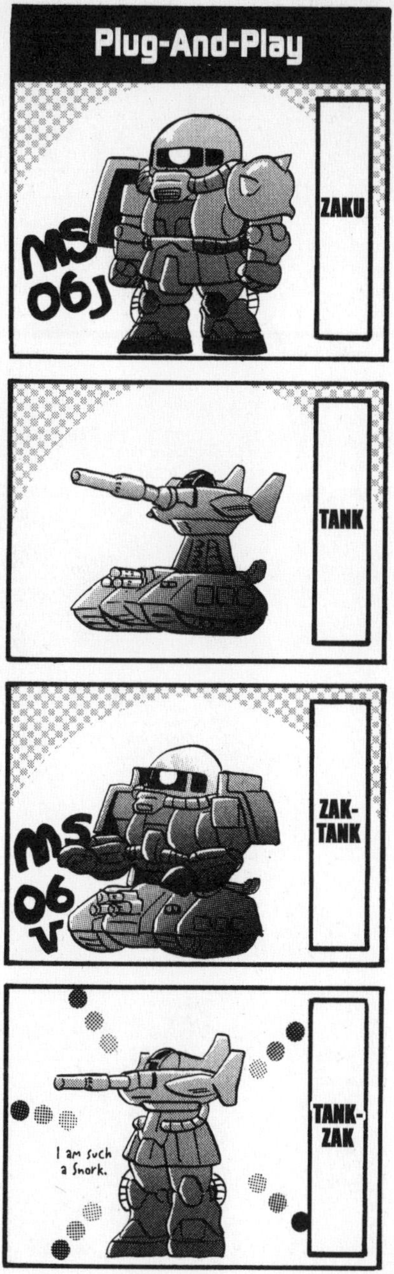
Plug-And-Play
ZAKU
MS 06J
TANK
ZAK-TANK
MS 06V
TANK-ZAK
I am such a Snork.

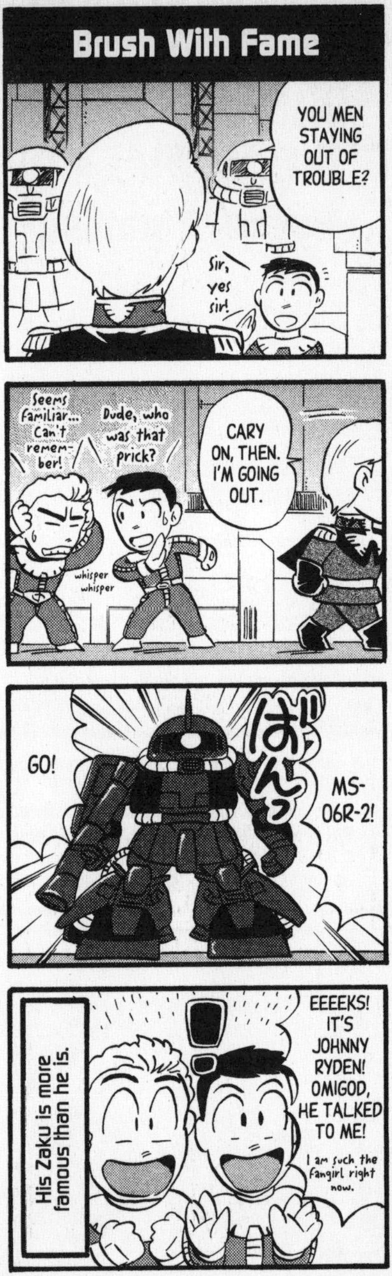
Brush With Fame
YOU MEN STAYING OUT OF TROUBLE?
Sir, yes sir!
CARY ON, THEN. I'M GOING OUT.
Dude, who was that prick?
Seems familiar... Can't remem-ber!
whisper whisper
ばんっ
MS-06R-2!
GO!
EEEEKS! IT'S JOHNNY RYDEN! OMIGOD, HE TALKED TO ME!
I am such the fangirl right now.
His Zaku is more famous than he is.

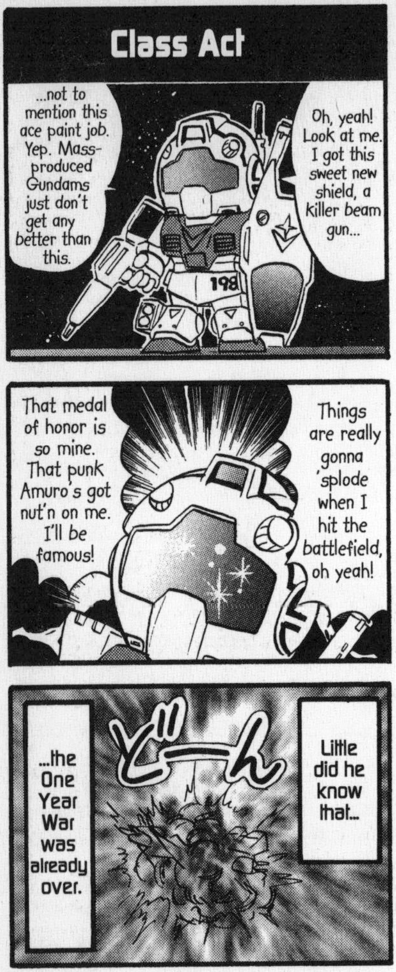
Class Act
Oh, yeah! Look at me. I got this sweet new shield, a killer beam gun...
...not to mention this ace paint job. Yep. Mass-produced Gundams just don't get any better than this.
198
Things are really gonna 'splode when I hit the battlefield, oh yeah!
That medal of honor is so mine. That punk Amuro's got nut'n on me. I'll be famous!
Little did he know that...
どーん
...the One Year War was already over.

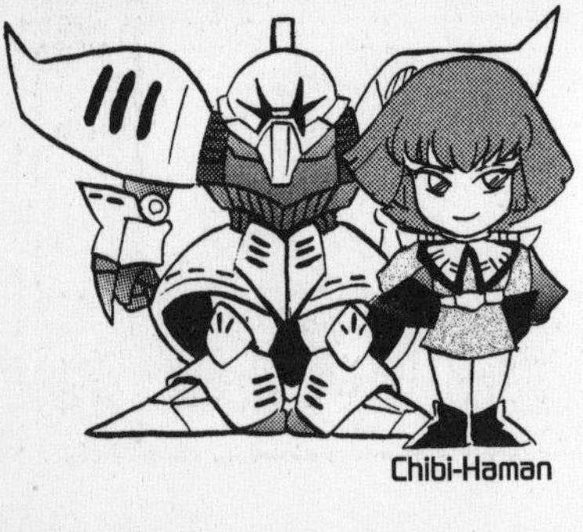
Chibi-Haman

FOUR-PANEL MADNESS

-GUNDAM PARADISE-

-Pocket Paradise-

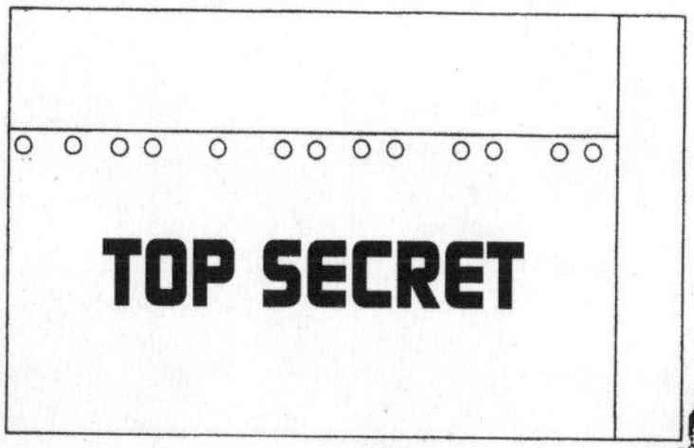
TOP SECRET

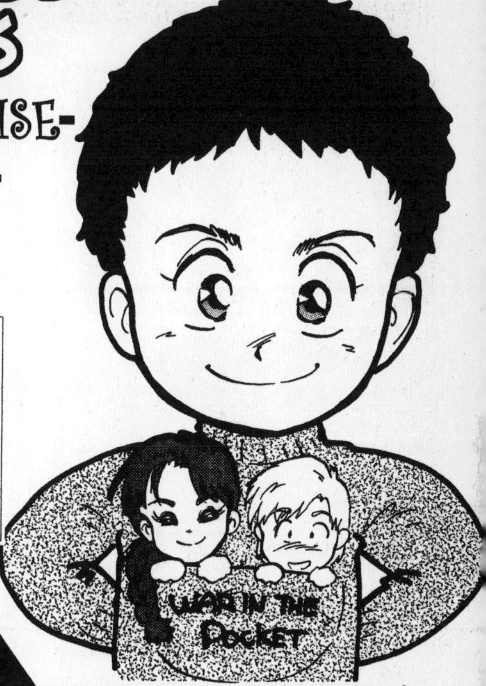
WAR IN THE POCKET

Mobile Suit Gundam 0080 War in the Pocket is...

...a Gundam side story which takes place in the final weeks of the One Year War. An elite team of Zeon soldiers called "Cyclops Force" track a newtype-compatible Gundam Prototype, the NT1 "Alex" to colony Side 6. The commandos infiltrate the Federation colony and go under cover to try and eliminate the new Gundam. The young Zeon pilot Bernie Wiseman meets the beautiful Federation pilot Chris McKenzie, and the two form a bond despite working for opposing sides.

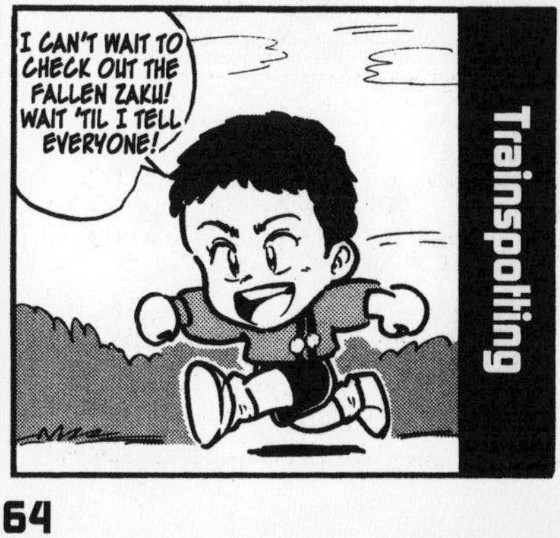
Trainspotting
I CAN'T WAIT TO CHECK OUT THE FALLEN ZAKU! WAIT 'TIL I TELL EVERYONE!

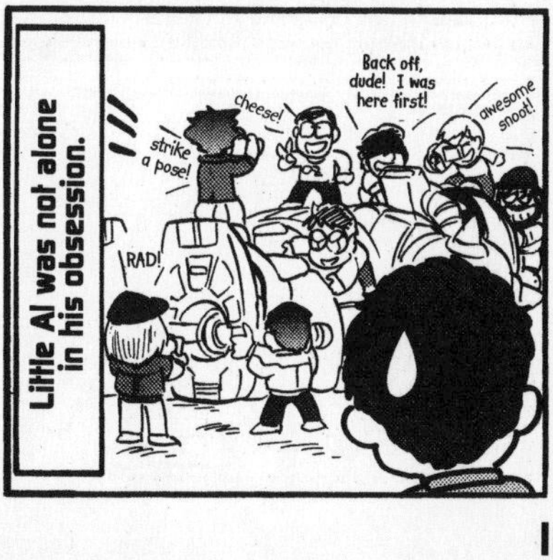
Little Al was not alone in his obsession.
awesome snoot!
Back off, dude! I was here first!
cheese!
strike a pose!
RAD!

The Boy Who Cried Wolf

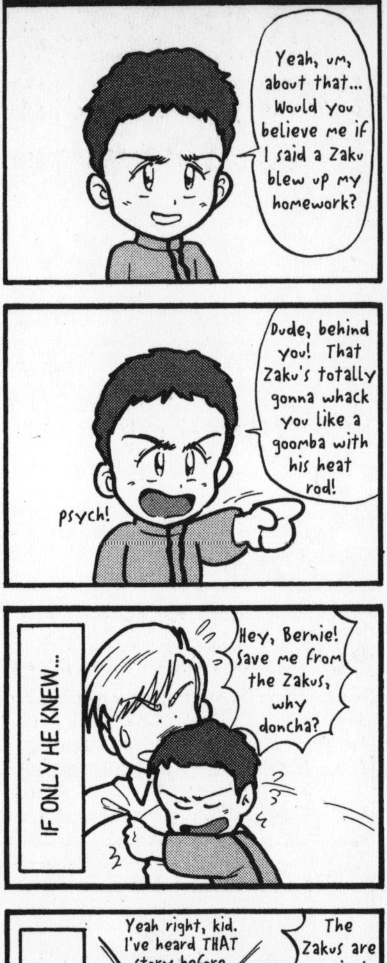

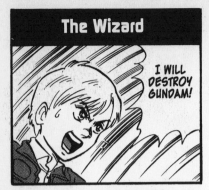

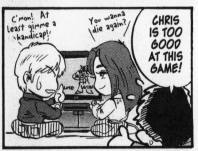

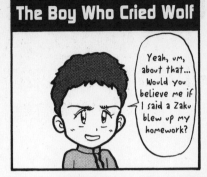

Yeah, um, about that... Would you believe me if I said a Zaku blew up my homework?
Dude, behind you! That Zaku's totally gonna whack you like a goomba with his heat rod!
psych!
Hey, Bernie! Save me from the Zakus, why doncha?
IF ONLY HE KNEW...
The Zakus are coming! The Zakus are coming!
Yeah right, kid. I've heard THAT story before.
SHIZZLE THAT FABLE, AESOP!

The Wizard

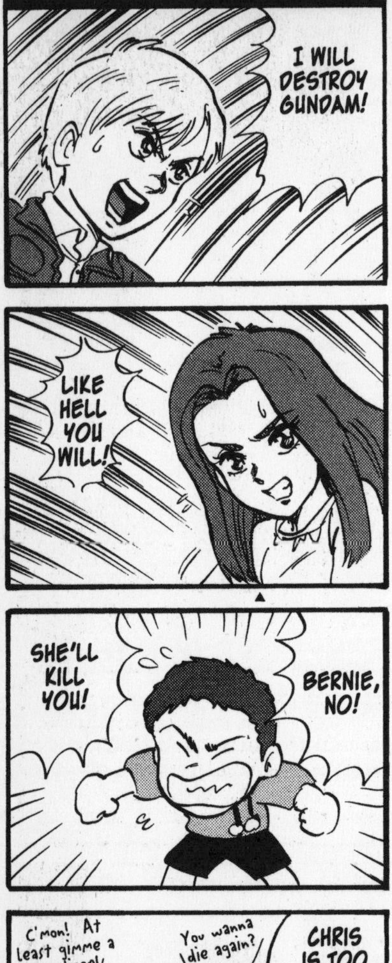

I WILL DESTROY GUNDAM!
LIKE HELL YOU WILL!
BERNIE, NO!
SHE'LL KILL YOU!
CHRIS IS TOO GOOD AT THIS GAME!
You wanna die again?
C'mon! At least gimme a handicap!

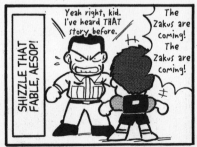

Secret Weapons

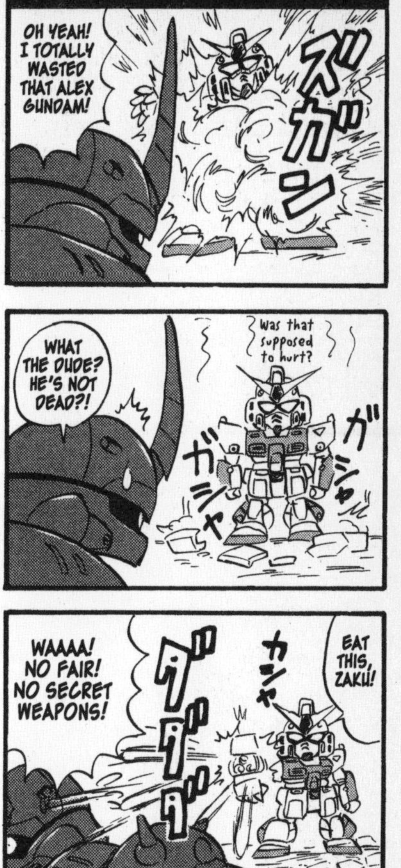
ズガン
OH YEAH! I TOTALLY WASTED THAT ALEX GUNDAM!
Was that supposed to hurt?
WHAT THE DUDE? HE'S NOT DEAD?!
ガシャ
ガシャ
EAT THIS, ZAKU!
カシャ
ダダダダ
WAAAA! NO FAIR! NO SECRET WEAPONS!
AW, DEUCE. THAT DOESN'T MEAN US, DOES IT?
Gundam Heavyarms
Leopard Gundam
NA, WE'RE ALTERNATE UNIVERSE. WE'RE EXEMPT.
These two couldn't live without their secret weapons.

When The Spirit Moves You

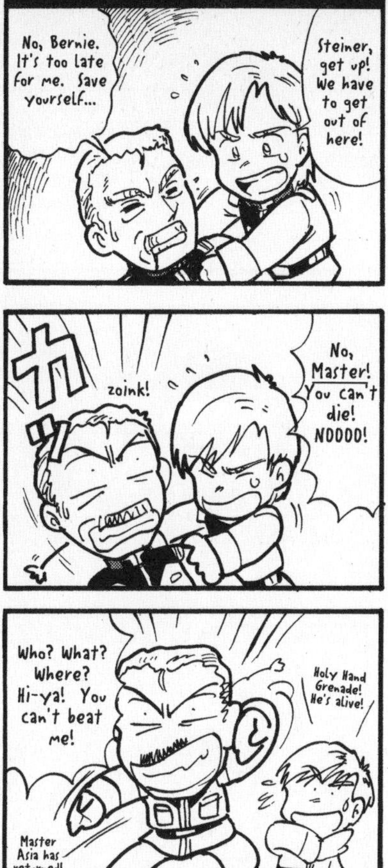
Steiner, get up! We have to get out of here!
No, Bernie. It's too late for me. Save yourself...
No, Master! You can't die! NOOOO!
zoink!
カッ
Holy Hand Grenade! He's alive!
Who? What? Where? Hi-ya! You can't beat me!
Master Asia has returned!
Yeah, so then he taught me the Ultimate Technique. I'm gonna waste that Gundam with my bare hands!
Yup. Master showed me how.
Awesome! Can I be your Padawan, Bernie? Huh? Can I?!

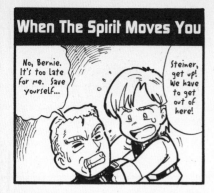

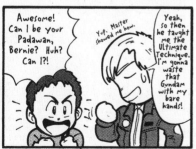

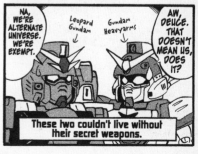

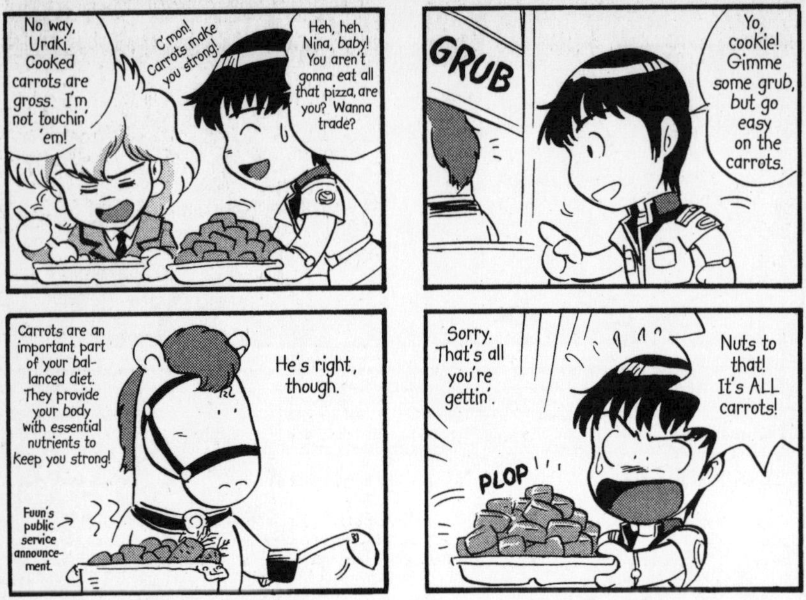
GRUB
Yo, cookie! Gimme some grub, but go easy on the carrots.
Heh, heh. Nina, *baby*! You aren't gonna eat all that pizza, are you? Wanna trade?
C'mon! Carrots make you strong!
No way, Uraki. Cooked carrots are gross. I'm not touchin' 'em!
Nuts to that! It's ALL carrots!
Sorry. That's all you're gettin'.
PLOP
He's right, though.
Carrots are an important part of your balanced diet. They provide your body with essential nutrients to keep you strong!
Fuun's public service announcement.

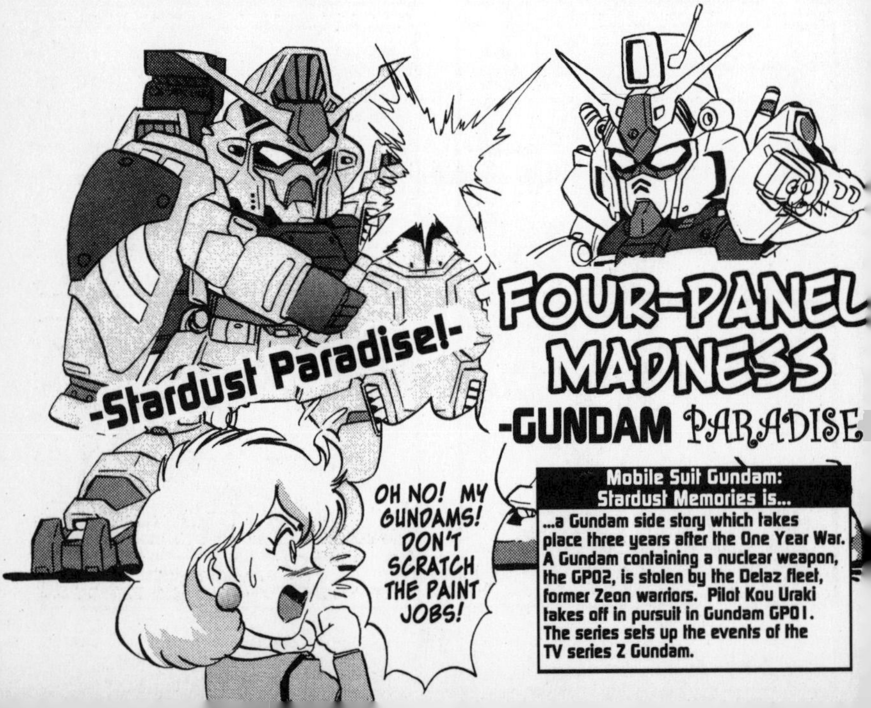
-Stardust Paradise!-
OH NO! MY GUNDAMS! DON'T SCRATCH THE PAINT JOBS!

FOUR-PANEL MADNESS
-GUNDAM PARADISE

Mobile Suit Gundam: Stardust Memories is...

...a Gundam side story which takes place three years after the One Year War. A Gundam containing a nuclear weapon, the GP02, is stolen by the Delaz fleet, former Zeon warriors. Pilot Kou Uraki takes off in pursuit in Gundam GP01. The series sets up the events of the TV series Z Gundam.

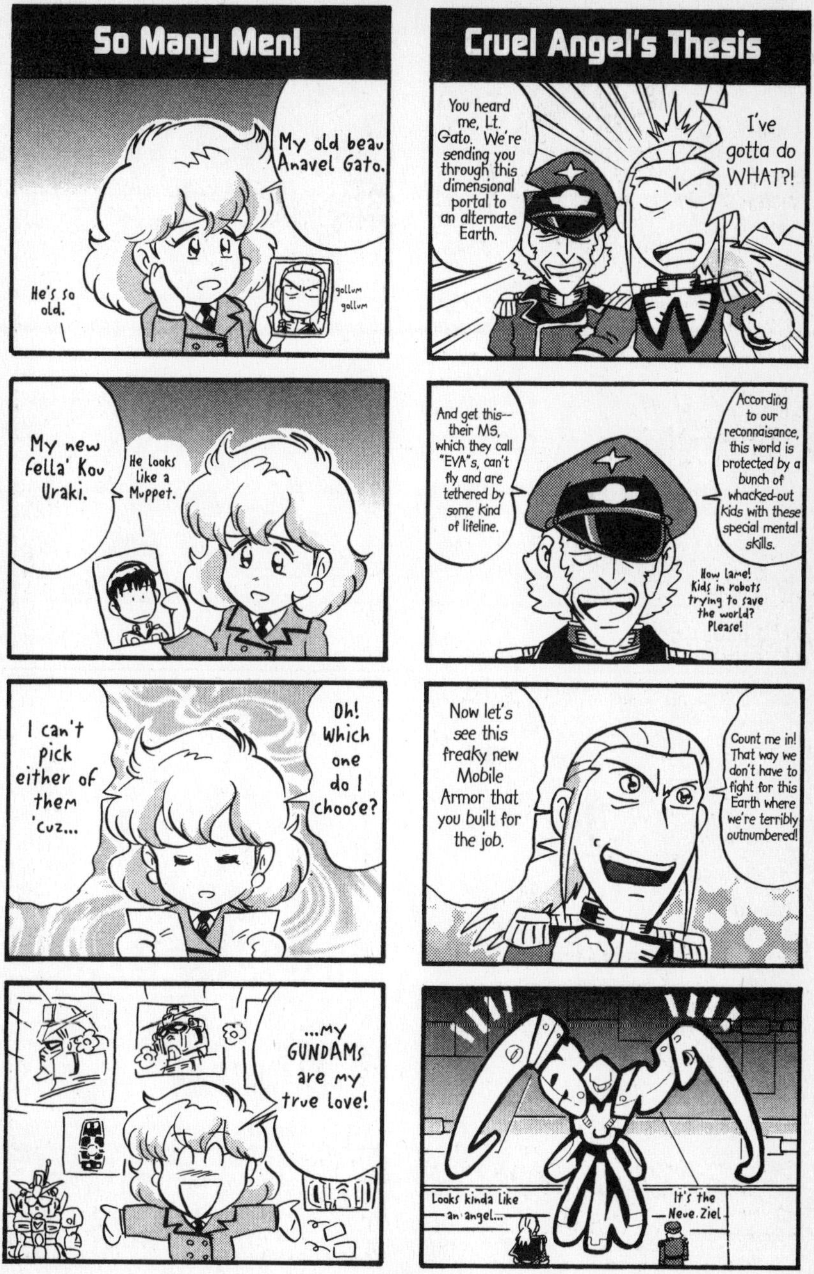
Cruel Angel's Thesis
I've gotta do WHAT?!
You heard me, Lt. Gato. We're sending you through this dimensional portal to an alternate Earth.
According to our reconnaissance, this world is protected by a bunch of whacked-out kids with these special mental skills.
And get this—their MS, which they call "EVA"s, can't fly and are tethered by some kind of lifeline.
How lame! Kids in robots trying to save the world? Please!
Count me in! That way we don't have to fight for this Earth where we're terribly outnumbered!
Now let's see this freaky new Mobile Armor that you built for the job.
It's the Neve Ziel
Looks kinda like an angel...
So Many Men!
My old beau Anavel Gato.
gollum gollum
He's so old.
He looks like a Muppet.
My new fella' Kou Uraki.
Oh! Which one do I choose?
I can't pick either of them 'cuz...
...my GUNDAMs are my true love!

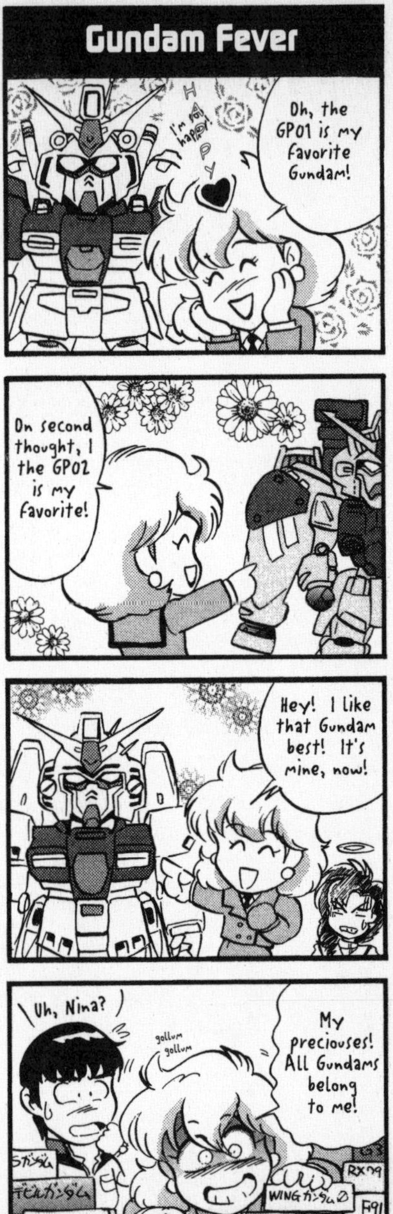
Gundam Fever
HAPPY
I'm so happy!
Oh, the GP01 is my favorite Gundam!
On second thought, I the GP02 is my favorite!
Hey! I like that Gundam best! It's mine, now!
Uh, Nina?
gollum gollum
My preciouses! All Gundams belong to me!
Sガンダム
デビルガンダム
νガンダム
ΖΖガンダム
GUNDAM RX78
ZGUNDAM
WINGガンダム
Gガンダム
RX79
F91
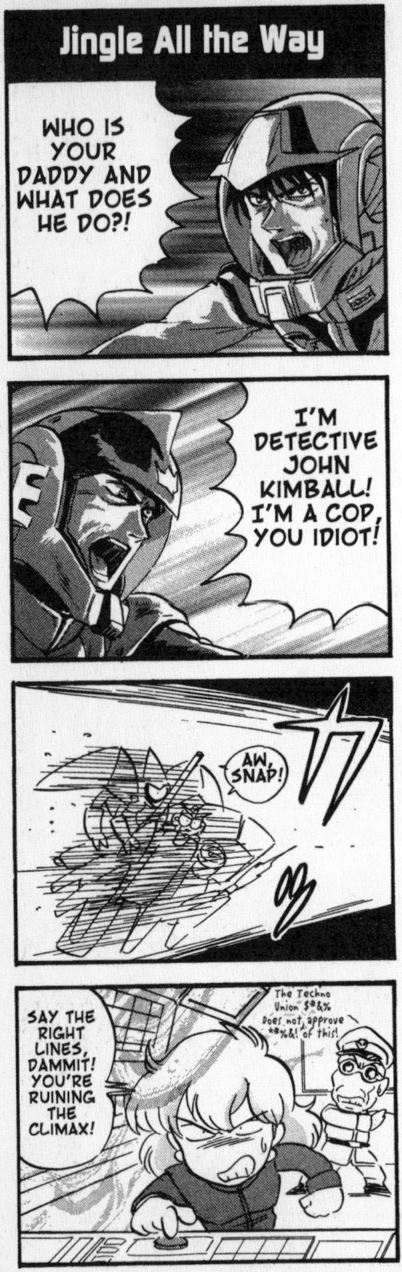
Jingle All the Way
WHO IS YOUR DADDY AND WHAT DOES HE DO?!
I'M DETECTIVE JOHN KIMBALL! I'M A COP, YOU IDIOT!
AW, SNAP!
SAY THE RIGHT LINES, DAMMIT! YOU'RE RUINING THE CLIMAX!
The Techno Union $#&% Does not approve *#%&! of this!

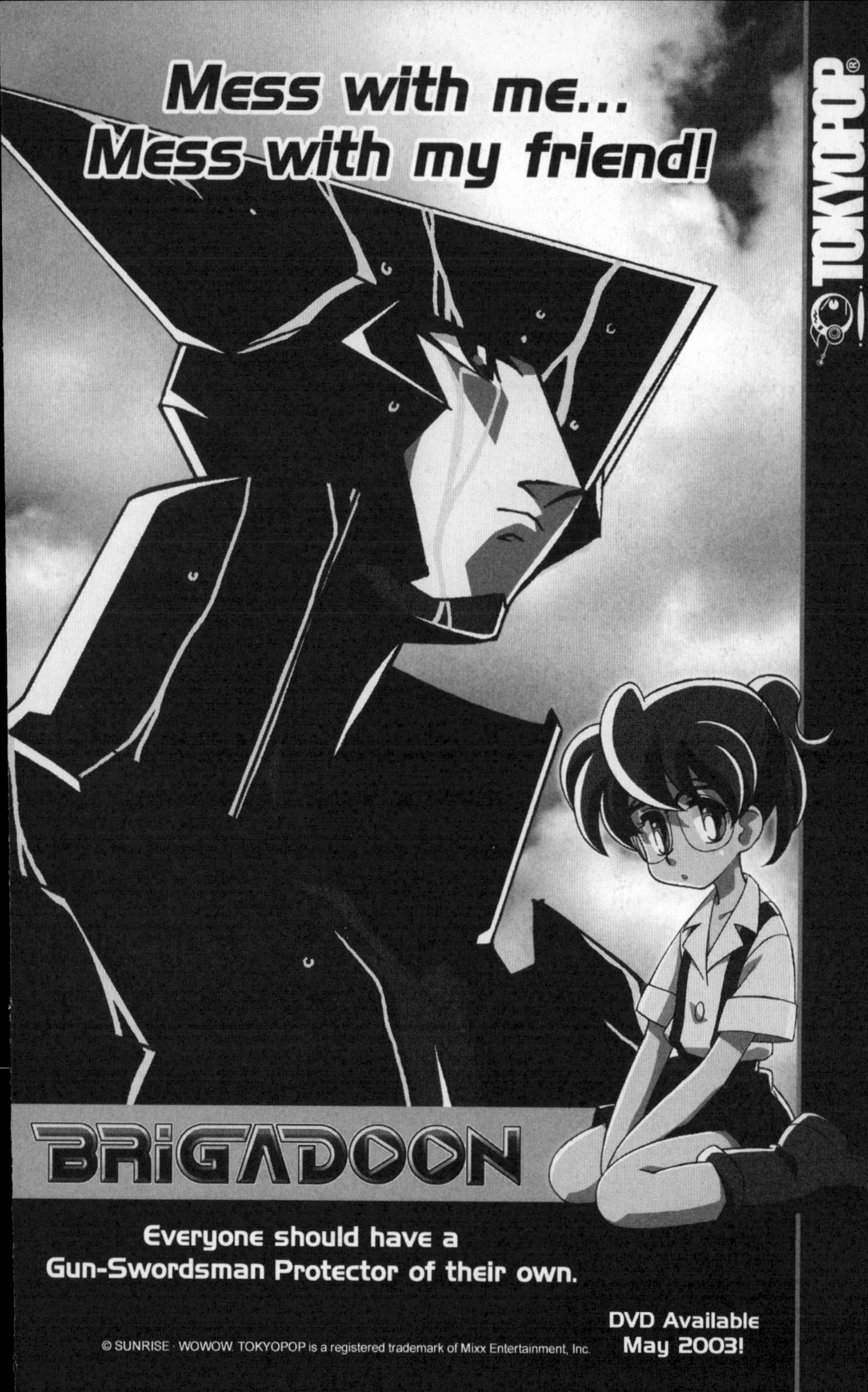

Mess with me...
Mess with my friend!
TOKYOPOP®
BRIGADOON
Everyone should have a
Gun-Swordsman Protector of their own.
DVD Available
May 2003!
© SUNRISE · WOWOW. TOKYOPOP is a registered trademark of Mixx Entertainment, Inc.

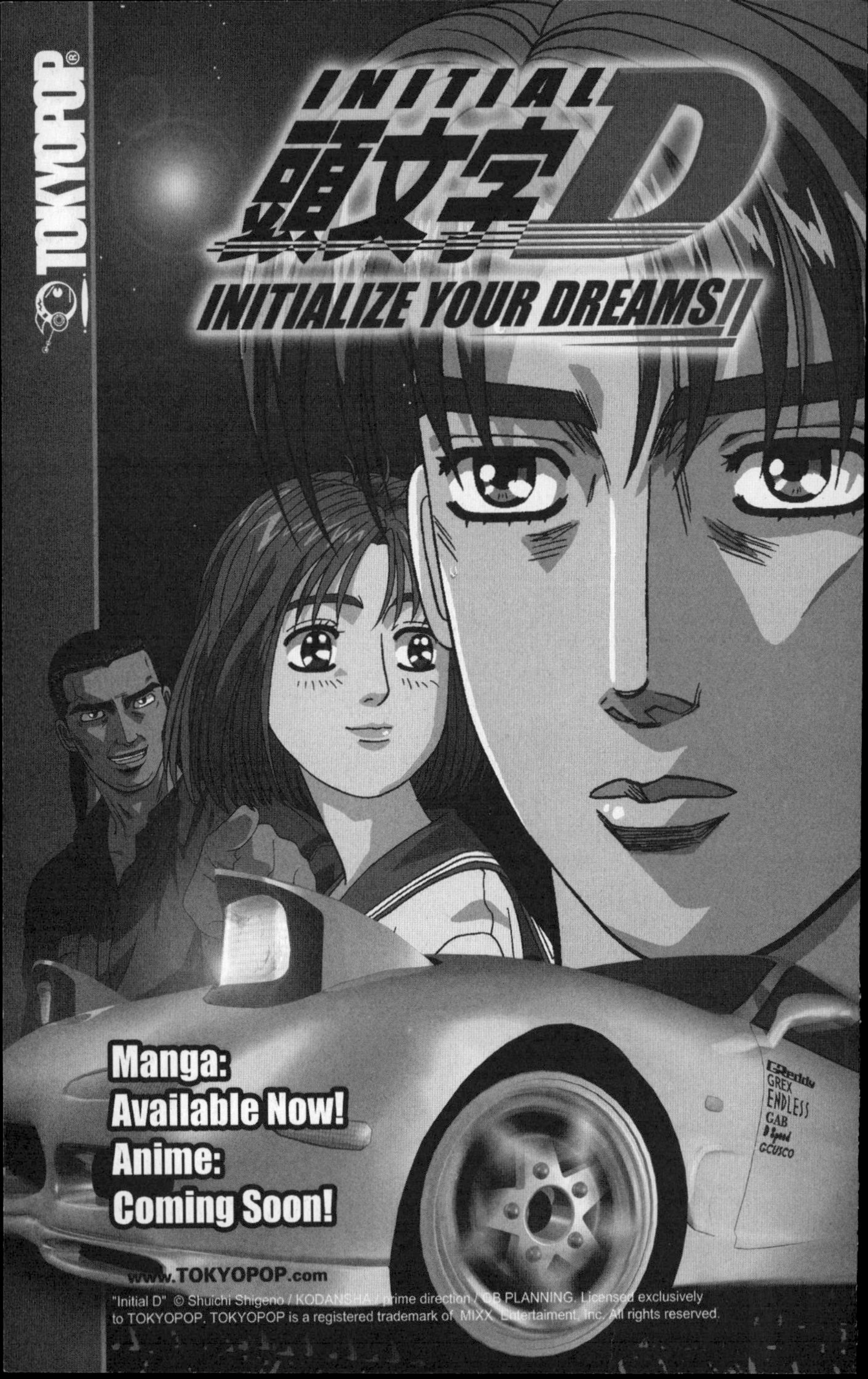
TOKYOPOP®
INITIAL
頭文字D
INITIALIZE YOUR DREAMS!!
Manga:
Available Now!
Anime:
Coming Soon!
www.TOKYOPOP.com
"Initial D" © Shuichi Shigeno / KODANSHA / prime direction / OB PLANNING. Licensed exclusively to TOKYOPOP. TOKYOPOP is a registered trademark of MIXX Entertainment, Inc. All rights reserved.

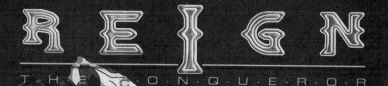

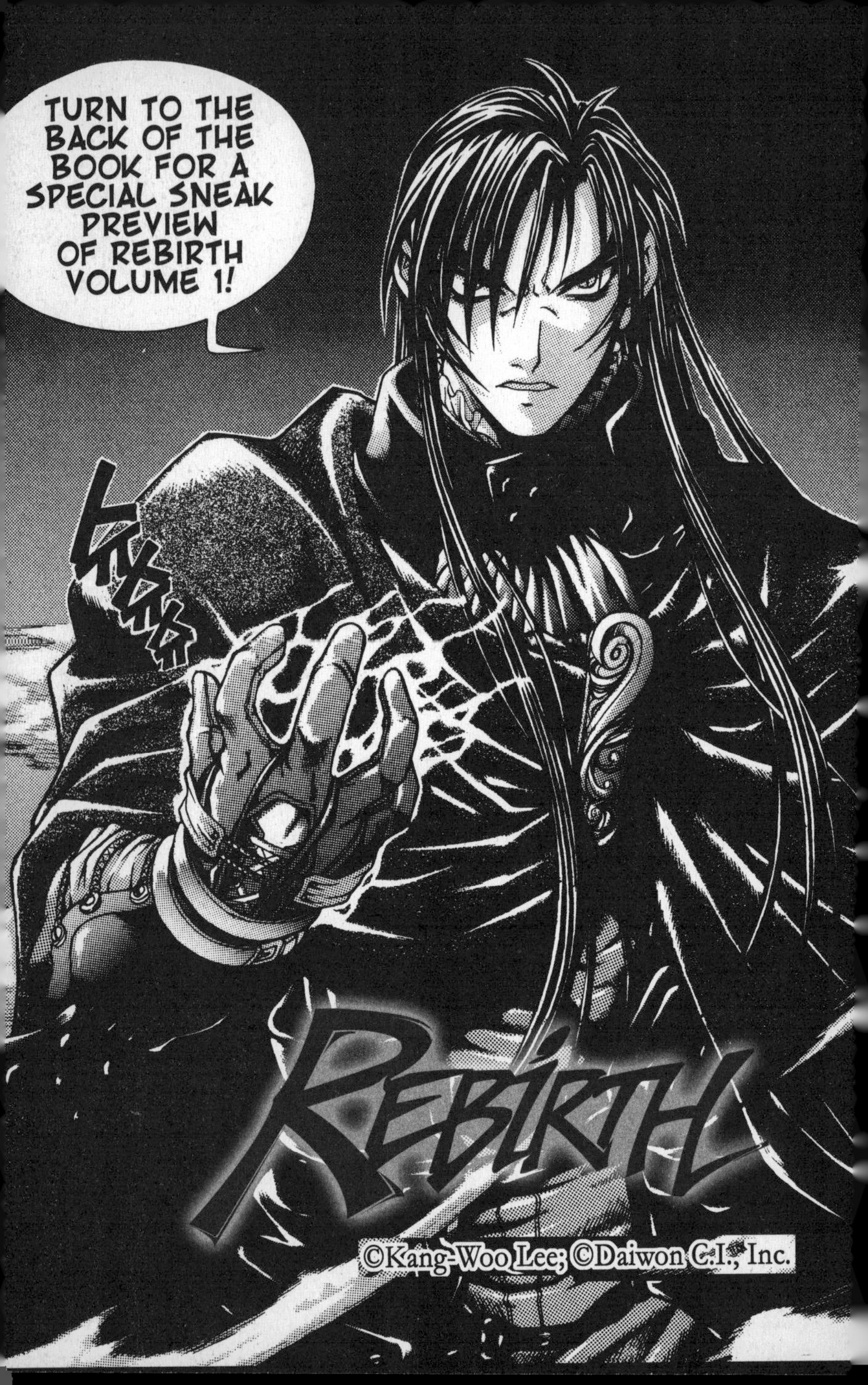
TURN TO THE BACK OF THE BOOK FOR A SPECIAL SNEAK PREVIEW OF REBIRTH VOLUME 1!
REBIRTH
©Kang-Woo Lee; ©Daiwon C.I., Inc.

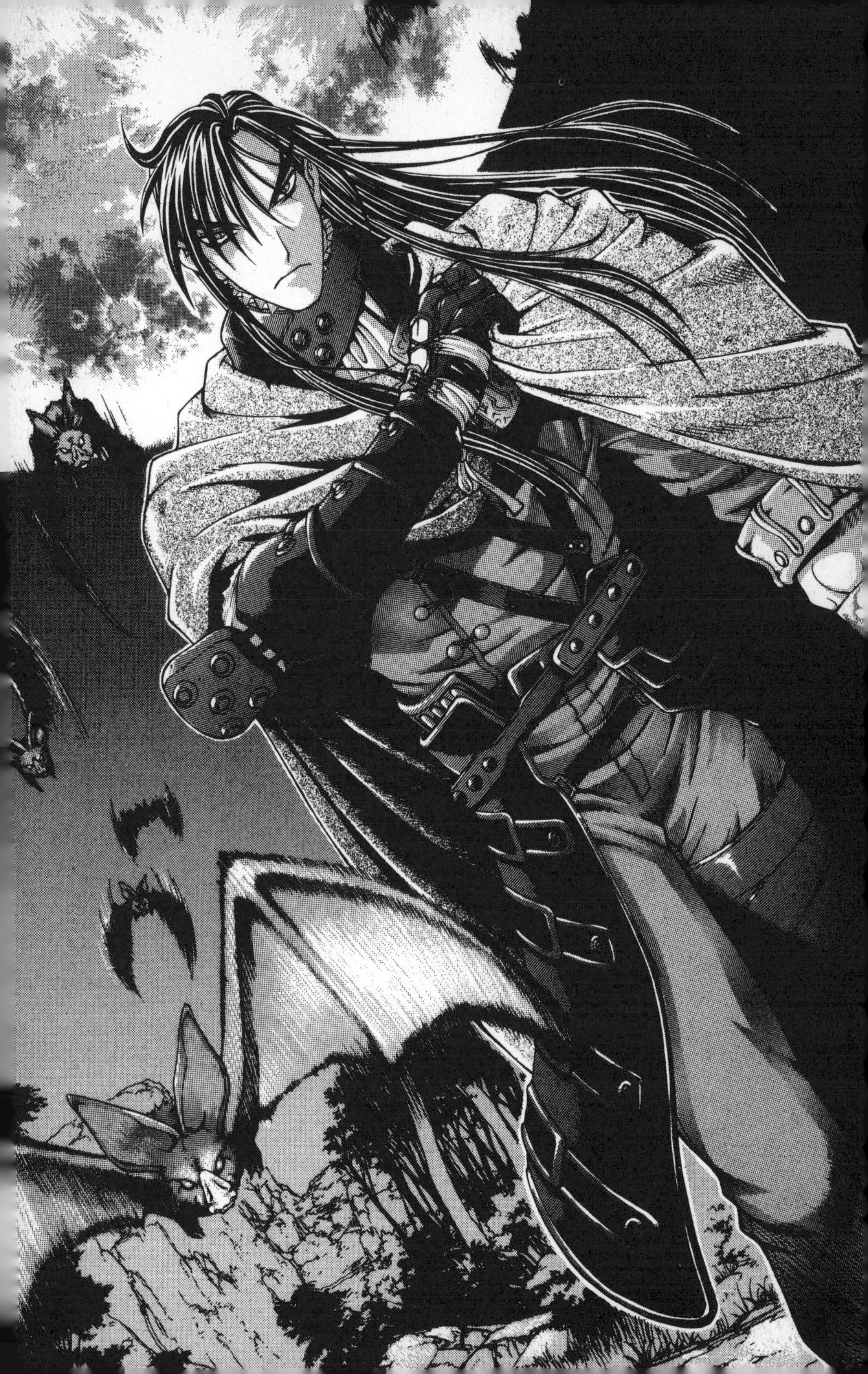

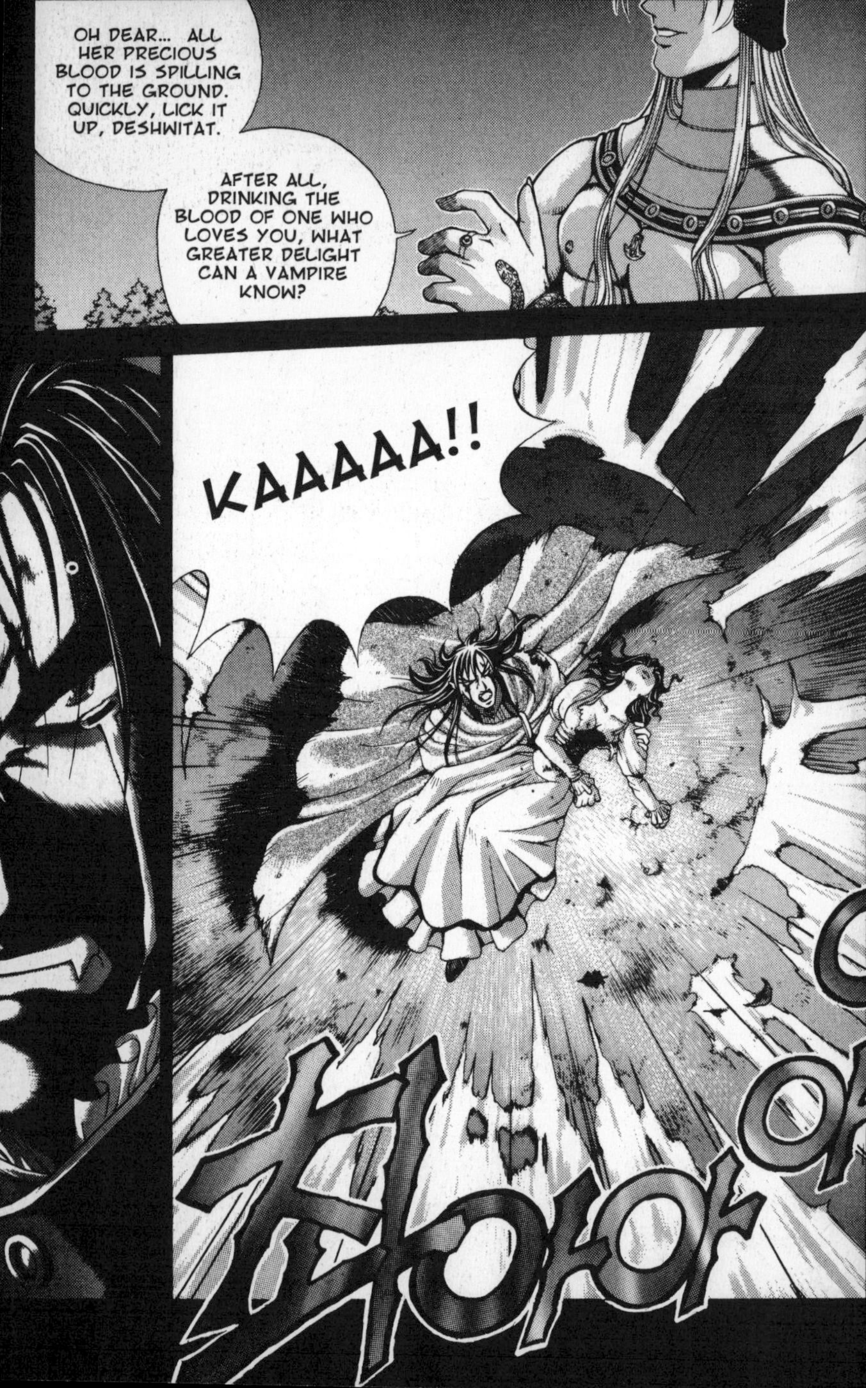
OH DEAR... ALL HER PRECIOUS BLOOD IS SPILLING TO THE GROUND. QUICKLY, LICK IT UP, DESHWITAT.
AFTER ALL, DRINKING THE BLOOD OF ONE WHO LOVES YOU, WHAT GREATER DELIGHT CAN A VAMPIRE KNOW?
KAAAAA!!

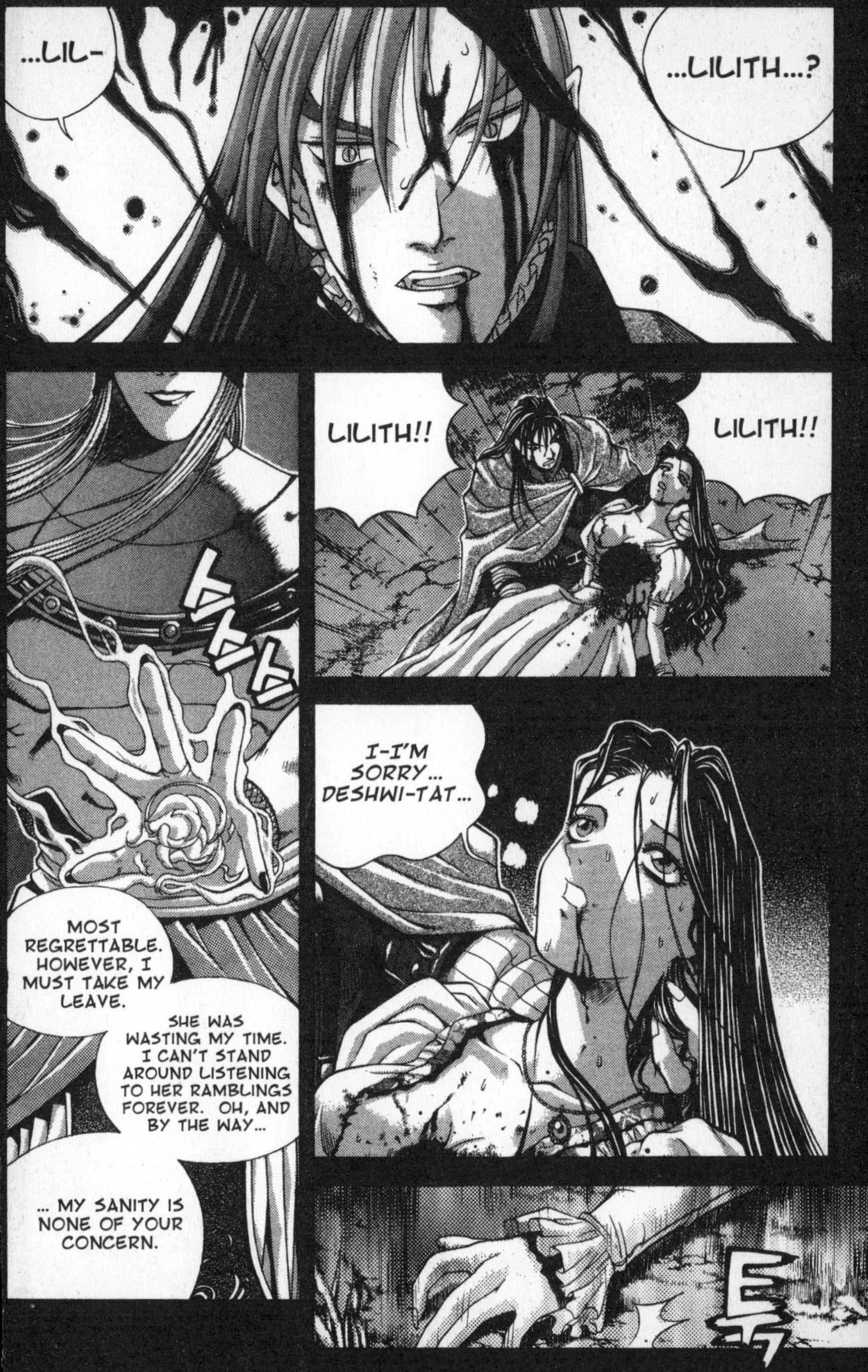
...LILITH...?
...LIL-
LILITH!!
LILITH!!
I-I'M SORRY... DESHWI-TAT...
MOST REGRETTABLE. HOWEVER, I MUST TAKE MY LEAVE.
SHE WAS WASTING MY TIME. I CAN'T STAND AROUND LISTENING TO HER RAMBLINGS FOREVER. OH, AND BY THE WAY...
... MY SANITY IS NONE OF YOUR CONCERN.

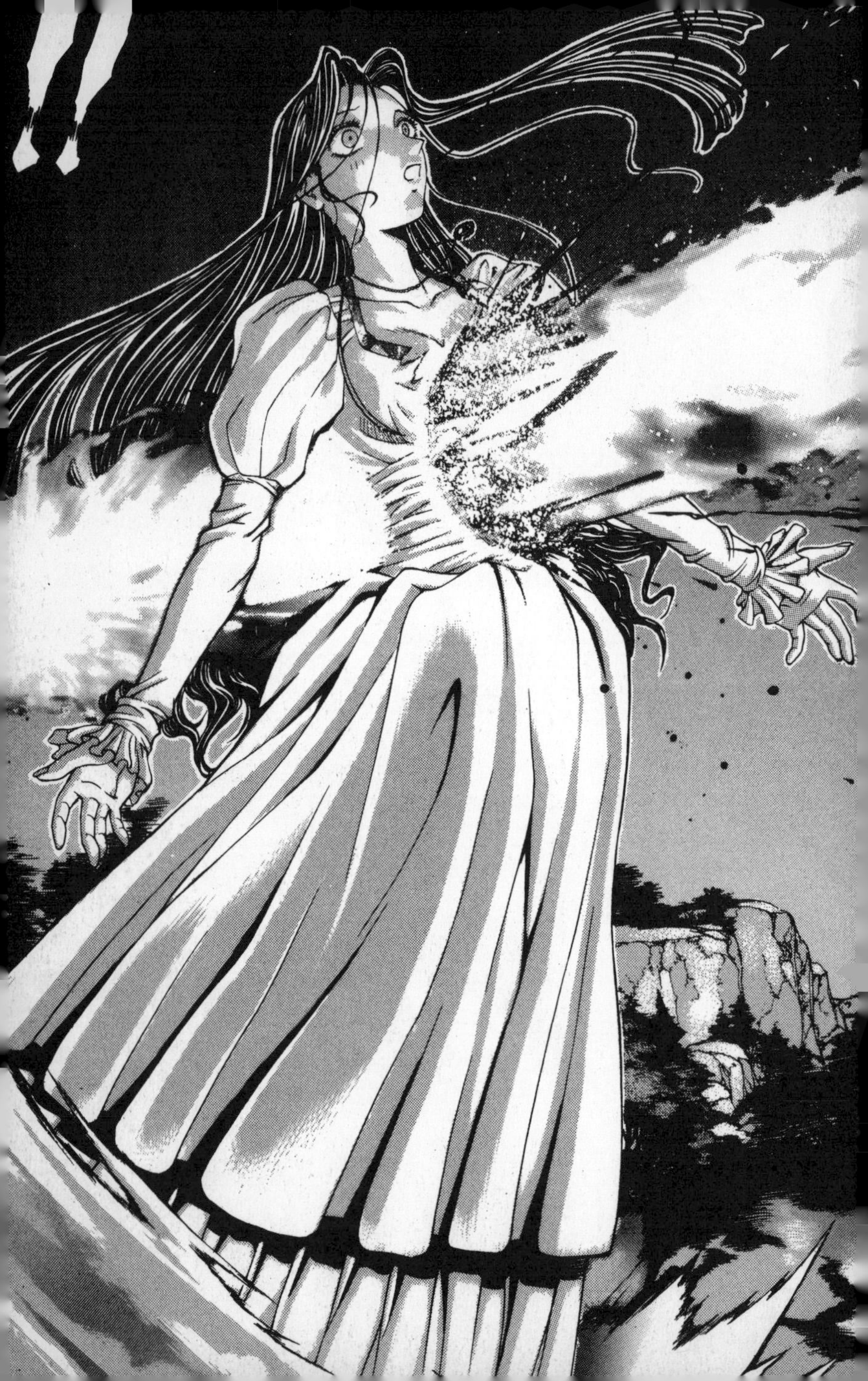
!!

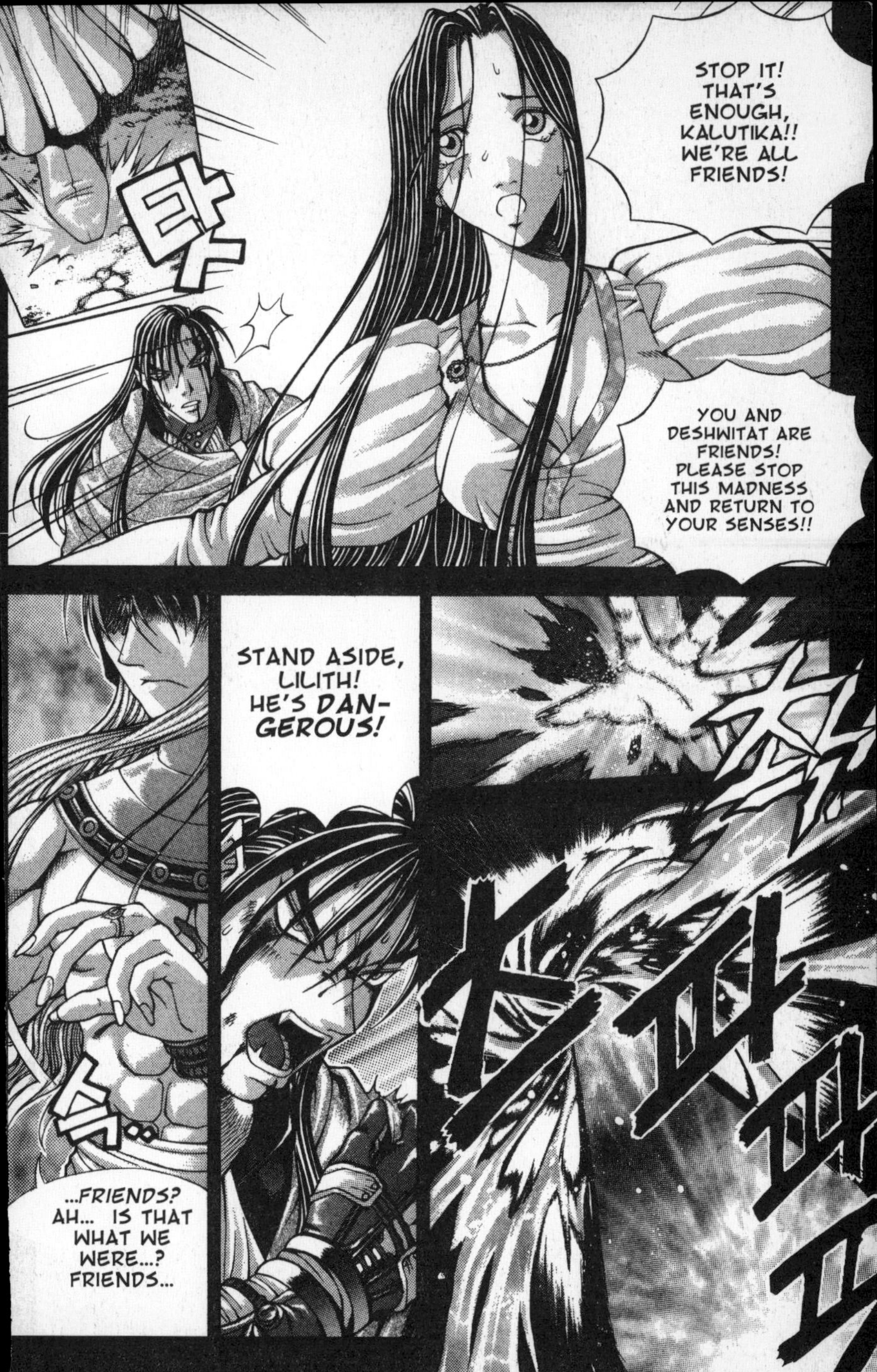
STOP IT! THAT'S ENOUGH, KALUTIKA!! WE'RE ALL FRIENDS!
탁
YOU AND DESHWITAT ARE FRIENDS! PLEASE STOP THIS MADNESS AND RETURN TO YOUR SENSES!!
STAND ASIDE, LILITH! HE'S DAN-GEROUS!
...FRIENDS? AH... IS THAT WHAT WE WERE...? FRIENDS...

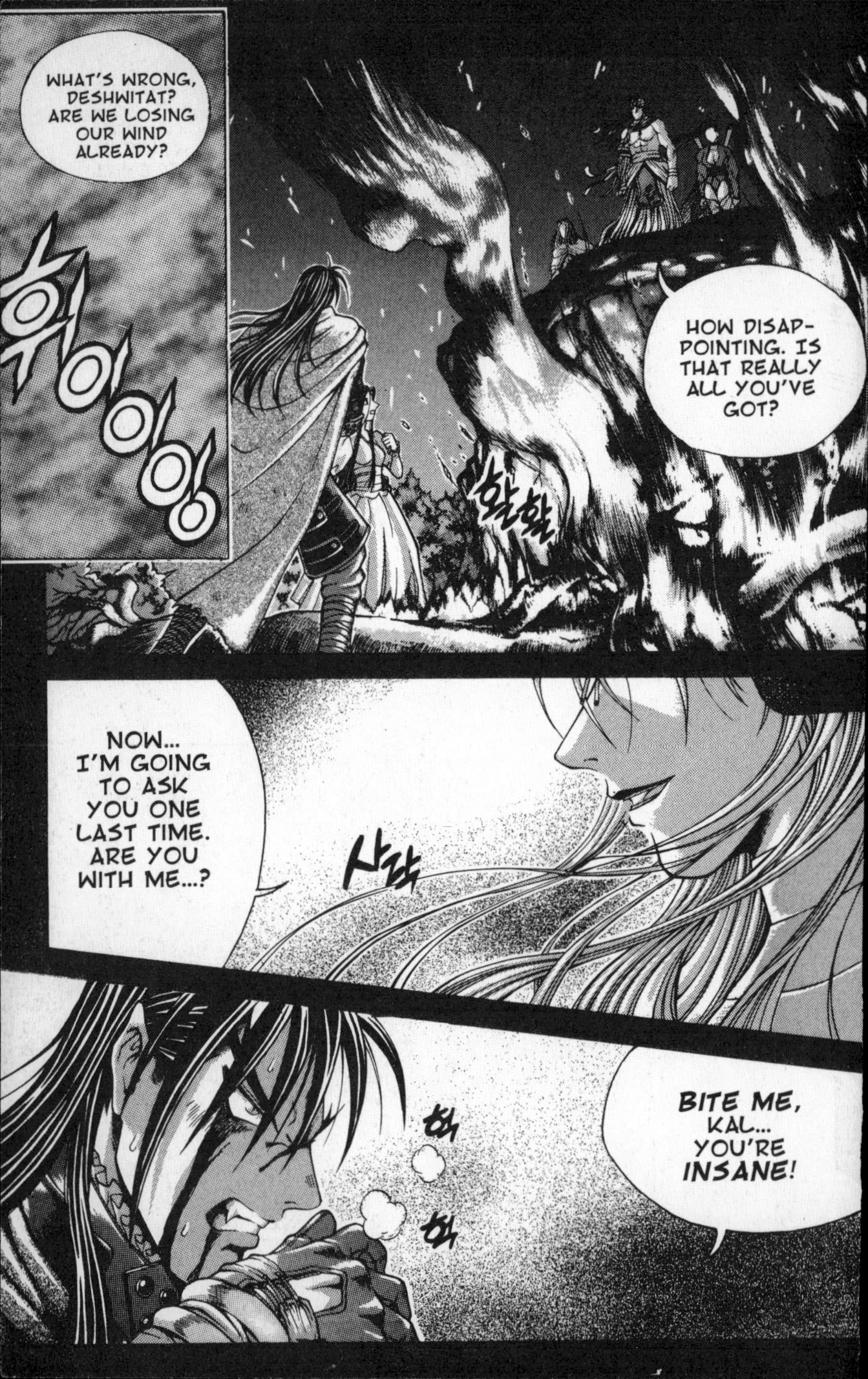
HOW DISAP-POINTING. IS THAT REALLY ALL YOU'VE GOT?
활활
WHAT'S WRONG, DESHWITAT? ARE WE LOSING OUR WIND ALREADY?
NOW... I'M GOING TO ASK YOU ONE LAST TIME. ARE YOU WITH ME...?
사락
BITE ME, KAL... YOU'RE INSANE!
헉
헉

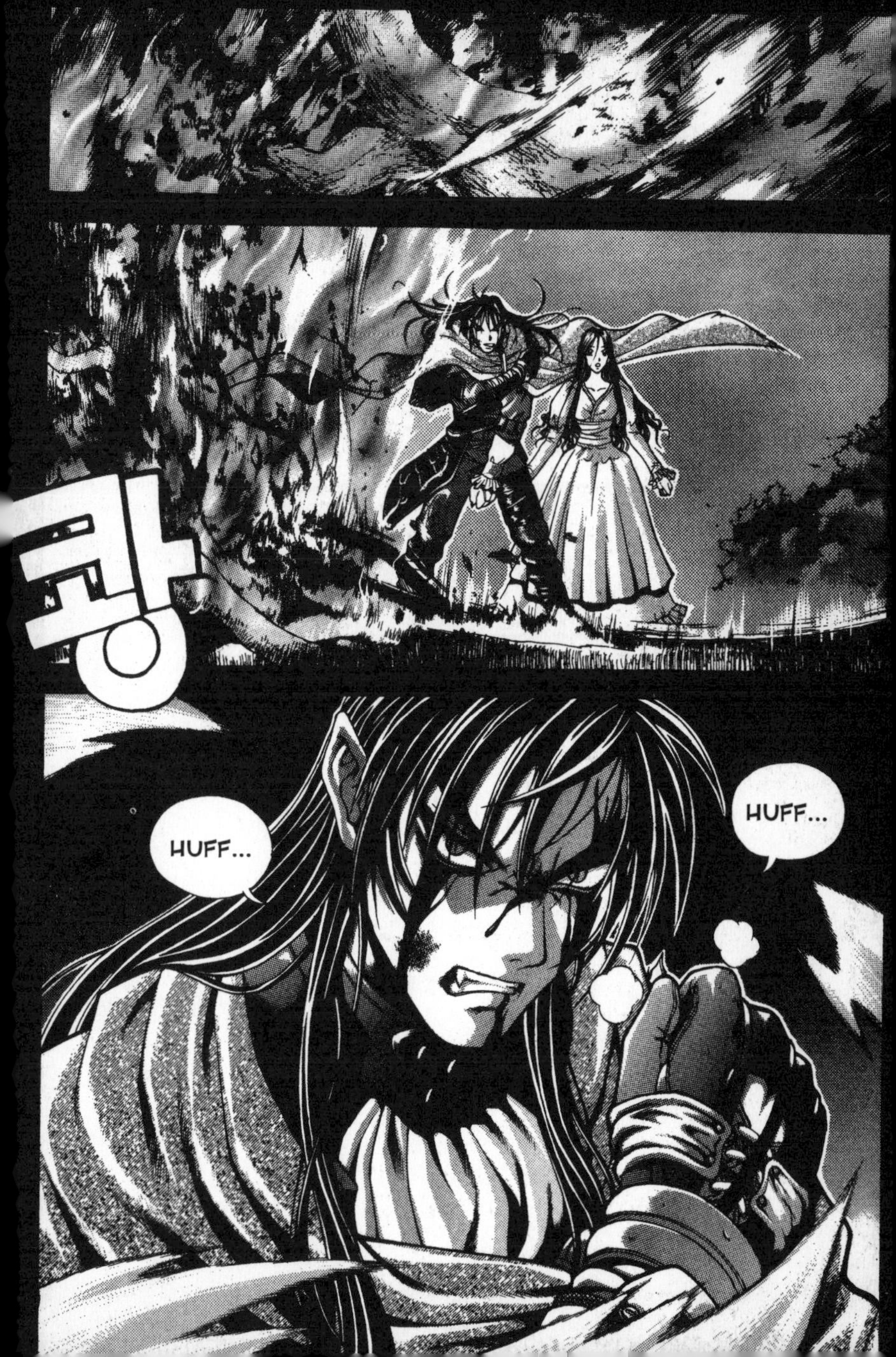
캉
HUFF...
HUFF...

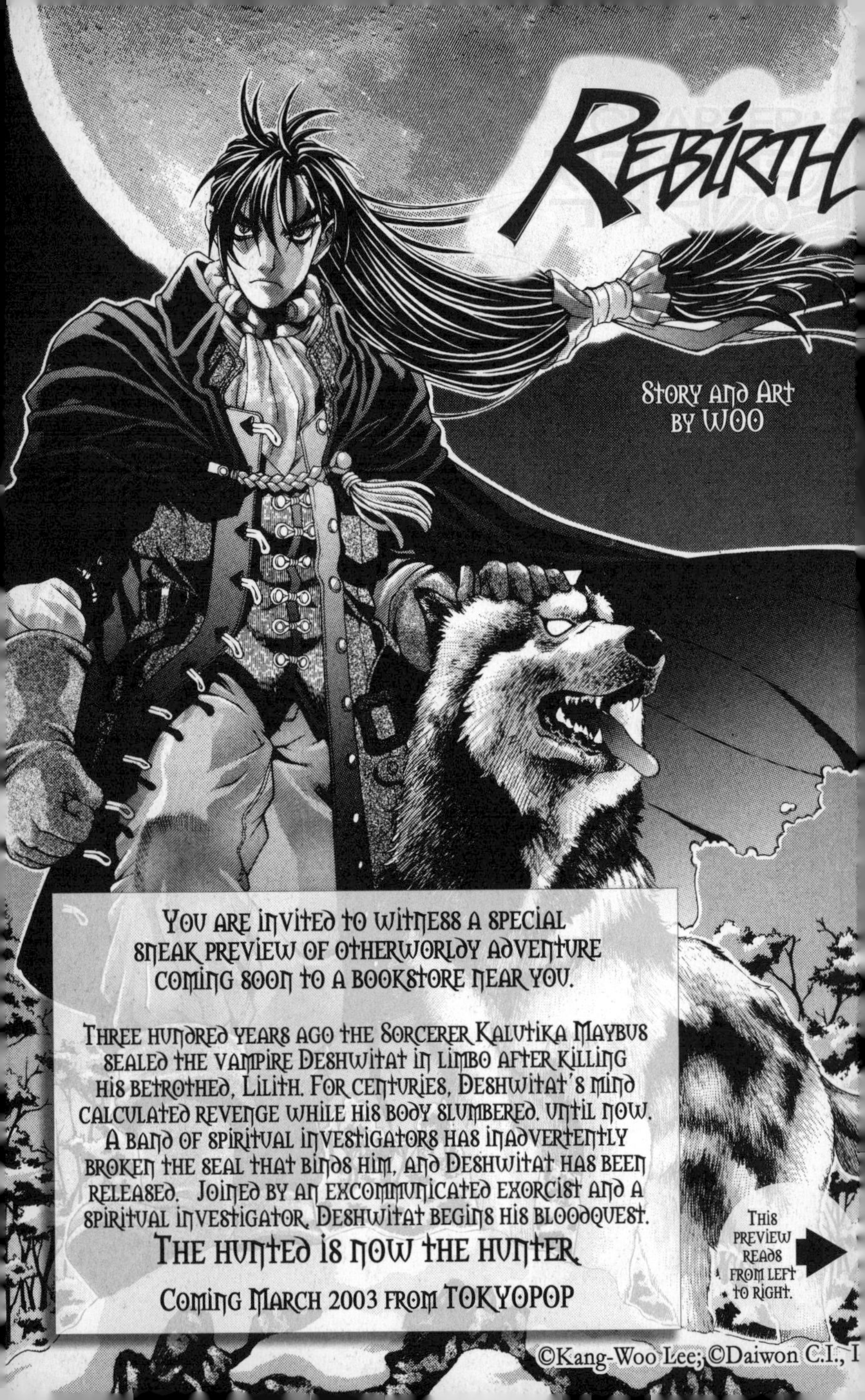
REBIRTH
Story and Art by WOO
You are invited to witness a special sneak preview of otherworldy adventure coming soon to a bookstore near you.
Three hundred years ago the Sorcerer Kalutika Maybus sealed the vampire Deshwitat in limbo after killing his betrothed, Lilith. For centuries, Deshwitat's mind calculated revenge while his body slumbered. Until now. A band of spiritual investigators has inadvertently broken the seal that binds him, and Deshwitat has been released. Joined by an excommunicated exorcist and a spiritual investigator, Deshwitat begins his bloodquest.
THE HUNTED IS NOW THE HUNTER
Coming March 2003 from TOKYOPOP
This preview reads from left to right.
©Kang-Woo Lee; ©Daiwon C.I., I

STOP!

This is the back of the book.
You wouldn't want to spoil a great ending!

This book is printed "manga-style," in the authentic Japanese right-to-left format. Since none of the artwork has been flipped or altered, readers get to experience the story just as the creator intended. You've been asking for it, so TOKYOPOP® delivered: authentic, hot-off-the-press, and far more fun!

DIRECTIONS

If this is your first time reading manga-style, here's a quick guide to help you understand how it works.

It's easy... just start in the top right panel and follow the numbers. Have fun, and look for more 100% authentic manga from TOKYOPOP®!

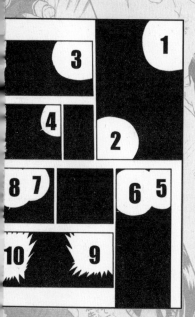

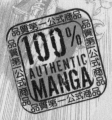